YELLOW STEEL

YELLOW STEEL

**The Story of the
Earthmoving
Equipment
Industry**

William R. Haycraft

University of Illinois Press
URBANA AND CHICAGO

Library of Congress Cataloging-in-Publication Data
Haycraft, William R. (William Russell), 1929–
Yellow steel : the story of the earthmoving equipment in-
    dustry / William R. Haycraft.
p.   cm.
Includes bibliographical references and index.
ISBN 0-252-02497-4 (alk. paper)
1. Construction equipment industry—United States—
History. 2. Mining machinery industry—
United States—History. I. Title.
HD9715.25.U62H39   2000
338.4'768176—dc21   99-6078
                                    CIP

C   5   4   3   2   1

CONTENTS

PREFACE

Retirement in early 1992 brought with it a welcomed opportunity to indulge more fully a lifelong interest in the reading of history. Not being a particularly systematic reader, in my browsing I happened on Wayne C. Broehl's *John Deere's Company*, which I found extremely absorbing. A well-written company history, the book deals primarily with agricultural equipment, and although my background is a thirty-five-year career in international marketing of earthmoving equipment, Broehl piqued my interest in delving further into the history of the machinery business.

In my search for more material, I found that histories have been written on all the major companies that pioneered the development of the American agricultural equipment industry. Many of these companies have commissioned works on their histories or have provided independent authors with access to corporate archives. Examples in addition to Broehl's book are *J. I. Case: The First 150 Years* by Michael S. Holmes; the Massey-Ferguson history, *A Global Corporation* by E. P. Neufeld; and C. H. Wendel's numerous books. As I began to focus more narrowly on the earthmoving equipment field, I found a similar situation—numerous books focusing on a single company or product. Examples are *The LeTourneau Legend* by Philip G. Gowenlock, *Benjamin Holt and Caterpillar: Tracks and Combines* by Reynold M. Wik, and a series of books published by Motorbooks International. In some of its own publications, Caterpillar does an excellent job of describing the evolution of the company and its earthmoving products from the first Holt crawler to the present, but that material is not intended to deal with the history and accomplishments of the company's competitors. I found a near total absence of historical work on the earthmoving equipment industry itself.

Thus, in the absence of a work that would knit together the diverse stories of the many companies, American as well as foreign, that created and make up the worldwide earthmoving equipment industry, I decided to write this book. It was an innocent decision, made without the foreknowledge of the thousands of hours over several years that would be required.

The book is unique in that it deals with all the important companies of the industry; their origins; how they grew, interfaced, and competed; and, in some cases how they failed. In a sense, it is a cautionary tale because it examines the gradual decline of some of the pioneer earthmoving equipment companies along with the rather brief careers of some latecomers.

Yellow Steel is a business history. It is more about companies than machines, so the works cited previously and other one-company books were invaluable sources. I have also drawn on my own experience, which covers most of the postwar fifty-year period I call the modern era of the industry. It is international in scope, although I do not pretend it is as comprehensive of foreign as it is of American companies. In telling the story of the companies, the book weaves the evolution of the equipment with developments in the construction and mining industries and relates how certain important economic and political events in the postwar period made an impact on the industry. In discussing specific machines, an effort has been made to avoid overly technical information so as not to bore nontechnical readers while at the same time supplying enough detail to illustrate how one particular machine would differ from others and so satisfy readers interested in that aspect. Thus, in general, technical descriptions do not go beyond horsepowers, weights, capacities, and unique features.

To those with an interest or involvement in the machinery business, I trust this book will provide a deeper insight into the evolution of a great industry. To those whose interest is limited to casual observation of "road machinery," I hope it will bring some appreciation of all that lies behind those big yellow machines.

Introduction

From prehistoric times, the drive to change the face of the earth to suit humanity's convenience has only intensified as civilization advanced. Starting with crude wooden tools, individuals have never ceased to seek improvement in the means to move earth in greater quantities, faster and with less expenditure of energy. But despite these strivings, little progress was made in earthmoving methods until the nineteenth century when steam was first harnessed to the task. That was the long-awaited breakthrough that opened the way to development of mechanized earthmoving tools. Trickling slowly through the nineteenth century and accelerating in the first half of the twentieth century, the flow of new earthmoving inventions became a flood in the years after World War II. Marvelously innovative machines of ever-increasing size and efficiency have poured from the factories of the earthmoving equipment companies, making possible feats of construction and mining considered impractical only a few decades ago.

This is the story of the earthmoving equipment industry, its companies, and the machinery they built. The story begins in the nineteenth century, tracing the pioneer farm implement companies into the early twentieth century, when, with the development of the crawler tractor, the manufacture of earthmoving equipment began to diverge from its farm machinery roots.

That trend is followed through the first four decades of the twentieth century until, after World War II, the industry emerged clearly as an entity separate from farm equipment. This book is primarily about the American companies that dominated the earthmoving equipment business until the rise of the Japanese in the 1970s, when American preeminence was first challenged.

How did American companies come to dominate the earthmoving equipment industry? A free and open economy, the pioneering spirit, and a wealth of entrepreneurs—these were the basic ingredients. Add to them the vast unsettled areas of the continent, the lack of roads, and a severe shortage of farm labor. The needs were great and the opportunity very large. These nineteenth-century conditions triggered the rapid development of the American farm implement industry, providing opportunities for countless inventors and entrepreneurs who responded by starting hundreds of enterprises to fill the needs of farmers. The successful companies were good at inventing mechanical devices, metalworking, and the "cut-and-fit" method of designing machinery. Growing out of the farm implement business, this deep-rooted and widely disseminated expertise was the base on which the earthmoving equipment industry was founded.

By the mid-1800s the relentless evolutionary process was already underway through which stronger farm equipment companies either absorbed those weaker or drove them under. By 1930 the North American farm equipment business had been distilled to seven substantial firms: International Harvester, Deere, J. I. Case, Allis-Chalmers, Massey-Harris, Oliver, and Minneapolis-Moline (the so-called long-line companies) and a host of smaller, more specialized short-line companies. The first thirty years of the twentieth century had also sharpened the distinction between earthmoving and farm machinery, primarily as a result of the development of the track-type tractor. So it was that of the long-line companies that existed in 1930, all except Minneapolis-Moline entered the earthmoving equipment business via the track-type tractor—International Harvester and Allis-Chalmers during the late 1920s, the others after World War II.

Caterpillar did not follow the pattern of the other farm machinery manufacturers. Its two predecessor companies, Holt Manufacturing and C. L. Best Gas Tractor, had origins similar to the old-line midwestern companies—McCormick, Deere, Oliver, and Case—started in the nineteenth century by inventors and entrepreneurs to build farm implements. But Caterpillar's predecessors were California companies, a critical distinction because customer needs in central California were quite different from those in Illinois, Iowa, and Wisconsin. Benjamin Holt was filling a local need for a low ground pressure prime mover when he put tracks on a steamer in 1904, not knowing that he was also developing what would become the basic earth-moving machine. With the track-type tractor as their principal product, the two California companies began to diverge from their midwestern cousins so that by 1925, when Holt and Best merged to form Caterpillar, the new company had little in common with the farm equipment makers. Although agriculture was still an important market for its crawlers, Caterpillar was already an experienced supplier of machinery for earthmoving applications. It had taken a lead that none of its competitors has been able to close.

But not all North American earthmoving equipment companies came from a farm equipment base, some entering the business directly. Euclid Road Machinery Company, R. G. LeTourneau, Frank G. Hough, and Clark Equipment Company are examples. In a separate category were the power shovel manufacturers. Bucyrus-Erie, Marion, P&H (Pauling and Harnisch-feger), Northwest, Lima, Koehring, Osgood, and others played an impor-tant role in the prewar construction and mining industries. But the postwar development of the wheel loader and hydraulic excavator put an end to the power shovel as a construction tool. In general, American shovel manufac-turers did not make a successful transition to hydraulic excavators and there-fore no longer compete in the construction market. Bucyrus-Erie, Marion, and P&H now participate only in the mining sector, while others either retired to the crane and dragline business or disappeared altogether.

In Europe, plenty of inventiveness existed in the nineteenth century to fill the need for more efficient agriculture, but no unsettled areas existed that would provide land for new farms, and the semi-feudal system of land tenure slowed mechanization. European manufacturers generally focused on their comparatively small home markets, and although some industry consolidation did take place, in the end no farm machinery giants emerged during the twentieth century to rival the North American firms. Thus, in Europe there was no parallel to the diversification into earthmoving equip-ment that occurred in the North American farm equipment industry. The economic devastation of two world wars further handicapped the Euro-peans.

During the recovery period following World War II, European farm machinery makers, along with International Harvester and Massey-Harris who had prewar plants there, were too busy rebuilding their shattered op-erations to think of new ventures. Europe's early postwar earthmoving equipment needs were met largely by American exports under the Marshall Plan. A few licensees were established by the Americans to add nominal local content, but it was only after strict exchange controls and import restrictions threatened loss of markets that the Americans in the early 1950s reluctantly began to establish earthmoving equipment manufacturing operations in Europe.

But the drastic shortage of hard currency and the desperate need for equipment spurred the development of a fledgling European industry. In the postwar, pre–Common Market period, European companies entering the business did so with short lines and generally concentrated on their own national markets. Some were able to contest the Americans locally but were unable to achieve the critical mass necessary to mount a challenge outside the home market. Lacking full product lines, Europeans found it difficult to develop effective distribution systems.

But American companies did not preempt one major European innovation—the hydraulic excavator. Introduced and refined in Europe during the late 1950s and early 1960s, the excavator was quickly adopted by contractors there, and European excavator manufacturers proliferated overnight. By the mid-1970s excavators were accounting for 30 to 40 percent of European equipment purchasing, and manufacturers lacking them in their product line were severely handicapped. The hydraulic excavator established the European equipment industry and made Demag, Poclain, Liebherr, and O&K significant players in the game.

———————

The unique conditions of Japanese agriculture never created a need for farm mechanization on the scale of North America or Europe, so no farm equipment base was ever formed from which a take-off into earthmoving could be made. Before the war, Komatsu had very modest experience with small track-type tractors, and Hitachi built power shovels. The other present-day participants in the industry—Mitsubishi, Kobelco, Kawasaki, Furukawa, TCM, Sumitomo, Yutani, and others—entered the business after the war and without a tradition of either farm or earthmoving equipment of the size and type used in the West.

In the early postwar period, the Japanese industry was based on borrowed Western technology to fill the need as the nation rebuilt its economy and, strongly encouraged by the government, as import substitutions. Beginning in the decade between the mid-1950s and the mid-1960s, Japanese manufacturers began legitimizing their use of foreign technology through numerous license agreements with U.S. and European equipment makers. Developing behind a impenetrable wall of tariff and non-tariff barriers, by the early 1960s Japanese equipment was good enough to compete with Western equipment on a price basis if not on a quality basis, particularly in developing countries. In 1965 Hitachi introduced the first Japanese-built hydraulic excavator, and by the mid-1970s Japanese hydraulic excavator technology was as good or better than that of the West. In the early 1980s a combination of favorable exchange rates and excellent product quality enabled Japan to mount a serious challenge worldwide to U.S. dominance while a deep recession in North America and Europe was drastically weakening the equipment industry there, causing the disappearance or realignment of numerous well-known names. Through the late 1980s a stronger yen and drastic restructuring by Western competitors created the worldwide industry of the 1990s in which Japan dominated the hydraulic excavator segment while the United States retained supremacy in all other segments.

In this book, chapter 1 reviews how the need was created for new methods and larger, more productive earthmoving equipment by increasingly ambitious civil works and the growth of the open-pit mining industry—how the evolution of canals, railroads, highways, dams, and open-pit mines has stretched the envelope of available equipment since the early 1800s and how manufacturers, badly behind the curve for most of that period, struggled to advance the state of the art.

Chapter 2 sketches a brief history of each of the North American companies that figured importantly in the industry, from their origins through 1941, although several of them did not enter the business until after World War II. Chapter 2 also covers the role of the American earthmoving equipment industry in World War II.

Chapters 3 through 7 take up the story at the end of World War II and encompass the modern era of the industry, decade by decade, to the mid-1990s.

Labor relations have been extraordinarily turbulent in the farm and earthmoving equipment industries. The influence of these important events on the companies is related separately in an appendix, and thus, to avoid redundancy, labor relations are mentioned only in passing in the body of the work.

A word about terminology. The reader will encounter the terms *earthmoving equipment, construction equipment,* and *industrial equipment* as this story unfolds. All are meant to apply to heavy equipment for the shaping, loosening, loading, and hauling of earth and rock materials, and all were and are used by different companies at different times to describe their products. The term *earthmoving equipment* is the most generic in that it takes in machines for both construction and mining, whereas "construction" implies an application to that industry alone. "Industrial" is the least descriptive and enters in only because some manufacturers have used the term to differentiate earthmoving products from their farm equipment lines. Unless the manufacturer specifically refers to equipment as "industrial" or "construction," the term *earthmoving* is preferred and used.

At some points in the book, manufacturers are ranked by size. These rankings are based on published information or in some cases, estimates, of dollar sales to the industry of all sizes of track-type tractors, track loaders, wheel loaders, wheel dozers, motor graders, wheel tractor-scrapers, off-highway trucks, dumpers, loader-backhoes, hydraulic excavators, power shovels, and attachments and parts for the foregoing products. Because most companies in this story also competed (and some continue to compete) in other industries such as logging (usually with derivative construction machines) and rarely break out their sales by industry, the figures used to arrive at size rankings are not completely pure. I believe, however, that the inclusion of some sales to other industries does not materially change the overall rankings given.

Let us begin the story now with an overview of how the need was created for the earthmoving equipment industry as we know it today.

YELLOW STEEL

Creating the Need

From the dawn of civilization, human beings have constructed civil works; indeed, until the advent of open-pit mining in the late nineteenth century, these works accounted for almost all of the earthmoving that took place. With nothing more than the most rudimentary tools, ancient civilizations of the Middle East, the Nile, and China accomplished impressive feats of construction through the forced mobilization of large masses of workers. Using similar methods, the Romans built their great civil works, many of which still stand. But the fall of the Roman Empire marked the end of civil works construction in Europe until the Renaissance, when the new wealth created by commercial expansion supported a revived interest.

In the ensuing years and through the seventeenth century, civil works activity increased slowly, but with few exceptions the scarcity of resources kept projects on a modest scale. Moreover, the various plagues that swept through Europe during the Middle Ages, along with the weakening of the feudal system, made it increasingly difficult to mobilize masses of forced labor, the traditional means of carrying out large projects. That labor shortage coupled with the nonexistence of labor-saving mechanical devices to strongly inhibit the scope of civil works involving earthmoving.

With the Industrial Revolution that began to change. The invention of the blast furnace and the steam engine in the eighteenth century and the ensuing industrialization launched a new era of mercantile trade in manufactured goods that demanded better means of transportation for bulk raw materials and finished products. That stimulated canal and subsequent railroad construction while the wealth created by the Industrial Revolution provided the capital to pay for these more ambitious civil works.

Despite these great industrial advances, earthmoving through the nineteenth century continued to be largely a pick-and-shovel process. The need was recognized for roads, dams, canals, railways, and other civil engineering improvements, and capital was becoming available to finance them. Despite these strong pulls, however, earthmoving machinery was quite slow to develop and continued to inhibit the scope of projects entailing the movement of large quantities of earth. Earthmoving machines needed two things that the technology of the day could not provide—a practical power source and mobility. The cumbersome steam engine could provide power but at a sacrifice in mobility, whereas the iron wheels of the day could not provide acceptable mobility for heavy vehicles in off-road conditions. Compared with the progress made in numerous other fields during the nineteenth century, earthmoving equipment badly lagged the need.

The combination of the internal combustion engine with the track-type tractor in 1908 was a giant step in resolving both power-source and mobility problems. As a drawbar machine, the crawler tractor quickly found a place in civil works, but the full potential of the crawler as an earthmover was not immediately perceived. Although most branches of the machinery industry were making great advances through the first three decades of the twentieth century, earthmoving equipment continued to lag. If anything, the vision of civil engineers was on a much steeper curve than the inventiveness of earthmoving machine designers during this period.

Adaptation of the diesel engine and the combination of the pneumatic tire with the scraper in the early 1930s were huge breakthroughs for the industry. Now the equipment was beginning to close the gap. The machinery inventiveness curve was becoming steeper than the civil engineer's ambition curve. By 1941 the earthmoving equipment industry was coming close to filling the need, and certainly by the early 1950s the lines had crossed. Thus, today engineers and builders can now conceive of virtually no project that cannot be built for want of adequate earthmoving equipment.

The evolution of civil works on an ever-grander scale since the late 1700s and the advent of large-scale, open-pit mining during the 1890s created a need for earthmoving equipment, which, as the state of the art permitted, a slowly emerging industry has filled. How that took place provides essential background for the story of companies that in responding to the need were to create the earthmoving equipment industry.

The Canal-Building Era

From the time humans learned to build boats until the development of the railroad in the 1830s, no easier, cheaper, or faster means existed to move people and goods from place to place than waterways, first on rivers and lakes and later supplemented by man-made canals. Canals were among the first major earthmoving projects in recorded history. Europe's first great canal project, Louis XIV's Midi Canal, opened in 1681. The 150-mile waterway connected the Atlantic and Mediterranean watersheds and used 101 locks to cross a 620-foot summit, a magnificent engineering feat for the time.[1] Taking advantage of their plentiful watercourses, England, France, and the Low Countries led the way in canal construction during the eighteenth century.

Beginning about 1785 and borrowing technology from England, America entered an era of canal construction that would last until about 1860. Early American waterways such as the Potomac Canal (later to become the Chesapeake and Ohio Canal) were lateral canals, closely paralleling a river and beginning where the stream ceased to be navigable. In some cases they were merely eliminating portages around short, nonnavigable sections. Earthmoving was minimized.

Soon American canal promoters and builders began dreaming of summit canals connecting different watersheds, boldly striking out across terrain that did not allow for the paralleling of natural watercourses but that would require unprecedented amounts of earthmoving. Unlike the roads of the time, canals, under the discipline imposed by the law of gravity, had to be constructed to an exacting gradient. For example, the Erie Canal had a slope of one inch per mile. That forced the engineer into trade-offs between deeper cuts versus additional locks, the latter being the usual choice. The limitations imposed by the shovel, wheelbarrow, and cart and the shortage of labor made mass earthmoving impractical. Some early canals in the United States were no more than three to four feet deep and fifteen feet wide, but even then each mile of advance through level terrain entailed more than twelve thousand cubic yards of excavation, a substantial amount for hand tools. Had it not been possible merely to sidecast most spoil material, early canal construction would not have been feasible. Alignments were chosen wherever possible to avoid rock cuts, but holes had to be drilled laboriously by hand when rock was unavoidable. Black powder was used for blasting.

Despite the primitive tools available, prodigious feats of engineering were accomplished. By almost any standard the Erie Canal, begun in 1817 and opened in 1825, was the outstanding success of the canal era from both engineering and financial standpoints. This 363-mile canal from the Hudson River north of Albany to Buffalo involved a total vertical lift of 688 feet through 83 locks. The original design provided for a width of twenty-eight feet at the bottom, forty feet at the waterline, and four feet of water. On level ground that cross-section entailed the excavation of more than twenty-five thousand cubic yards per mile. Material was sidecast to form a ten-foot towpath on one side and an eight-foot berm on the other. A sixty-foot right-of-way had to be cleared and grubbed through virgin forests over much of the line. The canal itself was dug entirely by contractors paid from 10 cents per cubic yard for dirt to $2 per cubic yard for solid rock. Lock construction was undertaken directly by the state of New York. Total cost of the original project was $7.1 million. Although no figures are available for the total amount of earthmoving, on the order of eight to ten million cubic yards must have been involved, surpassing anything yet attempted in North America. The canal was a great financial success, quickly returning its costs in tolls and becoming an important source of revenue to the state. In a much modified and improved form, the Erie Canal is still in use as the New York State Barge Canal.[2]

An even more ambitious project, the 395-mile Pennsylvania Mainline Canal from Philadelphia to Pittsburg, was conceived as a rival to the Erie Canal. Jealous of New York City's growing importance as a port, the Mainline backers intended to divert western commerce to Philadelphia. Begun in 1826 and completed in 1836, the Mainline exceeded the Erie as an engineering feat, actually reaching an elevation of 2,291 feet above sea level as it crossed the Alleghenies. In the highest section it used the horse-drawn, thirty-seven-mile Allegheny Portage Railroad and inclined planes to carry canal boats on cars over the summit. It also included a nine-hundred-foot railroad tunnel near Johnstown, Pennsylvania. But those dazzling engineering achievements were too costly, and the Mainline was a financial failure, its tolls never adequate to retire the construction bonds. To protect its canal investment against competition, the state levied a tonnage tax on the newly formed Pennsylvania Railroad. In 1857, to free itself of that burden, the railroad bought the Mainline system and quickly closed the uneconomic Portage Railroad.[3]

Throughout the American canal era, a constitutional controversy existed with regard to the powers of the federal government to fund internal improvements. As a result, canals were constructed either privately under state charters or directly by the states through the issuance of bonds. As carriers of agricultural staples from west to east and settlers and manufactured goods from east to west, canals were the mode of choice over roads—for shippers by reason of economy and for passengers by reason of comfort. The primitive roads of the day could not compete. In 1850, for example, the cost per ton-mile for agricultural staples by wagon was estimated at between 15 cents and 25 cents whereas the same products could move on canals for less than 2 cents per ton-mile. Indeed, with a network of largely state-owned canals already in being, the more populous states had very little incentive to fund road construction.[4]

The Railroad Supplants the Canal

In the 1830s, when canal construction was at its zenith, a new rival appeared—the railroad—which would quickly put an end to the supremacy of canals. By 1840 the United States already had 2,800 miles of railroad, a number that had increased to thirty thousand miles by 1860.[5] Initially, railroads, like canals, were encouraged if not actually underwritten by the states, but early eastern railroads such as the New York Central, Baltimore and Ohio, and Pennsylvania, quickly began attracting private capital. By the 1850s the eastern states had ceased providing financial support. Indeed, it was no longer needed because private investors poured money wildly into railroads, putting an end to canal construction entirely by 1860. In that year canals in America reached a peak of 4,254 miles but quickly began diminishing as competition from railroads grew.[6]

To encourage railroad construction in the thinly populated states of the Old Northwest and the South, in 1850 the federal government made the first railroad land grants in Illinois, Alabama, and Mississippi. That was followed by increasingly lavish land grants to railroads west of the Mississippi. By means of these indirect subsidies, in little more than three decades the entire nation had been laced together by railroad lines. The unprecedented speed and comfort of railways all but eliminated passenger travel by road, and intercity freight shipment by wagon virtually disappeared. Thus, during the latter half of the nineteenth century a burgeoning railway network removed any sense of urgency on the part of states to address the abysmal condition of their roads.

Railroads required a different set of disciplines from canal construction. Engineers were still under tight constraints with regard to gradient, but now radius of curvature also had to be considered. To gain elevation there was no alternative to using long reaches of gentle gradients; there were few tunnels. The first effort to drive a major railroad tunnel in the United States was the five-mile Hoosac Tunnel under the Berkshire Mountains of Massachusetts. Begun in 1855, it was too ambitious for the tools of the day and could not be completed until steam and later compressed-air drills were developed during the 1870s. It was opened in 1876 at a cost five times the original estimate.

Railroad construction across rolling terrain called for cuts and fills, which required the movement of material up and down the right-of-way in carts and wagons. On level terrain relatively little earthmoving was required because a low roadbed was merely cast up from the sides. In fact, early railroad builders frequently laid ties directly on the undisturbed ground. Initially, track was ballasted with dirt, and it would be decades before the advantages of clean, crushed-rock ballast were recognized. Hillside work could require displacement of substantial quantities, but that material was simply cast downhill. Although the rail-mounted steam shovel, invented in 1838, became an important tool in railroad construction, throughout most of the nineteenth century the primary earthmoving tools were no different from those used to build the canals: masses of men with picks, shovels, wheelbarrows, carts, and wagons. But the building of the American railway system, considering the tools at hand, was a civil engineering achievement that ranks with anything accomplished since, including the interstate highway system. By 1900, 193,346 miles of track crisscrossed the nation. The national system was essentially complete, although some sixty-eight thousand additional miles would be laid by 1929, the peak year. At the turn of the century, railways were almost the exclusive means of moving people and goods between cities.[7]

While the coming of the railroad slowed construction of barge canals in the latter half of the nineteenth century, inter-ocean canals for seagoing vessels were becoming technically feasible through the availability of steam-powered earthmoving tools. Examples were the Kiel, Corinth, Suez, and Panama canals, the latter two being the most important from an earthmoving standpoint.

The Suez Canal

The crowning achievement of the American railroad construction era was the link-up of the Union Pacific and Central Pacific at Promontory Point, Utah, in 1869, completing North America's first transcontinental railroad. Although that event was a milestone in American history, an event of even greater significance in world history was occurring the same year in Egypt with the opening of the Suez Canal. Evidence suggests that a canal connecting the Mediterranean and the Red seas existed during the times of the pharoahs, but early-nineteenth-century engineers believed that a substantial difference in elevation existed between the seas, precluding a sea-level canal. Subsequent surveys with more accurate instruments were to prove that false, and construction began in 1859 through the tenacity of the visionary Ferdinand de Lesseps and the support of Napoleon III.

French contractors employed more than twenty thousand Egyptian laborers, often equipped with nothing more than headbaskets, to move millions of cubic yards of sand. But for the first time in the history of earthmoving, machinery began to play the principal role. Recognizing that most of the material was loose sand, contractors brought in newly invented steam-powered floating ladder dredges. Once a pilot channel had been dug, they were able to use these machines to move the major part of the material. Also, by taking advantage of the dry desert lakes that lay along the alignment, less than half of the canal's hundred-mile length would have to be excavated from the sand. The highest point on the canal alignment was only sixty feet above sea level. Finished, the canal had a bottom width of seventy-two feet, a width at water line of 175 feet, and twenty-six feet of water. Almost one hundred million cubic yards of material was moved, making the Suez Canal the then-largest single earthmoving project in history. Aside from the monumental economic and political significance of the canal, it was also the first major earthmoving project to use machinery on a large scale.[8]

The Panama Canal

After his triumph on the Suez Canal, Ferdinand de Lesseps formed a group of French investors to build a sea-level canal across the fifty-mile Isthmus of Panama. Initial French estimates of the required earthmoving were wildly optimistic at only 120 million cubic yards, and they hoped to be able to apply the same dredging techniques so successful at Suez. But Panama was not Suez, and misdirected methods and inadequate machinery, along with tropical diseases, defeated the effort. The company went bankrupt in 1889 after nine years of work. Although a successor company continued work fitfully until 1902, a French canal was not to be.

In 1904 the United States purchased French rights for $40 million and began work on a lock canal. The principal obstacle was the nine-mile Culebra (later Gaillard) Cut across the spine of the isthmus, which would account for almost all the dry excavation. A few (probably less than ten) small, American-made steam shovels had worked on the canal during the French era.[9] But after 1904 the steam shovel became the primary excavating tool in the Culebra Cut, and more than seventy heavy machines, built by the Bucyrus and Marion companies, eventually operated there. The three-cubic-yard, ninety-five-ton, rail-mounted machines were capable of only a 180-degree swing, but that was all that was needed to load railroad cars on a parallel track. The overall system of excavation and haulage used in the Gaillard Cut was similar to that already in use for railroad construction and on the Mesabi Iron Range of Minnesota. It would be adapted for use in the growing number of large, open-pit mines being opened in the early twentieth century in North and South America and Europe.

When opened in 1914, the Panama Canal eclipsed any previous single

This view of the Culebra Cut illustrates the key role of the steam shovel in completing the massive excavation required for the Panama Canal. (Bucyrus International Inc.)

construction project in history in the amount of earth moved; indeed, few projects since have exceeded it. In twenty-two years the French had moved eighty million cubic yards, about one-third of the 232 million total the Americans moved in ten years to complete the work. Including the thirty million cubic yards of useful French excavation that could be incorporated, the final total for the canal as built was 262,440,945 cubic yards. In addition, the 4.4 million cubic yards of concrete poured in lock construction made the Panama Canal project the first to use Portland cement concrete on so massive a scale. This awesome challenge to American engineering might have ended in failure, like the French project, had it not been for the steam shovel.[10]

The Struggle for Roads: Enter the Automobile

Although the United States had almost no improved roads when it achieved independence, Western Europe already had a reasonably good road system, especially in France and England. During the seventeenth century, Louis XIV had established the corvée, a system of enforced peasant labor, and used it to build a fifteen-thousand-mile network of improved roads, and in 1733 Louis XV established a Department of Bridges and Roads (*Ponts et Chausées*). In England, Parliament had authorized a system of privately operated toll roads. In contrast, the U.S. Bureau of Public Roads was not established until 1904. In early-nineteenth-century Western Europe, overland travel and the transit of mail by regularly scheduled stagecoach were everyday practices. In the United States, however, the most reliable means of transport remained the saddle and the sailing ship.

The first federal involvement in roads occurred during the Jefferson administration, when federal funds were appropriated for the National Road from Cumberland, Maryland, to the Ohio River at Wheeling. Completed in 1818, the road proved popular, but with no provisions for maintenance it deteriorated rapidly. To provide funds for maintenance, Congress proposed to collect tolls, but that was vetoed by President James Monroe as an unconstitutional infringement of state sovereignty over the land on which the road was built. The principle of state jurisdiction over roads, regardless of the source of funding, has continued to the present. Control of the National Road was later transferred to the separate states, and a century would pass before federal support for roads reappeared.

Some states tried to meet the need by chartering private, for-profit toll roads. These roads, sometimes with only rudimentary improvements, were not financially successful and were gradually abandoned. But most states were singularly unaggressive in supporting road construction and left the matter largely to local authorities. By the Civil War the canal system and the railroad network well served the transportation needs of the more heavily populated states east of the Mississippi. Intercity travel by road was an unpleasant ordeal to be avoided, and state highway departments did not exist.

Still, in the latter half of the nineteenth century there was steadily growing recognition of the need for good roads. With the support of the National Grange and other farm organizations, that awareness led to the founding in 1892 of the National League for Good Roads. And under the unlikely leadership of bicycle enthusiasts, the American Road Makers, another lobbying organization, was founded in 1902 and changed its name to the American Road Builders Association in 1910.[11] These organizations began holding annual conventions, which led in 1909 to the first Road Show, an exhibition in Columbus, Ohio, by manufacturers of road-building machinery and materials. The thirty-seven exhibitors included J. D. Adams and Company, J. I. Case Threshing Machine Company, Galion Iron Works Company, Huber Manufacturing Company, Kelly-Springfield Road Roller Company, and several cement makers and asphalt suppliers.[12]

In 1892 Congress created the Office of Road Inquiry in the Department of Agriculture, and a year later, as an indirect stimulus to improved roads, authorized Rural Free Delivery, which required a gravel or macadam road for mail service.[13] But congressional support for federal aid for roads remained feeble.

Around the turn of the century, just when the railroad's supremacy seemed indisputable, a new challenger appeared that would change everything—the automobile. Suddenly, roads became important to wealthy city-dwellers who could afford cars and wanted good roads on which to drive them. In 1900 more than two million miles of roads existed in the United States, about half the network that exists today, but all-weather roads were virtually nonexistent outside cities and towns. The invention of the automobile made that situation unacceptable to a growing number of citizens, and the "good roads" lobby gained powerful new allies.[14]

The Birth of the Federal Aid Highway Program

In 1913, the year Henry Ford began mass production of his Model T, Congress passed a token federal appropriation for roads, providing $500,000 so the U.S. Post Office could participate with the states in building post roads. But when Model T production reached five hundred thousand in 1915 it was clear to Congress that a strong federal role in road-building could be delayed no longer. The breakthrough came in 1916 with the first Federal-Aid Road Act, under which Congress appropriated $75 million over five years for road-building, to be matched dollar-for-dollar by the states. An apportionment formula was devised based on area, population, and miles of post roads. With that act, Congress opened an era of road-building that still continues, creating the highway construction industry and a sustained demand for heavy construction equipment. Since 1916 the construction and maintenance of the federal aid highway system have created the need for more heavy construction equipment than any other sector of the economy.

The Federal-Aid Highway Act of 1921 improved on the 1916 act by substantially increasing appropriations and providing for nearly two hundred thousand miles of an integrated national system of federally aided primary highways. The 1921 act established the basics of the federal aid highway program, which would remain essentially unchanged until the passage of the Federal-Aid Highway Act of 1956. It also launched a sustained period of highway construction that lasted until the United States entered World War II. During the depression, road-building actually accelerated because the federal government used public works to provide employment, pumping $1 billion of unmatched grants into roads. Between 1921 and 1941 generous congressional appropriations, along with matching state funds, generated unprecedented amounts of highway construction.[15]

Between 1921 and 1941 the federal aid primary system of U.S. highways was largely put in place. Traffic could move between cities on relatively high-standard, two-lane concrete pavements, but the growth in numbers of vehicles was outstripping plans for new highways. By the late 1930s, higher traffic densities and vehicle speeds were making many portions of the system inadequate and unsafe. Modeled on the Frankfurt to Stuttgart autobahn built from 1933 to 1935, the prewar Pennsylvania Turnpike and the Merritt Parkway pointed the way to the future for American highways, although little civilian highway construction took place during the war years.[16]

The Alaska Highway

Early in the war, U.S. and Canadian contractors had an opportunity to demonstrate their competence during the emergency construction of the 1,420-mile Alcan (Alaska-Canadian) Highway. Beginning in May 1942, seven army engineer regiments combined efforts with civilian contractors and in six months punched through a pioneer road. During the 1943 construction season, a force of eighty-one contractors employing 14,100 workers and more than eleven thousand pieces of equipment completed a usable road the full length of the project. Although a Japanese wartime threat to Alaska proved to have been exaggerated, the crash-built highway continues to be the sole overland link to Alaska. Its successful completion was a severe test of the contractors and equipment that composed the road-building industry.[17]

Water Projects

Dams have been built since the dawn of history, and their builders have learned through trial and error the elusive science of building structures that would withstand the pressure, intrusion, and erosion of water. Early dams were made of earth, but as soon as the art of cutting stone was mastered it became the building material of choice, and cut stone continued in use into the twentieth century as a material for dams. But small dams continued to be built of earth, and builders by the nineteenth century had learned to construct earth-and-rockfill water retention structures of acceptable reliability.

The boom in canal construction during the first half of the nineteenth century led to the building of numerous dams for canal water supply and control. One, the South Fork Dam on the Conemaugh River in southwestern Pennsylvania, was built to supply water to a portion of the Pennsylvania Mainline Canal. Completed in 1839, it was an earthfill structure seventy-two feet high and 840 feet long, with a base 270 feet wide, making it one of the largest dams in the United States. When that portion of the Mainline served by the dam was closed in 1857, the dam was abandoned. The ensuing years of neglect culminated in failure of the dam during a heavy rain in 1889, resulting in the Johnstown disaster that cost the lives of more than 2,200 people.[18] Although the failure was not caused by flaws in the original design and construction, nevertheless the reliability of all earthfill dams was called into question. Earth as a material for the construction of high dams was almost totally eclipsed by a relatively new material: Portland cement concrete.

Cements had been used in masonry work in antiquity, but not until the early nineteenth century was a standardized process developed in England that would produce the high-strength, hydraulic cement that came to be known as Portland cement. The first Portland cement was not produced in the United States until 1871, and in 1889 the San Mateo Dam, the first in the United States built entirely of Portland cement concrete, was completed in California. An arch dam 170 feet high, 700 feet long, and 185 feet thick at its base, San Mateo was a marvel of its time and forerunner of a series of great concrete dams.[19]

The Bureau of Reclamation

By the Federal Reclamation Act of 1902, Congress established the Reclamation Service and gave it the mission of reclaiming for settlement the vast arid and semi-arid areas in the seventeen states lying wholly or partially west of the 100th Meridian. Reclamation meant irrigation, and irrigation meant dams and canals. Thus, an intensive dam-building era was launched in the western United States that only in the latter part of the century was slowed by a shortage of suitable sites and the resistance of environmentalists. From its inception until 1931, the Reclamation Service, which became the Bureau of Reclamation (BuRec) in 1923, built a series of relatively small earthfill dams (less than two million cubic yards) and a few notable concrete ones, including the 350-foot-high Arrowrock Dam in 1915 and the 301-foot-high Elephant Butte Dam in 1916. Through its first three decades of existence it had not made a large public impression, but Hoover Dam on the Colorado River brought national recognition to the agency. Authorized by Congress in 1928 and begun in 1931, when completed in 1935 it was the world's highest dam at 726 feet.[20] The $49 million construction contract, the largest civil contract awarded until that time, went to Six Companies, Inc., a consortium of contractors, some of whom would later come to dominate American heavy construction: Utah Construction Company, W. A. Bechtel, H. J. Kaiser, Morrison-Knudsen, and others. R. G. LeTourneau was a small subcontractor on the project. Before the completion of Hoover Dam, the Bureau had already started on its next great tour de force, the Grand Coulee Dam on the Columbia River. Begun in 1933 and completed in 1942 (the first stage), it was the world's largest concrete structure. The original dam contained more than ten million cubic yards of concrete.[21]

Notwithstanding the spectacular aspects of Hoover and Grand Coulee dams, the Bureau's most extensive (and perhaps most controversial) undertaking has been California's Central Valley Project (CVP). Bureau involvement was first authorized in 1935, and the work has continued into the 1990s. The first major CVP dams begun during the depression were the concrete Shasta and Friant dams. Following the war, however, the CVP's emphasis shifted to earthfill dams, including some very large ones: the Oroville Dam in 1959 with eighty million cubic yards; the Trinity Dam in 1962 with 29.4 million cubic yards; and the San Luis Dam in 1967 with 77.6 million cubic yards. When completed by the California Department of Water Resources, Oroville, at 774 feet, was the highest dam in the United States and the highest earthfill dam in the world.[22]

Although the Bureau had held fairly closely to its original charter as an irrigation agency until 1929, beginning with Hoover Dam and with the encouragement of the Roosevelt administration, it entered into construction of multipurpose dams. Electric-power generation took the lead role at Hoover, Grand Coulee, Glen Canyon, and several other major projects and was always an important secondary objective. Even on Central Valley projects it was justified on the basis that the sale of power helped pay the cost of the irrigation works. A list of accomplishments of the Bureau of Reclamation through 1978 included 11.4 million acres irrigated, 324 storage dams, 151 diversion dams, 7,064 miles of canals, and 50 hydroelectric power plants built over a span of seventy-six years.[23]

The U.S. Army Corps of Engineers

The assertiveness of the Bureau of Reclamation did not go unnoticed by the nation's traditional waterworks agency, the U.S. Army Corps of Engineers, which had exercised total responsibility for flood control and navigation on the major rivers and their tributaries since 1824. Despite the acclaim given to the newly activist Bureau of Reclamation, the Corps was not prepared to surrender its authority west of the Hundredth Meridian. Even though it received funding during the depression for a massive program involving hundreds of flood control projects all over the country—dams, levees, channels, and reservoirs—it still jealously guarded what it regarded as its historic areas of responsibility. As a result, it frequently clashed with the Bureau.

Corps work in the 1930s along the Lower Mississippi River, where there was no conflict between the agencies, accounted for 2,400 miles of levees and earthworks containing nearly one billion cubic yards.[24] But it was on the Upper Missouri River, where the Corps and the Bureau overlapped, that serious rivalries arose. Most early Corps dams were earthfills less than one hundred feet in height, although a major exception was the Fort Peck Dam on the Missouri River in Montana. Completed in 1939, it was then the world's largest earthfill dam: 250 feet high, 9,000 feet long, and containing 122 million cubic yards of fill placed hydraulically. The hydraulic-fill method had been pioneered on the Gatun Dam built between 1904 and 1914 to create Gatun Lake, the water supply for the Panama Canal.

Fort Peck was the opening round in a battle between the agencies concerning which would develop the Upper Missouri River Basin. Under a threat from Congress to create a TVA-like organization for the Upper Missouri that would cut out both agencies, in 1944 the Corps and the Bureau reached an agreement—the Pick-Sloan Plan—which defined their respective roles in the basin. Essentially, the Corps would build the main-stem dams and the Bureau would build the irrigation facilities made possible by these dams. On the tributaries, the agencies would split responsibility, depending on the principal purpose of the facility. The Bureau would administer all power facilities.

The Pick-Sloan Plan triggered a huge wave of dam construction, including the ninety-one-million-cubic-yard Oahe Dam that was completed in 1959.[25] Others included the Garrison Dam, Big Bend Dam, Fort Randal Dam, and Gavins Point Dam, all on the Missouri's main stem, as well as dozens of smaller dams, most of them earthfill, on tributaries. It was a bonanza for earthmoving contractors and equipment makers alike.[26]

The Tennessee Valley Authority

In 1933 Congress established the Tennessee Valley Authority, which launched a surge of dam construction in the southeastern United States. These were concrete dams with extensive earthen dikes in some instances and although not spectacular by the standards of many western dams, they entailed large quantities of earthwork and concrete. Thirty million cubic yards of excavation and 113 million cubic yards of concrete were required to erect 30 dams and build 1,300 miles of highway. But the TVA did not endear itself to contractors by carrying out its projects on a force account basis nor to private power companies by selling power directly. Thus, it has remained controversial throughout its existence.[27]

The Impact of Civil Works Projects on Construction Equipment: Early Road-Building Machinery

During the late nineteenth century, machinery began to play an important role in road-building. A key invention was the leaning-wheel road grader, brought out by J. D. Adams in 1885. The horse-drawn machine used an angled blade to cast up material from the roadsides and form a road-bed, simultaneously cutting ditches for drainage. Its unique feature was its ability to resist the sidedraft of the angled blade by leaning the wheels against the draft. The grader became indispensable for rural road construction and maintenance and was widely imitated. Heavier versions were developed for pulling by steam traction engines and later by crawler tractors. Several manufacturers offered the towed leaning-wheel grader until the introduction of the integral motor grader in the early 1930s brought about a rapid decline in its popularity. By the early 1940s it had fallen into disuse.[28]

A survey by the Office of Road Inquiry in 1904 showed that of roughly two million miles of rural roads only 153,000 had been improved. Of these, about thirty-eight thousand miles were "high-type" water-bound macadam; the remainder had lower-type surfaces of gravel and other material.[29] In 1815 John L. McAdam, a Scot, had introduced the technique of using well-graded broken limestone in roadbeds to form what became known as waterbound

The crawler tractor–towed grader combination was the premier rural road-building and maintenance tool well into the 1930s, when it began to be displaced by the self-propelled grader. (Courtesy of Caterpillar Inc.)

A crawler tractor with a hydraulically controlled bulldozer, around 1935. Rapid progress was being made in applying hydraulics to earthmoving machinery by the mid-1930s. After the war, stronger main frames allowed cable sheave or cylinder mounting to the engine cowling. (Courtesy of Caterpillar Inc.)

macadam. Limestone fines and dust filled the interstices of the surface, and moisture bound the materials into a dense, impervious surface.[30] Although a macadam road was the highest type of surface that could be built from commonly available materials, the need to break rock manually made macadam roads extremely labor-intensive. That problem was solved by Eli Whitney Blake's invention of the jaw-crusher in 1858, which made crushed rock available at a fraction of the former cost.[31]

Although little was known of the science of soil mechanics, early road builders recognized the benefits of compaction although they had no effective means of achieving it. In 1859 Lemoine, who was French, invented the steam roller, permitting another advance in the construction of macadam roads. Because it did not require a great deal of engineering to convert an already heavy steam traction engine into a roller, numerous manufacturers of steam tractors added steam rollers to their lines. Steam rollers made possible the first asphalt road surfaces in the United States during the 1870s.[32]

Another tool available but seldom used by turn-of-the-century road build-ers was the steam shovel. Invented in 1838 by William S. Otis of Massachu-setts, the cumbersome nineteenth-century machines had to be operated on rails.[33] That made them ideal for railroad work, and in the 1890s the rail-mounted steam shovel made feasible large-scale, open-pit mining. Yet despite steady refinement, the early steam shovel did not lend itself to road-building because of the requirement for rails. It was not until integral 360-degree, crawler-mounted machines became available after the turn of the century that shovels became sufficiently mobile and flexible to gain acceptance as a gen-eral excavating tool. But the rail-mounted steam shovel was the right tool for mass excavation and was able to prove that on the Panama Canal.

Through the first twenty years of the twentieth century, road-building was slowly mechanized; the basic tools were the crawler tractor and the towed elevating grader, which cast up roadbed from the sides. Rural roads tended to follow natural contours, and cuts and fills were minimized. But the new highway design standards established by the Federal-Aid Highway Act of 1921 mandated sharply increased quantities of earthmoving. Steam shov-els and belt-loaders, top-loading dump trucks, and crawler-mounted dump wagons pulled by crawler tractors became the earthmoving methods of choice until the appearance of effective crawler-drawn, cable-operated scrap-ers in the early 1930s.

The new standards also demanded improved compaction and paving equipment. The road-building boom triggered a dynamic burst of inventive-ness in the equipment industry during the 1920s and 1930s. Equipment grew in size and horsepower. Steam was replaced by gasoline and gasoline, in turn, by diesel power. The federal aid highway construction program stimulated many innovations that appeared during this twenty-year period: the bull-dozer and crawler-drawn scraper, motor grader, dump truck, bottom-dump wagon, self-propelled scraper, and the sheepsfoot roller as well as cable and hydraulic controls and concrete and asphalt plants and pavers.

Prewar Dam-Building Equipment

The combined activities of BuRec, the Corps of Engineers, and the TVA over the years before World War II had important implications for the earth-moving equipment industry. BuRec irrigation canals and the Corps of En-gineers' levee-building program of the 1930s created ideal work for bull-dozers, crawler-drawn scrapers, and draglines, and the predominance of concrete dams before the war stimulated demand for equipment for the production of aggregates. The massive quantities of concrete entailed the opening of large quarries that used the open-pit mining techniques of the day—steam shovels and rail-mounted or crawler-drawn haulage equipment. Yet overall the fifty years of dam building before World War II did not generate huge business for the earthmoving equipment industry. Good sites for concrete dams were still plentiful; the technology of building with concrete was well developed, whereas that of large, earthfill dam building was still developing; and the equipment industry lagged the potential for large, high-speed hauling units for dry-fill placement. More powerful, lighter-weight diesel engines, suitable transmissions, and large, off-highway earthmoving tires were not yet available. Engineers had years of experience with small earthfill dams and were confident that they knew how to build the really big ones, but until suitable machines were available the economics of doing so were not attractive to dam designers.

All of that began to change in the 1930s with the introduction of the wheel tractor–bottom-dump wagon combination, a product that had a major impact on the economics of dam building. It offered greater capacity and speed than any previous hauling unit, and its design simplicity made it relatively trouble-free and gave it a favorable ratio of payload to tare weight. It was a natural for dry-fill placement and was to become a favorite of dam

Introduced in 1934, the Euclid wheel tractor bottom-dump created a revolution in top-loaded earthmoving applications and greatly extended economical haul distances. (Historical Construction Equipment Association)

builders. The introduction of LeTourneau's Tournapull in 1938, the first integral wheel tractor-scraper, tipped the balance even more in favor of the feasibility of using fleets of wheeled hauling units to place dry fill.

The Hansen Dam in the San Fernando Valley of southern California was completed in 1940 by LeTourneau Tournapulls. It was the world's largest dry-fill dam at the time, exceeded in size only by hydraulic-fill dams, and demonstrated the feasibility of using rubber-tired hauling units for mass excavation.

Postwar Developments

Without question, the postwar event that had the greatest impact on the earthmoving equipment industry was the construction of the interstate highway system, the largest civil works project ever undertaken. Congress and highway planners had used the wartime construction respite to good advantage. The Federal-Aid Highway Act of 1944 envisioned the interstate highway system but did not provide specific funding or an integrated program for it.[34] In the postwar period, with federal-state cost sharing continuing at 50-50, states could not afford the higher construction costs of new-style, four-lane, limited-access highways. Some resorted to building them as toll roads financed by bonds. By 1955 five thousand miles of toll roads were in use, under construction, or planned. The obvious enthusiasm of motorists for the new highways sent a strong message to politicians: Voters wanted modern highways—immediately.

Congress responded with the milestone Federal-Aid Highway Act of 1956, establishing the forty-one-thousand-mile interstate highway system as a separate category of primary highways that qualified for construction cost-sharing on the basis of 90 percent federal and 10 percent state. The federal share would be covered by revenue from gasoline and excise taxes under the Highway Trust Fund that was established at the same time. On that more realistic funding basis, the construction of the system could begin in earnest. Completion would be scheduled for 1970. Compared to the original primary highways, the geometrical construction standards of the new four- and six-lane highways would require the movement of massive amounts of material. Limitations on gradient and curvature, limited access, interchanges, and grade separations entailed huge volumes of earthmoving. On level terrain the amount of embankment required for a single interchange or grade separation exceeded that required for literally miles of most traditional two-lane primary highways. Multimillion-cubic-yard interstate grading contracts became the norm. It was a contractor's dream come true. The first realistic estimate placed the cost of the system at $41 billion, but inflation, the addition of 1,500 miles, design changes, and various congressional mandates subsequently raised the final cost to nearly $100 billion and construction stretched out to more than twenty-five years. The gigantic project transformed the earthmoving equipment industry. [35]

Dams and Water Projects

The Hansen Dam was quickly eclipsed in size by postwar dry-fill dams. Earth and rockfill dams would henceforth be the preferred design, built by large fleets of mobile earthmovers. Dams such as Oroville, Oahe, Garrison, San Luis, and Trinity in the United States and Gardiner and Mica Creek in Canada called for bottom-dumps, rear-dumps, and scrapers in fleets of hitherto unheard-of size. Rivalry was intense among manufacturers to capture such large, high-profile orders.

The St. Laurence Seaway

Early settlers clustered along the St. Laurence River and around the eastern Great Lakes envisioned a continuous waterway for shipping from the Atlantic into Lake Erie, and as westward migration occurred that dream came to encompass all of the Great Lakes. But the dream had three physical obstacles: the rapids between Montreal and Lake Ontario, the 326-foot difference in elevation between Lake Ontario and Lake Erie, and a mile of rapids on the St. Mary's River at Sault Ste. Marie, the connection between Lake Huron and Lake Superior. The American Erie Canal had bypassed the first two obstacles, but Canadians viewed the canal as a dangerous rival that diverted western commerce to New York City, and they resolved to counter it. Thus, before the Erie Canal was finished Canadians began the Welland Canal, bypassing Niagara Falls across the twenty-eight-mile neck of land between Lake Erie and Lake Ontario. It was opened in 1830, only five years after the Erie Canal. The Canadians also dug small lock canals to bypass the St. Laurence River rapids above Montreal, but those were never adequate to carry ocean-going ships. Lacking the capital to go it alone, Canada awaited U.S. cooperation, which was not forthcoming because of opposition from the railroads.

Canadian interest in opening the Great Lakes to ocean-going shipping remained strong, but U.S. railroads successfully forestalled American cooperation until after World War II, when iron ore played a role in events. In 1948 a major ore find in the Quebec-Labrador area became vitally important to American steelmakers because of the approaching depletion of the high-grade Lake Superior ores. The last remaining obstacle, the St. Laurence rapids between Montreal and Lake Ontario, would have to be overcome. A U.S.-Canadian agreement was signed in 1954, and work began to open the 182-mile stretch of river to deep-water vessels. For difficult conditions, few construction projects have exceeded the Seaway. For example, the 3.5-mile Wiley-Dondero Canal, 442 feet wide at the bottom and 50 feet deep, was cut through sticky marine clay that could only be excavated by draglines and stuck stubbornly in the bodies of hauling units. Other excavations went through some of the hardest, most abrasive rock in the world. All of that, compounded by sub-zero winter temperatures, put construction equipment to the most severe test it had ever undergone as contractors worked around the clock to complete the project in four years.

From Montreal to Lake Ontario, the Seaway comprises seven locks, each 860 to 900 feet long and 80 feet wide; they provide a total lift of 246 feet with a 27-foot deep channel at a cost of $470 million. In addition, a $650 million complex of three dams created Lake St. Laurence, which flows through the Moses-Saunders Power Dam and generates 1,880 megawatts of power.[36]

Beginning with the Moses-Saunders Power Project on the Seaway, Canada became the focus of a series of spectacular hydroelectric developments over the next three decades: Daniel Johnson Dam on the Manicouagan River, Bennett Dam on the Peace River, Churchill Falls in Labrador, and the mammoth James Bay complex of dams in northern Quebec, to name only four of the largest. In 1968 the eighty-five-million-cubic-yard Gardiner Dam on the South Saskatchewan River was completed for irrigation and power, and several smaller power projects were completed on the Nelson River and Churchill River in Manitoba. Such projects, many in extremely remote areas and all constructed under difficult conditions of climate and terrain, tested contractors and equipment to their limits.

Postwar Equipment Developments

Equipment began to evolve quickly after the war. Although crude hydraulics had been used on earthmoving equipment before World War II, the 1950s saw rapid refinement and a proliferation of applications, the track-type and wheel-type front-end loaders and the hydraulic excavator being the outstanding examples. New hydraulically actuated scrapers were introduced, and hydraulics gradually began displacing cable controls for bulldozers as well as scrapers.

LeTourneau's prewar introduction of the integral wheel tractor-scraper was the beginning of the end for the power shovel as a tool for moving earth on construction jobs. The advantages of the scraper were so obvious that by the early 1950s all larger manufacturers had taken steps to add it to their lines. It became contractors' tool of choice for moving the vast amounts of earth involved in constructing interstate highways.

During the 1950s the trend accelerated to heavier, more powerful machines as larger engines, transmissions, and tires successively became available. As quickly as competitors could build or purchase the larger components, a new generation of larger, more productive machines inevitably followed. By the late 1960s, however, manufacturers were approaching the practical limit in the size of machines that could be reasonably moved from place to place, a requirement for the construction industry. Although machines for mining continued to grow in size, by the 1970s the emphasis in construction equipment had shifted to gaining increased productivity through increased horsepower and refinements in hydraulics, controls, serviceability, and operator amenities.

The End of an Era

Just as the start of construction of the interstate highway system had a huge impact on the equipment industry, so, too, did the completion of the system have an impact. In the late 1970s, with the highway system almost 90 percent complete, contractors and the construction equipment industry became aware that fewer and fewer new contracts involving heavy grading were being awarded. Although work continues on additions, modifications, and reconstruction, for all practical purposes the original interstate system was completed during the mid-1980s. Coupled with the deep recession of the early 1980s, the rather abrupt decline in large interstate grading contracts caused a severe shakeout among both contractors and manufacturers, and by the mid-1980s the nature of the highway construction industry in the United States had changed for good. Although spending on highways continued at high levels, emphasis shifted from new construction entailing heavy grading to improvements, reconstruction, and widening projects involving much smaller quantities of earthmoving. Such projects required different, more flexible methods and created demand for hydraulic excavators, articulated dumpers, elevating scrapers, and mid-sized equipment rather than the heavy crawlers and large scrapers used in new construction. Thus has the industry again been transformed.

Similarly but for different reasons, the nature of water projects also changed. The forty years following 1931 saw an unbroken succession of massive undertakings by the Corps, BuRec, TVA, and Canadian and international agencies for flood control, irrigation, power, navigation, and recreation. Rarely was a project successfully challenged until the environmental movement began to make itself felt during the 1970s. Now it is rare for a proposed water project to go unchallenged, and many are shelved or defeated by opposition from environmentalists.

Although the era of the big dam is unquestionably over in North America, it is still very much alive in the developing areas of the world. Lists of the world's greatest dams by height, volume, and size of reservoir or capacity include far more dams in developing nations than in industrialized ones. Tarbela and Mangla in the Indus Basin; Ataturk in Turkey; Yacyreta, Guri, Itaipu, and Tucurui in South America; Cabora Bassa in Mozambique; and Aswan in Egypt—to name only a few—have all been completed since 1965. Although few attractive sites remain in North America and Europe, great potential still exists in Africa, Southeastern Asia, and China.

Private Construction

While the foregoing discussion of the role of roads and water projects in creating the need for earthmoving equipment has focused on public works, the importance of private construction should not be overlooked. With the exception of a very few mega-projects such as the Trans-Alaska Pipeline, privately funded construction tends to be unspectacular, yet it has an impact by virtue of the sheer number of relatively small activities being undertaken. Every new building constructed, whether a single-family housing unit, shopping center, or industrial site, requires at least a small amount of earthmoving, and the collective impact on the equipment industry is enormous. Because of the usually modest size of the jobs, they are a principal source of demand for light-to-mid-sized construction equipment: loader-backhoes, small-to-mid-sized bulldozers, loaders, excavators, dumpers, and elevating scrapers.

Open-Pit Mining

While the postwar construction industry was being dazzled by a plethora of huge projects involving massive quantities of earthmoving, the mining industry had been routinely moving far greater quantities, year in and year out, in open-pit mines around the world. Coal, iron, copper, sand and gravel, and limestone historically have accounted for most of the activity.

The earliest efforts at mining took the form of scratching at mineral outcroppings with hand tools and then following veins into the ground. Until near the end of the nineteenth century all coal and metallic minerals, with the exception of placer mining, continued to be extracted from underground. In the case of metallic minerals, sufficiently high-grade surface deposits were rare, and ignorance of concentrating techniques made low-grade surface deposits unusable. Even if the concentrating process had been known, equipment did not exist until the latter part of the nineteenth century that would have made feasible the removal of heavy overburden and the surface mining of large quantities of ore. With coal, although the need for concentration was not a factor, even deposits near the surface required the movement of quantities of overburden far beyond the economic capabilities of then-available equipment.

Thus, until near the end of the nineteenth century, surface mining, like civil works projects, was inhibited in scope by the unavailability of necessary equipment. Because minerals were being supplied in adequate quantities from underground, however, the mining industry did not recognize that it was being inhibited. It was the discovery of the Mesabi Range of northeastern Minnesota, an iron ore body that forced development of surface-mining methods, that opened vistas to the mining industry through use of steam shovels and railroad cars. Soon after, the perfection of concentrating methods led to steam shovel and rail exploitation of low-grade surface porphyry copper deposits.

Iron Mining

Well before the introduction in the United States of the Bessemer Process in 1870, American producers knew that the then-identified ore supplies would not support a growing iron and steel industry. Prospecting was intensified, and in 1844 the Marquette Range, forty miles long and three to ten miles wide in the wilderness of Michigan's Upper Peninsula, was discovered. It was not only the largest deposit of iron ore yet found in North American but also over 60 percent in grade and very low in phosphorous. It would become direct-shipping Bessemer ore. With the opening of the canal and locks at Sault Ste. Marie in 1855, the first ore shipments came down the lakes to Cleveland in 1856. Iron-ore production in the United States totaled 2,873,000 long tons in 1860.[37]

Also in the 1860s, a second large deposit, the Menominee Range, was found to the south and west of the Marquette Range. The Panic of 1873 delayed its exploitation until 1877, when the first shipments occurred. In quick succession a third and fourth range were brought into production: the Gogebic, again in the Upper Peninsula, and the Vermillion, the first major find north of Lake Superior in Minnesota. By 1892 each was shipping more than a million tons, surpassing the Marquette Range.

The iron ore deposits in the four ranges found to this point were located in deep, sharply inclined veins that required mining by underground methods; by 1900 some mines in the Marquette and Menominee ranges were nearly two thousand feet deep. At the time, no prospector or geologist expected merchantable iron ore to occur in surface deposits—until the Mesabi Range was discovered in the late 1880s. More than a hundred miles long and two to ten miles wide, the Mesabi dwarfed the other ranges of the Lake Superior district. What was most astonishing was that the ore body was horizontal with sometimes only a few feet of overburden, and the ore itself was soft and powdery. At more than 60 percent iron and low in phosphorous, here was direct-shipping Bessemer ore with a vengeance. Nothing like it had ever been seen. The ore could be mined by steam shovels loading directly into standard-gauge rail cars for haulage straight to the Duluth loading docks.[38] An eight-man crew working a three-cubic-yard, rail-mounted steam shovel could handle three thousand tons per day. A similar amount from underground, using the methods of the day, required several hundred miners. Labor costs were drastically reduced, but that was partially offset by the much higher capital costs of open-pit mining. Thus was born large-scale open-pit mining. Whereas underground metals mines reckoned daily ore production in terms of a few thousand tons with very little waste, the new open-pit mines could produce tens of thousands of tons of ore daily yet often required perhaps two or three times that amount of waste in the form of overburden to be moved.[39]

The high capital costs of open-pit mining brought dominance of the industry by large corporations. Shortly after the first shipments of Mesabi ore in 1892, the Rockefeller interests gained control of a major part of the range as well as substantial holdings on the Vermillion and Gogebic ranges. By the late 1890s, however, the Carnegie interests had obtained, through leases of Rockefeller properties and outright ownership of other mines, a dominant position on the iron ranges. With the formation of U.S. Steel in 1901, Rockefeller and Carnegie holdings became part of that corporation.

Development of the Mesabi Range was so rapid that by 1895 it was the leading producer of iron ore in the United States. By 1902 it produced half the ore shipped from the Lake Superior district. As late as the mid-1920s, nearly half of U.S. iron ore continued to come from underground, but that proportion has steadily diminished and is now negligible. U.S. iron ore production peaked in 1953 at 118 million tons, but production in the early 1990s was about half that amount because of growing competition from imported steel and an increased use of scrap .

The richness and abundance of the Lake Superior deposits assured U.S. self-sufficiency in iron ore until the demands of World War II left the nation with diminished reserves of high-grade, direct-shipping ore. Techniques developed during the 1950s permitted the use of Minnesota's plentiful 25–35 percent taconite ore in the form of pellets containing more than 60 percent iron, and thus the district has continued to supply more than 75 percent of U.S. iron ore requirements. In fact, because pellets work better in blast furnaces than natural ore, they became the preferred feed over direct-shipping ore.[40]

To further secure ore supplies, U.S. producers undertook exploration programs in Canada and elsewhere outside the United States after the war, the most important find being the Quebec-Labrador iron range. A town and a 360-mile railroad were built to permit exploitation of that deposit in the trackless wilds of northern Quebec, and the first ore shipments to the United States began in 1954. Important finds were also made in Venezuela, Chile, and Liberia. By the 1990s, Canada, Brazil and Australia were the world's leading exporters of iron ore.

Copper Mining

Copper was humanity's first metal. Even before 6000 B.C., it was used for jewelry and ornamentation. The smelting process was being used to reduce copper from ore before recorded civilization. Copper's uses broadened when people learned to alloy it with tin to make bronze and with zinc to make brass. Until displaced by iron, bronze was the metal for weapons; indeed, bronze cannons were still in use during the American Civil War.

Although copper had long been valued for alloying with tin and zinc, its properties as a conductor went largely unappreciated until three events during the nineteenth century caused demand to soar: the invention of the telegraph in 1835, the electrical revolution of the 1880s, and the automobile radiator in the 1890s.[41]

Until the end of the nineteenth century, copper, like lead, tin, and zinc, the other base metals, was obtained from underground through the traditional mining of veins of high-grade, direct-smelting ores. Little was known about the concentrating of ores, and thus low-grade deposits were not considered commercially interesting. Around the turn of the century, however, there were major technical advances in beneficiation processes that made feasible the use of low-grade ore. Suddenly, previously known but neglected ore bodies became attractive. Yet there was one catch: If the grade of ore was low, the ore body would have to be very large to be commercially interesting. Utah's Bingham Canyon deposit was just that—a veritable mountain of low-grade copper ore. What was then considered low-grade ore at less than 2.5 percent was fairly evenly disseminated through hundreds of million of tons of host rock in what was called a "porphyry deposit." Techniques being used on the Mesabi Range solved the problem of how to mine it, and advances in selective flotation solved the problem of how to concentrate the ore. Exploitation of Bingham Canyon began in 1905 and still continues.

Through control of the American Smelting and Refining Company as well as through private holdings, the Guggenheim family had a hand in almost every major copper mining venture in the Western Hemisphere for the two decades following 1901. Beginning in 1907 they organized a syndicate to mine an underground copper deposit near Kennecott Glacier in Alaska and merged that company with Utah Copper Company of Bingham Canyon to form Kennecott Copper Company in 1923. They acquired the huge, undeveloped Chilean Chuquicamata porphyry property in 1910, paying for it with 26 percent of the stock in their newly formed Chile Exploration Company. Mine development financed by a $15 million bond issue began in 1914 and used steam shovels and railroad equipment from the Panama Canal as that project wound down. Thus, the Guggenheims were able to avoid large cash outlays as they opened the world's richest copper mine. In 1923 they sold controlling interest in Chuquicamata to the Anaconda Company for $70 million. With that purchase Anaconda likely obtained the greatest bargain in the history of mining. The mine would eventually produce at a rate of more than five hundred thousand tons of copper annually, but Chuquicamata was nationalized in 1971 after forty-eight years of Anaconda ownership.[42]

The magnitude of the large porphyry copper operations is sometimes difficult to grasp. In 1993, for example, Phelps Dodge Corporation's Arizona Morenci Mine moved more than 219 million tons of ore and waste, a rate of six hundred thousand tons per day, and milled nearly 130,000 tons of ore daily, with an average grade of .67 percent, to produce for the year just over four hundred thousand tons of copper. No construction earthmoving project in history has ever approached such volumes on a sustained basis.[43]

Other world-class open-pit copper operations include Spain's very old Rio Tinto Mines, Highland Valley in British Columbia, South Africa's Palabora, and mines in Zambia and Zaire on the African Copper Belt. Although Highland Valley and Palabora are relatively new, Copper Belt development began in 1906 when Union Miniere de Haute–Katanga began commercial exploitation in what was then the Belgian Congo, followed in 1909 by various British interests in Northern Rhodesia. The Copper Belt, 280 miles by 160 miles in area, was extremely rich not only in high-grade copper but also in lead, zinc, manganese, and cobalt. Following the independence of Zambia in 1969, operations there came under government control. Zambian copper production that year was seven hundred thousand tons, making it the Western world's third-largest producer after the United States and Chile. Production has fallen steadily since 1969, however, and the disturbances that followed independence in Zaire had a similar effect on mining operations in that country.

As older porphyry copper deposits were worked decade after decade and literally billions of tons of material were mined, the average grade of copper steadily dropped and the dimensions of the mines grew. To obtain the same amount of metal, two, three, or perhaps four times as much rock had to be moved as in the early days. Miners urgently needed either to find ways to reduce the cost per ton or face mine closure. The only answer, they realized, lay in use of bigger equipment. Thus, after the war the mining industry, like the construction industry, applied a strong pull on the equipment makers, although the slowly advancing state of the art permitted only a modest response.

Earthmoving Equipment and the Metals Mining Industry

By 1905, when Bingham Canyon was opened, the steam shovel had made possible a revolutionary change in both iron and copper mining. It was quickly to become the indispensable tool of the mining industry. Steam shovels used in early twentieth century mines were up to five-cubic-yard capacity. They were standard-gauge rail-mounted, which at 56.5 inches did not provide great lateral stability, and so used retractable stabilizers similar to those still in use on equipment today. Turn-of-the-century shovels used chain for operating hoist, crowd, and swing functions, but chain was supplanted by steel-wire rope in the early twentieth century. Because mining operations were rail-based, large crews were necessary to lay and take up track. The temporary nature of the trackage on working benches and waste dumps led to frequent derailments, the bane of railroad mining operations.

Aside from steam locomotives and steam-operated shovels and churn drills, early twentieth century mines contained little mechanical equipment. Later, central compressed-air systems would be installed for operating drills, with air lines running through the mine, but practical, portable air compressors of sufficient capacity would not be available for several decades. Large-diameter rotary and down-the-hole drills with integral compressors did not appear until the 1950s when ammonium nitrate came into use as a blasting agent.

The large metal mines opened before World War II stayed with rail haulage despite its drawbacks because they had no acceptable alternative. Heavy-duty off-highway trucks did not appear until the early 1930s but were limited in size by lack of horsepower and suitable tires. The astronomical number of fifteen-ton rear-dump trucks necessary to handle the daily tonnage of a large mine made converting to truck haulage impractical. In addition, the shovels in use were too large for small trucks. But other changes were made. Many mines converted from steam to electricity for rail haulage, and electric shovels of suitable size appeared during the 1920s. The introduction of more flexible crawler-mounted shovels around 1912 marked the beginning of the end for those that were rail-mounted. Once a practical bulldozer was developed during the 1920s, track-type tractors became an invaluable auxiliary tool for preparing railroad roadbeds and working around shovels.

Truck sizes rapidly increased after World War II. Using tandem rear axles, capacities had reached fifty tons by 1953. Larger tires allowed fifty-ton capacity on two axles by the late 1950s, and articulated units up to a seventy-ton capacity were in use. But the major breakthrough occurred during the early 1960s with the introduction of eighty-five-ton, diesel-electric-drive, two-axle units combining higher horsepower with a new-style vee body, a quantum advance that gained quick acceptance with miners. It produced the hauling cost reductions they had sought, and the remaining rail mines, with few exceptions, converted to truck haulage. As larger tires and engines have become available, truck sizes have risen through successive generations to more than three-hundred-ton capacity, and both electric and mechanical drives are available. Shovel equipment has grown proportionately, and since the 1970s large, hydraulic front shovels have taken their place alongside traditional cable-operated ("rope") shovels. Equipment manufacturers' responsiveness to the needs of the mining industry since the 1950s largely accounts for the miners' present ability to mine profitably the low-grade copper and gold ores that not many years ago would have been declared uneconomical.

On the iron range, the shift to taconite during the late 1950s and early 1960s had important implications for the equipment industry. The extreme hardness of taconite coupled with the need to crush and pelletize the ore required a change in mining methods, and railroad mining was discontinued in favor of more flexible truck haulage out of the pits.

Coal: "The Rock That Burns"

Through the end of the nineteenth century, coal was principally used for domestic heating, as a heat source for steam engines, and in the production of pig iron. U.S. coal production in 1891 was already an impressive 168 million tons, but production skyrocketed with the boom in development of electric utilities in the early twentieth century. By 1910, production had reached 500 million tons; by 1920, it was 658 million tons, a figure unsurpassed until World War II.

Until the early twentieth century all coal produced in the United States came from underground. Bureau of Mines production figures for 1914 show the first surfaced-mined bituminous coal at 1.28 million short tons compared with more than 420 million tons from underground. Thereafter, the amount of surface-mined coal as a percent of the total grew slowly but steadily, reaching 25 percent of total U.S. production in the mid-1950s. The shift to surface mining then began to accelerate—from 43 percent by 1970 to about 60 percent by 1980, where it stabilized. For the first time in history, total U.S. production in 1990 surpassed one billion tons, of which 605 million tons came from surface operations.

The rapid increase since the 1970s in both total production and the proportion furnished by surface mining is attributable to the discovery of huge deposits of low-sulfur coal in the West. Wyoming is now the largest coal producing state at more than two hundred million tons annually, all from surface mines. The number of producing coal mines in the United States has fallen by 50 percent since the 1970s, continuing the trend to large-scale, open-pit operations at the expense of numerous smaller, more labor-intensive underground mines.[44]

Early iron ore smelting used charcoal, but concern in England for the rapid depletion of the forests forced ironmongers there to begin using coal and later coke. The first iron was successfully smelted with coke in England in the early eighteenth century, and with its plentiful coal supplies England took a lead in the production of both coal and iron that was to last for more than 150 years. No doubt because of seemingly inexhaustible forests, U.S. ironmakers were slow to change from charcoal to coke. Not until the introduction of the Bessemer Process in 1870 did traditional American blast furnace practices begin to change. American ironmakers chose to locate in western Pennsylvania because of the availability of iron ore and, because of Pennsylvania's plentiful supplies of coking coal, remained there long after better sources of ore were found. Since the 1970s, an increased use of scrap to make iron and steel has steadily diminished the need for coke. Only twenty-four million tons were produced in 1991, comparable to the amount produced around the turn of the century.[45]

The Development of Coal Stripping Equipment

The ability to surface mine coal, beginning about 1914, is also attributable to the steam shovel, although rail mining like that carried on in iron and copper mines played a lesser role in coal mining. Records are not available, but it seems likely that the first surface-mined coal came from the contour mining of outcroppings. Steam shovels casting downhill could uncover the coal without stripping away excessive amounts of overburden. Shovels of the day could not reach more than about thirty feet, thus limiting the amount of overburden that could be stripped by this method. Large electric stripping shovels began to appear before World War II and became the favored stripping tool in the midwestern open-pit mines.

By about 1910 the dragline had been perfected, making feasible the surface mining of coal to previously unheard-of depths, and in 1913 the Monighan Company patented the walking mechanism for draglines.[46] Electric and steam draglines of four- to five-cubic-yard capacity were available by 1918. There followed a steady scaling up of draglines over the years, which permitted the economical mining of ever-deeper coal. Because of their below-grade digging ability and greater casting radius, electric draglines of more than a hundred-cubic-yard capacity have almost completely displaced large stripping shovels in large-scale coal stripping operations worldwide.

The huge machines, the largest mobile land machines ever built, economically strip coal to previously undreamed of depths.

The crawler tractor's role in coal stripping was limited to auxiliary work until after World War II, when tractors of more than three hundred horsepower were introduced. It then began to be used as a primary coal stripping tool in smaller operations, usually in the contour mines of Appalachia, where topography and depth of overburden favored the use of bulldozers. New environmental regulations largely put an end to that, however.

The Effect of Regulation on Equipment Requirements

Coal stripping in the United States had historically been unregulated, and coal companies were able to rape and pillage the land with impunity. States exerted little or no control over how stripping was conducted, and minimal reclamation, if any, was required. That began to change during the 1970s with the passage of reclamation laws of increasing stringency. Coal-strippers gloomily predicted that the new regulations would mean the demise of the industry, but as the foregoing coal production figures indicate such has not been the case. The new regulations did bring about radical changes in stripping methods, however, and have proven extremely beneficial to the equipment industry. Topsoil must now be stripped and stockpiled before mining operations can begin. Contour mines are no longer permitted to cast material downhill; it must be removed in hauling units and stockpiled for later backfilling after removal of the coal. Stripped land must be restored to approximately its original contours and topsoil spread and seeded. Runoff must be carefully controlled. The new regulations have not only required greater numbers of the largest bulldozers but have also created the need for types of equipment not previously used in coal stripping—the largest sizes of wheel loaders and hydraulic front shovels matched with fleets of off-highway trucks, along with large wheel tractor-scrapers for topsoil stripping and replacement.

Thus, the same factors driving open-pit metal mining to ever-larger machinery are also at work in the coal industry. More and more material must be moved to produce a ton of product, making the industry far more machinery-intensive than it was before regulation. The drive to substitute capital for labor has resulted in the virtual disappearance of small stripping operations and the industry being consolidated into fewer but larger producers. Twenty-four-hour-a-day, year-round operations under severe conditions make coal-strippers voracious consumers of some of the largest, most costly machines the equipment industry produces.

Other Minerals

Other minerals produced on a large scale from surface mines are baux-
ite, phosphates, gypsum and sand, gravel, and crushed-rock products for
construction and the production of cement and as concrete aggregates. Of
all products mined, sand, gravel, and rock products account for by far the
greatest tonnage. U.S. production of crushed rock totaled 1.117 billion short
tons in 1993, and sand and gravel totaled 895 million tons. The 4,800 producers, many of them comparatively small, were major consumers of earthmoving equipment.[47]

The earliest quarries were established in prehistoric times for the production of dimension stone for building. Before invention of the jaw-crusher
in 1858, crushed stone could only be produced by laborious and costly hand
methods. Until development of Portland cement concrete, gravel and crushed
stone were used principally in the surfacing of the few roads that received
any upgrading whatever. As concrete came into general use, limestone was
required for the manufacture of cement, and the demand for aggregates
increased, particularly crushed limestone, which produced concrete superior to that made with gravel. As a low-unit-value product, crushed rock
could not support the cost of transport over long distances, resulting in the
opening of numerous small quarries to supply local needs. Now the industry remains fragmented in comparison with other mineral producers, but
the overall trend is clearly to fewer and larger-scale operations. As the industry is driven by building activity of all kinds, locations in or near metropolitan areas are prized, but more remote sites must be used as those quarries are worked out or driven out by urbanization. Bulk crushed material
then has to be transported to centralized distribution points by rail or barge.

Unlike large-scale open-pit mines, pre–World War II quarry operations,
because of their more modest size, were reasonably well served by the equipment then available. A 1.5-cubic-yard power shovel and fifteen-ton rear-
dump truck were completely adequate for all but the largest quarries and
were considered state of the art in the industry. As larger equipment evolved,
quarry operators were not always quick to upgrade because of the need to
maintain balance with crusher capacity, which was the limiting production
factor. However, the same forces driving other minerals-producing industries were also driving the crushed-rock industry: the need to substitute
capital for labor, which entailed the scaling up of operations; the use of larger
equipment; and the elimination of small, higher-cost quarries. As a result,

equipment slowly drifted upward in size to thirty-five- to fifty-ton rear-dump trucks, and eight- to twelve-cubic-yard wheel loaders and hydraulic front shovels have become the loading tools of choice. Of course, very large operations may use even larger equipment. In addition to quarrying equipment, the industry is a heavy consumer of wheel loaders for working stockpiles of crushed materials. Overall, while many individual quarry operations tend to be conservative in their approach to replacing and upgrading equipment, the sheer number of operations worldwide makes the industry a leading consumer of machinery.

Conclusion

Thus is sketched how the will to rearrange the earth on an ever-grander scale and humanity's rising demand for raw materials created the need for earthmoving equipment, while the equipment industry, from primitive beginnings, struggled to respond to the need. The remaining chapters of this book will explore how the many companies that had important roles in the industry were born and how they grew and responded to the changing requirements of the construction and mining industries.

The Beginnings,
1831–1945

McCormick's invention of a practical mechanical reaper in 1831 was a seminal event in the evolution of the agricultural implement industry. As the first piece of mobile farm machinery, it was the forerunner of a series of revolutionary labor-saving inventions that transformed American agriculture during the nineteenth century and culminated in the introduction of farm tractors powered by internal combustion engines in the 1890s. As America's most dynamic manufacturing industry through the nineteenth century, the farm implement business gave birth to several pioneer companies of the earthmoving equipment industry. Thus, the history of these early farm implement companies is also the story of the beginnings of the earthmoving equipment industry.

International Harvester

An Industrial Dynasty

The reaper was the foundation of the McCormick family fortune, a powerful industrial dynasty that endured for more than 150 years and ended with the tragic breakup of the company in 1985. Cyrus Hall McCormick

Cyrus Hall McCormick (1809–84). Although there are other claimants to the invention of the first reaper, McCormick's flair for marketing made his machine and his company unrivalled commercial successes. (State Historical Society of Wisconsin negative no. WHi[X3]36818)

was born in 1809 into a prosperous farm family of Rockbridge County in the Shenandoah Valley of Virginia, and it was there that he built and demonstrated his first reaper. Recognizing that the center of grain-growing was shifting to the new lands of the West, he relocated his burgeoning business to Chicago in 1847. Although his talents as an inventor sparked the early years, the dynamic growth of the McCormick Harvesting Machine Company through the middle years of the nineteenth century was driven by his extraordinary talent for marketing and finance.[1]

The Dealer Franchise System

When McCormick's son Cyrus Junior joined him in the business in 1879, the company was the world's largest farm implement manufacturer. Working together in the early 1880s, the men began to revamp their distribution organization. At the time, the customary distribution system for farm implements was for regional agents to sell to small local businessmen, blacksmiths, hardware stores, and others who acted as sub-agents and retailed to farmers. These retailers frequently handled competing lines and had no particular loyalty to any one brand. The McCormicks introduced a contract into the relationship, granting a franchise to sell McCormick products but encouraging (if not requiring) the franchisee to refrain from selling competitive products.[2] Their franchised dealer concept was an important innovation and become the accepted method of retailing farm, and later construction, equipment.

The elder McCormick played a central role in the early mechanization of agriculture, and at his death in 1884 he was one of the leading industrialists of nineteenth-century America. Cyrus Junior, the CEO in the ensuing thirty-four years, would take the company to a dominant position in the farm equipment business.

The Formation of International Harvester Company

During the 1880s another Chicago-based harvester-maker, the William Deering Company, developed as a major rival. In those days, when the "trust" was considered a legitimate and desirable means of reducing competition, it was inevitable that McCormick and Deering, the two largest harvester manufacturers, would merge. In the event, a merger was effected in July 1902, taking in the two principals as well as three smaller firms: Plano Manufacturing Company; Warder, Bushnell, and Glessner; and the Milwaukee Harvesting Company. With $110 million in assets, the combine then controlled 85 percent of the harvester business in the United States. Like other large mergers then and now, it was facilitated by the intervention of Wall Street. George W. Perkins, a J. P. Morgan partner, named the combine the "International Harvester Company." Members were allotted shares proportional to their contribution in assets. McCormick received 43 percent; Deering, 34 percent; the three smaller members divided 9 percent; and Wall Street interests took 14 percent. Cyrus McCormick became president of the new company, but Wall Street nominees to the board retained a powerful influence until the McCormicks gained controlling interest in 1913.[3]

Expansion and Diversification

The company moved aggressively in several directions in the years immediately following the merger. The McCormick company had been an active exporter, but now Cyrus McCormick resolved to gain a greater share of the European opportunity by putting International Harvester (IH) plants there. Manufacturing operations were soon underway in Sweden, France, Germany, and Russia, and a plant was also established in Hamilton, Ontario.

But the event that was to have the greatest long-term impact on the fortunes of IH was its introduction of the Auto Buggy in 1907. This light truck, intended for farm use, gained such quick acceptance that an improved version, the Auto Wagon, was quickly brought out, and production reached 1,300 units in 1909.[4] The Auto Wagon was considered only a sideline, but it would set the company on a path to becoming the nation's leading maker of heavy trucks for many years. Eventually, trucks represented more than half of the company's sales.

Entry into the Farm Tractor Business

The steam engine had appeared on American farms before the Civil War, but it was not until development of large threshing machines in the 1870s that steam became a factor in farming. The threshing machine, belt-driven by a portable steam engine, became a common sight. Very quickly the portable steam engine evolved into the self-propelled engine that had a steering system, the true steam traction engine. By the 1890s special plowing versions were being developed, but for a variety of reasons the steam traction engine never supplanted the horse as the prime mover for fieldwork. Steam engines were expensive, extremely heavy, lacked maneuverability, and needed large amounts of solid fuel and water; other than on a few very large farms, they were primarily power sources for threshing. Yet they had provided a glimpse of what a powerful prime mover could do if ways could be found to overcome the steamer's disadvantages.[5]

Rapid development of the internal combustion engine in the last decade of the nineteenth century provided the solution, and inventors were not slow in perceiving it. As crude farm tractors using the new engine and petroleum fuels began to appear during the first years of the new century, it was clear to Cyrus McCormick that IH needed to enter that business. After several years of experimentation, in 1909 Harvester launched the Mogul line of gasoline-powered tractors from its new tractor works on Chicago's South Side, followed in 1910 by the Titan line. Moguls were sold by McCormick dealers and Titans by Deering dealers, the two dealer organizations having kept their separate identities.[6] It was none too soon; tractor manufacturers, like car manufacturers, were proliferating wildly. By 1921 there were 186 companies building farm tractors in the United States.[7]

The Fordson and the Farmall

In 1918 Cyrus McCormick chose to step down as president and CEO, becoming non-executive chairman and turning over the presidency to his younger brother, Harold. Between the firm's beginning and 1951—120 years—a member of the McCormick family would continuously either occupy the post of president or chair the board of McCormick Harvesting Machine Company and International Harvester.

Another event of 1918 that had sweeping impact on the industry was the U.S. introduction of Henry Ford's mass-produced, low-priced Fordson tractor. Although the industry had anticipated the Fordson, no one was prepared for the devastation it wrought in the tractor business. Within two years it had claimed two-thirds of the market, with sales of sixty-seven thousand units. Ford's market share peaked in 1923 at an incredible 76 percent.[8] Coupled with the recession of the early 1920s, the Fordson brought about a massive shakeout among farm tractor manufacturers; by 1930 only thirty-eight remained in North America.[9]

While Harvester's tractor business was hard-hit by the Fordson, the company was not caught totally unprepared. For several years Harvester engineers had been toying with the idea of an all-purpose tractor. Prototypes had been built, and the tractor had even been named the "Farmall," but nothing had been done to produce it. In 1921 the decision was made to go forward with the new concept. Introduced in 1924, the Farmall was an instant success. What made it revolutionary was a tricycle design and a high clearance that allowed it to work as a cultivator. Before the Farmall, tractors were used for seedbed preparation, but row-crop cultivation was still being done by horse-drawn implements.

In one of the most incredible industrial turnarounds ever, the Farmall rolled back the Fordson so quickly that late in 1928 Henry Ford discontinued producing it in the United States although he continued its production in Cork, Ireland, and Dagenham, England. That year the Farmall Works opened in Rock Island, Illinois, and International tractors gained a 47 percent market share. In 1929 the share of market reached 60 percent, and International Harvester became dominant in tractors as well as harvesters.[10]

The shakeout of the early farm tractor manufacturers in the United States was now almost complete, and survivors had been identified. The impact of the Fordson followed by the Farmall left little room for the scores of small producers who lacked full product lines and strong distribution systems. By 1930 the long-line producers—those who built tractors as well as a full line of implements—were down to seven companies: International Harvester, Deere, Allis-Chalmers, J. I. Case, Oliver, Minneapolis-Moline, and Massey-Harris.

IH and the Crawler Tractor Business

The 1920s were the best years in the company's history. The Farmall tractor and the opening of a large new truck plant in Fort Wayne, Indiana, were followed by a third important event in the dynamic expansion of the product line: the 1928 introduction of the first IH track-type tractor, the McCormick-Deering 10-20. A tracked version of the Model 10-20 wheel tractor, the new machine carried the trade name "TracTracTor." Renamed the T-20 in 1931, it was followed in 1932 by the T-40 TracTracTor version of the McCormick-Deering W-40, which had twenty-eight-drawbar horsepower, and in 1934 by the TD-40 TracTracTor, with an IH-built four-cylinder diesel engine. In 1937 a T-35 and TD-35 were added to the line.[11] Because the early machines were derivatives of wheel farm tractors, they were targeted primarily at the agricultural market. Although some TracTracTors

The 10-20 TracTracTor, introduced in 1928, was International Harvester's first crawler tractor, a track-type conversion of the McCormick-Deering ten-to-twenty-wheel farm tractor. (State Historical Society of Wisconsin negative no. WHi[X3]51379)

found their way into industrial applications, it was tough to compete with the heavier integral designs of Caterpillar and Allis-Chalmers. Nevertheless, the Harvester crawler line was new competition for Caterpillar, Allis-Chalmers, and Cletrac in the agricultural market as IH crawler production steadily rose to a prewar peak of nearly 8,500 units in 1937.[12]

In 1939 Harvester declared its intention to compete seriously in the industrial crawler tractor business by introducing the TD-18 TracTracTor, a twenty-three-thousand-pound, seventy-drawbar-horsepower machine designed from the ground up as a track-type tractor directly competitive with Caterpillar's D7 and Allis-Chalmers's HD-10. The TD-18 was followed in 1940 by the TD-14, TD-9, and TD-6, all integral track-type designs. Farm tractor-based machines were gradually phased out.[13]

The Depression Years: New Leadership

In 1929, the last year of prosperity before the depression, Harvester had a profit of $37 million. Incredibly, that level was not reached again until after World War II.[14] The company entered the 1930s as the dominant producer of farm equipment and emerged still the leader, but Deere and Allis-Chalmers had gained market share at the expense of IH. International Harvester also ended the decade as the leading producer of medium and heavy trucks, ahead of both General Motors and Ford.

The final important event in the story of prewar International Harvester was the accession of Fowler McCormick, forty-three, to the presidency in 1941. The son of Harold and Edith Rockefeller McCormick, he was thus a grandson of both Cyrus H. McCormick, Sr., and John D. Rockefeller. He would lead the company into the critical postwar period.

A Blue Chip Corporation

In 1941, 110 years after introduction of the McCormick reaper, International Harvester was one of the world's largest and most respected industrial corporations. On American farms, it had become an institution, meeting almost every conceivable machinery need of farmers from tractors to milking machines. Although not as dominant as it once was, IH still had the largest share of the American and the world farm equipment markets. It was one of America's first multinationals, with more than three decades of experience in overseas manufacturing and marketing. IH had become one of the blue chip companies in the Dow Jones Industrial Average in 1925, and its widely held stock was regarded as almost as secure as government bonds. The company had succeeded in everything it tried, and its future looked bright. Another new endeavor lay only three years ahead—the earth-moving equipment business.

Allis-Chalmers

The Young Entrepreneur

About the time Cyrus McCormick moved to Chicago, twenty-one-year-old Edward P. Allis arrived in Milwaukee from his home state of New York. He was intent on entering the leather business and soon had a thriving partnership in a tannery. But Allis was above all an entrepreneur and became dissatisfied with his prospects in the leather business; in 1856 he sold his interest to seek a larger opportunity on his own. He found what he was looking for in 1861, purchasing the Reliance Iron Works, a small Milwaukee machine shop and foundry specializing in flour-milling equipment. The booming wheat crops of Wisconsin and Minnesota made possible by the reaper and the threshing machine had created a demand for improved flour-milling equipment, and Allis quickly built his company into a leading supplier to that industry. By 1868 E. P. Allis and Company was one of the largest firms in the growing Milwaukee metalworking industry.[15]

Early Diversification

Unlike most founders of nineteenth-century industrial enterprises, Allis was not an inventor. He devoted his energies to finance and marketing, leaving product development and shop management to hired specialists. During the 1870s he shrewdly hired several outstanding inventors who established the company in the forefront in their respective fields: sawmill equipment, flour mill equipment, and steam engines.

Allis's most important catch was Edwin Reynolds, hired in 1877 to become superintendent of the company shops. Reynolds had been general superintendent of the Corliss Works, a leading producer of steam engines. Corliss patents had expired in 1870, so Reynolds was free to build Corliss-type engines with innovations of his own design. Soon Reynolds was applying his inventive genius to design massive blowing engines for steel works by using waste blast furnace gases. The company produced the largest engines of this type ever built, standing forty feet high with a seventy-six-inch air cylinder. Reynolds went on to build large pumping engines and pumps, mine hoisting machinery, reversing engines for rolling mills, and air compressors—all steam-powered.[16]

Going from triumph to triumph, his horizontal quadruple-expansion engine furnished the power for the 1893 Columbian Exposition in Chicago. Weighing 325 tons, it drove two 750-kilowatt alternators. The Allis company also furnished most of the steam engines for electrifying the New York subway system. Those engines included the largest ever built, rated at twelve thousand horsepower, the high point for reciprocating steam engines.[17] More than anyone else, Reynolds established the company as a leading manufacturer in the heavy engineering field. But the steam turbine had been perfected and within twenty years would completely supplant the reciprocating steam engine except in a few special applications.

The Formation of Allis-Chalmers

At the death of Allis in 1889 the company reorganized. Shares of stock were divided in varying amounts among his eight sons, with William, the eldest, becoming president of E. P. Allis and Company. Unfortunately, none of the sons provided the strong leadership of their father although some had distinguished careers in other fields.

The growth of the Allis company had always been limited by a shortage of capital, so owner interest was aroused in 1901 when a Wall Street promoter suggested a merger. Very quickly, three companies were merged with E. P. Allis and Company. The Fraser and Chalmers Company of Chicago brought mining machinery; Gates Iron Works, also of Chicago, contributed gyratory crushers and cement-making machinery; and Dickson Manufacturing Company of Scranton, Pennsylvania, added compressors, sugar mill, and coal mining machinery. The combination was called Allis-Chalmers Company, and its board included such Wall Street luminaries as Elbert H. Gary, Mark T. Cox, and Cornelius Vanderbilt.[18]

Common and preferred stocks were issued totaling more than $36 million on combined assets that were generously appraised at $9.9 million. Under terms of the agreement, the Allis family received $5.375 million in preferred stock and $1.66 million in cash—not bad for a company that had sales of only $4.8 million in 1899. Like all other principals in the merger, they did extremely well. William and Charles Allis were named chairman and president, respectively, but Wall Street interests controlled the important board committees.[19]

No sooner was the company organized than the recession of 1903 put it in financial straits and made it unable to meet the fixed charges on its preferred stock. Dividends were suspended in early 1904, never to be paid again until reorganization in 1913. No common dividends were ever paid in the company's twelve years of existence.[20]

Expansion

Despite financial problems, progress was made. The company began manufacturing steam and hydraulic turbines in 1904 and 1905, but General Electric and Westinghouse were already well established in that field. Both companies had greater resources than Allis-Chalmers and, a more critical concern, were able to build complete generating units—turbines coupled to generators. It was clear that Allis-Chalmers, to compete successfully, would have to enter the electrical business. Thus, in 1904 the company acquired control of the Bullock Electric Manufacturing Company of Cincinnati for $3 million in stock.[21]

During these years the large West Allis, Wisconsin, plant was built, and by 1907, with acquisition of Bullock, Allis-Chalmers had about 3.1 million square feet of manufacturing space, a large amount for the time.[22] Products included saw-milling and flour-milling equipment, steam and gas reciprocating engines, steam and hydraulic turbines, electric motors and generators, gyratory crushers, ball and rod mills, and cement-mill and sugar-mill machinery, making A-C one of the high-technology companies of the day.

Financial Reorganization: General Falk Takes Over

Notwithstanding its technical competence, the company was not sufficiently profitable to meet its obligations. Finally, in 1912 it was unable to pay the interest on its first-mortgage bonds, and a financial restructuring was unavoidable. Receivers were appointed, and a new company, the Allis-Chalmers Manufacturing Company, was incorporated in 1913. Gen. Otto Falk, a prominent Milwaukee businessman, was appointed a receiver and became president of the new company, and a new board majority of Wisconsin businessmen greatly reduced the Wall Street influence.

In Otto Falk the company had its first strong leadership since the death of Edward Allis twenty-four years earlier. A retired brigadier general of the Wisconsin National Guard with an authoritarian style of management, he guided the company until his death in 1940.[23]

Entry into Agricultural Equipment

One of Falk's first acts as president was to steer the company into manufacturing agricultural equipment. In 1914 efforts began on development of a farm tractor, but it was not until 1919 that a competitive three-bottom model was introduced. It was slow going for Allis-Chalmers farm equipment during the 1920s. The impact of the Fordson followed by the Farmall, the lack of a full line of implements, and a weak distribution system combined to bring steady losses in the Tractor Division, whose 1927 sales were a meager $2.26 million—only 6.8 percent of the company total.[24]

Track-Type Tractors and Motor Graders

During this period General Falk cast about for ways to improve the profitability of his Tractor Division, and one machinery company that must have caught his eye was the newly formed Caterpillar Tractor Company. During the late 1920s, Caterpillar was extremely profitable and averaged 22.4 percent net after tax on sales between 1925 and 1930.[25] Allis-Chalmers, however, typically made less than half that on comparable volume. Also, compared to the crowded farm tractor business, there were relatively few manufacturers of track-type tractors. Such considerations undoubtedly weighed heavily in Falk's decision in 1928 to acquire the Monarch Tractor Corporation of Springfield, Illinois, a maker of track-type tractors, for $500,000 cash.[26]

Monarch's two models, the Six-Ton and the Ten-Ton, formed the nucleus for Allis-Chalmers's expansion in the 1930s into a full line of track-type tractors. With the addition of the Monarch line, A-C Tractor Division sales more than doubled in 1928. The company quickly began development of new models, and nomenclature was revamped. The Ten-Ton became the Model 75 (Model F) and the Six-Ton became the Model 50 (Model H). These models were soon dropped in favor of new, distinctive Allis-Chalmers designs: Models K, L, and M, and, in 1937, the Model S. All were powered by Allis-Chalmers gasoline engines until 1937. In that year, the L-O and S-O with an optional "oil" engine were introduced, and both used a diesel injection system with spark ignition and a gasoline compression ratio.[27] The oil engine was not notably successful in responding to competitors' diesels.

In 1930 Allis-Chalmers made another move toward the earthmoving equipment business by acquiring rights to the road grader line of Ryan Manufacturing Company of Hegvisch, Illinois. Caterpillar had moved into the grader business in 1928 by acquiring the Russell Grader Manufacturing Company, and Allis-Chalmers followed Caterpillar's lead. Allis-Chalmers offered a two-model grader line of "Speed Patrols" through the 1930s: the No. 42 at forty-five horsepower and a larger No. 54. Both had a forward-mounted gasoline engine. The company planned to introduce its General Motors Detroit Diesel–powered Model AD in 1941, but World War II forced a postponement. No new Allis Chalmers graders were seen until 1946.[28]

The New Tractor Line

Recognizing that diesel power was necessary to compete successfully in the heavy-duty tractor business and lacking a diesel of its own, Allis-Chalmers began redesigning its track-type line in the late 1930s around the General Motors 71-Series Detroit Diesel engines (seventy-one cubic inches per cylinder). A new nomenclature using the HD prefix was adopted, and gasoline models were discontinued in 1942 and 1943. Powered by the GM 6-71 engine, the HD-14, first in the series, was introduced in 1939, followed in 1940 by the HD-7 (with a GM 3-71 engine) and the HD-10 (with a GM 4-71 engine). Future additions to the line would have to await the end of the war. These modern tractors were able to compete very successfully with comparable models in the industry.[29]

A major innovation introduced with the HD-14 was the "Positive Seal" Track Roller. Because the track-type undercarriage was in constant contact with a wide variety of ground conditions, it had always been the high-wear, high-cost part of the machine. As a result, it was the focus of a great deal of engineering effort. Track rollers were particularly troublesome. Despite daily greasing and the best seals that could be devised, dirt would work its way into rollers, shortening life and requiring expensive, sometimes premature replacement. Development of the Allis-Chalmers Positive Seal Roller was a major breakthrough.[30] After the war it would evolve into the "1,000-Hour Roller" that allowed a thousand hours of usage between lubrications. The roller was to cause considerable consternation and feverish engineering effort within Caterpillar, which did not introduce a better seal until 1958.[31]

The application of pneumatic tires to farm tractors was another of Allis-Chalmers's major innovations. The company worked with Firestone and Goodyear to make suitable tires available and in 1933 began offering them as an option to the steel wheels then standard on all farm tractors. At first, farmers were slow to accept rubber tires, but 95 percent of industry shipments of new farm tractors were supplied with them by 1940.[32] The Positive Seal Roller and pneumatic tires on farm tractors were just two of a number of Allis-Chalmers's major contributions to the advancement of earthmoving and farm equipment. The company did not lack for engineering talent.

A-C Becomes a Long-Line Company

In 1929 Allis-Chalmers filled out its agricultural line by acquiring for $275,000 the LaCrosse Plow Company, a distressed manufacturer of tillage tools.[33] That year it also adopted a new color, "Persian Orange," for its agricultural and earthmoving products.[34] The farm equipment line was now broad enough for Allis-Chalmers to be considered one of the long-line companies, but by market share it ranked last in the field. Compared to International Harvester and Deere, the A-C dealer organization was woefully weak. In 1931 that was corrected in one stroke by the acquisition of the financially troubled Advance-Rumely Corporation of La Porte, Indiana, for $4.5 million. The addition brought Allis-Chalmers not only an excellent line of harvesters and threshers but also, and most important, a network of about 2,500 dealers.[35]

Market Share Growth: New Diversification

The company's Tractor Division sales in 1930, including farm equipment, wheel and track-type tractors, and graders, reached more than $12 million—nearly 39 percent of the corporate total—but the depression cut division sales to only $5.1 million in 1933. After 1933 improving economic conditions on American farms coupled with the company's new products and stronger dealer organization led to a rapid sales growth that reached $45.5 million in 1938, 58.7 percent of the corporate total.[36] There is little doubt that the growth of its tractor and farm equipment business between 1934 and 1938 saved Allis-Chalmers during the depression. From a weak seventh in 1929, the company emerged third in market share among the long-line companies by 1936.[37]

Meanwhile, the company continued to diversify its industrial business and added circuit-breakers, switchgear, and transformers, yet it still ran a distant third to General Electric and Westinghouse. Although no other industrial enterprise in North America could match Allis-Chalmers in breadth of line, it was not the leader, except in relatively small fields such as flour-milling equipment, and had to compete with larger or more specialized firms that focused resources more narrowly. In inflation-adjusted terms, the Allis-Chalmers Power and Industrial Equipment Division was smaller in 1940 than in 1929. The only area to show real growth through the 1930s was the Tractor Division, which went from $10.6 million in sales in 1929 to $49.4 million in 1940, 57 percent of company business.[38]

The Death of Falk and the End of an Era

The death of General Falk in 1940 ended a twenty-seven-year era of almost one-man rule at Allis-Chalmers. He had acted, and the board had dutifully ratified his actions. He deserves great credit for his vision of diversifying the company into farm equipment, making Allis-Chalmers unique as the only long-line company originating outside agriculture. Most important for this story, Falk put the company in the earthmoving equipment business, second only to Caterpillar in breadth of line in 1941. General Falk made many astute decisions, but perhaps he erred in pursuing too many opportunities rather than too few. He left a dynamic and versatile company that had skills the nation would greatly need as war approached.

Caterpillar

Ben Holt's Tractor

It was Thanksgiving Day 1904 when Benjamin Holt tested his experimental steam-powered track-type tractor for the first time. It was heavy and cumbersome, but its endless tracks met his objective—the machine would work on ground too soft to support wheel tractors. Holt knew he had something that with refinement was commercially viable in the California Delta agricultural region. Soon he was selling Holt crawler tractors from his Stockton, California, plant under the copyrighted trademark "Caterpillar," unknowingly creating the name for a company that still bears it.[39]

Benjamin Holt did not invent the track-type tractor, but he did develop a practical application of previously known principles and was the first to commercialize the product successfully. The principle of a vehicle that ran on its own endless rails dated back to the eighteenth century and various patents had been awarded, but lack of practical motive power frustrated those early inventions. In 1901 Alvin O. Lombard of Maine patented a steam-powered track-type tractor for towing logging sleds during the winter. The machine was a mechanical success, but Lombard, lacking resources, never

Benjamin Holt (1849–1920). His 1908 gasoline-powered model was the first commercial success. The Holt Manufacturing Company was the leading producer of track-type tractors in the first quarter of the twentieth century. (Courtesy of Caterpillar Inc.)

promoted it outside the logging industry, and no more than two hundred were built.[40] Lombard later claimed that the Holt 1904 tractor infringed his patents, but he was never successful in obtaining a settlement or royalties from Holt. To strengthen its position in patent infringement litigation with Holt, the C. L. Best Gas Traction Company purchased Lombard's two most important patents for $25,000 in 1915.[41]

In contrast to Lombard, Holt had the resources of a large, prosperous company behind him. As president of the Stockton Wheel Company, established in 1883, and the successor Holt Manufacturing Company, his inventive and entrepreneurial talents had made his firm the nation's leading manufacturer of combines and California's largest producer of steam traction engines at the turn of the century. The company was noted for the prodigious size of its combines. The largest, built in 1893, had a fifty-foot cut and required thirty-six horses.[42] Holt, a native of New Hampshire, had been in California only since 1883 and was already fifty-five when he first put tracks on a steamer.

Holt had his experimental tractor in production less than two years after testing it, although he had already recognized the advantages of the internal combustion engine. In 1906 he organized the Aurora Engine Company in Stockton to develop and build gasoline engines, and by 1908 he was building track-type tractors powered by his own gasoline engine.[43]

In 1904 Holt converted one of his steam traction engines into this cumbersome crawler tractor. His goal was a low-ground-pressure agricultural tractor that would work in the soft conditions of the California Delta. (Courtesy of Caterpillar Inc.)

This gasoline-powered crawler, from around 1912, illustrates the immense progress Holt made in just eight years in track-type tractor development. The machine was technically more advanced than the wheel farm tractors of the time. (Courtesy of Caterpillar Inc.)

Holt's new tractor had a big boost in 1908 when the City of Los Angeles ordered one for work on the Los Angeles Aqueduct, then under construction. Additional orders followed in 1909 to a total of twenty-eight, but the job proved to be a severe testing ground for the tractors. Ultimately, project managers judged the performance of the machines less than satisfactory, although the experience accelerated development of a more reliable product.[44]

Expansion to Peoria

Until 1909 Holt's operations were centered in Stockton, with a small branch in Walla Walla, Washington, to serve the Pacific Northwest. That year the plant of a defunct farm implement maker, Colean Manufacturing Company, was acquired in the heart of the Midwest: East Peoria, Illinois. Credit for the move goes primarily to Pliny Holt, one of Ben Holt's nephews, who was encouraged by Murray M. Baker, a Peoria businessman who became the plant general manager. At a price of $75,000, the purchase was a great bargain.[45]

It is not clear what weight was given the various factors that drove the move. The Holt crawler tractor was replacing the steam traction engine as a prime mover in all kinds of drawbar applications in farming, freighting, and logging, but the Holt name was not well known other than on the West Coast. The tractor had been developed to meet a unique local requirement for a low-ground-pressure machine to work in agriculture in the Delta region of California, and Holt combines were designed for the dry California conditions. But he must have realized that the growth of his company would be limited if it were restricted to the California Central Valley and the wheatlands of eastern Washington. Grain growing in the Central Valley had already peaked and was declining as farmers diversified into other higher-value crops. Thus Holt's move to broaden his marketplace was timely.

By moving east, the company began its transition from being a purely regional concern to a national one. Although the timing may have seemed propitious for penetrating the midwestern farm belt, coincidentally 1909 was also the year International Harvester introduced its wheel farm tractor. Farm tractor manufacturers were mushrooming all over the Midwest. If an opportunity in the farm belt did exist for Holt in 1909, it was quickly frustrated by the wheel tractor. The onset of World War I with its heavy demand for Caterpillar track-type tractors may well have masked the failure of the Holt Company to penetrate the midwestern farm market in any significant way. In any case, the advent of all-purpose farm tractors in the 1920s virtually eliminated the track-type tractor as a major contender for the business of average midwestern row-crop farmers.

But a midwestern location was fully justified on other grounds. In contrast to the relative isolation of Stockton, Peoria was closer to population centers and closer to supplies of iron and steel. And as the track-type tractor/towed road grader combination became recognized as the premier road-building and maintenance tool of the day, the thousands of miles of midwestern dirt roads made it an ideal location.

The C. L. Best Rivalry

As Holt was getting established in Peoria, a new rival, the C. L. Best Gas Traction Company, was starting up back in California. C. L. (Leo) Best's father, Daniel, had been in the farm implement, combine, and steam traction engine business for more than thirty years. Operating from a San Leandro, California, plant, he had successfully competed with the Holt combines and steamers.[46] The rivalry had led to protracted patent infringement litigation that had been a drain on both companies.[47] That depletion, as well as recognition that the gasoline engine meant that the end was near for steam power, led Daniel Best, nearing seventy, to opt out. In 1908 he had accepted an offer from Holt for his business.[48]

Undeterred by his father's decision and after a short stint as a Holt employee, by 1910 the thirty-two-year old Leo Best was back in business on his own, building gasoline-powered wheel-type farm tractors and developing his own track-type tractor design. It might have been that his true intentions all along were to enter the track-type tractor business, which he did in 1913, five years after the sale of his father's company.

Best's first model was a "75," paralleling Holt's nomenclature system in which the model number approximated the brake horsepower of the machine.[49] Perhaps coincidentally, Holt introduced its Model 75 the same year, topping out a line that included Models 60 and 30.[50]

The Elimination of Tiller Wheels

In this period Holt was building crawler tractors at both Peoria and Stockton, as well as the combine line at Stockton. The engineering department at each plant had a wide degree of independence in tractor design. The Holt 30, introduced by Stockton in 1912, was designed for Central Valley farmers. Its engine was in the traditional extended forward position, and it had a low profile for orchard work and a front tiller wheel.[51] The forward position of the engine was a carryover from the steam traction design. That configuration required a front tiller wheel to support the extended overhung position of the engine as well as for steering. But the Peoria version of the Holt 30 introduced the following year had an altogether different and a revolutionary appearance. It was a short-coupled design, with the engine pulled back radically and the tiller wheel eliminated. Steering was effected solely by multiple-disc steering clutches and brakes. The Peoria 30 (the "Baby Caterpillar") had a profound effect on track-type tractor design, and henceforth the industry would adopt this configuration for new models.[52]

The period between the introduction of the gasoline-powered tractor in 1908 and the start of wartime demand for Holt track-type machines in 1916 was one of rapid growth for the company. It was becoming more and more apparent to management that crawler tractors had great potential in non-agricultural uses as well as in what had been the company's traditional field,

An early crawler without a tiller wheel. The 1913 Holt thirty-horsepower "Baby" Caterpillar was the first crawler to dispense with the front tiller wheel, assuming the configuration still in use. (Courtesy of Caterpillar Inc.)

The eight-ton, four-cubic-yard Holt side-dump ore wagon, introduced about
1910, when combined with a Holt crawler, formed the first mechanized off-road
earthmover from one manufacturer. (Courtesy of Caterpillar Inc.)

agriculture. As a start in exploiting the possibilities, in 1909 Holt introduced
a four-cubic-yard, eight-ton-capacity, side-dump wagon for use on the Los
Angeles Aqueduct project. Towed by a Holt crawler, it was likely the first
mechanized earthmoving hauling unit with off-road capability.[53]

World War I

With the onset of the war in 1914, Holt management recognized the
military potential of the crawler tractor as a prime mover for artillery and
supplies but initially was not successful in gaining the interest of the U.S.
Army. But it required only brief experience in the mud of Flanders for the
French and British armies to recognize the advantages of crawler tractors.
They quickly began ordering, and their example coupled with Holt's per-
sistent demonstrations led the U.S. Army to follow suit. To meet British and
French demand, production of standard products at the Peoria plant went
from ten tractors per month in mid-1914 to fifty per month by mid-1916.[54]
When U.S. government orders began to flow in the latter half of 1916, the
Holt Company was almost overwhelmed. Facilities at Stockton and Peoria
were wholly dedicated to the war effort but were unable to meet demand,

The high flotation and tractive ability of the crawler tractor made it a valuable tool on the Western Front during World War I. Holt supplied about ten thousand machines to the Allies. (Courtesy of Caterpillar Inc.)

so Holt licensed several manufacturers to assemble machines from Holt-supplied parts. To further complicate matters, the U.S. Army was unwilling to take the standard Holt commercial products and insisted on new designs sized specifically to match various artillery pieces. Thus, the 2½-ton, 5-ton, and 10-ton tractors were created to army specifications. Holt continued to build the commercial Models 60 and 75 and even some Model 120s, but they were of the older, tiller-wheel design. In total, Holt built 5,082 machines for the Allies, and with licensees assembled another 4,689. The bulk were five-ton tractors assembled by licensees and ten-ton tractors and Model 75s built by Holt. Stockton built engines, and final assembly was done in Peoria.[55]

Holt and the Tank

No discussion of Holt's role in the World War I production effort would be complete without addressing the origins of the tank because some Holt boosters have gone so far as to state unequivocally that the tank was a Holt invention. The principle of the crawler tractor undoubtedly provided the germ of the idea for an armored vehicle that could operate in difficult off-road conditions, but the British development of the tank occurred without direct involvement of the Holt Company. The company did collaborate with the U.S. Army in the development of several special-purpose military vehicles, but the war ended before any were in production. Holt personally never made any claims regarding his company's role in tank development.

Postwar Problems

To meet wartime demands, the company had almost recklessly expanded its facilities and increased employment in both Stockton and Peoria, and the rather sudden end of the war left Holt in serious disarray. Although its total dedication to meeting the demands of the military had been lucrative, it was now going to have to pay the price in several ways. First, it had manufacturing space well in excess of likely needs for peacetime production. Second, for all practical purposes Holt had been out of the civilian market for nearly four years and had neglected its dealer organization. Finally, its product line consisted of three modified military specification tractors: the two-ton, five-ton, and ten-ton as well as the obsolete prewar Models 60 and 75. The Holt Manufacturing Company was in serious trouble. From a peak of $23 million in 1918, sales fell to $15 million in 1919 and bottomed out at $8.9 million in 1921.[56]

To further complicate matters, Holt had to face competition that had been much less affected by the war, specifically the C. L. Best Gas Tractor Company. Soon after entering the track-type tractor business in 1913, Best had discontinued building wheel tractors to concentrate on track machines. He, too, had dispensed with the tiller wheel and was building machines technologically equal or superior to the Holt line. Business had been so good that in 1916, to meet the need for additional space, Best had purchased his father's old plant in San Leandro. To compound Holt's problems, in 1919 Best brought out a new Model 60 that was far better than anything in the Holt line. A companion Model 30 followed in 1921.[57] These were the two models subsequently contributed by Best in the 1925 merger with Holt. Their superiority is attested to by the fact that they were continued into the early 1930s before being replaced by diesel versions. In contrast, of Holt's contributions to the merger, the ten-ton was discontinued almost immediately, the five-ton lasted a year, and the two-ton was dropped in 1928 in favor of the new Model 20.[58]

Introduced in 1919, the Best 60 tractor had a modern appearance. A much-improved version formed the platform for the first Caterpillar diesel tractor in 1931. (Peoria Public Library)

The Death of Benjamin Holt

The most devastating event affecting the Holt Company after the war was the death in 1920 of Benjamin Holt at seventy-one. From his arrival in California in 1883 to head up the Stockton Wheel Company, he had devoted his life to the machinery business as an inventor and entrepreneur and built the Holt Manufacturing Company into the world's leading producer of track-type tractors. He became a prominent citizen of Stockton and maintained his home and company headquarters there even after Peoria had become the center of company manufacturing operations. Holt had four sons, but none ever occupied more than a minor position in the Holt Company. His youngest, William Knox Holt, would later become a successful Caterpillar dealer in Mexico City and San Antonio, Texas. Other members of the family, including two grandsons, also became dealers. At the time of his death, three nephews were active in the business: C. Parker Holt and brothers P. E. (Pliny) and Ben C. Holt. Pliny was to be a member of the first Caterpillar board and a vice president until his death in 1934. C. Parker also served as a Caterpillar vice president and executive vice president until his death in 1938.

Benjamin Holt's death caused considerable apprehension among the bankers who were holding the company's rather substantial debt, and they gave the directors little choice but to accept their candidate, Thomas F. Baxter, to succeed Holt. Baxter ran the company during the five-year interregnum until he was forced out in the merger with Best.[59]

The Merger of Holt and Best

Harry H. Fair was the moving force in consummating the 1925 merger of Holt Manufacturing Company and C. L. Best Gas Tractor Company. His firm, the San Francisco brokerage and investment banking house of Pierce, Fair and Company, was closely involved in the financial affairs of the Best Company, and Fair had become a Best board member and major stockholder. From that vantage point he saw the obvious advantages of a merger of the two bitter rivals and developed a plan to bring them together. In early 1925 a group made up of members of Pierce, Fair and Company, the Holt family, and Murray M. Baker, a vice president of Holt and general manager of the Peoria plant, gained control of the Holt Company. The event put Harry Fair on both sides of the equation. The group immediately opened negotiations with the Best company that culminated in the exchange of stock in the newly formed Caterpillar Tractor Co. for the assets of the two companies, to take effect on May 1, 1925. At the time of the merger, the Holt company was roughly twice the size of Best in sales and assets. Holt had forty acres of land, fourteen of them under roof, in Peoria and thirty-one acres, with thirteen under roof, in Stockton; Best had ten acres, with 5½ under roof, in San Leandro. Holt claimed a capacity to build 5,000 tractors per year compared to Best's 2,500. Combined sales in 1924 were about $17 million.[60]

About two-thirds of the 260,000 shares of Caterpillar common stock issued went to Holt stockholders and one-third to Best stockholders. Capitalization was $12.5 million. Leo Best became chairman, and Raymond C. Force, an attorney and member of the Best board, became president and CEO; Best, Force, and Fair composed the executive committee. In addition to members of the executive committee, directors were B. C. Heacock, first vice president; Murray Baker and Pliny Holt, vice presidents; O. L. Starr, manufacturing manager; A. L. Chickering, a San Francisco attorney; and J. A. McGregor, a California businessman. Although neither Holt nor Best was the surviving corporation, it is significant that most key positions were filled by men associated with Best, reflecting Fair's loyalties and dominance of the transaction. Caterpillar was incorporated in California and remained so until 1986, when it became a Delaware corporation. Although headquarters were established in San Leandro, the center of operations was to be Peoria. Corporate employment was 2,652.[61]

Early in its history, the new company decided that it would sell exclusively through independent, privately owned dealers, ratifying a practice both companies were already following. Because each company had about fifty dealers, many of them competitors, a painful selection process had to be carried out. By the end of 1925 there were eighty-nine Caterpillar dealers in the United States and abroad.[62] Holt's name was better known outside North America because the company had shipped thousands of tractors overseas during World War I. Holt already had a few overseas dealers, and a program was quickly started to find and appoint new "export" dealers. By the beginning of World War II, Caterpillar was represented in most of Europe as well as in Africa, Latin America, Australia, New Zealand, and India.

The first six years of the company's existence were extremely profitable despite prices actually being lowered every year through 1929.[63] The reductions were brought about in part by the general price deflation that took place in the economy during the period. But the fact was that the merger of the two leading manufacturers of crawler tractors had brought powerful synergisms in manufacturing and marketing that competition was finding it hard to match.

Early Competition

Shortly after the introduction of the Holt gasoline tractor in 1908, several firms had entered the track-type tractor business. In 1910 the Bullock Tractor Company of Chicago introduced a twelve-drawbar-horsepower model, the "Creeping Grip," and built machines under that name until being bought out by the Franklin Tractor Company in 1920. The Yuba Ball Tread Company of Yuba, California, built crawlers from 1914 to about 1928. The Electric Wheel Company of Quincy, Illinois, built several crawler models, including the large EWC 80 during the 1920s, but it exited the business in 1928.

In 1916 the Bates Tractor Company introduced its first crawler, the Model

C, under the brand name "Steel Mule." The Steel Mule line eventually included models ranging from thirty-five to eighty horsepower and largely gasoline-powered. Track-type tractors were built over a twenty-year period in a Joliet, Illinois, plant until the late 1930s, when the brand disappeared.

In 1918 the Monarch Tractor Company of Waterton, Wisconsin, was building three crawler models, the twelve-drawbar-horsepower, twenty-belt-horsepower (12-20) and eighteen-drawbar-horsepower, thirty-belt-horsepower (18-30) "Neverslip" and the six-drawbar-horsepower, ten-belt-horsepower (6-10) "Lightfoot" brands. The company went through reorganization, moved to Springfield, Illinois, and in 1928 was acquired by Allis-Chalmers. At that point it was building two models, a six-ton and a ten-ton.

Of all the companies to enter the track-type tractor business in the early years, only the Cleveland Tractor Company under the brand name "Cletrac" would survive as an independent manufacturer exclusively of crawler tractors. Numerous other names appeared and disappeared, among them Killen-Strait, Centiped, Bear, Leader, Austin, Laughlin, and Trundaar, but by 1920 only about ten companies out of a total of 186 were manufacturing track-type tractors. By 1930 only Caterpillar, Allis-Chalmers, International Harvester, Cletrac, and Bates remained as viable crawler competitors of the then thirty-eight U.S. companies building tractors. Under such competitive conditions it is little wonder that Caterpillar, a well-financed and experienced firm, was so profitable in the late 1920s.[64]

Why so few track-type competitors? Two principal reasons concerned limited size of opportunity and technical barriers to entry. The track-type market was comparatively small throughout the 1920s and 1930s and never exceeded 15 percent of the unit opportunity for wheel machines—in some years less than 10 percent. In 1937, for example, a record year for both wheel and track, 237,837 wheel tractors were built compared to 34,602 with tracks.[65]

Although engine and transmission technologies were directly transferable from wheel to track machines, steering systems, the final drives, and undercarriages of track machines were far more complex, creating a daunting barrier to entry. In addition, most wheel tractor technology was in the public domain, whereas certain aspects of the track-type machine, particularly details of its undercarriage, were a tangle of patents.

The Motor Grader

In 1928 Caterpillar took a critical step in diversifying its product line by acquiring for stock the Russell Grader Company of Minneapolis in a transaction valued at slightly more than $2 million.[66] Russell manufactured a line of towed road graders and had recently begun selling self-propelled versions based on farm tractors. Almost every county road department used graders to build and maintain rural roads, and crawler tractors, which have high tractive ability, were the preferred prime movers for towing graders. The acquisition made for a natural combination.

Three years later Caterpillar introduced the No. 10 Auto Patrol, the first integral, self-propelled, rubber-tired motor grader with an engine placed over the rear driving wheels and behind the operator. Previous self-propelled graders based on farm tractors had their engines forward, which restricted visibility and blade movement. The industry continues to follow the Auto Patrol's basic configuration. In 1934 Caterpillar further refined the product by introducing the diesel-powered No. 11 Auto Patrol, which had tandem rear drive wheels to improve traction and smooth grading ability. Four

Introduced in 1931, the No. 10 Auto Patrol combined engine-in-the-rear, powered controls, and pneumatic tires to form the motor grader configuration still in use. This diesel-powered version was introduced during the mid-1930s. (Courtesy of Caterpillar Inc.)

years later the No. 11 was succeeded by the No. 12, a model that continues to endure and the most popular grader ever built.[67]

The Diesel Engine: Product Development

Another revolutionary development of 1931 was the introduction of the Diesel 60 tractor powered by a massive 6⅛-inch-bore by 9¼-stroke, four-cylinder, Caterpillar-built, four-cycle engine—the first application of diesel power to the crawler tractor. In 1933 diesel Models 35, 50, and 75 were introduced, and by 1934 diesels were available in five models of Caterpillar track-type tractors and one Auto Patrol.

The introduction of the diesel engine was a key event in the evolution of earthmoving equipment. Patented by Rudolph Diesel in 1892, the diesel had certain important advantages over the gasoline engine when applied to heavy equipment.[68] To withstand the higher stresses induced by compression ignition, the diesel had to be substantially heavier than the spark-ignited gasoline engine, but that was not necessarily a disadvantage in a crawler tractor. Drawbar pull is a function of weight. The most important advantage of the diesel lay in its superior lugging ability compared to gasoline engines. As the load on the diesel-powered tractor increases and engine RPM begins to fall off, governor characteristics, the greater mass of the pistons, rods, crankshaft, and flywheel, and the slower burning nature of diesel fuel combine to allow an increase in engine torque. That gives an operator time to adjust the load without stalling or having to shift to a lower gear. This characteristic, called "torque rise," is minimal in a gasoline engine. In the days when all tractors were direct-drive, good operator technique relied on engine sound more than any other factor. As diesel engine technology has advanced, engineers have been able to enhance this lugging characteristic by lengthening the torque curve and increasing the percent of torque rise.

Finding a reliable and practical means of starting a heavy diesel engine in mobile applications had been a major barrier to its use, but Caterpillar solved the problem by providing a small auxiliary gasoline-starting engine and side-mounting it to the diesel. This was to prove a key sales feature for more than thirty-five years until it became too costly and was dropped in favor of direct electric starting in the late 1960s. The fuel injection system followed the Bosch principle but with a precombustion chamber, the latter remaining a feature of Caterpillar diesels for nearly fifty years until being phased out during the early 1980s in favor of direct injection.[69]

In 1932 the company discarded its gray and red trim paint scheme, in-

The prototype of the Caterpillar Diesel 60 tractor. The Diesel 60, here around 1931, led the way in the use of diesel power in earthmoving equipment. Its 1,090-cubic-inch engine produced only about sixty-brake horsepower. International Harvester and Cletrac followed three years later with their own diesel models. (Courtesy of Caterpillar Inc.)

herited from Holt, for "Hi-way Yellow," a high-visibility color that reflected the company's increasing concentration on the construction market.[70] Public identification of the color yellow with construction equipment eventually became so strong that almost all manufacturers adopted some shade of yellow for their machines.

Although the trend at Caterpillar was clearly to heavier, industrial-type tractors during the early 1930s, the company continued to build small gasoline-powered crawlers targeted at the agricultural market. Models 10, 15, 20, 22, 25, and 28 were introduced between 1927 and 1934, but most lasted only four or five years. During this period, the tractor line lacked stability and underwent frequent model changes, each new tractor having a new engine. Caterpillar built sixteen different gasoline engines from 1927 until gasoline-powered products were discontinued during World War II. Fearful that customers would not accept the higher-priced diesel power, the company offered optional gasoline engines until 1935. That year the line was stabilized with the introduction of the RD6, RD7, and RD8 crawler tractors, and the RD4 followed in 1936.[71] Until being discontinued in 1957, the D2, introduced in 1938, was the company's principal entry into the agricultural market. In 1938 the "R" was dropped, creating the tractor nomenclature that still continues.[72]

Caterpillar built its ten-thousandth diesel engine in 1935.[73] Its diesels were now being offered in industrial, marine, and generator set versions and were gaining acceptance as a power source in compressors, power shovels, crushers, and other original equipment manufacturer (OEM) construction equipment not built by Caterpillar.

Alliance with Deere

During the mid-1930s Caterpillar was in transition from an agriculturally oriented company to the earthmoving equipment company it was to become. But the agricultural market was still important to it, especially in California and the Pacific Northwest, where large-scale farming was conducted with crawler tractors and provided local Caterpillar dealers' principal source of business. In terms of territory size and financial resources, such dealers were large in comparison to typical farm equipment dealers in the area, but lacking a wheel tractor they were unable to serve the full needs of their farmer customers. Because Deere did not build competing track-type tractors, combined Caterpillar-Deere dealerships seemed a good fit. Caterpillar's 1935 annual report said the two companies "agreed to encourage certain of their respective dealers to supplement their sales activities by adding certain products of the other line." In 1936 Caterpillar appointed several hundred agricultural dealers, most of whom were also Deere dealers.[74] Restricted to sales to the agricultural market, these small dealers survived in steadily diminishing numbers until only a handful remained in the 1980s.

Crawlers continued popular for the hilly wheatlands of eastern Washington and the large irrigated farms of California but never successfully penetrated the huge midwestern farm tractor market. The typical midwestern farmer's need for an all-purpose row-crop tractor was being met by the wide selection of lower-cost wheel tractors available. Meanwhile, large-scale farmers began graduating into heavier, industrial-type crawlers modified for agricultural use. That left little opportunity on farms for track-type machines under forty horsepower.

The Depression: Consolidation in Peoria

The depression hit Caterpillar hard. Sales dropped steadily from a peak of almost $52 million in 1929 to a little over $13 million in 1932, when the company lost $1.6 million.[75] It was to be Caterpillar's only loss until the disastrous early 1980s. Beginning in 1927 as the Russians began their collective farm program, the depression's impact was softened for Caterpillar and other manufacturers by massive orders for thousands of tractors from the USSR.[76]

In 1930 B. C. Heacock moved up from first vice president to president, and Raymond Force became chairman of the executive committee. Heacock was to run the company until 1941, when Louis B. Neumiller took over as president and began twenty-one years as CEO. Neumiller had joined Holt Manufacturing Company in Peoria as a clerk in 1915 at the age of nineteen. After a tradition of Californians as CEOs of Holt, Best, and Caterpillar, Neumiller, a Peoria native, was the first midwesterner. Force continued on the board until his death in 1951. Heacock, the last surviving member of the original board, retired in 1962 after thirty-seven years as an officer and director of Caterpillar.

By 1931, with the exception of San Leandro, all manufacturing had been consolidated in Peoria, and Stockton and the Minneapolis Russell plant were closed. The emotional ties of a number of top management people, including Leo Best, to San Leandro and California no doubt saved the small plant there.

Auxiliary Equipment Manufacturers

The national road-building programs of the 1920s and 1930s and the large-scale civil works of the New Deal generated new contractor demands for heavy earthmoving tools. The track-type tractor was the prime mover of choice, but a tractor alone was of little use on a construction job. Tractors need bulldozers, scrapers, rock or dirt wagons, front buckets, or sidebooms to be useful tools, but Caterpillar made none of that equipment. During the 1920s and 1930s numerous small companies saw the need and filled it with a variety of attachments, both mounted and towed, that made crawler tractors a contractor's most versatile tool. Recognizing that the availability of well-built, reliable attachments enhanced the sale of tractors, in the 1930s Caterpillar began a program of assisting some small manufacturers that built good-quality products by providing the necessary engineering drawings and some technical support. Caterpillar dealers were encouraged to market these products, thus broadening the dealers' offerings and giving small manufacturers access to a strong distribution organization they could never create on their own. It was a mutually beneficial relationship, and other manufacturers also followed this practice. The selected companies were called "allied manufacturers," a term later changed to "auxiliary equipment manufacturers" because of the antitrust connotations of the word "allied." Caterpillar listed LeTourneau (bulldozers, scrapers, and cable controls), LaPlante-Choate (scrapers), Balderson (bulldozers), Trackson (cable-operated loaders), Cardwell (sidebooms), and others as allied manufacturers in 1941.[77]

LeTourneau's 1938 introduction of the Tournapull, the first integral rubber-tired earthmover, pressed home to Caterpillar the need and the opportunity for higher-speed equipment. In 1941 the company introduced its first rubber-tired earthmover, the hundred-horsepower DW10 tractor with a matched eleven-cubic-yard bottom-dump wagon, but wartime restrictions caused production to be suspended in 1942. Still, the DW10 was a straw in the wind for what would follow after the war.[78]

Earthmoving Leadership

In 1941 Caterpillar passed the $100 million mark in sales.[79] Although no official market share figures then existed, the company was clearly the leader in industrial and construction market sales of track-type tractors and motor graders. Its products were working on major civil engineering projects, county roads, farms and plantations, logging operations, and mines throughout the world. They were also supported by a well-established dealer organization. A conservatively managed company, it had been quite profitable after the three-year trough of the Great Depression. The war was about to make "Caterpillar" a familiar name to thousands in the American military service and to people scattered around the globe.

LeTourneau

An Earthmoving Genius

When Benjamin Holt developed his steam-powered crawler tractor in 1904, his objective was a machine that could pull things across soft ground. By the time of his death in 1920, his tractor had been greatly improved, but

Robert G. LeTourneau (1888–1969). No one made a greater contribution to the art and science of earthmoving. (Courtesy of Keith Haddock)

it remained essentially a machine that pulled—plows, combines, log haulers, dirt and rock wagons, road graders, scrapers, and anything else that needed a strong tractive force. The man who was largely responsible for making the crawler tractor a pusher as well as a puller was Robert G. LeTourneau, who developed a practical cable-controlled bulldozer. LeTourneau's unique contributions also included the large, crawler-drawn, cable-controlled scraper and the first integral wheel tractor-scraper. Benjamin Holt justifiably has received great recognition for his general-purpose track-type tractor, but no single individual made a greater specific contribution to the field of earthmoving than R. G. LeTourneau.

The Early Years

Born on a Vermont farm in 1888, LeTourneau shared common northeastern roots with Deere, Holt, Allis, and Case. In 1890 the family moved to Duluth, where he spent his childhood, and in 1902 another family move took him to Portland, Oregon. There, at fourteen, he dropped out of school to become a foundry apprentice and after sporadic foundry work over several years earned journeyman molder status. LeTourneau was sixteen when he became what is now called a born-again Christian, and that experience formed the basis for dedicated, lifelong evangelism.

Over the next fifteen years, LeTourneau worked at a variety of jobs and acquired skills as a machinist, electrician, welder, and auto repairman. With a partner, he established an auto repair business in Stockton, California, in 1911, and it was there that he perfected his skills at gas welding, then in its infancy. Unable to pass the army physical because of a childhood neck injury, in 1917 LeTourneau left the garage business in the care of his partner and took a job in the electrical shop at Mare Island Naval Shipyard, where he learned the basics of electricity. Returning to Stockton after the war, he found the garage business bankrupt, which forced him into other pursuits to pay off his debts.[80]

Finding a Vocation

In 1919 LeTourneau drifted into land-leveling work and discovered what was to be his life's vocation: earthmoving equipment. Beginning with rented equipment and later with his own Holt tractor and a primitive scraper, he became a land-leveling contractor in the Central Valley of California. It was his unsatisfactory experiences with the crude land-leveling scrapers of the day that led him to begin building scrapers that incorporated his ideas for improvement.

A Caterpillar 60 pulling five Euclid 1.5-cubic-yard scrapers in tandem during the late 1920s. This slow and expensive earthmoving method was state-of-the-art until LeTourneau's revolutionary Carryall scraper made it obsolete. (Historical Construction Equipment Association)

The earliest scrapers were essentially metal scoops (pans) drawn by a team of horses or mules. By raising on the rear of the scoop, a teamster, walking behind, would cause the front cutting edge to dig in, which filled the scoop as the team moved forward. Once full, pushing down on the rear would bring the cutting edge out of the ground, and the pan would be skidded to the fill area. Dumping was accomplished by raising the rear until the pan flipped over to empty itself by gravity. Perhaps as much as a half cubic yard of material could be moved in one cycle.

The next stage in scraper evolution eliminated the teamster's muscle power. A horse drawn scoop was mounted on two or four wheels, and a system of levers and pulleys operated the scoop. That allowed capacity to rise to as much as two cubic yards. One would expect the development of the gasoline-powered crawler tractor with hitherto unheard-of power and tractive ability to have brought an immediate increase in scraper capacity. Surprisingly, however, small models of less than two cubic yards continued in use in tandem trains that had up to eight units behind a single crawler. Operators in the cut and the fill jumped on and off scrapers being loaded and dumped in sequence—all to move perhaps twelve cubic yards per cycle. Compressed-air controls were being tried but did not prove satisfactory. LeTourneau's involvement began during this era of the scraper's evolution.

Early in his career as a land-leveling contractor, LeTourneau had conceived the idea of controlling a scraper electrically from the tractor operator's seat, and he made a successful installation on his own equipment. Soon he was designing and building electrically controlled scrapers and using them in his expanding contracting business. It was the first indication of a predilection for electricity that became almost an obsession for LeTourneau in designing machines after the war.[81]

The Bulldozer

In 1926, to meet the requirements of a particularly tough contract, LeTourneau built what he called a "rooter" (now called a ripper). Towed behind a crawler tractor, the device would rip up hard material so it could be dozed or loaded by a scraper. LeTourneau's next important development concerned the use of cable to control the bulldozer and scraper. As a means of pushing loose material, the bulldozer dated back to use with teams of oxen. It had been adapted for use with the crawler tractor but remained ineffectual because no fast-acting method had been devised to raise and lower the blade. In 1928, however, LeTourneau developed a cable winch

LeTourneau attachments made the crawler tractor of the 1930s a versatile tool. This Caterpillar Diesel 75 is equipped with a LeTourneau bulldozer, towed rooter, and double-drum, cable-control unit. (Courtesy of Caterpillar Inc.)

controlled by an electric motor, the first use of cable for that purpose.[82] Cable control gave operators quick-responding power to lift the blade, allowing gravity to lower it, making the crawler tractor an effective pusher as well as a puller.[83] From that point on, the bulldozer blade would evolve from a simple plate of flat steel to the hydraulically controlled, scientifically curved, box-section-reinforced, and heat-treated steel structure in use today. No other tool has been devised that will move material short distances as cheaply as the bulldozer.

The Formation of R. G. LeTourneau, Inc.

Throughout the 1920s and into the early 1930s, LeTourneau continued to work as an earthmoving contractor while at the same time developing and building earthmoving equipment for his personal use as well as for sale. In late 1929 R. G. LeTourneau, Inc. was formed, the company consisting of a small plant in Stockton that employed twenty people. Corporate sales in 1930 were $110,800.[84]

The Evolution of the Carry-All Scraper

The cable-controlled scraper was probably LeTourneau's single most important contribution to the field of earthmoving equipment. It required not only the development of the means to operate scraper functions by cable but also the tractor-mounted cable control unit itself. The first LeTourneau cable-operated scraper appeared in 1929.

As his scrapers evolved during the 1920s, they became larger and reached nearly six-cubic-yard capacity; steel wheels on the front as well as the rear eliminated partial skidding of the load. Even with LeTourneau's innovations, by the early 1930s scrapers were still basically scoops. They opened in front where the load entered, which resulted in a portion of the load being lost during transport. To correct that, LeTourneau developed the apron, a cable-actuated panel for the front of the scraper that brought about a major increase in efficiency. Another of LeTourneau's important contributions was to install pneumatic tires on scrapers, which significantly reducing rolling resistance compared to steel wheels

From the outset, scrapers had used the rollover, gravity-dump principle. That worked satisfactorily as long as the material was free-flowing, but with more cohesive or wet material a portion of the load sometimes remained stuck in the bowl. That led LeTourneau to develop a positive ejection sys-

A Caterpillar Diesel 50 crawler tractor pulling an early LeTourneau Carryall scraper, about 1935. The crawler tractor–towed scraper combination formed the first one-man mechanized system for moving earth in quantity. LeTourneau discarded steel wheels for rubber tires in 1932. (Courtesy of Caterpillar Inc.)

tem using the rear wall (initially the front wall) of the scraper as a bulldozer, forcing out material.[85]

In 1932 LeTourneau put all his innovations together—cable control, positive ejection, the apron, rubber tires, and all-welded construction—and created his eleven-cubic-yard Model B Carryall scraper. The operator could now control all scraper functions from his seat on the tractor, and scraper capacity could increase because the load was fully contained and carried free of the ground on rubber tires. It was a revolutionary advance in the field of earthmoving.[86]

The Move to Peoria and Relations with Caterpillar

As his manufacturing business grew in the early 1930s, LeTourneau had to recognize that in his activities as a contractor he was competing with his own equipment customers. He also realized that his manufacturing business was more profitable and less risky than contracting and that he had more to offer as an inventor than as a contractor. As a result, the contracting business was wound down. By concentrating his efforts exclusively on building earthmoving equipment, he was able to grow his business to more than $900,000 in sales in 1934.[87] But he had outgrown his facilities in Stockton and realized the need for a more central location. The decision was taken to move operations to Peoria, and the Stockton plant was closed soon after.

Peoria was chosen because LeTourneau officially had become an allied equipment manufacturer to Caterpillar. Under the agreement, he would design his equipment specifically for use on and with Caterpillar machines. Caterpillar, in turn, would encourage its dealers to sell LeTourneau products. Lacking his own dealer organization, LeTourneau gained access to the largest and most effective earthmoving equipment distribution organization in the world. Sales shot from $2 million in 1935 to $10.7 million in 1940, and after-tax profits on sales averaged 24 percent over the six-year period.[88]

The LeTourneau Foundation

By the mid-1930s it had become apparent to LeTourneau that his growing business would generate profits at an increasing rate. Seeking a systematic method of directing these funds into his evangelical work, he established the LeTourneau Foundation. Seventy percent of the 450,000 common shares of R. G. LeTourneau, Inc. were assigned to the foundation, with LeTourneau and his wife, Evelyn, as two of the three foundation directors. Remaining common shares were held by fewer than 1,400 shareholders. The directors were eager to begin the good works of the foundation, and in 1936 and 1937 paid corporate dividends of $5.50 per share on earnings of $5.84 per share. Subsequent dividends were more prudent.[89]

The Tournapull

LeTourneau's inventive genius contributed another important tool to the earthmoving industry when in 1937 he conceived the Tournapull, the first integral, articulated wheel tractor-scraper earthmover. The unique thing about the Tournapull was that the tractor had only a single axle, and the engine was "overhung" ahead of the driving wheels. Yet coupling it to a Carryall scraper gave the unit the necessary stability. Early units powered

LeTourneau's revolutionary Tournapull, introduced in 1938, was the first commercially successful wheel tractor-scraper and set the pattern for all future overhung-type machines. This Super C is matched to an eleven-cubic-yard Model LS
Carryall scraper. (Courtesy of Keith Haddock)

by the Caterpillar D17000 diesel engine were capable of speeds up to twenty
miles per hour as opposed to the three to four miles per hour of the crawler-
drawn scraper. It took a courageous or foolhardy operator to run one at
anything approaching twenty miles per hour, however, because the
Tournapull, like a track-type tractor, was steered by steering clutches. Nevertheless, it represented a quantum advance in earthmoving technology.[90]

Up to this point, LeTourneau, as an allied equipment manufacturer to
Caterpillar, had built nonpowered equipment for use with Caterpillar prime
movers. Now, suddenly, he had a prime mover of his own that some would
regard as competitive to the Caterpillar track-type tractor and crawler-drawn
scraper combination. Anxious to preserve his relationship with Caterpillar,
he attempted to interest Caterpillar president B. C. Heacock in his machine,
but according to LeTourneau he was turned down cold. In writing of the
event many years later, LeTourneau still showed a note of bitterness.[91]

The terms on which LeTourneau offered his Tournapull to Caterpillar are
not clear, nor are Heacock's reasons for rejecting it. It may have been that
Heacock believed the machine to be without commercial merit, or perhaps
Caterpillar already had plans for its own wheel tractor, the DW10, which
was introduced in 1941. But it would be thirteen years before Caterpillar
introduced a comparable, although substantially more sophisticated, ma-

chine: the DW21. By that time others were also building versions of an overhung tractor-scraper. In any case, beginning in 1938, after being turned down by Caterpillar, LeTourneau elected to produce and market the machine himself. It was the first machine of its kind to be exhibited at a Road Show in 1940. Industry acceptance was drastically accelerated by large wartime purchases by the military.[92]

Expansion

Needing more space for his fast-growing company, in 1939 LeTourneau added a new 160,000-square-foot plant in Toccoa, Georgia. The choice of that remote location was influenced by his wish to obtain a large tract of cheap land and build a Christian education and conference center along with a plant. That business decision, like others LeTourneau made over the years, reflected a desire to blend his business interests with his evangelical activities whenever possible. Although some would question such reasoning, no one could question his devotion to Christian works. Throughout his life LeTourneau lived simply, the bulk of corporate dividends going to church-related activities.[93]

In 1941 the company became international by forming R. G. LeTourneau (Australia) Proprietary, Ltd., a 75 percent-owned joint venture with an Australian partner. A small plant was established at Rydalmere near Sydney to supply American and Australian armed forces in the southwestern Pacific with earthmoving equipment for the duration.[94]

The Great Innovator

By the end of 1941 the LeTourneau company, with sales of almost $21 million, was a well-established player in the earthmoving equipment business.[95] Through his numerous innovations, his impact on the industry far exceeded the rather modest size of his business. He had taken the scraper from a primitive, semidragged scoop to an efficient, productive earthmoving tool. Cable controls helped make the crawler tractor into a bulldozer. And his crowning achievement, the Tournapull, became the model for all future integral wheel tractor-scrapers. Although LeTourneau would continue to innovate throughout the remainder of his career, nothing he would later do would eclipse his prewar contributions to the industry.

The Cleveland Tractor Company

From Sewing Machines to Steam Cars

Although Rollin H. White has never received the recognition extended to men such as Cyrus McCormick, John Deere, Benjamin Holt, and R. G. LeTourneau, he deserves to be included in that select group of inventors and entrepreneurs who led in building the American farm and earthmoving equipment industries. Born in 1872 and the son of Thomas H. White, founder of the White Sewing Machine Corporation, Rollin White personally held numerous patents during his thirty-year involvement in the design and manufacture of Cletrac-brand tractors.

Although most of the great names in the machinery business were self-made men who had little formal education, White, from a wealthy Cleveland family, graduated from Cornell University in 1894 with degrees in mechanical and electrical engineering. Following graduation, he joined his father's sewing machine firm, which was then expanding into bicycles, roller skates, and machine tools. But Rollin White's interest was in automobiles, first electric and later steam-powered cars. In 1900 he patented a flash boiler that allowed steam to be raised quickly and opened the way to development

Rollin H. White (1872–1962). Although largely forgotten today, White was a pioneer in the design and manufacture of track-type tractors. His Cletrac company was an important independent producer of crawlers in the prewar years. (Courtesy of Floyd County, Iowa, Museum)

of White's Stanhope-brand steam car. In 1901 the White Sewing Machine Corporation produced 193 steam cars, and by 1906 annual production had reached 1,500. That year the White automotive business was established separately. But with the rapid development of the internal combustion engine it became clear to Rollin White that the brief era of steam-powered cars was over. By 1910 the company had become the White Motor Company and evolved into the manufacture of gasoline-powered trucks.[96]

Geared to the Ground: Cletrac

About that time, Rollin White began experimenting with wheel-type farm tractors but soon became convinced that track-type tractors would be superior for agriculture. In 1915 he formed the Cleveland Motor Plow Company and introduced the Model R, a small crawler for farm use, with the slogan "Geared to the Ground." An improved version, the twelve-drawbar-horsepower Model H, was introduced in 1917. That same year, the company's name was changed to Cleveland Tractor Company, and the trade name "Cletrac" was adopted. In its first decade the company claimed to have produced forty thousand small farm crawlers, a figure that would rival the combined production of Holt and Best in number if not in size of tractors.[97]

During these years, White was not only the firm's CEO but also its chief designer. He patented controlled differential steering, which permitted a tractor to turn with power to both tracks, something not possible with the steering clutch design used by Holt and others.[98] Controlled differential steering was a feature of Cletrac machines throughout the life of the company. One of his earliest designs, the Model F, incorporated an elevated sprocket, a design Holt had tried on a small tractor in 1913. Caterpillar would adopt the concept for its tractors some sixty years later. Cletrac also had the distinction of being the first to have a crawler tractor tested at the Nebraska Tests in 1921.[99]

Product Line Expansion

Through the mid-1920s the company concentrated on tractors of twenty-belt horsepower and under, but by 1925 larger models began to appear. The twenty-drawbar Model 20K had twenty-seven-belt horsepower, and the thirty-drawbar Model 30A, which appeared in 1926, had forty-five-belt horsepower. By the end of the decade, Cletrac was producing a Model 40 and even introduced a Model 100 that weighed almost twenty-eight thousand pounds. The latter, built from 1927 to 1930, was the industry's largest tractor then in series production, although only a few were built. Models through the 20K used Cletrac's own gasoline engine, but the company did not develop higher-horsepower engines. It used a variety of purchased engines instead. Beginning in the early 1930s, most models were powered by Hercules gasoline and later by diesel engines; the Cletrac engine was discontinued.

Between 1929 and 1931 Cletrac's line—Models 20K, 30B, 40, 80, and 100—was more extensive than Caterpillar's Models 10, 15, 20, 30, and 60. Caterpillar introduced the Diesel 60, the first diesel-powered crawler, in 1931. Cletrac countered in 1934 with the twenty-four-thousand-pound Model 80D, a Hercules-powered diesel tractor.[100]

The Cletrac Company Orientation

From its inception, Cletrac was committed to the farm market but never expanded into a line of implements. Thus, its dealers were handicapped when competing with farm machinery dealers representing firms such as International Harvester, Deere, or Case that offered full implement lines matched to their prime movers. Caterpillar labored under the same disadvantage in the farm market, but by the early 1930s had begun to reorient its business and dealer organization to industrial and construction markets. Although Cletrac built larger tractors in sizes competitive with Caterpillar and Allis-Chalmers, Cletrac was less successful in pushing into the construction market and remained focused on farmers. Nevertheless, during the 1930s it was a formidable competitor for the business of those who favored track over wheel-type tractors.

Modernizing the Line

In 1936 Cletrac abandoned its numerical nomenclature for an alphabetical one and restyled its tractors to have a more modern look. The former numerical models were redesignated A through H; the suffix G or D indicated gasoline or diesel. The largest model, the FD, was powered by a Hercules six-cylinder diesel and weighed more than twenty-six thousand pounds, placing it between the Caterpillar RD7 and RD8 in size. It has been estimated that only four hundred Model FDs were built.[101]

The twenty-six-thousand-pound Model FD tractor was Cletrac's strongest bid to break into the heavy industrial crawler business. Introduced in 1936, it was produced in small quantities until discontinued in 1952 in favor of the Oliver OC-18. (Courtesy of Floyd County, Iowa, Museum)

Cletrac: A Crawler Tractor Specialist

Throughout its existence as an independent company, Cletrac remained a closely held, family-owned firm. Without access to the capital of its publicly owned competitors, the company grew very slowly, however. In 1937, a record year for industry sales, Cletrac employed only 1,500 and was entirely devoted to building track-type tractors that had purchased engines.[102] At the beginning of World War II, Cletrac was the only firm exclusively manufacturing track-type tractors; in its field, only Caterpillar exceeded it in experience. Unlike Caterpillar, however, the company remained farm-oriented. Its days as an independent company were numbered.

The Euclid Road Machinery Company

The Early Years

The Euclid Crane and Hoist Company, established by George Armington in 1909, and its offshoot the Euclid Road Machinery Company, remained closely held, family-controlled businesses throughout their lives. The original company entered the scraper business during the 1920s, building small rotary and other towed models up to about two cubic yards. It also built towed dump wagons mounted on crawler tracks. A separate off-highway equipment division was set up in 1931 under George Armington's son Arthur and became the Euclid Road Machinery Company.

The Off-Highway Rear-Dump Truck and the Bottom-Dump Wagon

During the 1930s, operating from a small plant in Euclid, Ohio, Euclid made two major contributions to the development of earthmoving equipment: the modern heavy-duty off-highway truck and the wheel tractor–bottom-dump wagon. In 1934 Euclid introduced its $^{10}/_{11}$-ton "Trak-Truk," the first rear-dump truck designed from the ground up for heavy-duty off-road service. That was followed in 1936 by the much improved fifteen-ton Model 1FD truck. With a diesel engine, modern drive line, planetary final drives, leaf-spring suspension, and pneumatic tires, the truck established a new industry baseline and made obsolete the heavy, gasoline-powered, chain-drive Macks, which had solid rubber tires and had been standard for work under power shovels in severe construction and mining applications.

The truck was quickly followed by the wheel tractor–bottom-dump wagon combination. Capable of haul road speeds of as much as thirty miles per hour, more than six times that of crawler-drawn scrapers and dump wagons, bottom-dumps brought a new dimension to the economics of earthmoving. They extended haul distances well beyond what previously had been thought economically feasible and at the longer haul distances also would have an advantage in cost per cubic yard over wheel tractor-scrapers. Along with the Tournapull, the Euclid bottom-dump brought fundamental change to earthmoving. They were major advances.

In the late 1930s the company experimented with integral wheel tractor-scrapers in both overhung and three-axle configurations, but the war intervened and ended the development program for the duration. Although a

Introduced in 1934, Euclid's off-highway truck was the industry model for more than twenty years. This later, fifteen-ton unit illustrates the full leaf-spring suspension with six pneumatic tires, a one-piece welded scoop body with canopy, and heavy-duty main frame. (Historical Construction Equipment Association)

small company (prewar sales probably never exceeded $20 million), Euclid's contribution of rubber-tired vehicles to earthmoving ranks with that of LeTourneau.[103]

The Power Shovel Companies

Throughout the nineteenth and early twentieth centuries and before the development of the bulldozer and scraper, only one method existed for dry excavation: to dig the earth, lift it, and place it in some type of conveyance for movement. Until the invention of the rail-mounted steam shovel by William S. Otis in the late 1830s, the hand shovel was the sole excavating and loading tool. Otis's invention was without question one of the most important breakthroughs in the history of earthmoving. Until development of practical bulldozers and scrapers during the 1920s and 1930s, the power shovel and its derivative the dragline were indispensable tools for almost any earthmoving job.

Three American companies predominated in the development of the power shovel: Bucyrus Steam Shovel and Dredge Company, Marion Steam Shovel Company, and P&H. Of the many American companies that would enter the shovel business, only these would survive.

The three companies were founded within a four-year period in the 1880s. Bucyrus Foundry and Manufacturing Company was founded by Daniel Parmelee Eells, an Ohio industrialist, in 1880 in Bucyrus, Ohio, and became Bucyrus Steam Shovel and Dredge in 1890. Two years later the company moved to Milwaukee, which has been its home ever since. After a financial reorganization in 1896 the name was changed to the Bucyrus Company, and it remained under the control of the Eells family until 1911. That year a merger with a competitor, the Vulcan Steam Shovel Company, resulted in a dilution of the Eells holdings, although family involvement in the company continued until 1952. Already a leader in the shovel industry, Bucyrus further consolidated its position in 1927 by merging with Erie Steam Shovel Company, the leading manufacturer of small shovels, to become Bucyrus-Erie Company. In 1931 the company acquired control of the Monighan Manufacturing Company and gained important walking dragline patents that gave Bucyrus-Erie a unique advantage over its rival Marion in large draglines. The company entered the blast-hole drill business in 1933 when it purchased the Armstrong Drill Company, which had a line of churn drills.[104]

Based on Henry M. Barnhart's patent for an improved swing mechanism, the Marion Steam Shovel Company was founded in 1884 in Marion, Ohio. Financial backing came from Edward Huber, a Marion industrialist and threshing machine manufacturer who would later build farm tractors, static road rollers, and motor graders under the Huber brand. Early Marion shovels were marketed under the Barnhart name. The Marion company remained closely held until its acquisition by Dresser Industries in 1977.[105]

Alonzo Pawling and Henry Harnischfeger founded their company in Milwaukee as a small machine and pattern shop in 1884. In 1887 the E. P. Allis Company commissioned an electric traveling overhead crane, putting P&H into what would be its principal business until after World War II. After the turn of the century the company entered the shovel business and pioneered in the introduction of gasoline engines. In 1911 Harnischfeger bought out Pawling, and the company remained family-controlled into the 1980s.[106]

From their beginnings, both Bucyrus-Erie and Marion concentrated on the shovel business and would certainly qualify as pioneers in the earthmoving equipment industry. Both played major roles in the successful digging of the Panama Canal.

Between 1900 and 1915, many important innovations and technical advances were made in power shovels, including the development of full revolving machines first on traction wheels and then on crawler tracks and the installation of gasoline engines. The dragline was invented by John W. Page in 1903 and the walking mechanism by Oscar J. Martinson in 1913. Electric-powered machines also came into production. By the 1920s these innovations had been adopted industrywide, and a continuous process of refinement and scaling-up in size began that still continues.

In 1936 Bucyrus-Erie diversified into the manufacture of bulldozer blades, crawler-drawn scrapers, and controls as an auxiliary equipment manufacturer to International Harvester.[107]

Before World War II numerous manufacturers of small power shovels competed in the construction market, where shovel size was limited by the difficulty of moving heavy, bulky machines from place to place and by the small hauling units then available. A ¾-cubic-yard machine was considered the standard of the day for prewar construction work. As shovel size rose,

This tractor-tandem wagon combination likely hauled only five or six bank cubic yards of earth per cycle. A key machine in the typical earthmoving spread of the 1920s, the power shovel was gradually displaced by the scraper in earth applications. (Historical Construction Equipment Association)

the number of competitors fell off drastically because of the much higher capital requirements for the manufacture of the larger components. In the second decade of the twentieth century Bucyrus-Erie and Marion were already competing to meet the demands of the mining industry for larger, heavy-duty electric shovels and draglines.[108] P&H lagged somewhat and did not introduce its first electric mining shovel, the five-cubic-yard 1400, until 1944.[109] The timing was right for P&H because shovel companies without a strong postwar position in the mining industry would not survive.

At the beginning of the 1940s Bucyrus-Erie was the leading shovel manufacturer, but Marion and P&H were well established ahead of numerous smaller companies. The power shovel remained the indispensable loading tool of the open-pit mining industry and continued to hold an important position as a construction tool, but during the 1930s improvements to the crawler-drawn scraper and the introduction of the Tournapull began to cut into the power shovel's work as an earth excavator. The crawler tractor-mounted, cable-operated, front-end loader attachment had also come into use. Although initially crude and limited in effectiveness, the device had great scope for improvement, which would only mean further erosion in the role of the power shovel in construction. It was clear that the construction industry was intent on finding new tools to lower the cost of earth excavation, but such portents seemed to be lost on power shovel manufacturers.

All of the foregoing companies were in the earthmoving equipment business when World War II ended and the industry's modern era began. Several other companies with long histories in the farm equipment business would only become major players in earthmoving equipment after the war, but it is appropriate to include the stories of their origins.

Deere & Company

The Steel Plow: Early Years

In 1836 a nearly penniless thirty-two-year-old blacksmith named John Deere moved from his birthplace in Vermont to the frontier town of Grand Detour, Illinois, where he hoped to find a better opportunity to practice his trade. There he quickly came to appreciate the farmers' need for a moldboard plow that would scour cleanly in the heavy, wet midwestern soil, something the cast iron plow then in use would not do. In 1837, using a

discarded piece of steel saw blade, he successfully fashioned a clean-scour-
ing steel plow and created a sensation among local farmers. During the
Grand Detour years between 1837 and his move to Moline, Illinois, in 1848,
Deere prospered and built steel plows in partnership with others. In Moline,
he formed a new partnership but on a more substantial basis. A shop was
built and equipped, and by 1850 production consisted of more than three
hundred plows per month. John Deere was on his way.[110]

The Charles Deere Years

In 1853 the Deere partnership dissolved, and John Deere entered the plow
business as sole proprietor for the first time, joined by his sixteen-year-old
son Charles in 1854. Although the Deere company was already one of the
six or eight largest plow manufacturers, when the Panic of 1857 struck it
experienced a severe cash flow squeeze that brought it near insolvency.
Through a complex series of legal maneuvers in 1857–58, the company was
able to protect its assets and emerge intact. There was one major difference,
however: Twenty-one-year-old Charles Deere became head of the firm and
would lead it for forty-nine years until his death in 1907.[111]

In 1868 the firm incorporated under the name Deere & Company, with
capital stock of $150,000 divided among four major shareholders. Charles
Deere had 40 percent; John Deere, 25 percent; son-in-law Stephen Velie,
14 percent; George Vinton, a relative of John Deere's wife, Lucenia, had
10 percent; and two other minor stockholders received the remainder. In
the first year of incorporation the company recorded almost $650,000 in
sales.[112]

A Period of Consolidation

The Deere product catalog of 1866 included a total of thirty-one implements, including walking and riding plows and cultivators, harrows, drills
and planters, and wagons and buggies. At the turn of the century the number of product families was essentially unchanged although the number of
models within each family had been greatly expanded.[113] During this period,
Deere, like its competitors, had put its greatest efforts into improving manufacturing operations and making advances in tooling, jigs and fixtures,
metallurgy, heat treatment, and factory organization.[114] Implements were
improved and refined, but the next big breakthrough in farm machinery
awaited the development of the internal combustion engine.

The Death of John Deere

In 1886 John Deere died at eighty-two. He was, of course, the founder of the company and the moving force through the early years of its growth, part of that time with partners who are now largely forgotten. After ceding controlling interest to Charles in 1858, John's influence waned. In evaluating his contributions one must credit him with laying a solid foundation for the company, but his relatively short tenure of leadership (1837–58) has to be balanced against the forty-nine-year contribution of Charles Deere. Overall, although John Deere has received a great deal of well-deserved recognition, perhaps greater credit is due his son, who took what was a small, regional company in 1858 and built it into a leading national producer of tillage equipment by the turn of the century.

The Third Generation

The death of Charles Deere, seventy, in 1907 brought son-in-law William Butterworth to the presidency. Butterworth, a lawyer, had been influential as a director and treasurer of Deere since the 1890s and was clearly the heir-apparent. Although Charles Deere was noted for his conservatism in business affairs, Butterworth was even more so. His dual roles as Deere CEO and trustee of the Deere family's controlling interest in the company were not always compatible.[115]

The Modern Deere Company

The last four decades of the nineteenth century were marked by a steady consolidation of the agricultural implement business. According to the 1900 U.S. Census, 715 implement firms produced substantially more implements than the 2,116 firms reported in 1860. But the combination that shook the industry to its core occurred in 1902 with the formation of the International Harvester Company. When Deere's net assets of $3.7 million in 1900 are compared to Harvester's total assets of $110 million in 1902, one can appreciate the consternation that must have existed within Deere and throughout the industry.[116]

Deere directors realized that something had to be done to assure the survival of their company, but eight years of uncertainty, indecision, and drift had ensued. Finally, in 1910 the board took decisive action to formulate a plan for Deere's future. The main points of the plan were:

—consolidation of the company and elimination of outside ownership
of branches;

—an acquisition program to bring Deere closer to being a full-line
company;

—an increase in the capital base of the company to provide funds for
the acquisition program (without sacrificing family control);

—and an entry into the harvester business, either through acquisition
or internal development.

At that point, Deere & Company assets were valued at $22.7 million,
and descendants of John Deere controlled about two-thirds of the common
stock, either through outright ownership or as trustees of family trusts.
Acting with uncharacteristic speed, the board agreed to issue $22.1 million
in preferred stock and $16.8 million in common stock.[117] A number of ac-
quisitions were quickly made but none brought with it a harvester, so in
1912, despite misgivings of Butterworth and other members, the board voted
to enter the business through internal development. Funds from the stock
issue were appropriated to build a harvester plant in East Moline, Illinois.[118]
From that point forward, International Harvester and Deere were destined
to compete across a steadily broadening front.

Entry into the Tractor Business

By 1910 International Harvester and several smaller companies were producing farm tractors powered by internal combustion engines. As production increased and the new machines became increasingly affordable to farmers, they brought revolutionary changes to American farming and ultimately
to the nation. Following on the decision of 1912 to enter the harvester business, the Deere board was faced with a new dilemma created by the farm
tractor. Again, Butterworth was reluctant to spend money to enter a new
business, and another period of drift ensued. Finally, in 1918 Deere bit the
bullet and acquired a tractor manufacturer, the Waterloo Gasoline Engine
Company of Waterloo, Iowa, for $2.35 million. The firm built two models
of kerosene-powered, two-cylinder tractors, the Models N and R, under the
trade name "Waterloo Boy." The two-cylinder engine would become almost
sacrosanct at Deere. Long after other manufacturers had gone to four- and
six-cylinder engines Deere stayed with the two-cylinder design, building the
last one in 1959.[119] The two cylinders gave Deere tractors a characteristic
sound, leading to the affectionate nickname "Poppin' Johnnies."[120]

With the introduction of harvesters and tractors, Deere became a full-line manufacturer but throughout the 1920s continued to run a distant second to International Harvester. Although Deere gained market share in almost every category, IH held or gained as well. Federal Trade Commission figures for 1929 showed Deere holding 21 percent of the tractor business compared with IH's 60 percent; for binders, the difference was 26 percent to 68 percent.[121]

In 1924 Deere introduced its bellwether Model D tractor, which was to stay in the line for thirty years. Although very popular, it proved no match for Harvester's Farmall as an all-purpose tractor. Five years later the Model GP (general purpose) was introduced in another effort to counter the Farmall. But not until the Model A in 1934 and the smaller Model B in 1935 did Deere produce an adequate response to the Farmall for row-crop farmers.[122]

The Accession of Charles Deere Wiman

In 1928 William Butterworth chose to give up the direction of day-to-day affairs as president of Deere and become chairman. His replacement was Charles Deere Wiman, nephew of Charles H. Deere and grandson of John Deere. Wiman, thirty-six, had held a number of increasingly responsible jobs within the company and was well prepared for his new role.[123]

Ties with Caterpillar

The reasons for the 1935 Caterpillar-Deere alliance are related in the discussion of Caterpillar. Deere welcomed the opportunity to sell through the large, well-established Caterpillar dealerships, particularly in California. The arrangement also helped Deere in Latin America, where most countries already had a strong Caterpillar dealer presence.[124]

Although representation by Caterpillar dealers in California may have produced a short-term benefit for Deere, it was not advantageous in the longer term. As the construction market grew in importance to the joint Caterpillar/Deere dealers, the Deere line sometimes received secondary attention. Common dealerships began disappearing after World War II in the United States but continued into the 1960s in some Latin American countries.

Caterpillar and Deere also had dealings in another area during the 1930s. When Caterpillar was formed in 1925, a line of Holt combines was continued in a subsidiary, the Western Harvester Company. By 1935 the company's growing industrial orientation made it anxious to exit the combine business.

Deere now had its own line of combines but was granted a nonexclusive license to Western's hillside model. Caterpillar discontinued the other models, marking the end of fifty years of Holt/Caterpillar involvement in the harvesting equipment industry.[125]

Deere's First Crawler Tractor

Passing almost unnoticed in the mid-1930s was Deere's first entry into the track-type tractor business. To fill a need in local orchards for a small crawler tractor, in 1935 Lindeman Manufacturing Company of Yakima, Washington, began making and installing a track-type undercarriage conversion on Deere's ten-drawbar-horsepower Model GPO orchard tractor. When that model was discontinued, the BO Model was used in the conversion. In 1940 Deere began marketing this conversion as the "John Deere–Lindeman," giving the dealer organization its first crawler tractor to sell. Thus, perhaps inadvertently, Deere had planted the seed for future entry into the construction equipment business.[126]

At Home in the Midwest

With the depression ending and war looming, Deere entered the 1940s in a comfortable second position to International Harvester in U.S. farm equipment business. It remained a very conservative, family-controlled business focused narrowly on the North American agricultural market. No overseas operations had been contemplated. Farmers liked the conservative design of Deere products, which helped the company gain ground steadily from International Harvester in the 1930s. Although Deere had added a small crawler tractor to its line, entry into the earthmoving equipment business was not part of the company's plans in 1941.

J. I. Case

The Young Thresherman

Jerome Case was to threshing what Cyrus McCormick was to harvesting and John Deere to plowing. Born in 1819 on a farm in western New York state, Jerome Increase Case was exposed very quickly to the rigors of hand-reaping grain ("cradling") and the subsequent flailing and winnowing necessary to separate the grain from the straw and chaff. Primitive mechanical threshers had been invented in the late eighteenth century, and an improved version, called the "Ground Hog," drew young Case's interest. When operated by horse-tread power, the machine could thresh 150 to 200 bushels daily, a great advance over hand methods.[127] Using this machine, Case as a young man engaged in the custom-threshing business for six seasons in his native Oswego County. But the breadbasket of the nation was moving west, and reports of huge grain crops from the new lands led Case to migrate in 1842, joining a stream of other entrepreneurs that included McCormick and Deere.[128]

Case did not go west to farm. His experience working with the Ground Hog had kindled his interest in developing an improved machine, and he set out to do so shortly after his arrival in Rochester in Wisconsin Territory. Early threshers used various methods to free the grain from the straw and chaff but did not actually separate or winnow the grain. It was about this time that horse-powered fanning machines began to appear as a method of winnowing grain. The obvious solution was to combine the two functions in one machine, something for which John and Hiram Pitts received a patent in 1837.[129] Jerome Case's initial contributions were improvements and refinements of ideas originated by others and based on rights he purchased from patent holders.[130] Case was never to claim the invention of the separator, as the thresher was then called.

Manufacturing Begins: Early Growth

In 1844 Case began building his improved threshing machine in a small shop in Racine, where he had moved to obtain a site that had access to water power, and established a business in the town that is still home to the company that bears his name.[131]

The 1850s brought huge increases in acreage sown to wheat. Rapid improvements had been made in the plow and reaper, and European immigration contributed to a swelling population. Case prospered and became one of the country's leading thresher manufacturers by the mid-1850s. After the Panic of 1857, the Civil War brought an increase in the price of grain and a shortage of farm labor, creating renewed demand for implements. In 1860 Case sold three hundred machines and in 1865, six hundred.[132]

Enter the Steam Engine

The antiquated treadmills and sweeps that were the traditional methods of transferring the power of horses to threshers limited Civil War–era threshing machines to three to four hundred bushels per day.[133] The Case company recognized the potential for increased thresher productivity by belt-driving the machine from a steam power source, and in 1869 Case cautiously introduced its first steam engine. The eight-horsepower machine was the forerunner of more than thirty-five thousand steamers Case would build over the next five decades. The last Case steam traction engine was built in 1926.[134]

Early portable steam engines required horses for movement from place to place, but self-propelled models began appearing in the early 1870s. Even then, horses were required for steering until the 1880s, when self-steering devices were invented that finally eliminated horses altogether from the threshing operation. A custom-threshing rig could be moved from place to place in a "train" composed of a self-propelled steam traction engine towing a water tender followed by the threshing machine itself. Early machines were wood-burning, but soon the straw burner was introduced, an important innovation on the prairies.[135]

The Golden Age of Steam

By the late 1870s the manufacture of steam traction engines was booming, launching a forty-year era of supremacy for steam power as the motive force for threshing. Use of steam power in the 1870s immediately doubled the output of threshers to about eight hundred bushels per day.[136] What had been eight to ten horsepower in the 1870s gave way to twenty to twenty-five horsepower by 1900. The advent of steam plowing around the turn of the century brought on engines of forty to fifty horsepower, and Case was building a 110-horsepower giant in 1910.[137]

A great many companies entered the business, but no other manufacturer came close to matching Case's total production over a fifty-year span. Many steam traction engine makers attempted to make the transition to gasoline tractors, but with the exception of Case none survived as an independent farm equipment company. Few farmers could afford the expensive steamers, whereas mass production, beginning in the second decade of the twentieth century, quickly brought the price of gasoline tractors into the range of many. The rapid increase in the number of sales prospects meant that only manufacturers with extensive distribution organizations and full lines could achieve the necessary volume to survive. Henry Ford's first foray (1918–28) into the U.S. farm tractor business was enough in itself to eliminate most small farm tractor competitors.

The Transition to Kerosene/Gasoline

One of the reasons J. I. Case was able to survive while other steam traction engine makers disappeared was that Case was quicker to realize the threat to steam posed by the internal combustion engine. In 1892 the company began experimenting with a tractor powered by an internal combustion engine, but nothing practical resulted. Its first tractors appeared in 1911.[138] Case, like most steam engine makers, built them on the frame of steam engines, a design that was unsuccessful due to their weight and cost. The most successful pioneers of kerosene or gasoline tractors, Hart-Parr, International Harvester, and Waterloo, were not steam traction engine manufacturers and thus unburdened by preconceived notions. But by the end of the decade Case had produced new designs more in line with the trend to smaller, lighter, and cheaper farm tractors. That, along with its well-known name and established distribution system, enabled it to survive the turbulent 1920s.

The Formation of Separate Case Companies

In 1876 Jerome Case decided to diversify into the plow business and organized a company that in the mid-1880s became the J. I. Case Plow Works, with Jerome Case as principal stockholder. In 1890 he distributed the majority of his stock to his son Jackson, who became president, and three sons-in-law.[139] The existence of two companies bearing the Case name would lead to interesting consequences.

The Death of Jerome Case

Since the 1860s the thresher company had been operating as an equal partnership among Jerome Case, Stephen Bull (Case's brother-in-law), and two others. In 1880 J. I. Case Threshing Machine Company incorporated with a capitalization of $1 million, and each partner received 2,500 of the ten thousand shares issued.[140] In 1891 Jerome Case, seventy-three, died. His contributions to the development of threshing rounded out the cycle of labor-saving machinery in grain growing, and thus he ranks as one of the handful of pioneers that changed the face of agriculture in the nineteenth century. His shares in the threshing machine company were divided among his widow Lydia, his son Jackson, and three daughters, Henrietta, Jessie, and Amanda. Jackson soon sold his shares to support an extravagant life-style, leaving him only with an interest in the smaller plow company. Stephen Bull, at this point the only survivor of the original partners, now held the largest block of stock and took control.[141] He and later his son Frank were to run the J. I. Case company for many years. Henceforth, the two Case companies had no commonality of management and would become competitors.

Although Jerome Case had seen the need earlier to diversify into plows, the divergence of the Plow Works had left the company a manufacturer of threshing machines and prime movers only while its principal competitors were becoming full-line companies. To broaden its line, in 1919 Case acquired Grand Detour Plow Company of Dixon, Illinois, a lineal descendant of the 1837 partnership between John Deere and Leonard Andrus.[142]

Massey-Harris and the Plow Works

The two Case companies had a reasonably peaceful coexistence, but the Grand Detour acquisition aroused considerable hostility at the Plow Works. Both companies were already competing in the tractor business, the Plow Works having introduced the Wallis tractor in 1916. But the smaller Plow Works was fighting a losing battle against the larger, better-managed Case company and was in serious financial trouble when it was acquired by the Canadian Massey-Harris Company in 1928. The Case threshing machine company, anxious to have sole control of the Case name, paid Massey-Harris $700,000 for it.[143]

Recapitalization: New Leadership

During the early years of the new century, Case had grown so rapidly that major borrowing was required for the first time. The company was recapitalized at $40 million in 1912; Case shares by World War I were being listed on the New York Stock Exchange and were widely held.[144] But all was not well with the company. Its great success with the threshing machine and steam traction had brought complacency. It was slow to adopt new technology and tended to be a follower. By the early 1920s those tendencies were beginning to create profitability problems, and at the initiative of Morgan Stanley, Inc., investment bankers then influential in Case affairs, it was decided to seek new, more aggressive leadership.[145]

Morgan Stanley found its man in Leon Clausen, forty-seven, and for the next thirty-four years he would hold Case in a strong grip as president and later chairman. While other companies in the industry were led by lifetime employees, Clausen was already forty-six and a vice president of Deere when he was hired as CEO by Case in 1924. He had joined Deere in 1912 from the Chicago, Milwaukee, and St. Paul Railroad and had quickly moved up in the organization, becoming vice president of manufacturing and a board member in 1919. He was instrumental in overcoming the reluctance of the conservative Deere board to phase out the obsolete Waterloo Boy farm tractor line and bring to market the Model D tractor in 1923.[146] The decision proved crucial to the future of Deere.

Clausen was known for his tough, almost fanatical resistance to labor unions, an attitude that eventually led to his estrangement from the more benevolent Deere board and carried over throughout his years at Case. A dynamic and determined individual, he initially sparked the company out of its lethargy. During the early years of his tenure, he built Case into a full-line competitor, developed the dealer organization, and modernized the factories and product line. But the company suffered from Clausen's autocratic management style and rabid antiunionism. He stepped down as CEO in 1948 at the age of seventy but continued to exercise influence as chairman and a board member for another ten years. Retirement came in 1958 at eighty-one.[147]

In 1928 Case bought the implement business of Emerson-Brantingham Corporation in Rockford, Illinois, which had been established in 1852. Case was now a full-fledged long-line company. The purchase of the Rock Island Plow Company in 1937 rounded out the company's line of implements.[148]

Tentative Moves to Diversify

During the steam era Case had offered a line of steam rollers and other road-building equipment, but with the phaseout of steam products, those machines were dropped. A move was made toward the industrial market in the 1930s with modified versions of farm tractors for warehouse and towing applications, but that was regarded as a sideline. During the mid-1930s, Case, like Deere, introduced a track-type conversion of one of its wheel tractors, the seventeen-horsepower Model C (the "CD"). Intended for farm use, no attempt was made to market the tractor as an earthmover.[149]

Case and the Combine

The development of a practical combine for the midwestern grain belt in the mid-1920s spelled the end for the threshing machine business, although Case continued to build them until 1953. Diminishing thresher business coupled with slowness in developing competitive tractors made Case a shrinking company in the late 1920s. The depression compounded its problems, but Clausen's conservative financial management and Case's cash reserves carried it through. A government study of the industry placed Case fourth after International Harvester, Deere, and Allis-Chalmers, with a 7.8 percent share among the long-line companies of the U.S. farm equipment business in 1936.[150]

Survival and Consolidation

The latter half of the 1930s were good years for the farm equipment industry and for Case. In 1941 it was a solidly entrenched, full-line competitor in the middle of the pack. Reasonably modern plants were located in Racine, Rockford, and Rock Island, but it had yet to venture outside the United States for manufacturing facilities. Case's leadership had brought it safely through the depression, but overly conservative management was beginning to handicap the company. After the war, difficulties would multiply.

Massey-Harris

The Founding of an Institution

When Daniel Massey began manufacturing agricultural implements in 1847 in a small town in what is today the province of Ontario, little did he know that he was founding a company that would become a Canadian institution and the country's first multinational. Ten years later, Alanson Harris bought a small factory in Beamsville, Ontario, and started the company that would join with Massey Manufacturing Company in 1891 to form the Massey-Harris Company. At the time of the merger, the two companies together held more than half of the farm implement business in Canada. Unlike their nineteenth-century U.S. counterparts, neither laid claim to inventing or developing anything revolutionary. Both companies were content to acquire technology in the United States and modify it to suit Canadian conditions.[151]

In Canada, migration to the western prairies was made difficult by a geographical barrier, the hundreds of miles of trackless Precambrian shield that lay north of Lake Superior. Settlers trickled west by lake steamer or through the United States, but it was not until the early 1880s, when the

Canadian Pacific Railroad reached the prairies, that large-scale settlement in that area began. Until nearly the end of the nineteenth century, U.S. implement manufacturers centered in the Midwest had better access to western Canada than did Canadian farm equipment companies concentrated east of Lake Huron. That may have accounted for the slowness of U.S. implement makers in establishing plants in Canada in the last half of the nineteenth century. It was not until 1904 that International Harvester opened a plant in Hamilton, Ontario, but by that time the Massey-Harris Company, the largest Canadian implement company, was prepared to hold its own.

A Foothold in the United States

In the early years, the Massey and Harris companies' strong interest in exporting put them ahead of their U.S. rivals in this respect.[152] Because U.S. duties on agricultural implements were prohibitive throughout the nineteenth century, both companies focused on Europe. Still, neither made a move to circumvent the U.S. tariff by establishing operations in the world's largest implement market. The reasons are not clear, but fear of retaliation likely played a role. International Harvester's move to Hamilton in 1904 galvanized Massey-Harris to counter with a move into the United States, and in 1910, after several years of hesitation, Massey-Harris acquired controlling interest in Johnson Harvester Company of Batavia, New York. The purchase provided a foothold, but Massey-Harris failed to take advantage of it by integrating the Johnson operations or introducing its own models into the United States. Johnson would turn out to be a perpetual money-loser for Massey-Harris—its first venture into the United States was a failure.[153]

The Acquisition of Case Plow Works

From 1915 to 1925 Massey-Harris, without a tractor line, watched the U.S. farm tractor population skyrocket and recognized its vulnerability to U.S. competition. Again, indecision reigned. Finally, negotiations were started in late 1926 with the J. I. Case Plow Works of Racine, Wisconsin, to obtain the rights to Case's well-regarded Wallis "Certified" tractor. The talks culminated in 1928 with Massey-Harris's outright purchase of the financially distressed Case company for $1.3 million cash.[154]

A side-effect of Massey-Harris negotiations with J. I. Case Plow Works was surrender of company control by the Massey family. During negotiations it was rumored that Case was attempting to gain controlling interest in Massey-Harris by purchasing the Massey family stock. The "sell-out" of one of Canada's premier companies to Americans created an uproar, and a syndicate of Toronto investors was formed to buy the Massey shares. Thus control passed out of family hands.[155] Vincent Massey had resigned the presidency of the company in 1925 to enter public service and would have a long and distinguished career, becoming the first Canadian-born governor-general of Canada in 1952.

Overseas Manufacturing

The export orientation of the Massey and Harris companies had continued after the 1891 merger, with particular success in France, but the company soon learned how vulnerable the business could be to forces beyond its control. Company exports to Europe, peaking in 1920 at $9.2 million, began dropping off sharply due to protectionist tendencies and local competition that included International Harvester in France. Massey-Harris faced the classic dilemma of exporters—abandon what had been a profitable export market or establish a manufacturing presence. The company chose the latter and set up a small plant in northern France in 1925. Concurrently, a parts manufacturing operation in Germany was expanded to begin building implements.[156]

Depression, Retrenchment, and Reorganization

With acquisition of Case Plow Works, Massey-Harris was able to compete successfully in the United States and by 1930 was third-largest longline company after IH and Deere. But the depression was to change all that. In the absence of a New Deal–style support program, Canadian farmers were hit harder than Americans. Beginning in 1930, Massey-Harris experienced six consecutive years of losses totaling $16.4 million.[157] Common stock dividends were suspended and not resumed until 1946, and preferred dividends were withheld until after a financial reorganization in 1941. The company retrenched everywhere and in the process lost market share. During the mid-1930s the board decided to close its unprofitable U.S. operations and would have done so except for the intervention of J. S. Duncan, general sales manager.

Joining Massey-Harris in 1910 at seventeen, Duncan had spent most of his early career in the company's overseas businesses, an experience that gave him an appreciation of international operations long before the term *multinational* was coined. Called back to Toronto headquarters in 1935 to become general sales manager, he found an atmosphere of gloom induced by several years of losses, a board policy of retrenchment, and the plan to close U.S. operations. Realizing that it would be a monumental and probably fatal error to do so, Duncan was able to convince the board to rescind the decision. By year's-end, after events proved him right, he was made general manager and then became president and CEO in 1941. Duncan's overseas experience made him unique among the leaders of the machinery companies of the day.[158]

Sales in 1939 were $21 million. The company had returned to profitability, but losses during the depression had accumulated a capital account deficit of $20.7 million, rising to $21.3 million with the write-off of European properties lost in 1939–40. No dividends of any kind had been paid for several years, and preferred stockholders were becoming extremely restive. A financial reorganization in 1941 eliminated the deficit, largely at the expense of the common stockholders, and put the company back on a reasonably sound footing.[159]

The Self-Propelled Combine

Massey-Harris always emphasized market leadership in harvesting equipment and had pioneered the development of the combine harvester in the 1920s. But a self-propelled machine suitable for midwestern conditions was not perfected until the late 1930s, when Massey-Harris introduced the Model 20. Its successor, the Model 21, introduced in 1941, was responsible for reestablishing the company as a leading agricultural equipment manufacturer.[160]

In 1944 Massey-Harris used a clever marketing scheme to persuade the U.S. and Canadian wartime governments to allow it to build an additional five hundred combines. They would be sold to custom-combine operators who would guarantee to harvest at least two thousand acres with each machine. The operators were formed into the well-publicized "Massey-Harris Harvest Brigade" that began moving from the South in the spring up through the plains to reach the Canadian border in September. That public relations coup boosted Massey-Harris's standing with American farmers at a critical time, just as the war was ending.[161]

A Budding Multinational

From its Racine, Wisconsin, base, Massey-Harris was fairly well established in the United States by the end of the 1930s—strong in harvesting equipment but weak in tractors and without its own engines. The company had been international in outlook well before its U.S. competitors, both as an exporter and an overseas manufacturer, and derived 40 percent of its 1939 sales outside North America.[162] Massey-Harris focused entirely on the agricultural equipment business, with no activity in track-type tractors. After the war it would have to rebuild its shattered European operations.

Thus, the base was laid for the emergence of the modern earthmoving equipment industry after the war. In 1941 Caterpillar, Allis-Chalmers, International Harvester, and Cletrac were offering a wide range of track-type tractors, and Caterpillar and A-C added motor graders. LeTourneau had a line of towed scrapers and had introduced the Tournapull, the first integral wheel tractor-scraper. Euclid was solidly established with its off-highway trucks and bottom-dumps. And the power shovel, an indispensable tool in the mining industry, still occupied a prominent position in the construction market.

Deere, Case, and Massey-Ferguson, who would enter the earthmoving equipment business in the late 1950s, were still totally focused on agricultural equipment.

The War Years, 1942–45

As American rearmament began in 1940 and gathered speed in 1941, the farm and construction equipment industries, representing a huge pool of manpower, technical skills, and manufacturing facilities, were quickly drawn into the production of war material. As early as mid-1940, industry firms were receiving government contracts that immediately began a competition within the companies for manpower and facilities normally devoted to building civilian products. Although the production of war material was vital, so, too, was the need for increased production of food. The drain of manpower from farms into the armed forces made labor-saving farm equipment all the more necessary. Were the demands for weapons to override the requirements of farmers for production-enhancing tractors and implements? And would the firms burdened with the largest war contracts have to watch helplessly while their civilian business was lost to other, less capable or perhaps less patriotic firms? Could the supply of construction equipment be cut off in the face of the need to build war plants, increase power supplies and produce more raw materials? The Office of Production Management (OPM), established in late 1940, was responsible for deciding such questions, establishing priorities, allocating raw materials, and attempting to maintain some degree of equity among producers in the same industry. After the United States entered the war, the OPM was succeeded by the War Production Board (WPB), which along with the War Labor Board and Office of Price Administration controlled every facet of American industry until war's end.

The Government and Civilian Production

In late 1941 the OPM issued an order to the farm machinery industry limiting production for 1942. Using 1940 as a base year, production of new machines would be limited to 80 percent of the 1940 level, parts to 150 percent, and exports to 96 percent. New models introduced in 1941 could not be produced at all and had to be dropped. But by mid-1942 shortages of almost all critical materials caused the WPB to order severe cutbacks in civilian production. That created an uproar among farmers, who, with the backing of Congress, forced the WPB to temporize. The upshot was that in late 1942 the WPB introduced the concept of concentrating farm machinery production with the small- and medium-sized producers to free large firms for war production. The idea likely made sense to an industry with substantial excess capacity to produce farm equipment, but it was not well received by the larger firms. The concept was only partially implemented in that International Harvester, Deere, Case, and Allis-Chalmers, although limited, never actually ceased producing farm equipment; Minneapolis-Moline, Oliver, Massey-Harris, and Ford-Ferguson did benefit, as evidenced by their enhanced market shares at war's end.[163]

The Shift to Military Products

Caterpillar and Cleveland Tractor (Cletrac), as producers of track-type tractors, were differentiated from the farm equipment manufacturers in that the military did have a need for track-type machines although it had little need for farm tractors. The government, however, was tardy in recognizing the important military role of crawler tractors in beachhead consolidation, air field construction, and road-building. In 1941 and early 1942 both com-

panies were awarded major war contracts that would draw on their expertise but absorb a significant portion of their resources. Cletrac was prime
contractor for the MG-1, an aircraft-towing tractor with a tank-type undercarriage, and built thousands of them during the course of the war. The
contract tied up Cletrac's manufacturing capacity for the duration and effectively destroyed its civilian business. Government restrictions relaxed in
1944 and the company was again able to build tractors for civilian use, but
it was clear to the owners that they would lack the resources to rebuild after the war. Rollin White, the seventy-two-year-old founder and chair, was
convinced that his company could only survive as part of a larger firm, so
in 1944 a merger with Oliver Corporation took place. White retired and
lived until 1962.[164]

In July 1941 Caterpillar was awarded a contract to convert a radial aircraft engine to a diesel tank engine and to produce it in quantity. By January 1942 a prototype was ready, and in February the Caterpillar Military
Engine Company was formed, a wholly owned subsidiary, to produce a
thousand engines a month in a new army ordnance plant in Decatur, Illinois. But only 120 engines were built. By mid-1942 the military had come
to realize that using Caterpillar's full capacity to build track-type tractors
would be far more valuable to the war effort than production of an unproven
tank engine when alternative engines were already available. Caterpillar was
ordered to phase out its military contracts and concentrate on producing
tractors. The D7, at ninety-three-flywheel horsepower and twelve tons, was
selected as the largest tractor that navy landing craft could reasonably bring
ashore. Although the International TD18 and the Allis-Chalmers HD10,
both similar in size and horsepower to the D7, were also supplied to the
military, the majority of the tractor equipment of the Army Corps of Engineers and Navy Construction Battalions was Caterpillar. From 1942 on, the
government took 85 percent of the company's production. What little civilian production remained was allocated to contractors working on high-
priority government contracts. Until government demands began to ease in
late 1944, Caterpillar dealers had almost no new machines to sell and survived by supplying parts and labor to overhaul older machines.[165]

Throughout the war, bulldozers, cable, and hydraulic controls for use on
Allis-Chalmers, International, and Caterpillar-built tractors were supplied
by others because these companies built only prime movers. The wartime
supplier of bulldozers and cable controls for Caterpillar machines was R. G.
LeTourneau from his Peoria, Illinois, plant. In addition, LeTourneau supplied more than ten thousand crawler-drawn Carryall scrapers to the mili-

Earthmoving equipment played a vital role in World War II. Caterpillar and LeTourneau were the largest suppliers of earthmoving equipment to the military. (Courtesy of Caterpillar Inc.)

tary, along with almost 2,200 of his rubber-tired Tournapull Super C tractor-scrapers.[166] Like Caterpillar, LeTourneau's contribution to the war effort, at the request of the government, centered on building its standard products. Indeed, the war years were no doubt the most productive and rewarding in the twenty-four-year life of the company. R. G. LeTourneau would claim that his company was the largest wartime supplier of earthmoving equipment to the military.[167] In terms of pieces of equipment, that may well have been the case; in value terms, however, Caterpillar's contribution was substantially larger.

Like Caterpillar and LeTourneau, the Euclid Road Machinery Company was also allowed by the government to continue to build its standard products.

Although the military had little use for International Harvester's farm equipment, it did need trucks by the hundreds of thousands, and IH contributed 122,000 to the war effort. In addition, the company produced track-type tractors and a variety of war material, including half-tracks, tank transmissions, gun carriages, torpedoes, ammunition, and many other items.[168] It was during the war that Fowler McCormick, who had become president in 1941, determined to take the company into the construction equipment business after the war. The company had taken a four-model line of track-type tractors into the war—the TD6, TD9, TD14, and TD18, which roughly corresponded to the Caterpillar D2, D4, D6, and D7—but knew it would need a bigger tractor to match the Caterpillar D8. Accordingly, plans were laid to introduce the TD24 as soon as practicable after the war.[169]

As purely a farm equipment manufacturer, Deere's war contracts involved production of material unrelated to its regular products. The company took on a large contract to produce transmissions and final drives for the M-3 tank, forming a subsidiary to handle that business, and was a major subcontractor to Cletrac on the MG-1 towing tractor. That subcontract apparently gave rise to an idea by Charles Wiman, Deere president, to merge with Cletrac. Although the idea was debated by a dubious Deere board at a meeting in early 1942, it never went beyond that stage. In the spring of 1942 Wiman accepted a commission as a colonel in the Ordnance Corps and left for Washington. Early in 1944 the War Production Board obtained his release to serve as director of the WPB's Farm Machinery and Equipment Division. Although he served in that capacity less than six months, that was long enough to become embroiled in controversy over production quotas for farm equipment manufacturers. Wiman inherited a situation in which quotas had been established based on each manufacturer's prewar production, with International and Deere, of course, having the lion's share. But with demands for war material winding down, neither company was able to reconvert to civilian production quickly enough to use its full quota. Smaller companies demanded that these unused quotas be split among them, and after unfairly accusing Wiman of a conflict of interest they carried the day. Shortly after that imbroglio, ill health forced Wiman to resign his WPB position and return to Moline.[170]

Case became one of Wisconsin's largest defense contractors, producing more than fifteen thousand wheel tractors in various industrial and military versions for the government as well as items as diverse as ammunition, wings for B-26 bombers, gun mounts, and aftercoolers for aircraft engines. Case had lagged its competitors in developing an all-purpose farm tractor, bringing its two key models to market in 1940 and 1941, but the timing caused them to be affected by wartime restrictions on the production of new models. As a result, the company went through the war with a competitive handi-

cap, yet it did receive quotas to build nearly sixty thousand tractors of earlier designs for the civilian market.[171]

Of all the companies in the industry, none had a more diversified manufacturing capability than Allis-Chalmers, and most of its product lines were
vital to the war effort. Government contracts poured in for steam turbine
propulsion systems, electric motors and generators, electrical controls, and
crawler tractors. In addition to its regular products, A-C had major contracts to design and build the M-4 and M-6 high-speed track-type prime
movers for heavy artillery and to produce aircraft superchargers. The company also had a role in producing material for the Manhattan District
Project, the atomic bomb.[172]

Increased Sales, Slim Profits

Wartime contracts ballooned the sales volume of all farm and construction equipment companies. Allis-Chalmers's sales shot up from $87 million
in 1940 to $365 million in 1944, more than a fourfold increase.[173] Cater-
pillar's sales went from $73 million to $242 million in the same period.
LeTourneau, only a $10.7 million business in 1940, grew to $42.2 million
in 1944.[174] International Harvester, whose prewar volume had never exceeded $360 million, saw sales peak at more than $640 million in 1944.[175]
With war contract cancellations beginning in 1944, all the companies saw
sharply lowered sales in 1945. Although sales generally began to recover in
1946, it would be three or four years before most companies would be able
to exceed their 1944 peaks.

Although industry sales boomed during the war years, profits, under tight
government constraints, did not. Caterpillar, one of the industry's most
profitable companies, averaged 13 percent after tax on sales for the years
1934 through 1941 but only 3.8 percent for 1942 through 1945.[176] Caterpillar's total tax burden reached more than 70 percent on pre-tax profits
during the war, a figure typical of the industry as a whole. Although the
companies generally accepted profit limitations on wartime government
contracts without murmurings, little did they know that they would never
again see the lower prewar rates.

Bulldozers, Scrapers, and Controls

In 1944 Caterpillar announced that after the war it would begin building its own bulldozers, scrapers, and cable controls. Driven by a realization

that its postwar business would be heavily construction-oriented, the company was determined that it would no longer be dependent on other manufacturers to supply those essential and profitable items.[177] The announcement was fraught with significance for R. G. LeTourneau, who up to that point, as one of Caterpillar's allied manufacturers, had distributed his products through the Caterpillar dealer organization. The relationship would change from one of collaboration to competition. LeTourneau realized that his postwar survival was dependent on establishing his own dealer organization and set out to do so on a crash basis. By the end of 1944 he had appointed fifty-three dealers in the United States and seven in Canada, and new export dealers were being selected as rapidly as wartime conditions would permit. Only a handful were also Caterpillar dealers.[178]

The Race to Reconvert

As government requirements eased in 1944, the race began to convert back to civilian production. Companies with the greatest proportion of their capacity devoted to war contracts were, of course, the most disadvantaged in the race—International Harvester, Allis-Chalmers, Deere, Case, and Cletrac. Caterpillar, LeTourneau, and Euclid, which produced standard products for the government, needed little reconversion. But all the companies faced great turmoil and disruption in their factories as government contracts were wound down, employment reduced, and facilities revamped. With an eye to the postwar period, most companies had carried on research and development programs on a reduced basis during the war, but the immediate postwar emphasis was on satisfying pent-up demand with prewar models.

The War Years Summarized

Overall, only relatively modest changes occurred in the construction equipment industry between 1942 and 1945. On the product side, the government's ban on the introduction of new models froze product lines at the 1941 level. Probably the biggest winner, from a product standpoint, was LeTourneau. Aided by large military orders, the LeTourneau Tournapull proved itself and gained wide acceptance as the first high-speed wheel tractor-scraper earthmover. One competitor, Cletrac, who had never established a strong position in earthmoving, was taken over by a farm equipment manufacturer and would become even more strongly farm-oriented. Caterpillar had announced plans to broaden its earthmoving line for the first time since it entered the motorgrader business in 1928, forcing LeTourneau to establish its own distribution system. Coming out of the war, the principal players were Caterpillar and Allis-Chalmers with track-type tractors and motorgraders and International Harvester with a competing line of tractors; a strengthened LeTourneau specializing in wheel tractor-scrapers; and Euclid with a growing line of off-highway trucks and bottom-dumps. All had big plans for the postwar period.

THREE

The Postwar Decade, 1946–55

After nearly four years of war, the nation was longing to resume normal peacetime pursuits. As wartime rationing ended, consumers were in a fever to buy anything and everything that had been denied them for the duration, and manufacturers, eager to begin satisfying that pent-up demand, were scrambling to reconvert to the production of civilian goods. Contractors were ready to tackle the huge backlog of deferred public works projects but needed to renew worn-out equipment. And labor unions had plans for a catch-up in wages they believed had been unfairly withheld through wartime restrictions.

Although government price controls were still in effect in 1946, corporate profits did begin to improve as companies completed their war contracts and an increasing proportion of sales were to the civilian market. Tax rates were lowered as the confiscatory wartime excess profits tax was phased out, giving corporations a four-year respite until 1950 when it was reimposed for the Korean War. The year 1946 set a record that still stands for the number of man-hours lost to strikes, as unions demanded large wage increases and attempted to lock in concessions obtained through government wartime intercession.

The Economy

In 1946, with the huge cuts in government military spending, the U.S. economy went through a severe postwar readjustment and contracted 11.9 percent.[1] But from 1947 through 1955, gross national product in real terms grew 41 percent while the contract construction component of the GNP was growing at a record-breaking 61 percent, from $12.9 to $20.8 billion (in 1958 prices).[2] In the four decades following 1955, growth in construction activity never came close to matching the first postwar decade. It is little wonder that the earthmoving equipment industry attracted several new entrants during the 1950s.

The Postwar Struggle for Better Roads

In July 1945 the War Production Board ended quotas on farm machinery production, and in September it lifted controls on highway construction.[3] Anticipating a postwar increase in unemployment, President Harry S Truman followed with a recommendation to Congress to release funds authorized for the highway program in the 1944 Federal Aid Bill, which had provided for $500 million for FY 1945 through 1947, and Congress complied.[4] Thus began a decade in which federal aid funds for highways, even when matched by state funding, were totally inadequate to the highway needs of the nation. The four-year wartime moratorium on highway construction, inadequate maintenance during the war, and the postwar boom in vehicle registrations combined to create a huge deficiency in the road system and a growing clamor for action. As late as 1952, only 53 percent of the nation's three million miles of roads were paved.[5]

A powerful roads lobby took shape, including the National Good Roads Association, American Road Builders Association, National Highway Users Conference, American Association of State Highway Officials, American Municipal Association, U.S. Mayors Conference, and others. Private industry with a stake in highway construction not only supported the lobbying groups with contributions but in some cases also took direct action to mobilize public opinion. Goodyear Tire and Rubber Company began an advertising campaign in 1951 in support of roads, followed by Caterpillar.[6] Alfred P. Sloan, chair of General Motors, headed the National Highway Users Conference. Despite pressure from these groups, Congress dithered for ten years until the passage of the 1956 act that authorized and funded

the interstate highway system. In the interim, many states, desperate to relieve highway congestion, resorted to construction of bond-financed toll
roads.

Restarting Water Projects

In addition to the nation's postwar highway needs, a huge backlog of
Bureau of Reclamation and Corps of Engineers water projects had been
halted or deferred by the war. The Corps alone had plans for more than 250
flood control and rivers and harbors projects costing $750 million await-
ing appropriations by Congress. Overall, plans were ready for $2.5 billion
in public works construction to be undertaken beginning in 1946.[7] By late
1952, Hungry Horse Dam, the first major postwar project of the Bureau of
Reclamation, was dedicated. Located on the Flathead River in northwest-
ern Montana, the 564-foot concrete dam was the world's third highest after Hoover and Shasta.[8]

Manufacturers and Machine Allocation

Contractors, starved for machinery for four years, began ordering heavily
as soon as controls were lifted, swelling company order backlogs to record
levels. To provide equity among dealers in the distribution of new machines,
companies set up allocation systems. The phrase "on allocation" was the
industry's byword into 1948 and beyond. It was a seller's market—sales and
profits were limited only by the industry's capacity to build machines.

The Ford-Ferguson Suit

An event followed intently by the nation's business community was the
massive lawsuit filed in 1948 by Harry Ferguson Incorporated against Ford
Motor Company. Ferguson claimed treble damages totaling $342 million,
alleging that Ford had destroyed its North American business and infringed
its patents.

Beginning in the 1920s, Ferguson, a maverick Irish inventor, had developed a new farm tractor concept called the Ferguson-System, in which the
plow, instead of being towed by the drawbar, became an integral part of the
tractor. Mounted on a Ferguson-developed three-point hitch, the implement
was controlled by a hydraulic system integral to the tractor, including valving
that provided automatic draft control. The system created a pull-down ef-

fect on the rear wheels, which increased traction and gave the lightweight tractor the pulling power of a much heavier machine. Henry Ford, who had withdrawn from farm tractor manufacture in North America in 1928, became interested in the Ferguson concept, giving rise to the famous "gentlemen's agreement" of 1939 between Ford and Ferguson. Incredibly, nothing was put in writing, but the understanding was that Ford would produce the tractor for sale in North America by Harry Ferguson Incorporated, a marketing corporation established for the purpose.

American farmers quickly recognized the advantages of the Ferguson-System. Sales shot up, reaching almost sixty thousand tractors and $80 million in 1946, but Ford was becoming increasingly dissatisfied with the arrangement and demanded full control of the enterprise. When Ferguson demurred, Ford established Dearborn Motors Company and began building essentially the same tractor for sale through its own distribution organization. By mid-1947 Ferguson had lost its North American source of supply, and many of its dealers had deserted to Ford.

The suit, some aspects of which reached the U.S. Supreme Court, was settled in 1952 in a consent judgment when Ferguson agreed to accept $9.25 million in settlement of the patent infringement portion of his claims. Although largely a moral rather than a material victory, Ferguson nonetheless believed he had been fully vindicated. The power of his concept has been amply demonstrated by the fact that after his patents expired, every major farm tractor manufacturer offered a similar system.[9]

The Government and Industry Distribution Practices

While the nation followed the Ferguson-Ford suit closely because of the David and Goliath aspects and the extremely large sum involved, another 1948 lawsuit riveted the attention of the farm and earthmoving equipment industries when the Justice Department filed a civil complaint against International Harvester, Deere, and J. I. Case for violation of the antitrust statutes. The government charged the manufacturers with coercing their dealers into exclusive relationships by refusing to sell to those who handled competing lines, thereby acting in restraint of trade. In its complaint, the government asserted that the three companies produced 75 percent of U.S. farm equipment, a concentration of business in the hands of a few manufacturers that was itself anticompetitive to the detriment of small manufacturers, dealers, buyers, and the general public.

This action called into question the very basis of the dealer franchise system in use for nearly a century for distribution of farm equipment and later adopted by the earthmoving equipment industry. It shed doubt on the rights of manufacturers to select their dealers and to refuse to sell to others, as well as to maintain stability within their distribution organizations. If a manufacturer could not refuse to sell at dealer net prices to anyone who wished to buy for resale, the entire dealer franchise system would be quickly destroyed.

In the event, the Justice Department elected to bring only J. I. Case to trial, perhaps believing the practices of that company were more egregious or that Case, as a smaller company, would make easier prey. In 1951, after a two-month trial in Minneapolis before District Court Judge Gunnar H. Nordbye, the Justice Department, unaccustomed to losing antitrust cases, was shocked by the outcome: Nordbye totally rejected the government's case. The manufacturers breathed a deep sigh of relief.[10]

The Korean War

By 1950 the supply of construction equipment had caught up with demand, but in June the Korean War began, putting the nation back on a war footing. Numerous new and sometimes overlapping federal agencies were set up to control materials, prices, and wages, including the Office of Price Stabilization, the Wage Stabilization Board, the National Production Authority, the Office of Defense Mobilization, and the National Security Resources Board.[11] The excess profits tax was reestablished at 77 percent of the "excess," and corporate profit rates quickly slid back to World War II levels.[12] Although numerous government contracts for war material were awarded to the machinery companies, mobilization for war work on the scale of World War II was never required. Production of machines for the civilian market continued but was limited by government controls on steel supplies and by strikes in the steel industry. Earthmoving equipment was again in short supply, and some manufacturers were back on allocation. A combination of war contracts and civilian business swelled sales of industry companies in the Korean War years, albeit at lower profit rates.

With the winding down of the war, the last price controls were removed in March 1953. Unlike the end of World War II, a major reconversion to civilian production was not needed, and the companies quickly returned to normal. But without the stimulus of high government spending on armaments, the economy slid into a shallow recession in 1954.

The Companies

In the latter half of 1944, with the end of the war in sight, military procurement began to taper off. That was reflected in 1945 corporate results when nearly every company showed sharply reduced sales and profits. But the industry's troubles were only beginning. In late 1945 and early 1946, as companies began the costly task of reconverting to civilian production, strikes started and brought substantial shutdowns throughout the industry. Yet despite the turmoil created by reconversion and labor strife, all the companies were quick to launch postwar expansions.

International Harvester

At its annual meeting in early 1946, International Harvester announced a $145 million expansion that would add eighteen thousand jobs. About $30 million of it would be spent on expansion of its Construction Equipment Division, established in 1944. That included the 1945 purchase from the government of a former Buick aircraft engine plant in Melrose Park, Illinois, for $13.5 million. Track-type tractor and diesel engine production, to be moved from the old Chicago Tractor Works, was planned to begin at Melrose Park in the summer of 1946. Eleven new parts depots were also to be added.[13] At this point, the company decided to enter the consumer refrigeration and air-conditioning business in a big way, buying another former war plant in Evansville, Indiana, in 1946 for that purpose.[14] The unwise decision siphoned off capital badly needed for other diverse enterprises while management deluded itself into thinking it could create an effective appliance distribution organization from a nucleus of farm implement dealers and that the International Harvester name had recognition value among city-dwellers. After ten years of growing frustration, the business was sold to Whirlpool-Seeger for $19 million.[15]

IH did withdraw from one peripheral business when in 1947, due to persistent labor problems, it sold its iron mines near Hibbing, Minnesota, to Cleveland Cliffs Iron Mining Company, announcing that henceforth it would supply the iron ore needs of its Wisconsin Steel Division from the open market.[16] But Harvester continued to believe that it made sense to produce its own steel from this small, inefficient mill and poured capital into it for another twenty-five years.[17] The company was to enjoy the illusion of prosperity for a short period after World War II, but well before the end of the first postwar decade it became clear that its costs were out of line with those of its competitors.

In 1949 Harvester took a step that nearly all of its competitors would later follow when it set up International Harvester Credit Corporation. At the time, it was planned that the credit operation would function as a last-resort source of financing of dealer floor plans and customer notes, but soon it became clear that this business not only augmented sales but also was very profitable in its own right. The company's good credit rating enabled it to borrow at the lowest rates, and it financed dealers and customers at much higher rates.[18] The credit corporation portfolio would eventually become the company's largest asset.

A Power Struggle in the Executive Suite

In 1946 Fowler McCormick became chairman of Harvester, retaining the title of CEO, and John McCaffrey, fifty-four, was named president and chief operating officer.[19] McCaffrey had joined Harvester at seventeen, advancing through the company on his abilities as a salesman and coming on the board as sales vice president in 1941. In the late 1940s a power struggle began between McCormick and McCaffrey, apparently triggered by, among other things, McCaffrey's resentment at the large amount of time McCormick spent away from his desk. Confident of his ground, in 1951 McCormick demanded the board choose between the two, not reckoning on the influence of the outside directors. He was stunned when the board proposed to change the corporate bylaws, stripping the chairman of the CEO title and giving it to the president, McCaffrey. McCormick resigned, McCaffrey succeeding him as CEO, and for the first time since the formation of International Harvester in 1902 a McCormick was not running the company.[20]

Product Development

The opening gun of Harvester's postwar challenge to Caterpillar was the introduction of the TD-24 track-type tractor in 1947. Initially at 130-draw-bar horsepower, it matched Caterpillar's D8 but quickly topped it when IH raised the horsepower to 140 just before the 1948 Road Show. At 37,500 pounds, it outweighed the D8 by more than three thousand pounds. More important, it offered an exciting new feature: two-speed planetary power steering. Unlike conventional crawler tractors that required one track to be declutched to make a turn, the TD-24 used a new steering system that allowed turns with power to both tracks. It was a great concept, and the flagship TD-24 carried the high hopes of Harvester to overtake Caterpillar. But it was not to be. In its haste to bring the machine to market, Harvester had made the fatal mistake of insufficiently field-testing the new steering system, and under job conditions it proved mechanically unsound. Warranty costs were very high as the company was forced to rebuild or buy back hundreds of tractors.[21] Eventually, the TD-24 became a reasonably reliable tractor and remained in the line until it was replaced by the TD-25 in 1959, but the initial fiasco had taken its toll. The tractor never became a credible challenger to the Caterpillar D8. Instead, it became a symbol of Harvester's failed hopes for its Construction Equipment Division.

Without adequate product development money, the IH Construction Equipment Division tried to make do with auxiliary equipment manufacturer products to round out its line. It had used Bucyrus-Erie bulldozer blades, controls, and scrapers since the mid-1930s, purchasing the rights to those products in 1953. Likewise, it used attachments built by Drott Manu-

Featuring novel two-speed planetary power steering, the TD-24 was International Harvester's first major postwar earthmoving product. Initially, it was plagued with mechanical problems. (State Historical Society of Wisconsin negative no. Whi[I]-7015-MM)

facturing Company of Wausau, Wisconsin, to convert its crawler tractors into track-type loaders. In the mid-1950s Drott developed an ingenious patented multipurpose loader bucket called the "4-in-1," for which Harvester obtained marketing rights, giving it a valuable exclusive feature for a few years. But it was not until the early 1960s that the company introduced integral track-type loaders of its own design.

Recognizing the wheel tractor-scraper as essential to a full line of products but lacking funds for in-house development, the IH Construction Equipment Division tried a shortcut to entry by the 1953 purchase of the rights to two models built by the Heil Company of Milwaukee. Poorly designed and underpowered, the machines were never competitive, earning the company a poor reputation for scrapers and forcing later in-house development. Harvester never became a major player in the scraper business.[22]

The one and only bright spot in Harvester's postwar product development resulted from the acquisition of the Frank G. Hough Company of Libertyville, Illinois. An inventor and entrepreneur, Hough had developed and brought to market in 1944 the "Payloader," a rubber-tired, hydraulic front-end loader. What made Hough's loader unique was that he put the engine in the rear, behind the operator, where it did not impair visibility to the front and acted as a natural counterweight to the bucket load. It was an idea whose time had come, and the word *payloader* became almost generic for the wheel loader. Hough's company grew fast, reaching $20 million in sales in 1952 when he agreed to sell out to Harvester for $7.8 million in stock. Under IH ownership, the Hough brand of wheel loaders continued its tradition of leading-edge technology, making its machines the strongest products in the IH earthmoving line.

Lacking confidence in its own Construction Equipment Division, Harvester management decided not to integrate its new acquisition with the rest of its construction equipment, establishing instead a separate Hough Division with its own dealers. That inexplicable move deprived Harvester construction equipment dealers of a profitable line that would have substantially strengthened the organization. It also created an anomaly whereby some Hough dealers who had other lines competed with IH dealers and required the costly administration of two separate dealer organizations.[23] Twenty-two years later the dealer organizations were finally integrated, but by that time Hough had long since lost its leadership position in wheel loaders.[24]

An example of the innovativeness of Hough engineers was the unconventional Hough No. 12, a track-type loader modeled after the wheel loader with the engine in the rear; all other crawler loaders had front-mounted

This one-cubic-yard Hough HF wheel loader was state of the art when introduced in 1947. Hough's engine-in-the-rear design set the pattern for all future wheel loaders. (State Historical Society of Wisconsin negative no. WHi[X3]51377)

engines. The machine had other unique features, but as with most unconventional designs it also had mechanical problems, although they did not appear to be serious. Introduced in 1956, only a few were sold. Perhaps because Harvester feared another TD-24 debacle, the machine was withdrawn in 1958. But it created interest in at least one competitor. Caterpillar acquired one for testing, and the Hough No. 12 may well have been the germ of the idea for a new line of rear-engine track loaders later introduced by Caterpillar.

Harvester was never to develop a motor grader, leaving its dealers to pick up an independent line. Many carried the Galion line.

The Construction Equipment Division: Third Fiddle at IH

Throughout the first postwar decade, the Construction Equipment Division of International Harvester, launched with such great expectations in

1944, was afflicted with the ailment from which it was to suffer throughout its ill-starred life. A weak third fiddle behind farm equipment and trucks, the CE Division never was given the resources to mount an aggressive product development program. As a result, it was unable to grow volume and gain market share at the rate necessary to challenge Caterpillar. Without adequate volume, the division rarely made a good profit. It was a cycle from which IH was never to escape.

Caterpillar

Having announced in 1944 that it would begin building its own bulldozer blades, scrapers, and cable controls, Caterpillar began first shipments of bulldozers in late 1945, followed by scrapers and controls in early 1946. But the company was strapped for floor space in East Peoria in which to build those additions to the line. In 1946, CEO Louis Neumiller announced a $30 million expansion plan that would add 1.8 million square feet of space, all in East Peoria, and include an engine factory of nearly a million square feet.[25] In 1947 the program was increased to $43 million—two million square feet of new space in East Peoria, including a new fabrication and tractor assembly building and modernization of 3.4 million square feet.[26] When the program was completed in 1949, the company had gone from 79 acres under roof in 1946 to 128 acres, all but the small San Leandro plant located in East Peoria.[27]

Recognizing the potential for crippling labor problems if it continued to concentrate in one location, Caterpillar's next wave of expansion during the early 1950s took place outside Peoria when more than a million square feet were added in 1951 in Joliet, Illinois, and 360,000 square feet in 1952 in York, Pennsylvania.[28] In 1954, 909,000 square feet were added in Decatur, Illinois. Between 1945 and 1955 more than $200 million were spent on land, buildings, and equipment.[29]

In 1950 Caterpillar made its first overseas investment when it set up a British subsidiary, the Caterpillar Tractor Company Limited, with an initial investment of £100,000. With devaluation of the pound and rigid exchange controls, U.K. Caterpillar dealers were not able to obtain dollars to import parts and were fast losing the market to independent British suppliers. Cat Limited was originally established to procure Caterpillar parts from British sources for resale to U.K. dealers. The modest venture was the first of a series of foreign investments that were to follow.[30]

In 1954 a Brazilian subsidiary was formed with a $3 million investment, also planned as a small parts manufacturing operation. Caterpillar recognized the great promise of Brazil and was the first American earthmoving machinery manufacturer to invest there. Over the next forty years, the parent company invested substantial additional sums and plowed back local earnings, attaining the position of market leader there.[31]

Caterpillar deepened its commitment to the United Kingdom in 1955 when it announced that it would build a 650,000-square-foot plant in Glasgow despite all indications at the time that it needed to be on the Continent.[32] Eventually, the company was to have three large plants in the United Kingdom, a commitment out of proportion to the importance of that market or to its advantages in access to the Continent. That overcommitment ultimately led to costly consequences when two of the three plants had to be closed during the 1980s.

Protectionist measures by the Australian government led Caterpillar to establish a small manufacturing subsidiary there in 1955, with a $4.9 million investment.[33]

Product Development

Caterpillar was absorbed in the early postwar years with getting its bulldozers, controls, and scrapers into production. That entailed bulldozers and a matching crawler-drawn scraper model for each tractor model, as well as several types of cable and hydraulic controls. By 1947 the job was largely done.

The DW10 wheel tractor with matching bottom-dump wagon, which had been on the market briefly before the war, was reintroduced in 1947 in an upgraded version and was Caterpillar's first entry in the wheel tractor-scraper business. Horsepower was raised from 100 to 115, with a matched nine-cubic-yard (heaped) Caterpillar scraper.[34] Although the three-axle DW10 tractor-scraper unit performed reasonably well, it was clear that the two-axle, overhung-type wheel tractor scraper (the LeTourneau design) had superior traction and maneuverability characteristics. That fact had not been lost on the Caterpillar engineers who were deep into the development of such a unit.

The only other major development in the first five years after World War II was the modernizing of the company's small-bore engine line. All motor graders and tractors with the exception of the D7 and D8 received new engines and a modest horsepower increase. Only minor improvements were made to the D7 and D8 until 1948, when competitive pressures forced a twelve-horsepower increase to 144 horsepower for the D8. But overall, with the exception of the revamped DW10, not a single new engine-powered model was added to the line until 1950.[35]

In that year the HT4 track loader was introduced, which used the D4 as a base for a hydraulic loader attachment from the Trackson Company of Milwaukee, an auxiliary equipment manufacturer.[36] Trackson had been building cable-operated loader and pipelayer attachments for Caterpillar machines since the mid-1930s, but the HT4 was a substantial technical advance. In late 1951 Caterpillar acquired Trackson for stock valued at $2.6 million.[37] The HT4 was followed in 1953 by the No. 6 Shovel, an all Caterpillar track loader built around the D6 tractor. These products led to the introduction in 1955 of a three-model line of integrated track loaders—the 933, 955, and 977 Traxcavators—which with updates were to continue into 1981–82.[38] The solid machines put Caterpillar into the lead in track loaders.

In 1951, thirteen years after the appearance of LeTourneau's Tournapull, Caterpillar finally began production of its response: the 225-horsepower DW21 overhung tractor and a sister unit, the two-axle DW20 tractor and matching 18.5-cubic-yard (heaped) scrapers. Caterpillar's large diesels, of the heavy, medium-speed type, were unsuitable for this type of service, so a new high-output engine that was lighter had been required—a new experience for the engineers. The result was the temperamental D337 engine with Roots blower supercharging. The engine ran hot and was plagued with cylinder-head cracking until a wide-head conversion kit was made available. A more stable turbocharged version of the D337 was installed in 1955.[39] The DW20 and DW21 were very competitive, state-of-the-art machines when introduced and quickly became market leaders, but during the late 1950s they began to lose ground to the more modern Euclid scrapers.

From 1947 to 1954 the Allis-Chalmers HD-19 (followed by the improved HD-20) held the crown as the world's largest crawler tractor, but in 1954 Caterpillar reclaimed the lead when it announced the D9 tractor, which, at 286 horsepower and fifty-eight thousand pounds, was more than 40 percent larger than anything else on the market. Caterpillar pioneered the use of turbochargers on diesel engines, with the D9 being the first piece of earthmoving equipment to be so equipped. And after criticizing torque-converter drive for seven years, Caterpillar offered it in the D9. As D9 shipments began in 1955, a new series D8 and D7 were also announced that had updated engines and higher horsepowers, the first major updates to these tractors in ten years.[40]

The first successful semiautomatic transmission in heavy earthmoving equipment, the General Motors Allison Division Torqmatic transmission,

When introduced in 1954, the 286-horsepower Caterpillar D9 was 40 percent larger than any other tractor on the market and had the first turbocharged engine to be used in earthmoving equipment. Some thought it too big to sell successfully. (Courtesy of Caterpillar Inc.)

was introduced on a Euclid wheel tractor-scraper in 1949. Before that, manually shifted direct-drive transmissions that had large, friction-type master clutches mounted to the engine flywheel were standard equipment. The dry friction surfaces wore rapidly and were a high-maintenance item. Beginning in 1953, Caterpillar began installing its new oil-type clutch, first on the D6, D7, and D8 and later on other models of tractors and motor graders. That clutch, running in a bath of oil, was a major advance in power-train technology; it radically reduced wear on the friction surfaces and eliminated frequent clutch adjustments. Oil-cooled steering clutches and brakes followed in the mid-1950s, but it would be 1958 before the first Caterpillar-built powershift transmission appeared.[41]

Ten Years of Solid Growth

During the postwar decade, under Neumiller's leadership, Caterpillar aggressively expanded its manufacturing capacity but was slow off the mark with new products. Through the first five years of the decade, powered products—crawler tractors and motor graders—did not change materially from those in the prewar line, but new vehicular products did begin to flow after 1950 with the DW21 and DW20 tractor-scrapers in 1951 and the D9 and the Traxcavator line coming near the end of the period between 1946 and 1955. During those years, Caterpillar established a pattern in product development that the company has generally followed to the present: to be bold in innovations, refinements, and improvements to products already in its line but to be a more cautious follower in adding totally new products.

Allis-Chalmers

During his twenty-seven years of autocratic rule of Allis-Chalmers, General Falk had held the reins so closely that on his death in 1940 there was no obvious heir-apparent who had the training in general management to qualify for the job. After floundering for two years, the board gave the job to Walter Geist, forty-seven and a vice president with a well-rounded background at Allis-Chalmers in engineering, manufacturing, and sales but no prior general management or board experience. Geist, because of family hardship, never completed high school and had joined the company as a messenger at fifteen, but as a young, self-taught engineer he made his name at A-C by developing the multiple V-belt drive. When he was named president in May 1942, the company, like all other heavy machinery manufacturers, was already a captive of the War Production Board. Thus, until the war's end, Geist had very little latitude in shaping the company's operations. He led the company as president and CEO through the difficult 1945–46 period of violent labor strife and the early postwar years but died from a heart attack at fifty-four in 1951.[42]

Geist was succeeded by William Roberts, a veteran of the Tractor Division and the first nonindustrial machinery man to head the company. Roberts gave the company some much-needed dynamic leadership until he, too, succumbed to a heart attack in 1955.[43]

Postwar Expansion

Allis-Chalmers's postwar expansion took more the form of acquisitions to broaden the already broad product line than large additions of new floor space. New plants were purchased rather than built, usually bringing with them new product lines so that the number of manufacturing locations proliferated. By 1953 Allis-Chalmers had sixteen factories.[44] The company continued to scatter its shots without attaining a leadership position in any one important field. Production of the postwar construction equipment line of track-type tractors and motor graders was centered in Springfield, Illinois, and a major expansion took place there in 1952, when the company added three hundred thousand square feet and modernized at a cost of $15 million.[45]

Like others in the industry, Allis-Chalmers also opted for the United Kingdom as its first overseas investment. In 1950 it bought a plant in Essendine, England, where it planned to build construction and farm equipment and industrial products.[46]

Product Development

Although a bitter strike completely shut down A-C at all locations during the spring of 1946, the Springfield construction equipment plant was back to work in early fall. The war had forced postponement of the introduction of new A-C motor graders, so in 1946 two models were quickly ready to go: the seventy-eight-horsepower AD-3 and the fifty-horsepower BD-2. They had a unique tubular mainframe, GM Detroit Diesel engines, mechanical controls, and the "Roll-Away" moldboard that was claimed to impart a special rolling action to the material being graded. These machines were later upgraded to 104 horsepower and 78 horsepower as the AD-4 and BD-3, and a small fifty-horsepower Model D was added in 1949, giving A-C good coverage of the motor grader market.[47]

The big news, however, came in 1947 with the introduction of the world's largest track-type tractor, the HD-19. Powered by a Detroit Diesel engine, it had 163 horsepower and weighed more than forty thousand pounds, 20 percent more than the Caterpillar D8, but its unique feature was a torque converter in the drive train. Heavy loads tended to lug and stall the engine of a direct-drive tractor, sometimes forcing the operator to declutch, but the hydraulic torque converter of the HD-19 prevented engine stall as the load increased. Instead, drawbar pull automatically increased as the tractor slowed under load. It was a major breakthrough and made the HD-19 ideal for jobs such as push-loading scrapers. In contrast to the TD-24, the HD-19 also proved to be a reliable tractor.[48] With nothing comparable to offer, IH and Caterpillar criticized the torque converter as inefficient, but the HD-19 had undeniable advantages and was tough competition.

A-C was not slow in picking up on Hough's new wheel loader and in 1950 combined with Tractomotive Corporation, an auxiliary equipment manufacturer, to bring out the TL-10, which was modeled on Hough's rear-engine design.[49] Although it was the first wheel loader with torque-converter drive, in other respects it was less sophisticated than the Hough. A-C/Tractomotive had a four-model line by 1955, but the machines did not match the features of Hough and Clark-Michigan.[50] A-C never became a major player in the wheel loader business.

A-C, like Harvester, tried to shortcut the in-house development process to enter the scraper business. It acquired the LaPlante-Choate Manufacturing Company of Cedar Rapids, Iowa, in 1952, and incorporated its two rather uncompetitive scraper models, the TS-200 and TS-300, into the A-C line.[51] Like Harvester, this entry strategy doomed A-C to being a perennial also-ran in the scraper business. By the late 1950s, when improved models were introduced, it was too late. Contractors had settled on other brands. A-C relied far too long on auxiliary equipment manufacturers for its bulldozers, controls, towed scrapers, and track loader attachments. Baker Manufacturing Company of Springfield, Illinois, its longtime source for bulldozers, was finally acquired in 1955. It was not until after 1959, when Tractomotive Corporation was acquired, that A-C began to produce loaders of integrated design.[52]

The Acquisition of Buda Diesel

Before World War II, A-C had designed GM Detroit Diesel engines into its earthmoving products as exclusive engine power. That dependence on an outside supplier for a vital component was a concern to A-C, but it was tolerable as long as General Motors remained outside the earthmoving business. Concern rose to a crisis in 1953 when GM acquired Euclid Road Machinery Company, making A-C's sole supplier of engines an earthmoving competitor. Less than a month after the GM-Euclid deal was consummated, A-C stockholders approved the acquisition of the Buda Company, a manufacturer of diesel and gasoline engines and lift trucks located in Harvey, Illinois. In an exchange of one share of A-C for 2.5 shares of Buda, the deal was valued between $10 million and $11 million and became effective November 1, 1953.[53] A-C lost no time in designing Buda diesels into its earthmoving products and phasing out the Detroit Diesel engines. The acquisition also put A-C into yet another business—industrial lift trucks. Following the pattern of other A-C businesses, the lift-truck operation was never to have the muscle to make it an industry leader.

A-C: Too Many Businesses, Too Few Dollars

In many ways A-C's postwar product development strategy closely paralleled that of Harvester. The diversified nature of both companies created fierce intracompany competition for scarce product development funds. Both tried to circumvent the problem by heavy dependence on auxiliary equipment manufacturers and by acquisitions. Ultimately, they learned there was no substitute for in-house design control in achieving an integrated product line and were forced, belatedly, into spending the product development dollars anyway.

R. G. LeTourneau

At the end of the war, LeTourneau had more than seven hundred thousand square feet of manufacturing space in his main plant in Peoria as well as smaller plants in Toccoa, Georgia, and Vicksburg, Mississippi. The space had been able to support a wartime production peak of $42 million in 1944, a level unlikely to be reached for several years in the postwar civilian market.[54] Nevertheless, in 1945 LeTourneau began construction of a new fabricating plant at Longview, Texas. In keeping with his interest in education, he also purchased the government surplus Harmon General Hospital at Longview for one dollar and converted it into the LeTourneau Technical Institute.

Construction began on a plant at Stockton-on-Tees, England, in 1946, but slow progress and a shortage of cash forced abandonment of the project in late 1947. These questionable investments in additional manufacturing space came at a time of shrinking sales and, aggravated by heavy product development expenses, put the company in serious financial straits by 1948.

Product Development

At peak wartime production, LeTourneau was shipping seventy to eighty Tournapulls a month to the army.[55] By the end of the war LeTourneau had more experience building rubber-tired earthmovers than all of his competitors combined. Drawing on that experience, before the war ended he began developing the scraper line that would supplant the original unsophisticated Tournapull after the war. By the end of 1947 he had introduced three new machines: the Model B Tournapull at a thirty-five-ton capacity, the Model C-11 Tournapull at sixteen tons, and the Model D Roadster at nine tons.[56] In keeping with his predilection for things electrical, the tractor-mounted cable control was abandoned. Scraper functions and steering were controlled by separate electric motors, and an air-actuated semiautomatic "Tournamatic" transmission was an option on the B and C models. By the end of 1948 he had added a larger Model A Tournapull and three models of Tournatractor skid-steer wheel dozers, the first of their kind in the industry.[57] His new products were in a class by themselves, clearly on the leading edge of the technology of the day, but initially they were plagued by a host of mechanical problems. Although LeTourneau could advance many reasons for the superiority of electrical controls, the reality was that few mechanics in the field could repair them. No other manufacturer chose to use electrical controls, and, ultimately, fast-developing hydraulic technology became the industry's choice for controls.

Throughout his career, LeTourneau's product development processes tended to be somewhat chaotic, as illustrated by the nearly sixty different models of Carryall scrapers produced between 1933 and 1947.[58] The tendency was to arrive at a design, build a few, and then begin making engineering changes. Wartime military procurement brought a discipline to engineering changes, but LeTourneau returned to his old habits in his postwar product development program. The unstable product line of the early years after the war almost bankrupted the company.

Costly warranty expenses in 1947 resulted in a $3 million loss on $24.5 million in sales. An accumulation of unsalable inventory resulted in LeTourneau's being unable to obtain a clean opinion from his auditors for 1948. Heavy write-offs brought another loss of $2.7 million for the year on $19.2 million in sales.[59] The business appeared shaky indeed. But the worst was behind him. The product line was stabilized, and sales began to grow, reaching $55 million in 1951 with help from government procurement for the Korean War. Still, it was clear that a short-line manufacturer like LeTourneau would face heavy going as larger companies began entering the scraper business.

The Electric Wheel and LeTourneau

In 1950 LeTourneau announced the electric wheel, a revolutionary development in which an electric-drive motor and gearing were installed in the hub of a wheel.[60] Believing it would make all other drives obsolete, LeTourneau henceforth directed his primary product development efforts toward perfecting this product. Confidence in the electric wheel concept was likely a contributing factor in his decision in 1953 to sell his business to Westinghouse Airbrake Company for $31 million. The sales agreement included the current product line and the Peoria and Toccoa plants. It also called for R. G. LeTourneau to serve as a consultant and refrain from reentering the earthmoving equipment business for five years.[61] Rights to the electric wheel were retained by LeTourneau, and it formed the basis for a new line of earthmovers when he did reenter the business in 1958 from his plant in Longview, Texas.

The Westinghouse Airbrake Company

George Westinghouse had founded his company in 1869, based on his patents for a railroad airbrake. Although he did not invent the first railroad airbrake, his was the first commercial success because of its fail-safe features. He went on to found the Westinghouse Electric Company in 1886 but lost control of it in the bank panic of 1907, although he retained the airbrake company until his death in 1914.[62] Still the leading manufacturer in its field in 1952 with $93.6 million in sales, the company was seeking to diversify out of the railroad equipment business. The predicted boom in highway construction attracted Westinghouse Airbrake to earthmoving equipment, just as it did General Motors. That year the company had acquired the LeRoi Company, a maker of compressors and concrete mixers, and its acquisition of LeTourneau in 1953 put it squarely in the earthmoving equipment business.[63]

The company would be known as LeTourneau-Westinghouse, apparently in the belief that the LeTourneau name would continue to have drawing power in the construction industry. Merle R. Yontz, vice president, treasurer, and a longtime employee of LeTourneau, was named president.

The Adams Motor Grader Acquisition

LeTourneau-Westinghouse moved to further broaden its product line when, in January 1955, it acquired for $8 million the J. D. Adams Manufacturing Company of Indianapolis, an old-line manufacturer of motor graders.[64] J. D. Adams, the founder, is credited with inventing the towed leaning-wheel road grader in 1885. After the acquisition, some grader production was moved to Toccoa. LeTourneau-Westinghouse retained the well-known Adams name on its motor graders for a few years before finally phasing it out, marking the disappearance of a venerable name in the machinery business.

The Short-Line Handicap

In 1955 LeTourneau-Westinghouse sales were $172 million, only slightly more than the sum of sales of the component companies before the acquisitions.[65] Although the line had been broadened, the company's dealers still suffered from lack of track-type products, which, at the time, were judged to be the fundamental building blocks of an earthmoving product line.

The Euclid Road Machinery Company

Wheel Tractor-Scrapers and "Twin Power"

In the postwar years Euclid expanded, building a new plant and purchasing another, both in the Euclid, Ohio, area. Soon after the war, an off-highway truck of twenty-two tons was introduced, establishing a new standard size in the industry. In the late 1940s a line of three-axle, hydraulically actuated scrapers was introduced using the FDT and TDT two-axle tractors

The Euclid Model 8TDT-14SH three-axle scraper was introduced in the late 1940s. Operated by hydraulically actuated cables, the machines were simple in design and very rugged. (Historical Construction Equipment Association)

The forerunner of all twin-powered scrapers, the 1949 Euclid Model 51FDT tractor-13SH scraper was made technically feasible by the development of the Allison Torqmatic transmission. Pictured here is a 1950 version. (Historical Construction Equipment Association)

developed earlier as prime movers for bottom-dumps. In 1949 Euclid made a major breakthrough with the introduction of the first wheel tractor-scraper that had a separate engine powering the scraper wheels. That development became technically feasible through the 1948 introduction of the Allison Division of GM's first semiautomatic "Torqmatic" transmission, which had a torque-converter drive. With Torqmatic transmissions mounted to both engines, the tractor and scraper driving wheels could be kept in synch, something previously not practical with direct-drive transmissions. The sixteen-cubic-yard (struck) Model 51FDT-13SH with 190-horsepower Detroit Diesel 6-71 engines front and rear was the inception of the Euclid Twin Power concept.[66]

The concept was extended to the off-highway truck line in 1949 when the Model 1FFD 34-ton truck with tandem rear axles was introduced with two 6-71 190-horsepower engines mounted side by side, each driving a separate transmission and axle. Using the same design approach, in 1953 Euclid began production of the fifty-ton 1LLD truck, which had two three-hundred-horsepower Cummins engines.[67] With the trucks there was no operational advantage to the two-engine concept. There simply were no engines of adequate size then available, but Twin Power gave Euclid a big lead in trucks.

The company established a British manufacturing subsidiary in 1950, and by 1953 Euclid was a $33 million business that had 1,600 employees building 170 off-highway vehicles per month.[68]

General Motors and Euclid

In a move that shook the earthmoving equipment industry, General Motors acquired the Euclid Road Machinery Company from the Armington family in 1953 for stock in a transaction valued at $20 million. Euclid president Raymond Q. Armington became general manager of the new Euclid Division of GM.[69] Although a very small company by GM standards, Euclid brought with it a well-known name, valuable know-how in its field, and a dealer organization; it was also the market leader in off-highway trucks and bottom-dumps. Without an engine of its own, Euclid had offered both GM Detroit Diesel and Cummins engines as options in its products.

At the time, General Motors, the largest U.S. corporation, was a perennial target of the U.S. Department of Justice and a favorite whipping boy of Congress because of its dominant position in the automotive, locomotive, and coach businesses. The acquisition of Euclid brought a storm of criticism. In hearings before the Senate Antitrust and Monopoly Subcommittee in 1955, GM was accused of "swallowing up" a small, family-owned company. Armington, the principal witness, told the senators that his company had not had the capital to compete with others in the industry in development of new products, and he had no choice but to merge with a larger company. But a Cummins official testified that Euclid's purchases of engines from that company had dropped to about 25 percent of their former level in the two years following the GM takeover, the difference going to Detroit Diesel.[70] The fact was not lost on the Justice Department.

Early GM Involvement with Machinery

General Motors's first brush with the machinery business was prompted by the success in the farm tractor business of its chief rival, Ford. In 1917 General Motors decided that it, too, would enter the farm tractor business by acquiring the Samson "Sieve Grip" line, but ensuing losses brought about a quick withdrawal and the business was liquidated in 1922.[71]

GM Diesel Engine Development

During the early 1920s, the great automotive innovator of General Motors, Charles F. Kettering, became interested in the diesel engine and began a development program in the GM research laboratories. One of his objectives was to lower the weight-to-horsepower ratio of heavy diesel engines to make the diesel suitable for mobile use. His work led him to conclude that only with the two-cycle design could he achieve the reduced weight-to-horsepower ratios he was seeking. Thus, General Motors committed early and exclusively to the two-cycle engine while the rest of the industry chose the four-cycle design.[72]

By the end of the 1920s GM believed it had a viable design that would be suitable for locomotive service. In 1930, with a view to commercializing the engine, GM acquired two Cleveland-based companies: the Winton Engine Company, probably the leading U.S. diesel engine manufacturer at the time; and the Electro-Motive Engineering Company, an engineering, design, and sales firm. In 1935 the decision was taken to enter the diesel locomotive business, the Electro-Motive Division was formed, and a plant was built in LaGrange, Illinois.[73] At the end of World War II, when U.S. railroads began converting en masse from steam to diesel, Electro-Motive Division locomotive technology was far ahead of competition and GM dominated the market.

In 1937 the Detroit Diesel Division was set up to build a smaller range of two-cycle diesels, and the very successful 71-Series was introduced, a line that still endures.[74] These lightweight, reliable, low-cost engines, from two to sixteen cylinders, have been widely used by original equipment manufacturers in all forms of construction equipment.

Early Euclid Division Products

Despite the clamor, General Motors lavished funds on Euclid Division, launching an ambitious product development program while the industry waited apprehensively to see what this powerful new competitor would do. It did not have long to wait. In 1954 the first Euclid overhung scraper—the small, seven-cubic-yard (struck) S-7—was introduced, quickly followed by the eighteen-cubic-yard S-18.[75] Although these modern, hydraulically actuated scrapers clearly had been well along in development when GM acquired Euclid, it was now all too obvious to the industry that Euclid, with the resources of GM behind it, was spending heavily on development of new wheel-type hauling units, Euclid's traditional line. But no one expected the giant corporation to be content competing only for that portion of the industry. These expectations were confirmed in 1955 when Euclid made headlines by unveiling the TC-12 track-type tractor. At fifty-six thousand pounds and 365 horsepower, it dethroned Caterpillar's 286-horsepower D9 as the world's largest tractor. The unique design incorporated two Detroit Diesel 6-71 engines, side by side and driving separate Allison semiautomatic transmissions, which made it the first big tractor with powershift. Rear-mounted radiators gave the tractor a distinctive streamlined look. But despite its size and features, the two engines and power trains proved costly and less reliable, and the tractor never came close to unseating the D9 in popularity.

Also introduced in 1955 was the TS-18 wheel tractor-scraper, the first of Euclid's overhung all-wheel drive designs that used a second engine mounted on the scraper and driving the rear wheels. It, too, was powershift, whereas the rest of the scraper industry was still largely direct-drive. The TS-18 set new industry standards for traction and gradeability.

At the end of 1955 there was little doubt that GM was driving for leadership in the earthmoving equipment industry.

Oliver-Cletrac

During the 1860s, James Oliver developed and patented "chilling," a process for casting iron plows by which the heat was drawn as the casting was poured, resulting in a case-hardened product that would take a mirror finish. His company, the Oliver Chilled Plow Works of South Bend, Indiana, became a major factor in the plow business. It successfully competed with the steel plows of Deere and others but never diversified out of tillage implements.

The Oliver Corporation, the surviving corporation in the 1944 merger with Cleveland Tractor Company, was formed by the 1929 merger of four companies, each of which had a long heritage as a farm equipment manufacturer. Other participants in the 1929 combination were smaller companies. The Hart-Parr Tractor Company, Nichols and Shepard Company, and American Seeding Machinery Company were specialists who, like Oliver, were finding it more and more difficult to compete with large, long-line farm equipment companies. Hart-Parr, generally credited with being the first successful builder of farm tractors powered by internal combustion engines, contributed a good line of tractors. Nichols and Shepard, an early steam traction engine and threshing machine maker, brought combines, and the American Seeding Machine Company added grain drills. Thus, from these diverse manufacturers the Oliver Farm Equipment Corporation was formed, changing its name a few years later to the Oliver Corporation.[76]

At the time of the merger with Oliver, the Cletrac line consisted of five basic models of track-type tractors of pre–World War II design, ranging from the tiny eleven-drawbar-horsepower gasoline Model HG to the 27,000-pound, 113-belt-horsepower diesel Model FD.[77] Oliver made a $3.5 million investment to upgrade the old Cleveland plant and continued to use it to build the Cletrac line with minimal changes except that the tractors were marketed under the trade name Oliver-Cletrac.[78]

Product Development

Oliver planned to exploit the Cletrac acquisition as a vehicle to enter the earthmoving equipment business. Initially, efforts were made using auxiliary equipment manufacturer attachments to adapt the tractors for earth-moving applications, but the results were unsophisticated and sometimes too light for industrial service. Even if the adaptations had been more successful, the farm-oriented Oliver dealer organization was not in touch with contractor users of heavy equipment. Thus, at the outset the Oliver-Cletrac line merely complemented the Oliver line of wheel farm tractors in the agricultural market rather than giving Oliver a hoped-for entry into industrial equipment.

Modernizing the Line

Recognizing that the line would have to be redesigned if Oliver were to have any chance to penetrate the industrial market but working with very limited resources, in 1951 the company began introducing its new OC Series of crawlers. By 1956 it had replaced the original Cletracs with a five-model line of tractors that ranged from the eighteen-drawbar-horsepower OC-4 to the 33,000-pound, 133-drawbar-horsepower OC-18. These tractors were a marked improvement over the former line. The smaller models continued to be offered with gasoline option, and all were available with Hercules diesel engines. Rollin White's unique controlled differential steering continued as standard equipment. Other innovations included levers that

actuated both steering and brakes, a feature Caterpillar added to its tractors several years later, and "Hi-Life" track rollers with a thousand-hour
lubrication interval.[79]

In a further attempt to push into the earthmoving business, in 1952 Oliver
acquired the Be-Ge Manufacturing Company of Gilroy, California, a small
manufacturer of towed scrapers, land-levelers, and hydraulic cylinders.[80]
With improved tractors and a line of scrapers the company began to con-
nect with soil conservation contractors who were known to Oliver farm
equipment dealers, but Oliver was never a player in the heavy construction
field.

The Clark Equipment Company

In the early 1950s a new competitor arrived to challenge the Hough wheel
loader. Founded in 1903 and organized as the Clark Equipment Company
in 1916, the company made steel castings, wheels, and axles and in the late
1920s pioneered the lift-truck business and began building transmissions.
After the war and under the leadership of CEO George Spatta, Clark expanded its transmission and axle business, deriving three-quarters of its
revenues from that source. In 1953, in an effort to diversify from its heavy
dependence on the automotive industry, it acquired the Ross Carrier Corporation, a maker of straddle carriers, and a Ross subsidiary, the Michigan
Power Shovel Company, which had an embryonic line of wheel loaders.[81]
That year Clark corporate sales were $122 million.[82] In early 1954 Clark
announced that it was entering the wheel loader business under the brand
name "Michigan" with a six-model line from fifteen cubic feet to 2½ cubic
yards. It would build a new plant for its construction equipment line at
Benton Harbor, Michigan.[83]

Patterned after the Hough machines, Michigan loaders had the rear-engine, rear-wheel steer configuration, and some had Clark semiautomatic
transmissions. The machines were well received, and the Benton Harbor
plant was quickly expanded to nearly triple its original size. Loader sales
grew from $12 million in 1954 to $33 million in 1955. Corporate sales grew
48 percent during the same period, reaching more than $150 million in 1955.
That year, 70 percent of Clark's business was from materials handling and
earthmoving equipment, and the company had plans to expand even further into earthmoving.[84]

Deutsche Maschinenfabrik AG (Demag)

An event that was little noticed in the United States was the 1954 introduction by the German firm Deutsche Maschinenfabrik AG (Demag) of the Model B-504.[85] In terms of impact on the earthmoving equipment industry, this product, along with the wheel loader, rank with Holt's track-type tractor and the LeTourneau scraper. By the mid-1970s the hydraulic excavator and the wheel loader would each account for more than a third of all heavy earthmoving units sold.

Throughout the decade, Deere, Case, and Massey-Ferguson were still totally reliant on the agricultural market. U.S. production of farm tractors had reached a historic peak in 1951 of almost six hundred thousand units, nearly double the prewar high of 1940, but pent-up demand had been met, the market was saturated, and production dropped steeply after 1951. By

The Demag B-504, introduced in 1954, was the first fully hydraulically controlled excavator. There has been remarkably little change in basic configuration except for the much longer track on today's machines. (DemagKomatsu GmbH)

1954 it was down to about 250,000 units, and except for brief upticks the trend in U.S. farm tractor unit production continued down over the next four decades although the average size of tractors steadily grew.[86] Deere did not exceed 1951 dollar sales until 1958.[87] Case, losing market share through the early 1950s, began a desperate search for a merger partner.[88]

Deere & Company

Postwar Expansion

At its 1946 annual meeting, Deere announced that the new $10 million Dubuque, Iowa, plant was under construction, with completion expected in October.[89] In 1945 Deere had purchased Lindeman Manufacturing, Inc., a small company in Yakima, Washington, which since the mid-1930s had been converting a Deere wheel farm tractor into a crawler. In 1947 production was moved from Yakima to the Dubuque plant, which began producing the Model MC crawler based on Deere's new 14.4-drawbar-horsepower Model M wheel tractor.[90] In the late 1950s, when Deere began to introduce its earthmoving line, production was centered in Dubuque. Also in 1947, Deere purchased the former Des Moines ordnance plant for $4.15 million for additional agricultural implement capacity. By the end of the 1947 fiscal year, the depreciated value of Deere's land, buildings, and equipment had increased from $21.6 million in 1944 to $52 million. Fearful that spending for expansion was getting out of hand, CEO Charles Wiman reined it in during 1948.[91]

A Move Overseas or Diversity at Home?

Wiman's reticence did not last long. By 1950 he was contemplating a manufacturing venture in Scotland. Up to that point, Deere had been strictly an exporter from North America into overseas markets. Although the company had done quite well with this strategy in Latin America, Asia, and Africa, its market share in Europe, the largest overseas opportunity, badly lagged that of International Harvester and Massey-Harris, both with many years of manufacturing experience there.[92]

Like many other U.S. manufacturers wanting to get their feet wet in Europe during this period, Deere opted for the United Kingdom for a variety of reasons. The farm equipment business there was somewhat more advanced than on the Continent; a U.K. location gave access to the sterling area of the British Empire (Imperial Preference); the government was encouraging foreign investment through loans and subsidies; and finally, and perhaps most importantly to Americans inexperienced in Europe, there was no language barrier. Although these seemed cogent reasons at the time, a location on the Continent would have been a wiser choice. The more dynamic economies of Western Europe quickly outpaced the faltering U.K. economy after 1950, and with decolonization the sterling area as an economic bloc steadily lost importance. With the signing of the Treaty of Rome in 1957 without British participation, a U.K. location was hardly more advantageous from the standpoint of market access than exporting to Western Europe from the United States.

In any case, Wiman was determined on Scotland, and he dragged a dubious board with him. But before any final commitments were made, Wiman suddenly gained a new interest—the fertilizer business. In 1952 he proposed to the board that Deere enter a joint venture with Amoco to produce artificial nitrogen fertilizer from a plant to be built in Oklahoma. Although farm equipment and fertilizer had one commonality in that both were purchased by farmers, the venture into chemicals would take Deere in a wildly divergent direction from its traditional business. Wiman prevailed despite an even more dubious board, and $20 million was invested in the venture.[93]

In the meantime, a change in attitude of the British government toward concessionary assistance to foreign investors torpedoed the plans for a plant in Scotland. Deere would wait another five years before gaining a lodgment in Europe.

New Leadership

In 1954 Charles Wiman learned that he had a terminal illness and would have only a few months to live. At the time, Deere had, for all practical purposes, an "inside" board, consisting of members of the Deere family and close connections and key executives. There was never any question but that Wiman would be free to pick his own successor nor that the successor, more than likely, would be a member of the family. In the event, the choice fell on forty-year-old William A. Hewitt, Wiman's son-in-law. Hewitt, a University of California graduate, had been with Deere only six years, all in branch operations. He was unanimously elected to the newly created post of executive vice president in June 1954 and became president and CEO a few days after Wiman's death in May 1955. Although there were strong overtones of nepotism in his selection, Hewitt proved to be an extremely

William Hewitt (1914–98)
(Deere & Company)

able CEO and during his twenty-seven-year tenure presided over a sea change at Deere that transformed the company into a modern multinational. It was Hewitt who took Deere into earthmoving equipment.[94]

During the Wiman years, Deere had continued its conservative ways and remained a narrowly focused, midwestern-based North American agricultural equipment manufacturer that nonetheless steadily gained U.S. market share. Perhaps unfairly, Charles Wiman's obituary in the *New York Times* on May 13, 1955, gave more recognition to his accomplishments as an international yachtsman than to his twenty-seven years as president of Deere & Company.

Massey-Harris

Massey-Harris had barely survived the depression, but large government war contracts both at Canadian and U.S. operations had returned the company to reasonable financial health at war's end. M-H prospered through 1951 and became the world's third-largest farm equipment maker, largely on the strength of its technological lead in self-propelled combines. Sales that year amounted to nearly $250 million, of which $80 million were outside North America. But as competition closed the gap on combines, the weakness of Massey's tractor line became glaringly apparent, volume began dropping, and profits fell disastrously.[95] These events led to the 1953 merger with Harry Ferguson, the aftermath of which became the subject of numerous business school case studies.

The Merger with Ferguson

After his battle with Ford, Ferguson had reestablished himself in the United States and built a plant in Detroit. Superficially, it appeared that Massey-Harris and Ferguson were a good fit from a product standpoint, but apparently little advance thought was given to the specifics of how the product lines and dealer organizations were to be rationalized. As a result, when Massey-Harris issued $16 million in shares for all the shares of Ferguson, no firm plan existed as to how to proceed. In the end, the two companies were not really merged. Instead, it was decided to follow a "two-line" concept in which both product lines and dealer organizations would coexist. After three years of growing friction between the Massey and Ferguson groups, chaos in the distribution system, and deepening losses, the Argus Corporation, a Canadian holding company and major stockholder, brought about the resignation of J. S. Duncan as CEO and the appointment of W. E. Phillips as chairman and CEO and A. A. Thornbrough as president. Thornbrough, a product of the Ferguson organization, reorganized the company, taking the steps that should have been taken at the time of the merger. He would later lead Massey-Ferguson into the construction equipment business.[96]

J. I. Case

In early 1946 Case was hit by a bitter UAW strike that lasted 440 days at Racine and caused Case to lose a full season of farm equipment sales when demand was at record highs. The dealer organization, with little or nothing to sell for more than a year, was decimated, and many of the best dealers defected to other brands.[97]

After settling the strike in 1947, the company was able to participate, along with all the other farm equipment manufacturers, in a strong market that lasted through 1951. But when the market turn came it was clear that

Case was in for some very tough times. With no overseas operations and minimal exports, the company was going to have to fight for a share of the shrinking North American market against some powerful competitors.[98] By the end of the postwar decade, Case would be desperately seeking a merger to survive.

The 1948 Road Show

Sponsored by the American Road Builders Association (ARBA), a grouping of roads advocates that formed the spearhead of the good roads lobby, Road Shows had been held regularly since 1909. Along with the machinery exhibition, the ARBA conducted its convention, which provided a forum for pro-highway speeches by prominent politicians and road authorities and produced a blizzard of news releases exhorting Congress and the general public to action in support of roads. But the real drawing card was the machinery show organized by the Construction Industry Manufacturers Association (CIMA), a division of the ARBA. The association represented manufacturers that had a stake in highway construction: machinery builders, component and parts manufacturers, tire companies, oil companies, and a myriad of smaller fringe players in the business of roads.[99]

The July 1948 Road Show was a celebration after an eight-year hiatus of the industry's new postwar vitality; sales were booming, and the companies anticipated even better years ahead. Spread over thirty acres at Chicago's Soldier Field, the 355 exhibits dwarfed any previous show. With product lines frozen throughout the war, enthusiastic manufacturers were eager to showcase their new developments to the crowd of a hundred thousand contractors, highway officials, and the general public that trooped through the nine-day event. Interest was high even though pent-up demand for equipment had pushed deliveries out as much as three years.[100]

Attendees expected to see some sensational new products and were not disappointed. R. G. LeTourneau dazzled them with his new line of articulated wheel tractor-scrapers, including the huge, five-hundred-horsepower Model A Tournapull. But unlike 1940, when he had the field to himself, in 1948 several other overhung scrapers were shown, including new models from the Heil Company and LaPlante-Choate. Euclid was there with its new rear-dump truck, twenty-two tons, along with the 22½-ton model of its rival, Mack. Euclid also displayed a big belt-loader for top-loading bottom-dumps. The Frank G. Hough Company displayed a revolutionary line of rear-engine Payloaders that had a capacity of up to 1.25 cubic yards. The centerpiece of International Harvester's display was, of course, its new TD-24 tractor, and Allis-Chalmers countered with the even larger HD-19. Caterpillar, as the largest of the earthmoving equipment manufacturers, smarted from the attention lavished on its rivals' big new tractors but nevertheless had an impressive display of its new line of crawler-drawn scrapers and bulldozers matched to its tractors, along with its new DW10 tractor-scraper and updated motor graders. Caterpillar also displayed, prematurely as it developed, prototypes of the DW20 and DW21 wheel tractor-scrapers; it would be another three years before they were ready for production. And the expansive display area was a virtual forest of high booms from the numerous power shovels, cranes, and draglines.[101]

Although the huge crowd and large number of orders taken made the 1948 show seem a smashing success, manufacturers were not totally pleased. The record number of exhibitors and a demand for exhibit space, in the absence of an adequate indoor site, had dictated an outdoor location. Exhibitors were at the mercy of Chicago's intemperate summer elements, however, and the show fell during the middle of the busy construction season, an inconvenient time for the very people for whom it was being conducted. Still, Chicago remained the location of choice because of the concentration of industry manufacturers in the Illinois-Wisconsin area. But the manufacturers who paid the bills for the Road Show were determined to exercise more control over future events.

The outcome of these concerns was that in 1949 the CIMA broke away from the ARBA and became an independent trade association of the manufacturers that would henceforth have full control of future Road Show machinery exhibitions. Nine years would pass before the next show, and that would be held in the enlarged International Amphitheater on Chicago's South Side.

Summary, 1946–55

By the end of the first postwar decade, the earthmoving equipment industry, no longer merely an offshoot of the farm equipment business, had taken on a distinct identity. Caterpillar's 1944 decision to build its own scrapers, bulldozer blades, and controls had signaled corporate recognition that its future lay in earthmoving and a determination henceforth to concentrate its resources there. International Harvester had transformed its prewar track-type tractor business from an agricultural offshoot to an earthmoving orientation by providing separate manufacturing facilities and establishing a construction equipment division with its own dealers. Similarly, Allis-Chalmers put new emphasis on its Springfield-built earthmoving line as separate from its West Allis agricultural line.

A wave of mergers and acquisitions took place as established competitors sought to broaden their lines and new competitors entered the field, the most formidable being General Motors. Toward the end of the decade a new name appeared. The Clark Equipment Company, with its Michigan line of wheel loaders, challenged International Harvester–Hough, which had had the field almost to itself.

New integrated construction equipment made its appearance. The track- and wheel-type hydraulic front-end loaders and hydraulic excavators were developed, and the wheel tractor-scraper became contractors' machine of choice for moving dirt. Of these developments, the wheel loader and the hydraulic excavator, from small beginnings, would in time outstrip the track-type tractor to become the two most important product segments in value terms of the full range of earthmoving equipment. By the end of the first postwar decade, all the major types of earthmoving equipment that now exist were in general use. The next forty years would see a steady scaling up and refinement of these tools. By the mid-1950s the decline of the power shovel as an earth excavating tool in construction was nearly complete, but its displacement from rock jobs by large wheel loaders and hydraulic front shovels was some fifteen years in the future.

Driven by a dynamic construction industry that expanded 61 percent between 1946 and 1955, the earthmoving equipment business in the United States experienced steady if not spectacular growth through almost the entire period. After a mild downturn in 1953–54, sales recovered strongly in 1955. Meanwhile, the rapid economic recovery taking place in Europe during the early 1950s offered increased export opportunities for U.S. earthmoving equipment producers. It also encouraged the entry of new European suppliers. Overall, the industry had every reason for optimism as it entered the second postwar decade.

FOUR

The Interstate Decade, 1956–65

The second postwar decade opened with the most important event of the century for the U.S. earthmoving equipment industry: the passage of the Federal-Aid Highway Act of 1956. Signed into law by President Dwight D. Eisenhower on June 30, 1956, the act set in motion the greatest construction program in the history of the world, the building of the forty-one-thousand-mile interstate highway system over the next thirteen years at an estimated cost of $33.5 billion. Cost-sharing for the interstate would be 90 percent federal and 10 percent state in contrast to the historic 50-50 ratio for all previous federally aided highway programs. The earthmoving equipment industry, contractors, and other members of the roads lobby were jubilant. The Associated General Contractors bullishly predicted that the program would peak in 1960, with work underway totaling $8 to $9 billion; 435,000 to 450,000 would be employed on highway construction compared to the 300,000 employed in 1956.

The average person likely did not realize the full significance of the act but may have been aware that it raised the federal tax on gasoline from 2 to 3 cents per gallon, which was expected to cost the average motorist only $6 to $9 per year. The key point, however, was that highway-user taxes (federal gasoline and diesel fuel taxes plus revenues from excise taxes on other highway-related items) would flow into a new highway trust fund that would be wholly dedicated to the federal aid highway program. Up to that point, congressional appropriations for highways had come from general funds, and earmarking tax revenues for a particular purpose was something Congress had traditionally shunned. It was a smashing breakthrough for the roads lobby and for the American people as well. But there was one caveat: The program was strictly pay-as-you-go. Annual apportionments to the states would be limited to the money available in the trust fund.[1]

The manufacturers, expecting immediate increases in the amount of highway work let to contract, were euphoric. But these expectations proved premature. What they failed to reckon on were the long leadtimes entailed in major highway projects, the months and even years required for design and right-of-way acquisition. The fact was that, initially, a disproportionate amount of the funds available would have to be spent for right-of-way acquisition. Instead of the anticipated boom in construction contracts driving steeply rising equipment sales, the economy suddenly slid into a recession during the third quarter of 1957, and sales fell precipitously. Manufacturers, caught unawares, saw factory inventories surge, and layoffs became widespread. The earthmoving equipment industry was extremely disillusioned.

In 1958 the recession deepened, and with it the gloom of the manufacturers. Sales in 1957 had been below 1956 levels, and 1958 would be below 1957. Ominously, the Bureau of Public Roads (BPR), the federal agency administering the highway program, had announced in August 1957 that the highway trust fund was falling short of the expected income. Despite the fact the interstate system, at its inception, had been envisioned as entirely toll-free, the BPR incorporated 2,102 miles of existing toll roads.[2] It was clearly a cost-cutting measure. Of course, the affected states demanded that trust fund money be used to retire their toll road construction bonds, making the roads free, but the money was not there. As a result, almost four decades later most of these roads remain toll.

But the worst was yet to come. In January 1958 the BPR brought in a more definitive cost estimate for the system—$37.6 billion, an increase of a round $10 billion in the federal share—and raised its projected construction period to twenty-one years. Although it was unpleasant news for Congress, it was also a long-overdue injection of realism.[3] There was simply more work there than could be done for the money and in the time of the original 1956 estimate. In March 1958, as an anti-recession measure, Congress approved extra highway funding for fiscal years 1959 through 1961. By mid-

1958 the pace of road-building had begun to pick up, and it appeared the recession was near an end. Companies began recalling laid-off workers.

But the new BPR cost estimate forced Congress to face up to the mounting crisis of inadequate funding for the program. In early 1959 the administration proposed a 1.5 cent increase in the federal gasoline tax, and Congress, after considerable bickering, in September approved a "temporary" increase in the Federal-Aid Highway Act of 1959—from 3 to 4 cents per gallon.[4] That put the program on a sound financial footing, at least for the present, and it was finally off and running.

Water Projects

In addition to interstate highway construction activity, the decade was also marked by a steep rise in large earthfill dam construction. In 1958 the $380 million Oahe Dam on the Missouri was closed. Part of the joint Corps of Engineers–Bureau of Reclamation Pick-Sloan Plan, the ninety-two-million-cubic-yard Oahe was then the world's largest rolled earth fill dam. Big Bend Dam, the last of six main stem dams on the Missouri, was also underway.[5] The same year also saw the start of the eighty-five-million-cubic-yard Gardiner Dam on Canada's South Saskatchewan River. In 1960 the voters of California passed a referendum authorizing the $1.75 billion California State Water Project that would bring water from the north to the arid Los Angeles Basin. That triggered a series of mammoth dams and canal projects, beginning with the seventy-eight-million-cubic-yard Oroville Dam on the Feather River north of Sacramento.[6] That was followed in 1963 by the start of the similarly sized San Luis Dam in central California.[7]

In 1964 the United States and Canada reached agreement on the development of the Upper Columbia River Basin that launched new dams on the Columbia and Kootenai rivers, starting with the Mica Dam in British Columbia in 1965. The Libby, Arrow Lake, and Duncan dams followed.[8]

The dam-building pace was beginning to pick up outside North America as well. In the early 1960s the World Bank's agreement to assist in the development of the Indus River Basin in Pakistan brought a $354 million contract for the building of the eighty-three-million-cubic-yard Mangla Dam by a consortium of U.S. contractors led by Guy F. Atkinson.[9] With superior know-how gained in construction of Corps and BuRec dams in the United States and greater resources, American contractors were able to win most of the major postwar projects in the developing world until around the mid-1960s, when the growing strength of Italian, French, German, and British contractors began to make itself felt. But the huge fleets of equipment were invariably made in the United States.

An exception to the dam-building successes of U.S. manufacturers and contractors was the Aswan High Dam on the Nile. The heavy-handed diplomacy of Secretary of State John Foster Dulles resulted in the withdrawal of a U.S. offer of assistance on the huge project. Begun in 1960 and completed in 1968, the dam was built with equipment from what was then the USSR.

Mining

Southern Peru Copper, a joint venture of Asarco, Cerro de Pasco, Phelps Dodge, and Newmont Mining, began development of its large Peruvian copper property in the late 1950s. An estimated four hundred million tons of ore had been outlined, but the ore body was thought to be as much as one billion tons. An Exim Bank credit of $115 million supported the construction of a concentrator and smelter, and the initial stripping of 130 million tons was underway in 1958 by means of a large fleet of Euclid trucks.[10]

The Economy

After the sharp, painful recession of 1957–58, the U.S. economy experienced healthy growth through 1965. Gross national product in real terms (1958 prices) rose 41 percent during the decade, outstripping the period between 1947 and 1955. But the contract construction component of GNP, after the phenomenal 61 percent rise in the previous eight years, only grew from $20.8 billion to $23.5 billion, an anemic 13 percent in the ten years through 1965.[11] Fortunately for equipment manufacturers, a greater proportion of construction spending was concentrated in machinery-intensive activities such as road-building. Inflation remained under reasonable control, with the consumer price index rising only 14.3 points: from 80.2 in 1955 to 94.5 in 1965 (1967 = 100).

The Formation of the European Economic Community

Following the success of the European Coal and Steel Community, formed in 1952, the six member nations—France, West Germany, Italy, Belgium, The Netherlands, and Luxembourg—agreed to examine the possibilities for further economic integration. That led to the signing of the Treaty of Rome in 1957, forming the European Economic Community (EEC). The treaty mandated the elimination of trade barriers among member nations over a twelve-year period, the adoption of a common external tariff for imports from the rest of the world, and a common agricultural policy among member nations. Because of certain supranational aspects of the treaty, Great Britain declined to join. In response, Great Britain and six other non-EEC nations formed the European Free Trade Association (EFTA) in 1960, which, as essentially a customs union, was free of any aspirations toward eventual political integration.

The establishment by the EEC of a 17.5 percent common tariff on earth-moving equipment sent a strong message to U.S. manufacturers: If they wanted to continue to participate in the Western European market, they could not long postpone a manufacturing presence on the Continent. By the mid-1960s most major U.S. competitors had established at least nominal manufacturing or assembly operations within the EEC.

Great Britain, recognizing the economic success of the EEC, made efforts during the 1960s to join on its own terms. Because of its close ties to the United States, however, its membership was vetoed by DeGaulle until he resigned as president of France in 1969. Great Britain, Ireland, and Denmark joined in 1973 in the first expansion of what had by then become the European Community (EC).

The Companies

The boom in highway and heavy construction during the 1950s intensified the race within the earthmoving equipment industry to produce ever-larger and more powerful machines. Design engineers, encouraged by management, eagerly accepted the challenge to top the competition with new, record-breaking (and more profitable) products. As established companies focused on bigness, their interest in the smaller, less dramatic machines diminished, leaving that segment of the market poorly served and creating a situation ripe for exploitation by new entrants. Thus, in the early years of the second postwar decade, a new sub-industry, light construction equipment, was born with the entry of J. I. Case, Deere & Company, and Massey-Ferguson.

J. I. Case

The immediate postwar seller's market when farmers were in a virtual feeding frenzy for equipment had given Case a brief illusion of prosperity. Case's sales and U.S. market share had peaked in 1949 at $170 million and

9.9 percent, putting it in third place after Harvester and Deere.[12] But as the market saturation point neared, the company's weaknesses became all too evident. Chief among these were an outmoded product line, a weak dealer organization, and overly conservative management. Under the influence of CEO Leon Clausen, Case had been slow to update its tractor line during the 1930s, and it was these outdated models that the company brought into the postwar period. They were "good enough" when strong pent-up demand existed, but farmers soon started looking for something more modern. The dealer organization, never as strong as Harvester's or Deere's, was severely damaged by the 440 day postwar strike when many of the best dealers defected. Even though seventy-year-old Clausen's heavy hand was lifted by his retirement in 1948, his replacement as president and CEO was sixty-six-year-old Theodore Johnson, a lifelong Case employee. Johnson was not the dynamic leader Case so desperately needed. Alarmed by the steady deterioration in the company's condition, Morgan Stanley and Company, Case's longtime underwriter, intervened in 1953 to bring about a change. Johnson was replaced by John T. Brown, fifty-four.[13] Sales, however, continued to plummet and dipped to $94.8 million in 1955.[14] Case was in serious trouble.

The Merger with the American Tractor Company

A desperate board seized on the idea of a merger, leading to talks with Minneapolis-Moline and then Oliver, both smaller than Case. But it was all too clear that a merger with either of these weak companies was not the solution.[15] Encouraged by Morgan Stanley to seek diversification, in the fall of 1956 Case finally found a willing partner in the American Tractor Company, a small manufacturer of construction equipment in Churubusco, Indiana. Thirty-eight-year-old Marc B. Rojtman, the company's president, had organized the company in 1950 and built sales to $10 million. Rojtman controlled 42 percent of the stock. Although Wall Street estimated the value of the company at no more than $4.5 million based on earnings, by the terms of the merger agreement it appeared that Case was paying almost $15 million in stock. Rojtman said Case was "buying potential," but others thought Case was paying a $10 million premium to get Rojtman, a "boy wonder" who, as part of the package, became executive vice president, general manager, and a director of Case.[16] The flamboyant and aggressive Rojtman would bring a drastic change to the straitlaced management of Case.

The American Tractor Company's product line had started with two small conventional crawler tractors, the GT25 and GT32, marketed under the trade name "TerraTrac." These had been superseded by a three-model line, the 400, 500, and 600, and the company was in the process of introducing two additional models, the 800 and 1000. Introduced at the 1957 Road Show with great fanfare, the 800 and 1000 had a revolutionary new "Terramatic" power train that was, in effect, a separate power-shift transmission for each track, enabling the tracks to counterrotate and providing a 180-degree spot turn. Although that made good advertising copy, it was a feature of little value in normal tractor operation. The 1000, the largest in the line at eighty-seven-flywheel horsepower, weighed a little more than thirteen thousand pounds, slightly more than the Caterpillar D4. The Terramatic transmission was to prove mechanically unreliable, which forced Case into a $10 million rework and buy-back program in 1959 and 1960.[17]

The Loader-Backhoe

Although Case's focus was on the acquisition of the ATC crawler tractor line, another event growing out of the merger would later take on much greater significance. For some time, Case had been building industrial versions of its farm tractors equipped with a light-duty front-end loader attach-

The 1957 Case 320 loader-backhoe was the first machine of its type to be offered factory-assembled and fully warranted by one manufacturer. Case has held loader-backhoe world leadership ever since. (Courtesy of Case Corporation)

ment. In fact, Case claimed to have been the first to offer this as a factory-installed package. Meanwhile, the American Tractor Company had recognized the utility of a rear-mounted hydraulic backhoe attachment. The idea of installing the backhoe on the rear of the Case wheel tractor-loader was born about the time of the merger, and the first Case loader-backhoe, the Model 320, was displayed at the 1957 Road Show. There is some dispute about who was actually first with the loader-backhoe concept, but there is no doubt that Case pioneered in offering a complete factory-installed and warranted package in the United States.[18]

Few products have had a greater impact on the construction industry than the loader-backhoe, and Case led the way in developing that invaluable utility tool. It was a low-cost machine because initially it was a derivative product based on a high-volume farm tractor. Its affordability made it the entry-level machine for thousands of would-be excavating contractors. Loader-backhoes could excavate, dig trenches, load trucks, perform rough grading, and be run on the road from job to job without the need for a transport trailer. It was a tool whose time had come. Marc Rojtman and the loader-backhoe put Case into the construction equipment business.

The 320 was succeeded by 430 and 530 "Construction King" loader-backhoes in 1963, based on Case's new 30-Series farm tractor.[19] Production of the 530 also began at the company's Vierzon, France, plant, putting Case on the ground floor with that product in the European Common Market.[20] In 1965–66 models 430 and 530 were superseded by the 480, 580, and 680 "Construction Kings," establishing the nomenclature that continues to the present.[21] Beginning with the 80-Series, the machines were no longer derivatives of farm tractors although they continued to benefit from low-cost parts and components drawn from the farm tractor line.[22]

As much as any product in the construction equipment industry, the 80-Series established the standard by which all other loader-backhoes were measured. Utilitarian in design, the machines were simple, durable, reliable, and cheap to build. They dominated the industry and held more than half the North American market for more than two decades. Case's Burlington, Iowa, plant became the loader-backhoe capital of the world.

The Demise of Rojtman

Meanwhile, Rojtman was busy dragging a somewhat reluctant Case into the modern age. In addition to the new emphasis on construction equipment, he spent heavily on development of new farm equipment, reorganized marketing, and established the Case Credit Corporation to finance dealer inventory and customer paper. Before Rojtman, Case had almost no business outside North America. He quickly established J. I. Case International S.A. and organized subsidiaries in France, Great Britain, and Australia. Rojtman believed that additional volume was the solution to Case's problems, and he set about producing it with a series of dealer extravaganzas the likes of which the staid farm equipment industry had never seen. Dealers liked what they saw, and orders poured in.[23] The Case board liked what it saw, too, and rewarded Rojtman with the presidency in May 1958.[24] But orders from dealers were not the same as retail sales. Dealers' yards were full, and Case receivables skyrocketed. Sales rose from $87 million in 1956 to a record $200 million and a $6.2 million profit in 1959, but debt escalated from $40 million to $236 million.[25]

Even though Rojtman had put Case back in the black, the growing debt burden was too much for the still-conservative board and the company's bankers. On February 1, 1960, he was ousted. According to the news release that announced the event, "To free Mr. Rojtman from detail and routine administration, he [will] assume the important new post of special adviser to the president and the Case executive committee." His advice was never sought.[26] Case had had enough of Rojtman, yet he had undeniably left his imprint on the company. Despite his P. T. Barnum–like promotional flair, Rojtman was responsible for great positive change at Case that without question contributed to the long-run viability of the company.

Rojtman's replacement, William J. Grede, sixty-three and an outside member of Case's board and executive committee, had been influential in bringing about the ATC merger. His job was to bring Case's runaway debt under control. Production schedules were cut, plants were consolidated, and dealers were granted special discounts to move inventory and reduce Case receivables. Traditionally, Case had normally not resorted to discounting, but after 1960 the company came to use it routinely and all too frequently to unload inventories or reduce receivables. Ironically, a six-month strike in 1960, the first since 1946–47, helped with the inventory problem.[27] Despite drastic retrenchment, however, Case lost a record $39.8 million in 1960 and $32.3 million in 1961 on $128 million in sales.[28] The patience of the bankers was exhausted.

As the price of granting Case a new bank agreement, Grede had to go. His replacement was Merritt D. Hill, a former Ford vice president and general manager of its Tractor and Implement Division. Under Hill, the company was completely restructured, more operations were consolidated, and

Case returned to profitability but at meager levels. The company had not made a good profit in more than ten years.

The Case Dual Distribution System

During the early 1960s Case pushed hard to develop its industrial dealer organization, and company stores began to appear. Under the intense profit pressure of its bank agreement, Case could not afford to have open sales territories, even for short periods while it sought suitable dealer candidates. It needed the volume immediately. As a result, it resorted to setting up company-owned Case Power and Equipment stores to fill open territories or cover key urban areas. By 1963 there were already forty-nine of them in North America, a number that would continue to grow.[29] The company store gradually ceased being an expedient and became an accepted if not preferred distribution channel for Case construction equipment. Thus, Case was alone among the major competitors in the North American market to operate a two-track distribution system—company-owned stores and privately owned dealers—with all the built-in conflicts that entailed. A potential private investor in a Case dealership was understandably leery of having to compete with a company store in the next county. Deere, who entered the light construction equipment business at about the same time, shunned company stores in favor of privately owned dealers. In fairness to Case, during the early 1960s Deere could afford the luxury of the longer view but Case could not. In later years, however, when Case could have withdrawn from company stores had it been determined to do so, the company persisted in its two-track system. It was hooked and unwilling to endure the withdrawal pains to kick the habit.

The two-track distribution system had a great deal to do with the inability of the Case Construction Equipment Division, over the years, to generate good, consistent operating profits. The fundamental problem was that Case company stores, in contrast to independent dealers, were not required to produce an operating profit to survive. Other manufacturers with privately owned dealers understood the need, long term, for their distribution systems to operate at a profit, and that produced a healthy discipline largely absent at Case. With the greater part of its retail organization under in-house control, the temptation was always present to snap on that special overnight program to "move the iron." Case Power and Equipment stores could respond more quickly than dealers, especially when profitability was not a prime consideration. The company-owned stores had an abysmal record of operating losses, year after year.

The Merger with Kern County Land Company

By 1964, despite $46 million in tax-loss carry-forwards, the company was not generating sufficient profits to cover interest expense and still provide for future growth. Its survival depended on finding a merger partner. Number four in the farm equipment business, Case had a promising construction equipment business, but for acquirers its most attractive feature was its tax-loss carry-forwards. Through a director common to both boards it found the perfect suitor in the well-heeled Kern County Land Company (KCL), which was able to use the carry-forwards to shield its healthy oil royalties. In May 1964 KCL acquired a majority of Case common shares through a tender offer at $14.50 per share, ending Case's 122-year existence as an independent company. Case acquired financial respectability through the transaction but little else changed. Low profitability continued to plague the company.[30]

A New Life for Case

By the end of 1965 Case had been in the construction equipment business for nine years, specializing in lighter, utility-type machines, and had carved out a niche with smaller excavating, sewer and water, and residential housing contractors. It now had a three-model line of crawlers topped by the 1150, the successor to the ill-starred 1000, and a crawler loader version of each; a five-model line of wheel loaders from the one-cubic-yard W5 through the 2.5-cubic-yard W12; and a three-model loader-backhoe line of the 480, 580, and 680.[31] It was the fourth-largest maker of construction equipment after Caterpillar, International Harvester, and Allis-Chalmers, but those manufacturers hardly regarded Case as a competitor. They were focused on medium-to-heavy construction machines and generally ignored the fast-growing lighter segment of the market where Case was getting most of its business. Case had 140 construction equipment dealers and was approaching one hundred company-owned Case Power and Equipment locations.[32] In 1965 the majority of its sales still came from farm equipment, but the faster-growing Construction Equipment Division would soon predominate. The company had done a remarkable job of transforming itself in the decade, and with a new parent the future looked bright.

Deere & Company

Under the leadership of William Hewitt, the Deere company was transformed in the second postwar decade. Three major accomplishments stand out. The company became a multinational and established several manufacturing operations outside North America; it became the world's largest manufacturer of agricultural equipment, passing International Harvester in market share; and it entered the earthmoving equipment business.

Hewitt, taking control in 1955, was shrewdly perceptive of the needs of the company. He recognized that Deere needed to be shaken out of its narrow, parochial, midwestern perspective. One of his first actions was to persuade the board to approve the construction of a new administrative headquarters in Moline. Designed by Eero Saarinen, the dramatic modernistic building, occupied in 1964, was to contribute significantly to changing the way the company saw itself.[33]

Merger Talks with Massey-Ferguson

Hewitt had hardly taken office when he was approached privately by J. S. Duncan, CEO of Massey-Harris-Ferguson about the possibility of a merger. The Massey-Harris and Ferguson combination had occurred in 1953, and the events growing out of that merger are related elsewhere in this book. At the time, Deere had no overseas plants, and Hewitt, perhaps not fully aware of the severe internal problems of M-H-F, was attracted by M-H-F's strength in world markets outside North America. But in the end, the problems of merging what were in effect three organizations and product lines proved too daunting, and talks, which had been kept very quiet, were broken off. Shortly thereafter Duncan was forced out at M-H-F.[34]

The Lanz Acquisition: A Move Overseas

Hewitt knew that Deere could not hope to compete successfully in the fast-growing European agricultural equipment market unless it manufactured there. In 1953 the company had been offered the opportunity to buy controlling interest in Heinrich Lanz A.G. The old-line manufacturer of farm equipment in Mannheim, West Germany, had fallen on hard times and was going downhill fast, but the name was still well known and respected in Europe. The Deere board, unprepared to take the plunge into what for it were unknown waters, turned down the proposal. Three years later and still without an initiative in Europe, the board reconsidered. This time it approved the proposal, and for \$5.3 million the company acquired 51 percent of Lanz. Thus, Deere launched its first overseas manufacturing operation, a venture that for the next two decades would bring it nothing but pain, suffering, and substantial losses. The Deere-Lanz market share in Western Europe was lower in 1965 than the Lanz market share of 1955.[35] With the benefit of hindsight, it is now clear that a "green field" approach to starting up in Europe would have been preferable to assuming all the problems that the Lanz acquisition brought. But in 1956, with no previous overseas experience, Deere lacked confidence in its ability to operate outside North America.

The Need for More Horsepower

Throughout the 1950s Deere tractors continued to be powered exclusively by the company's two-cylinder engines, a tradition that had begun with the acquisition of the Waterloo Boy line in 1918. The Deere two-cylinder engine had an excellent reputation for dependability. It was extremely simple in design and thus could be repaired by farmers themselves, many of whom were almost fanatically loyal to the "Poppin' Johnny." Still, the design had its drawbacks, the principal one being a practical limitation in size and horsepower. In the early 1950s the trend to higher farm tractor horsepower was obvious, and no one knew where it would end. Deere competitors, using four- and six-cylinder engines, were well positioned to meet the trend. Fearing that it would be left behind if it stayed with the two-cylinder engine, around 1953 Deere set up a highly secret engineering group to design new four- and six-cylinder engines. Secrecy was imperative because marketing for the next six years had to continue to extoll the virtues of Deere's exclusive two-cylinder engines.[36]

In 1952 and 1953 Deere introduced a new line of farm tractors, the Models 40, 50, 60, 70, and 80, which replaced the original, alphabetically designated models dating back to the 1920s and early 1930s. Growing out of this as a derivative of the Model 40 was the new fifteen-drawbar-horsepower 40C crawler, which replaced the MC, Deere's first crawler.[37] Between 1956 and 1958 Deere again revamped its farm tractor line, bringing out the six-model 20-Series, 320 through 820, and a thirty-horsepower crawler version of the 420 replaced the 40C.[38] The two-cylinder engine continued as the power source. The company was creeping into the crawler tractor business but had not yet built a true industrial tractor.

The Move into Construction Equipment: The First Road Show

Deere's intentions became clearer in 1957 when it first displayed at a Road Show. A modest 3,800 square feet (compared to Caterpillar's 24,400 and International Harvester's 21,400 square feet) were shared with the Hancock Manufacturing Company, which made elevating scrapers, and the Henry Manufacturing Company, a maker of loader and backhoe attachments.[39] Hancock had developed a self-loading scraper using sprocket-driven, chain-mounted horizontal flights to elevate loose material into the scraper bowl. The prime mover was the Deere 820, a derivative of the 820 farm tractor, which drove the scraper elevating mechanism from the tractor power take-off. It was unsophisticated but it worked. Deere pioneered the elevating scraper as a factory package, but others soon followed. The company was clearly pitching to small rural conservation contractors rather than road builders because the latter regarded the light Deere machines, with their two-cylinder engines, as farm equipment.

The pivotal year of 1957 marked the establishment of an engineering group and a small marketing organization for the industrial line. The decision had been made to enter the construction equipment business, and with it came the requirement for a distribution organization. Deere began the long and arduous job of building a separate dealer organization for its industrial line. The industrial organization was headquartered in the old Moline wagon works, where industrial attachments were made and assembled to basic machines built in Dubuque and Waterloo to convert them to industrial configurations. In 1965, with the introduction of integral designs, production of industrial equipment was centered in Dubuque.[40]

Deere entered the finance business in 1958, setting up the John Deere Credit Company. Other companies in the industry had preceded Deere into financing, but antitrust constraints prevented Deere from doing the same until it disposed of a block of stock it held in a Moline bank.[41] Having an in-house financing capability was indispensable in establishing its industrial dealer organization and supporting dealer retail sales of construction equipment. Overall, Deere has used its credit operation more effectively in the dual roles of stimulating sales and creating interest income than any other company in the industry.

In 1958 Deere produced its first industrial machines, the 440 crawler and wheel tractors, each with a factory-installed loader and backhoe attachments. At this point Deere began to differentiate its construction equipment with yellow paint.[42] It and Case were now running neck and neck for position in the light construction equipment business.

The "New Generation of Power"

The real turning point in Deere's efforts to build construction equipment came in 1960 when it introduced its "New Generation of Power": the 10-Series farm tractors powered by Deere's new four- and six-cylinder engines. Two crawler derivatives were a part of the new line: the forty-horsepower 1010 and fifty-two-horsepower 2010, each offered in bulldozer and loader versions. The industrial wheel tractor versions of the 1010 and 2010 were offered as loader-backhoes. The 5010 replaced the 840 as the prime mover for the Hancock elevating scraper.[43] The last two-cylinder engine was built in 1959, and thus, to the dismay of many loyal customers, a long Deere tradition died.

Despite the new models, the Deere industrial line continued to be derivative of the farm tractor line and used the same nomenclature. Recognizing the need to help customers distinguish between the farm and industrial lines, in 1964 Deere adopted the JD prefix and new nomenclature for the industrial line. A year later the first integrally designed industrial machines were introduced: the JD350 and JD450 crawler bulldozers and loaders and the JD300, JD400, and JD700A loader-backhoes. The JD760 replaced the 5010 in the scraper package.[44]

Deere and Farm Equipment Leadership

Deere had made steady gains in its share of the U.S. farm equipment market since the end of World War II, and in 1958 it topped International Harvester for the first time. But the latter's strength outside the United States kept Harvester in the overall lead. After the introduction of the New Generation of Power in 1960, however, Deere sales spurted. They reached a new high of $688 million in 1963, surpassing Harvester's total farm equipment sales for the first time.[45] Harvester would never again top Deere in farm equipment sales.

Deere's Transformation

The second postwar decade had been one of great change at Deere. The company had become multinational, with farm equipment manufacturing operations in West Germany, France, Spain, South Africa, Mexico, and Argentina. It had also begun to part with its cherished concept of decentralization and face up to the reality that a large manufacturing multinational required a high degree of centralized control. Deere had diversified, first into construction equipment and then in 1963 into consumer products, a business that, surprisingly, would grow as fast as its construction equipment.

In 1965 the fledgling construction equipment product line consisted of two small crawlers, four loader-backhoes, and an elevating scraper, but the next decade would see impressive expansion of the line.

Massey-Ferguson

In 1956 Massey-Harris-Ferguson was a well-established multinational corporation with farm equipment sales of $372 million, almost 20 percent more than Deere.[46] No other farm equipment maker could begin to match the scope of its worldwide enterprise. Its 1953 merger with Ferguson had not worked out well, but the new management team of W. E. Phillips, CEO, and A. A. Thornbrough, president, was taking steps to correct the problems. In a move to diversify, in 1957 the company acquired Mid-Western Industries, Inc. of Wichita, Kansas, for $3.4 million. Mid-Western, which made loader attachments, small ditchers, and other light equipment, became the Industrial Division of M-H-F, and the company entered the construction equipment business with its own loader-backhoe.[47]

The Acquisition of Perkins and Landini

New developments began coming quickly. In 1958 the Harris name was dropped, and the company became Massey-Ferguson.[48] In 1959 M-F made an important strategic move when it acquired the F. Perkins Manufacturing Company of Peterborough, England, for the bargain price of $12.6 million and assumption of debt. M-F had its own source of engines for the first time. In 1958 Perkins built 77,000 engines, and five years later it was building 250,000.[49] Also in 1959, M-F purchased the tractor operations of Standard Motor Company of Coventry, England. Standard, as a contract manufacturer, had been the company's U.K. source of farm tractors, and the move brought in-house a capacity for a hundred thousand tractors a year.[50] In 1960 M-F acquired Landini S.p.A. of Italy, a small manufacturer of tractors that began production of M-F's first crawler tractor in 1961. Initially, the small Landini crawlers were targeted at the Italian farm market, but by the mid-1960s two industrial models were in production. Landini remained a small operation and built only 2,252 crawlers in 1965.[51]

A Growing Taste for Industrial Products

The Industrial Division of Massey-Ferguson was moved from Wichita to Detroit in 1961, where it shared manufacturing facilities with farm tractors until 1964 when M-F, with expansion in mind, acquired a 330,000-square-foot plant in the Detroit area for its newly named Industrial Products Operation.[52]

Sales of industrial products, beginning in the low $20 million range in 1957, had grown to more than $60 million by 1965, primarily in North America. M-F had developed a taste for the industrial business and would move into it aggressively on an international scale during the coming decade.

Caterpillar

During the better part of the first postwar decade Caterpillar products had been on allocation to dealers, and 1956 was more of the same. Supply limitations were costing the company business, and dealers were frustrated by long deliveries that often sent customers to competition. Despite $200 million in capital spending from 1946 through 1955, demand and the product line had grown faster than capacity could be added. Determined to rectify the situation, the company embarked on a massive $535 million investment binge for additional manufacturing capacity over the next ten years.[53] Manufacturing floor space went from 9.5 million square feet to nearly 17 million square feet, yet still, in the mid-1960s, products were frequently on allocation.

Overseas Expansion

Although most of the capital spending was in the United States, it was in this decade that Caterpillar established an overseas manufacturing base. Initial emphasis was in the United Kingdom, where in 1956 Caterpillar purchased the Birtley Company, a Caterpillar licensee that manufactured scrapers and bulldozer blades in Newcastle.[54] The same year, construction was started on a six-hundred-thousand-square-foot plant in Glasgow, where D8 production began in 1958.[55] Although Great Britain had not signed the Treaty of Rome, Caterpillar was betting heavily on the near-term British

entry into the newly formed European Economic Community. When it became clear in 1963 that this was not going to happen, the company already
had more than 1.3 million square feet of manufacturing space and 3,200
employees in Great Britain. It had hedged its bet in 1960 when it bought
out a small manufacturer of crawler tractors, Richard Freres, in Grenoble,
France, providing a base within the Common Market. The 150,000-square-
foot plant was quickly expanded and in 1961 started production of the D4
tractor, a model already being built in Glasgow.[56] Its heavy investment in
the United Kingdom during the 1950s had not given Caterpillar the presence it needed in the EEC, and the company was forced to make substantial additional investments within the EEC during the 1960s.

It was fortunate for Caterpillar that it could afford such investments. In
1965 the company announced a major new plant to be constructed at
Gosselies, Belgium, at a reported cost of $80 to $85 million. At the time,
U.S. corporations were being pressured by the Johnson administration's
shortsighted policy of refraining from direct foreign investments that entailed
an outflow of U.S. dollars, but Caterpillar obtained financing in Europe for
the new plant. The Belgian government, anxious to remedy high unemployment in the Gosselies area due to the closure of old, high-cost coal mines,
provided certain short-term financial incentives that were the controlling
factors in Caterpillar's selection of Belgium as the site for its largest European operation.[57]

Too Much Floor Space?

A contributing factor to the insatiable appetite for additional manufacturing space was Caterpillar's highly integrated nature, which gave rise to
the practice of making all but the most specialized components of its products. The manufacturing department had unbounded faith that there was
almost nothing it could not make cheaper and better than anyone else when
it came to tractors. Make-or-buy analyses were conducted, but the results
almost always called for more space and machine tools. Although it is conceivable that Caterpillar was the low-cost source almost every time during
the late 1950s and early 1960s, a steady escalation in UAW wages and
benefits made it increasingly unlikely that such would continue to be the case.
The lesson would be learned painfully and the price paid with the closure
of substantial amounts of floor space in a downsizing that would begin in
1983.

Growing Exports and Counter-Cyclical Protection

Additional emphasis on foreign business came in 1956 when Caterpillar established two overseas trading companies. Caterpillar Americas Company was a Western Hemisphere trading corporation, and Caterpillar Overseas C.A. was a Venezuelan corporation with responsibility for the rest of the world. In 1960 Caterpillar Overseas was reincorporated in Switzerland and became an active marketing company with a large staff based in Geneva. For the years 1956 through 1965, Caterpillar's business outside the United States as a percentage of its total was never less than 37 percent and was usually in the range of 42 to 46 percent. That gave the company a high degree of insulation, not enjoyed by its competitors, from U.S. business cycles. In the mild 1960–61 recession, for example, Caterpillar's domestic sales for 1960 were down 21 percent, $96.5 million lower than the previous year. That drop, however, was nearly offset by an increase in foreign sales, which were up 26 percent and $70 million, resulting in only a 3.5 percent downturn in the total.[58]

A Burst of New Products

The years from 1958 through 1963 were probably the most prolific in the history of the company in terms of major new product introductions. It began with the bellwether D8 Series H in 1958 that a year later was equipped with the company's first semiautomatic powershift transmission. In 1959–60 Caterpillar finally entered the wheel loader business with three models: the 922, 944, and 966. Although these machines were of the conventional rear-wheel steer design, they set a new industry standard by having lift arms that were front-mounted instead of alongside the operator, a hazardous position. The company really showed its muscle in 1962 when it introduced its new nine-model family of 600-Series hydraulic wheel tractor-scrapers, from eighteen- to fifty-four-cubic-yard heaped capacity. The timing was right to take advantage of the interstate highway program, where construction was reaching a sustained high level, and the worldwide surge in the construction of large earthfill dams. At the 1963 Road Show, Caterpillar introduced its first articulated wheel loaders, the three-cubic-yard 966C and the six-cubic-yard 988; its first off-highway truck, the thirty-five-ton 769; the big 225-horsepower No. 16 motor grader; and two models of wheel bulldozers. It was an impressive line-up of large equipment, but with the ex-

Caterpillar's 769 had unique oil-disc brakes, a strut-type suspension, and molded fiberglass cab and cowling. Low body side height was a design goal to permit loading by wheel loaders. (Courtesy of Caterpillar Inc.)

Caterpillar's first articulated loader, the 988 (here in 1963) had three hundred horsepower. (Courtesy of Caterpillar Inc.)

ception of the No. 16 the new models only brought Caterpillar up to the sizes that some competitors were already selling.[59]

Discontinuing the D2 Tractor

During the development of new products in the late 1950s Caterpillar became increasingly preoccupied with large machines. The construction and mining industries were demanding them, and competitors were steadily leap-frogging each other in the horsepower and capacity race. Meanwhile, Caterpillar's smallest track-type tractor, the D2, was, aside from a new engine in 1947, yet to be updated from its original 1938 design. Within the company it was considered essentially an agricultural tractor, and by the mid-1950s technical advances in wheel farm tractors, compounded by the antiquated design of the D2, were cutting into its sales. In 1957 the D2, along with a small motor grader, was dropped from the line. The company said, "Demand for them at prices which would recover the cost of this quality was not sufficient to warrant their continued manufacture."[60]

It was a telling admission that Caterpillar doubted its ability to build a competitive machine in that size class. The decision was also an indication of the degree to which the company had turned away from the agricultural market, but more critically Caterpillar badly misread the fast-growing segment of the construction market that wanted a small bulldozer. Case and Deere happily filled the void and soon began chipping away at larger Caterpillar models. Sixteen years later when it decided to reenter the business with the D3, Caterpillar found the going hard indeed. Case and Deere were solidly entrenched.

Dealer Financial Growth: The Parts Business

As Caterpillar grew and prospered through the decade, so did its dealers. Dealers had made good profits during the first decade after the war, and by the mid-1950s the 110 North American Caterpillar dealers had an average net worth of $1.4 million. By 1965 that had grown to $2.5 million. The 150 dealers outside the United States had similar financial resources. Caterpillar had organized a credit corporation in 1954, but dealers rarely needed or used it. In 1965 it was carrying just $15 million in receivables.[61]

A major source of manufacturer and dealer profits was the parts business derived from the steadily growing machine population. Although manufacturers liked to talk in terms of ten thousand operating hours over five years as the normal economic life of a piece of heavy earthmoving equipment, the reality was that only on the very largest construction jobs and in mining and quarry operations did machines get that kind of usage. The majority of the field population consisted of mid-range and smaller machines that usually accumulated hours at a much slower rate and remained active for as long as fifteen to twenty years. An owner could easily spend several times more in parts over the life of a machine than its original cost. Typically, equipment dealers had a 25 to 30 percent gross margin on parts, and retail parts were not discounted. With a growing machine population the parts business provided a steady source of profit for dealers, although they could not afford to be complacent.

The lucrative nature of the parts business naturally attracted after-market competition, especially for the profitable undercarriage segment. Caterpillar recognized the vital necessity of protecting its parts business and was constantly striving to stay one step ahead of competition by developing proprietary items that would be difficult to duplicate. Thus, it introduced "Lifetime-Lubricated" track rollers and idlers in 1958, Sealed Track in 1962, and Sealed and Lubricated Track in 1974.[62] There was also growing competition for filters, bearings, and cutting edges, but the company never conceded its parts business.

The Towmotor Acquisition

Merger and acquisition mania was at a peak on Wall Street during the mid-1960s. Corporate raiders were running amok, and a new kind of corporation, the conglomerate, had been born. Caterpillar had no interest in becoming a conglomerate, but it had become very growth-oriented and was not averse to expansion by means of merger into new opportunities that seemed to fit well with its core business. Caterpillar executive William Blackie led the push for growth by merger and targeted the Hyster Company as an acquisition candidate in the early 1960s. Hyster, already one of Caterpillar's auxiliary equipment manufacturers of winches and logging equipment, had a good line of lift trucks and was entering the compactor business. The combination was a natural, but no agreement could be reached in private negotiations.

Continuing the pursuit of acquisitions, in 1965 Caterpillar entered the lift-truck business by acquiring Towmotor Corporation of Cleveland, Ohio, through the issuance of about 1.9 million shares of common stock in a transaction valued in excess of $69 million. It seemed a good fit. Lift trucks were capital goods, dealers sold them to industrial users, and they were products the company was sure would fit well with its current line. Towmotor became a wholly owned subsidiary.[63] Its direct sales force was closed down, and the rather spotty Towmotor dealer organization was quickly augmented when most Caterpillar dealers in the United States and Europe were appointed as Towmotor dealers. Although they knew nothing whatever about the lift-truck business, they were prepared to take the account on faith. Products with the Caterpillar name had always been profitable, and Caterpillar was confident that its strong dealers would cause sales to skyrocket. But that did not happen. Gradually, the dealers became aware that lift trucks were not a high-margin business like tractors. It was not the kind of business at which they excelled. It also became evident that Towmotor, although strong in large lift trucks, was woefully weak at the high-volume low end and that a good part of the line was obsolescent. Thus began more than two decades of travail as Caterpillar poured money into manufacturing facilities, revamped the line, added electric trucks, and periodically infused additional working capital. All in all, it was to be probably the most painful and costly experience in the company's history.

Expansion into Japan

During the latter half of the 1950s, the Japanese construction equipment industry had developed rapidly and kept pace with the resurgent Japanese economy. U.S. manufacturers were eyeing Japan with interest, but a shield of protection erected by the Ministry of International Trade and Industry (MITI) severely limited opportunities for export sales. Import licenses were not issued for products of a type and size manufactured in Japan, and by 1960 Komatsu and Mitsubishi Heavy Industries, the two leading Japanese manufacturers of construction equipment, had extended their lines to cover all but the largest sizes of machines. But a dynamic industrialized nation of nearly one hundred million people was too attractive to be ignored. Western manufacturers, seeking ways to participate in the Japanese market, found that it would require an investment in facilities in a joint venture with a Japanese majority partner. That could be achieved only after long and intricate negotiations. Wholly owned foreign investments in manufacturing were not welcome. At the time, Japanese manufacturers were more anxious to acquire Western technology than Western business partners. As a result, several American and European manufacturers settled for royalty payments from license agreements and minority joint ventures as the extent of their participation in the Japanese home market. Examples were International Harvester, Clark Equipment, Cummins Engine, and Bucyrus-Erie.

Caterpillar, uninterested in licensing its technology to a potential competitor, was prepared to invest in Japan but not on a minority basis. In July 1963 it announced that it had concluded an agreement with Shin Mitsubishi–Heavy Industries (MHI) to form a 50-50 joint venture, Caterpillar Mitsubishi Ltd., to manufacture Caterpillar products in Japan. The rare instance of a foreign company being able to negotiate and obtain approval from MITI for a venture in which the Japanese interest was not controlling was likely attributable to the power of the Mitsubishi name and Caterpillar's position as a world industry leader. Products of the venture would be sold in Japan and designated areas of the Far East. A 1.3-million-square-foot plant was constructed, and production of the first two models, the D4 tractor and 955 track loader, began in 1965.[64]

A New Headquarters, a New CEO

During the mid-1960s Caterpillar, an important multinational ranking about fiftieth on the Fortune 500, still maintained its corporate headquarters in a rabbit warren of old factory buildings in the East Peoria plant. In 1964 the company announced that it would construct a new headquarters building in downtown Peoria. Unlike Deere's new administrative headquarters, which received a great deal of favorable exposure in the media, company officials kept the Caterpillar building low-key. It was even rumored that some begrudged the "addition to overhead." The building was occupied in 1967.

In 1962 chairman and CEO Louis Neumiller reached the mandatory retirement age and was succeeded by Harmon S. Eberhard, sixty-one, who had been president since 1954. The affable Eberhard, another former Holt employee, had come up through engineering, the only Caterpillar CEO to do so. William Blackie, fifty-six, succeeded Eberhard as president. Joining Caterpillar from Price Waterhouse in 1939, Blackie, an astute financial man, had become vice president and chief financial officer in 1944 and executive vice president in 1954.[65] It was largely through his vision and drive that the company emerged as a true multinational during the 1970s.

A Secure Position in World Markets

Caterpillar's most important accomplishment in the decade was the establishment of an overseas manufacturing base. By 1965 it had two major plants in the United Kingdom, one in France, and had begun construction of its Belgian plant, which would become its largest overseas operation. The company was now well-entrenched in the EEC. It was also expanding its Brazilian facility and had a more than adequate plant in Melbourne, Australia, considering the rather small opportunity there. In addition, its important new Japanese joint venture was just getting underway. The company was now "on the inside" in all the industrialized world's largest markets, making it relatively secure from the vagaries of currency movements and capricious tariff and non-tariff barriers. None of its U.S. competitors had been able to match that strategy. The principal earthmoving competition in the industrialized world outside North America was now coming from indigenous companies.

The other major accomplishment of the decade was the broadening and strengthening of the product line. The product development program of the late 1950s had borne fruit in the early 1960s in an outpouring of new models, the most notable being the nine-model scraper line, an off-highway truck, and a four-model wheel loader line topped by the large 988.

The company had crossed the billion-dollar mark in sales in 1964, and in that year and in 1965 had an after-tax profit on sales of more than 10 percent, a figure not seen since prewar days.[66] Although perhaps it had made some missteps, overall it came out of the decade far stronger than it went in.

International Harvester

In 1950, when farmers' postwar buying spree was nearing its peak, International Harvester profits reached a new high of $66.7 million, 6.5 percent on sales of $942.6 million. The next year's sales were up 36 percent to a record $1.277 billion, but profit fell to $63 million, only 4.6 percent on sales.[67] It would be 1959 before Harvester could top the profit and volume highs of 1951, the peak of the industry's farm equipment sales. Growth in the company's truck and construction equipment businesses helped offset the downturn in farm equipment so that corporate volume throughout the 1950s hovered at a little more than $1 billion, but profits stagnated in the 3 to 4 percent range. In a resurgent farm market Harvester's 1959 sales of

$1.363 billion generated a profit of $83.9 million, more than 6 percent, but that was the high-water mark.[68] In the remaining years of its existence the company would never again equal its 1959 profit rate.

Harvester's Cost Problems

Beginning in the early 1950s, Harvester was a company that had a serious profitability problem. Its costs were higher than those of its competitors. A confrontational relationship with the UAW had created costly work stoppages until after 1959, when Harvester began buying labor peace with concessions on work rules. Management came to believe that it had a less favorable agreement with the UAW than its competitors but did not come to grips with the problem until it was too late.

Until 1961 Harvester was still making farm implements at the old McCormick Works, an eighty-acre, 3.5-million-square-foot complex that included some five-story buildings erected during the 1870s after the Chicago fire destroyed McCormick's original plant. Other plants still in use in the 1950s were acquired as part of the 1902 merger. During the 1950s and 1960s Harvester belatedly closed most of these older plants. Its profitability was not helped by a steady loss of farm market share to Deere.

Truck Sales and Farm Equipment

John McCaffrey, the consummate truck salesman, had taken over as CEO after the 1951 board revolt led to the resignation of Fowler McCormick. During the McCaffrey regime, the truck business received heavy emphasis, and Harvester truck sales exceeded farm equipment for the first time in 1955.[69] By 1959 trucks accounted for 47 percent of sales; farm equipment, 34 percent; construction equipment, 13 percent; and steel, 5 percent.[70] Harvester was determined to hold its position as the leading heavy truck manufacturer, so during the 1950s, with McCaffrey's encouragement, the number of truck types, sizes, and configurations proliferated. That helped market share but almost assured higher costs and lower profitability.

Construction equipment never exceeded 18 percent of Harvester's business, and its Construction Equipment Division was running a distant second to Caterpillar. For example, the 13 percent of Harvester's 1959 sales contributed by construction equipment amounted to $173 million, just 23 percent of Caterpillar's $742 million. As the market leader, Caterpillar never hesitated to increase its prices for product improvements and to recover inflation, and that aggressive pricing policy provided a comfortable umbrella under which the rest of the industry, including Harvester, sheltered. It was not that Harvester's prices were too low, it was that costs were too high. With usually less than 20 percent of Caterpillar's volume, Harvester's Construction Equipment Division could not match Caterpillar's costs.

The Wisconsin Steel mill produced about one million tons annually in its outdated South Chicago facilities. Rather than sell or close the mill, in the early 1960s Harvester poured scarce capital into it in an effort to improve efficiency by installing a new rolling mill, basic oxygen furnaces, and later a new coke plant. But the small mill could never match the costs of the big producers and the new mini-mills, and Harvester would not face up to closing Wisconsin Steel, which had high, unfunded pension liabilities.[71]

The Acquisition of the Solar Aircraft Company

Overall, Harvester was not the low-cost producer in any of its businesses and may well have been the high-cost producer. Its consistently low margins during the 1950s and 1960s called for drastic action, but management seemed paralyzed. When McCaffrey retired in 1958, President Frank Jenks, sixty-two, moved up to become chairman and CEO. Jenks, with a financial background, had started as a clerk at Harvester in 1914. Steeped in the past glories of Harvester, he was not the man to turn the company around. His most notable action was the acquisition of Solar Aircraft Company in 1960.[72]

During the 1950s, the automotive industry and mobile equipment manufacturers, including International Harvester and Caterpillar, began investigating a potential new power source, the gas turbine. Many engineers believed the turbine promised to replace gasoline and diesel engines in mobile applications, and not to be left behind the companies began turbine research programs. Solar, a small, high-technology San Diego firm, was a leader in the field and already produced gas turbines for the U.S. Navy. Confronted with an unwelcome takeover attempt in 1959, Solar found a "white knight" in International Harvester. In an exchange of stock valued at about $12 million, Harvester acquired Solar in 1960. Frank Jenks said, "We anticipate that Solar will find a market for a number of its present or future products among the Harvester Company and its subsidiaries."[73] But it was not to be. The early promise of the gas turbine as a mobile power source was never fulfilled because of its voracious appetite for fuel. Harvester had acquired a fifth business when it was already struggling to manage the other four.

The Troubled Construction Equipment Division

Harvester's Construction Equipment Division chafed under Caterpillar's dominance of the large tractor business with its D9 and launched a challenger in 1961 when it introduced the TD30, a 320-horsepower tractor. But like the TD24 of 1947, inadequate testing resulted in costly field failures, and it was later withdrawn from the market.[74] In 1957 two off-highway trucks were introduced, the eighteen-ton 65 and the twenty-four-ton 95 Payhaulers, but the units brought nothing new to the industry.[75] In 1959 the company introduced its thirty-four-cubic-yard 295 and 495 Payscrapers. Although the new models were much improved over the former Heil scrapers, most large earthmoving contractors had already settled on Euclid or Caterpillar scrapers. In 1965 Harvester brought out its unique 180 Payhauler off-highway truck at forty-five tons, with all-wheel drive and dual tires front and rear.[76] It appealed to contractors working in poor underfoot conditions, but the mining industry had well-established haul roads and was not seeking the all-wheel drive feature. Harvester could not keep pace in the competitive horsepower race because of limitations imposed by its largest diesel engine, the DT-817. IH tended to stretch the engine beyond its natural capabilities, which created additional problems and forced the company to use purchased engines in its larger products.[77]

Going back to its first crawler tractor of 1928, International Harvester's construction equipment had always proudly shared the bright red color of its farm equipment, but in 1961, swallowing its pride and bowing to the near-universal acceptance of yellow as the color for construction equipment, the Construction Equipment Division began offering yellow as optional paint.[78] It later became standard.

Although the Construction Equipment Division had its problems, the Hough Division continued to produce consistently good products. Its machines were always the shining stars of Harvester's trade show displays. The patented Z-bar loader linkage came in 1955 on the four-wheel-drive HU, HH, and HO Payloaders. The geometry of the design provided much more powerful bucket breakout force than other linkages, an exclusive feature Hough retained for many years. In 1958 Hough began introducing a new, nine-model line of wheel loaders, but it was slow in adopting articulated steering. That did not appear on Payloaders until 1964 on the five-cubic-yard H-120C and big ten-cubic-yard H-400. In 1965 Hough was advertising a sixteen-model wheel loader line that included four articulated and

Introduced in 1961, the huge, articulated International Harvester–Hough D500, at 700 horsepower and 72.5 tons, was targeted to compete with large crawlers in bulldozing and scraper push-loading. Here it is being used with IH 295 Payscrapers. (State Historical Society of Wisconsin negative no. WHi[X3]51376)

twelve straight-frame models.[79] Wheel bulldozers were added in 1961, including the giant D500 Paydozer.[80]

The Struggling Giant

In 1962 Harry O. Bercher, fifty-six, replaced Frank Jenks as CEO. Bercher, another lifetime employee, came from a background at Wisconsin Steel. He, like Jenks, was not equipped to turn the company around. Profit per share rose on rising volume during his early years as CEO, but there was little improvement in the profit rate. That did not deter Harvester, the company that could least afford it, from paying out a higher percentage of its profits in dividends through the 1960s than either Deere or Caterpillar.[81]

At the end of 1965 Harvester, with sales of more than $2 billion, could look back ruefully on fifteen years in which its profitability, with very few exceptions, had been consistently lower than its chief competitors'. Such a state of affairs, if continued, risked the very existence of the company, but three different CEOs in the same decade had not found a solution to Harvester's high costs. In fact, it was not clear, at least through 1965, that any of them had identified the true dimensions of the problem.

Allis-Chalmers

When Robert S. Stevenson was promoted from vice president of the Tractor Division to president and CEO in 1955, Allis-Chalmers was a half-billion-dollar company made up of thirty diverse businesses.[82] The Tractor Division, which included agricultural and construction equipment, accounted for the bulk of company sales, making most of the remaining businesses very small indeed.[83] And that was the company's problem—too many small businesses attempting to compete with much larger or more specialized companies. It was third in construction equipment after Caterpillar and International Harvester, third in farm equipment after Harvester and Deere, third in steam and hydraulic turbine generating equipment after General Electric and Westinghouse, and fourth in materials handling after Clark, Yale, and Hyster.

The company was attempting to operate all these diverse businesses through two divisions, Tractors and General Machinery. One of Stevenson's first acts was to split the company into five divisions, creating a separate identity for construction equipment for the first time since the acquisition of Monarch Tractor twenty-seven years earlier.[84] The Construction Equipment Division's facilities in Springfield, Illinois, with more than three thousand employees, had been increased in capacity by about 50 percent in the early 1950s.

Overseas Expansion through Acquisition

Stevenson had ambitious plans to expand overseas, augmenting the plant in England purchased in 1950. In 1957 Allis-Chalmers International was formed and, needing a base inside the Common Market, Vendor S.p.A. of Cusano, Italy, a small manufacturer of crawler tractors, was purchased in 1959. Vendor had five hundred employees.[85] A-C acquired controlling interest in Ets. de Construction Mecanique de Vendeuvres S.A. in France in 1960 and had plans to build generator sets and motor graders. But without the resources to follow up with investments to expand these small companies, A-C's efforts to become a true multinational failed. During the early

1960s the company had overseas operations that manufactured various products in seven countries, but they accounted for only 15 percent of the company's volume.[86]

During the second postwar decade, using periodic touch-ups, A-C was able to maintain a representation in all the popularly sized classes of construction equipment, but the company did not venture out of its previously established product lines. After the 1959 acquisition of Tractomotive Corporation brought fully integrated track and wheel loaders, an improved, six-model line of articulated wheel loaders was introduced, beginning with the TL-645 in 1964.[87] The company's prototype of the five-hundred-plus-horsepower HD-41 crawler made a splash at the 1963 Road Show, but another eight years would pass before the machine was in production. Allis-Chalmers came out of the decade with virtually the same product line, although updated, with which it went in. It did not have the resources to mount an aggressive product development program and was losing ground in both construction and farm equipment.

A Candidate for Takeover

The decade was one of stagnation for A-C. Already a half-billion-dollar corporation in 1955, sales did not top $600 million until 1964, when they reached a new high of $631 million.[88] Efforts at overseas expansion had not contributed significantly to growth. The company had lost its way badly, but a major reorganization had taken place in 1963 that promised improved results. A-C remained an underperforming company of many diverse businesses—an ideal candidate for takeover and breakup. Corporate raiders were already eyeing it as the decade ended.

The Euclid Division of General Motors

New Facilities, New Products

In 1956 the Euclid Division announced that it would build a new, 582,000-square-foot plant in Hudson, Ohio, at an estimated cost of $60 million. The plant was expected to employ 1,500. In 1959 the company began a 335,000-square-foot parts warehouse in Hudson to consolidate several operations around Cleveland.[89]

The TS-18 scraper was quickly superseded by the larger TS-24 when, beginning in 1957, Euclid began to update its line of overhung and three-axle scrapers and add larger models. The new Euclid machines and the Twin Power concept were the talk of the 1957 Road Show, and contractors were impressed. By 1961 the line included nine models, extending from the twelve-cubic-yard S-7 through the fifty-two-cubic-yard SS-40 and including two twin-powered models, the TS-14 and the TS-24. It was a formidable line of hauling units.

In 1959 a second track-type tractor appeared: the C-6. Essentially half of a TC-12, it was targeted at the two-to-three-hundred-horsepower class of the D8, HD21, and TD25.[90] New products were flowing, and with the vast resources of General Motors behind it Euclid seemed intent on toppling Caterpillar from industry leadership.

The Justice Department Suit

Suddenly, the bubble burst. In a bombshell, the Justice Department announced in October 1959 that it would sue General Motors to force dives-

The D9's reign as the largest crawler was short-lived after the Euclid TC-12 was introduced in 1955. The TC-12, at 365 horsepower and fifty-six thousand pounds, outclassed the D9 in horsepower and weight but never surpassed it in popularity. (Historical Construction Equipment Association)

The industry's first overhung, twin-power scraper, the Euclid's TS-18 (here in 1955) set new standards for power, traction, and gradeability. At this point, Euclid was several years ahead of competition in scraper design. (Historical Construction Equipment Association)

titure of Euclid. The government contended that the acquisition tended to create a monopoly and was in restraint of trade. The pattern of GM activity being attacked was the acquisition of an established but not dominant company in a non-GM line of business and the development of that company to a position of dominance. Why the government had waited six years to take such action has never been clear. GM protested that it was being unfairly prosecuted because the government had not objected to the acquisition in 1953, but the Justice Department denied ever giving prior approval. Euclid was a tiny fraction of GM's 1958 sales of $9.5 billion—$644 million profit and 520,000 employees. The plaintive claim of Frederick Donner, the company's chair, that the Euclid Division had only a 5 percent market share was no doubt correct when the market for all types of earthmoving equipment is considered, but it had a higher share of the fairly narrow portion for which it competed.[91]

Ebb Tide for Euclid

Thus began more than eight years of litigation that clearly dampened GM's enthusiasm for major new investments in the core product line of off-highway trucks and bottom-dumps obtained in the purchase of Euclid Road Machinery. They received little attention because of the likelihood that they would have to be divested in the event the government was successful. As a result, Euclid, once the unchallenged off-highway truck market leader, steadily lost ground to LeTourneau-Westinghouse, Caterpillar, International Harvester, K-W Dart, and Unit Rig. In 1965 the six-model truck line extended from twelve to sixty-two tons, but basic design and appearance the units had changed little in ten years. That year, in a modest response to the sweeping changes competitors had made in truck design, a new R-35 was introduced that incorporated a vee body and modifications to Euclid's venerable leaf-spring suspension.[92]

Despite these difficulties, Euclid had the distinction of being the first major competitor to produce articulated wheel loaders when the 2.25-cubic-yard L-20 and the 3.0-cubic-yard L-30 came out in 1962.[93]

After the dynamic period of the late 1950s when it appeared that General Motors was driving for leadership in earthmoving equipment, the 1960s saw a significant slowing of the pace of new product introductions while competitors were accelerating. Clearly, the spark was gone. Caterpillar's outpouring of new products between 1959 and 1963 put an end to any dreams General Motors may have had of dominating the earthmoving equipment business.

The LeTourneau-Westinghouse Division of Westinghouse Airbrake

In 1956 the LeTourneau-Westinghouse (L-W) line of scrapers, wheel bulldozers, and motor graders generated about $66 million of parent WABCO's $214.6 total sales, unimpressive growth from R. G. LeTourneau's $55.5 million in 1952, the year before the merger. In the decade preceding 1965, despite the interstate highway construction program, L-W's construction equipment sales stagnated and reached only $76.5 million in 1965.[94] The reasons were not hard to find. In an industry with several full-line manufacturers, short-line manufacturers must offer differentiated products to attract buyers, and L-W never succeeded in doing so with its scrapers and motor graders. Euclid, also a short-line manufacturer, offered some highly differentiated machines in the late 1950s and made itself a strong second to Caterpillar in the scraper business, relegating L-W to a weak third. Dealers found it difficult to survive on the L-W line alone, so many carried other lines and diluted effort on L-W products.

The Haulpak Revolution

Recognizing the need to diversify and broaden its product line, shortly after the merger L-W began concentrating product development resources on off-highway trucks, an initiative that culminated in 1958 with the introduction of the revolutionary Haulpak, a quantum advance in design. Using hydro-pneumatic "Hydrair" struts, the Haulpak suspension system made leaf springs obsolete, just as the optimized, variable-section, fabricated main frame made the heavy, rolled-section, straight-frame design obsolete. The new-style main frame also made possible a deep vee-type body for better

The revolutionary 1957 Haulpak off-highway truck brought several new concepts and forced all other truck manufacturers to reevaluate their designs. (Komatsu Mining Systems)

load retention.[95] Overall, the Haulpak set a new standard that all other off-highway truck makers were forced to emulate. The designer, Ralph Kress, subsequently moved to Caterpillar, where he had a hand in the development of its first off-highway truck, the 769, which was introduced in 1963.

The first Haulpaks, in the twenty-five- to thirty-two-ton range, were too small to be useful in large open-pit mines, but they received good acceptance from contractors. By 1960, however, L-W was offering a sixty-five-ton unit, and in 1965 a seventy-five-ton unit was introduced. At the 1965 Mining Show, L-W introduced its first electric truck, the 120A, a 105-ton-capacity, two-axle unit that used General Electric electrical components. A 160-ton prototype electric truck, then the world's largest, was put in the field in 1966 based on the 120A with a fifth-wheel semi-trailer dump body. The trailer wheels were also electrically driven.[96] These large new mechanical and electric trucks were just what the mining industry was looking for, and miners were buying them in fleets.

Management Changes

L-W's business was down sharply in 1960, and, citing differences with the parent over policy, Merle Yontz, L-W president since the merger, resigned. His replacement was Lewis J. Burger, a former G.E. division chief.[97] Yontz moved down the street to Caterpillar.

Haulpak: The Key L-W Product

By the end of 1965 the Haulpak line had solidified L-W's otherwise rather weak position in the industry. Truck sales had maintained construction market volume at 25 to 28 percent of WABCO's total, and the mining market was now contributing more than 10 percent and growing. L-W products, chiefly Haulpaks, were being built in Canada, Belgium, South Africa, Brazil, and Australia in wholly owned or joint-venture operations. The company still lacked track-type products and wheel loaders. In the next decade it would try to correct these deficiencies and would undergo another change in ownership.

The Reappearance of R. G. LeTourneau

In 1958, five years after the sale of his business to Westinghouse Airbrake, R. G. LeTourneau announced that he was reentering the earthmoving equipment business from his base in Longview, Texas. WABCO sued successfully

to prevent his use of the LeTourneau name, to which it believed it had acquired exclusive rights. As it developed, LeTourneau's reentry proved a non-
event. He was obsessed with building ever-larger machines and poured
money into developing huge electric wheel machines. The extreme was
reached in 1966 with his LT-360 Electric Digger—three seventy-two-cubic-
yard scrapers (driven by twelve electric wheels) in tandem with eight engines,
totaling 5,080 horsepower, an empty weight of 240 tons, and a length of
200 feet. LeTourneau returned to his old habits and built about thirty different types and configurations of scrapers between 1959 and 1966.[98] Contractors were understandably cautious about buying such massive machines,
and eventually, to get the machines out on jobs, LeTourneau was forced to
offer them for lease or rental.

He also attempted, unsuccessfully, to enter the rear-dump truck business
and built several articulated electric-drive models with large single tires in
capacities up to a hundred tons. That unconventional configuration was not
attractive to miners when compared to the large Unit Rig and WABCO electric-drive trucks then coming on the market. Several different models of electric wheel loaders were built; the largest, the Pacemaker SL-40, was rated at
a forty-ton capacity. With a strong prejudice against hydraulics, LeTourneau
insisted on his beloved electrically driven, rack-and-pinion design for bucket
functions. What resulted were probably the most ungainly machines ever

Few earthmoving jobs could accommodate LeTourneau's LT-360 Electric Digger.
(Courtesy of Keith Haddock)

built. Few, if any, were sold. Ultimately, his staff prevailed upon him to accept hydraulic cylinders for bucket functions, and the result was the introduction of the thirteen-cubic-yard L-700 in 1967. It was the first successful LeTourneau loader and a forerunner of several larger models.[99]

LeTourneau pioneered the design and construction of offshore drilling platforms and delivered the first one to Zapata Petroleum in 1956.[100] It was this activity that kept the company solvent for a number of years, but in 1966 the company entered a financial crisis. The costly but unproductive earthmoving product development program had been a continuing drain. Also, land development projects in Peru and Liberia, started in the 1950s for commercial and philanthropic purposes, had never become self-supporting, creating a further drain on company resources. The final straw, the death of R. G. LeTourneau at eighty in June 1969, led to the purchase of the company by the Marathon Manufacturing Company in August 1970.[101] Marathon added larger models to the line of L-Series electric wheel loaders, acquired the "Titan" line of large off-highway trucks from GM, and with these products gained a share of the mining market.

Oliver-Cletrac

Of Oliver's 1959 total sales of $114.6 million, $82.8 million were farm equipment and most of the balance were Oliver-Cletrac industrial sales.[102] Of the seven long-line farm equipment companies, only Minneapolis-Moline was smaller. Oliver's larger competitors' sales in 1959 ranged from Deere's $577 million to Case's $200 million. It was a losing battle and Oliver knew it. In 1960 it accepted an offer from the White Motor Company to purchase its farm equipment business for 655,000 shares of White plus $9 million cash, a transaction valued at about $27 million.[103] White took a two-year option on the purchase of the Cletrac assets, which it picked up in 1961 for $5.5 million.[104]

From White to White: The End of Cletrac

Ironically, Cletrac had now come full circle. Founded in 1917 by Rollin L. White as an offshoot of the White Motor Company, Cletrac now returned to the White Motor Company, albeit neither was any longer controlled by the White family. White Motor's purchase did not include the antiquated Cleveland Cletrac plant. The OC crawler line was moved to Charles City,

Iowa, where the Hart-Parr farm tractor had originated in 1901.[105] Struggling with low market share and an inadequate dealer organization, White discontinued production of OC crawlers altogether in 1965.[106] Thus, after forty-eight years of life, the Cletrac brand disappeared. About the time Cletrac died, two new brands of light-to-medium crawler tractors, Case and Deere, were becoming established in the marketplace. The Oliver-Cletrac machine was probably technically superior to either, and its disappearance is an object lesson in the importance of marketing and distribution.

The Disappearance of the Oliver, Minneapolis-Moline, and Cockshutt Brand Names

White, with 1959 sales of $333 million, claimed 25 percent of the U.S. heavy truck business, second only to Harvester.[107] Its reasons for wanting to enter the crowded farm equipment business remain obscure. Following its acquisition of Oliver, White picked up Cockshutt, a Canadian farm equipment company, and then Minneapolis-Moline. White rationalized the three product lines while continuing the brand names for a brief period, but gradually phased out old models in favor of new White-brand machines. By the mid-1970s all vestiges of the famous old brand names Oliver, Minneapolis-Moline, and Cockshutt had gone the way of Cletrac.

The Clark Equipment Company

Between 1956 and 1965 Clark intensified its drive into the earthmoving equipment business with its Michigan-brand products. With only three years in the earthmoving equipment business, it had a large, impressive exhibit at the 1957 Road Show, including a six-model line of wheel loaders, from the 1.25-cubic-yard 75A to the 375A, a six-cubic-yard machine considered massive by the industry standards of the day. Hough, whose largest model was a 2.5-cubic-yard machine, had been leapfrogged by Clark both in the size and technology of its wheel loaders. Also introduced were a totally new three-model line of hydraulic wheel tractor-scrapers and a line of wheel bulldozers, derivatives of the three largest wheel loaders, that were new for the industry. The loaders and bulldozers were all straight-frame machines that had rear-wheel steering. All were equipped with Clark semiautomatic transmissions, and Waukesha, Cummins, and Detroit Diesel engines were offered as options.[108]

The "All-Rubber" Concept

Clark was selling hard on the idea of the "all-rubber" earthmoving spread because the company did not manufacture track-type machines but was never successful in getting the construction industry to buy into the concept. In average soil conditions, a wheel bulldozer had to be as much as 50 percent heavier than a crawler of equivalent horsepower to produce the same pushing power. A wheel bulldozer, however, was more successful as a utility machine, particularly in open-pit mining, because of its ability to move quickly from place to place.

Clark dealers worked sand, gravel, and crushed-rock producers very hard, and Michigan loaders became well entrenched in that industry. Perhaps because they came later on the scene, however, Clark products were less successful with earthmoving contractors. Despite their clean, modern appearance, Michigan scrapers never gained a significant share of the market.

In 1962 the wheel loader line was upgraded with the introduction of the Series II models. These up-rated versions of earlier machines had more horsepower and bucket capacity but remained straight-frame and rear-wheel-steer even though the industry was beginning to convert to articulation.[109]

A Fast-Growing Company

Clark sales went from $150 million in 1955 to $350 million in 1964, of which an estimated $90 million was from construction equipment.[110] During the decade, it established a joint-venture wheel loader manufacturing operation and a company-owned distributor, Equipco, in France. Since its entry into the business Clark had staked out a strong position in the fast-growing wheel loader market, however the openness of technology made for ease of entry. By the mid-1960s, in addition to Hough, Allis-Chalmers, and Clark, who were early entrants, Caterpillar, Case, and Euclid had added comprehensive wheel loader lines. A half-dozen other short-line companies were also building wheel loaders in the United States, including Trojan, Pettibone-Mulliken, Lorain, Nelson, and Scoopmobile. Clark's challenge during the coming decade would be to hold on to the high market share it had won in the previous ten years.

Komatsu

Organized in 1921, through its early years Komatsu Ltd. produced a variety of heavy industrial material and equipment and specialized in large hydraulic presses. It pioneered the track-type tractor in Japan, producing a small crawler farm tractor in 1931, however tractors remained a minor sideline until after World War II. Immediately after the war, surplus U.S. military construction machinery made up the Japanese construction industry's equipment fleet until the government encouraged Komatsu to begin producing the D50 in 1947. Modeled on the Caterpillar D4, the D50 bulldozer was the first true industrial crawler tractor built in Japan. The following year Komatsu began building diesel engines.[111]

Broadening the Product Line

From the D50, the company gradually extended its line of crawler tractors upward; by 1960 it had models through the two- to three-hundred-horsepower class. During the 1950s it had added motor graders, track loaders, vibratory rollers, and lift trucks.[112] All of that took place behind a barrier of protection from foreign competition. As it developed its line, Komatsu modeled its products heavily on Caterpillar, so much so that Komatsu castings sometimes carried Caterpillar part numbers. Komatsu was able to upgrade the engines in its products through a 1961 license agreement with the Cummins Engine Company.[113]

In 1965 Komatsu and International Harvester/Hough formed Kimco, a joint venture company to build wheel loaders in Japan.[114] The addition of wheel loaders broadened the product line to cover all the popular types and sizes of machines in the home market, with the exception of excavators. Introduced in Japan by Hitachi during the mid-1960s, the hydraulic excavator was accepted quickly. Komatsu was already developing its own line based on technology it had acquired through a license agreement with Bucyrus-Erie. Although it was working very hard to improve quality, at this stage most objective observers still considered Komatsu construction equipment to be inferior in quality to American-made equipment.

Komatsu and the Push for Quality

Ryoichi Kawai became president of Komatsu in 1964, and it was at this point that the company's focus really became international, perhaps galvanized by the perceived threat to its home market share by the Caterpillar Mitsubishi joint venture. Kawai understood extremely well the vital necessity for superior quality if Komatsu were to be successful in export markets against North American and European competition. That year the company was awarded the prestigious Deming Prize for quality control by the Japanese government, and Komatsu embarked on a fanatical campaign to excel the competition in quality.[115] The company began winning export business during the 1960s in developing countries, often on the basis of tied Japanese development loans and trading company package deals, but Komatsu machines in North America and Western Europe were still a rarity. Using a hybrid distribution system of direct sales, dealers and sub-dealers in the home market, Komatsu had little experience in setting up an independent dealer organization, the traditional channel for construction equipment in the Western industrialized world.

Komatsu, the dominant producer in Japan, had little impact outside the country through 1965 but was working feverishly to prepare itself to challenge Western manufacturers on their home grounds. The Western industry, slow to perceive the impending threat, would be shaken out of its complacency before the next decade ended.

The 1957 Road Show

Coming less than a year after the launch of the interstate highway program, the 1957 Road Show reflected the strong feeling of optimism that pervaded the industry. The impressive product evolution that had taken place in the nine years since the last show was underlined by the fact that most machine models exhibited in 1957 did not exist in 1948. Sponsored by the Construction Industry Manufacturers Association (CIMA), the six-day show was held at the end of January and featured 277 exhibitors on twenty-two acres of indoor floor space in Chicago's cavernous International Amphitheater.

The stars of the 1957 show were clearly Clark-Michigan and the Euclid Division of GM. Two new Michigan wheel loaders—including the big six-cubic-yard 375A, two new wheel bulldozers, and three new wheel tractor-scrapers—were highlighted in this industry newcomer's impressive display. Euclid showed its recently introduced TC-12 track-type tractor and the new TS-24 wheel tractor-scraper and unveiled the new C-6 tractor and its top-of-the-line, fifty-five-ton, off-highway truck, the R-55. Marking a new departure in off-highway truck design, LeTourneau-Westinghouse displayed its prototype LW-30.

International-Harvester showed its new eighteen-ton 65 and twenty-four-ton 95 Payhauler off-highway trucks but found its line of Hough wheel loaders seriously upstaged by the new Michigan models. Although it had the largest exhibit, Caterpillar, the industry leader, failed to impress knowledgable industry observers with a display that notably lacked new products. Although their exhibits were small, the presence of Deere and Case signaled their intentions to enter the earthmoving equipment business. Case shared its space with the newly acquired American Tractor Corporation. Overshadowed by the fanfare directed at the new TerraTrac 800 and 1000 tractors, the Case 320 loader-backhoe attracted little notice.[116]

The 1963 Road Show

After the 1957 show, the manufacturers had agreed to conduct the show every six years. The site chosen was again Chicago's International Amphitheater.

After the lackluster display of 1957, Caterpillar dominated the 1963 show with its new 769 off-highway truck, 988 and 966B articulated wheel loaders and wheel bulldozers, and big 225-horsepower No. 16 motor grader. It was also the first opportunity to display the recently introduced 600-Series wheel tractor-scraper line in a major show.

In an attempt to steal the spotlight, Allis-Chalmers showed a prototype HD-41, the world's largest track-type tractor and some new 45-Series articulated wheel loaders.

Hough, playing catch-up since 1957 when it was outclassed by Michigan, topped its competitor by displaying the Hough H-400 ten-cubic-yard machine, the world's largest wheel loader. New wheel bulldozers were also shown, including the giant, seventy-two-ton 500 Paydozer.

The Euclid Division of General Motors broadened its line and showed its new L-Series wheel loaders, but the fast pace of new model introductions of the 1950s clearly was not being sustained.

Compared to 1957, the light construction equipment segment was better represented. Small crawler bulldozers and loaders were shown by Case, Deere, and Oliver-Cletrac, and Case, Deere, and Massey-Ferguson each showed a range of loader-backhoes.

Fed by more than five years of interstate work, the construction equipment industry at the 1963 Road Show was showing newfound affluence, increased competition, and a remarkable growth in the size, variety, and sophistication of its products.[117]

Summary, 1956–65

As the second postwar decade began in 1956, the companies recognized as the principal earthmoving equipment competitors were Caterpillar, International Harvester–Hough, Allis-Chalmers, LeTourneau-Westinghouse, and the Euclid Division of GM, with Oliver-Cletrac on the fringe. Aside from some ownership changes, the hierarchy was not greatly different from 1946. Worldwide, the industry was still dominated by U.S. companies, but foreign competition was beginning to stir. The coming decade was to bring great changes.

Early in the interstate decade, the aggressive product program of the Euclid Division threatened to upset the industry's equilibrium until the bubble burst in 1959, when the government sued to force divestiture. In the meantime, Clark was successfully establishing its wheel loader line and claiming a 50 percent market share by 1957. Between 1959 and 1963 Caterpillar brought on a mass of new products and product updates and entered the wheel loader and off-highway truck business.

The highway program, with literally billions of cubic yards of earthmoving, favored Caterpillar and Euclid, which had strong scraper lines, but all heavy equipment manufacturers benefited. The seemingly endless miles of concrete pavement and thousands of structures required hundreds of millions of tons of aggregate, favoring International Harvester and Clark whose Hough and Michigan lines of wheel loaders were strong in the quarries. The big Caterpillar motor graders were standard equipment on most interstate jobs.

With few exceptions, the large earthfill dams were built by Caterpillar or Euclid scrapers and bottom-dumps, and Caterpillar got the lion's share of track-type machines and graders.

While all this was happening on the heavy equipment side, a new phenomena was taking place: the beginnings of what would become a major subindustry for light construction equipment. The birth of the light construction equipment industry was the most significant event of the years between 1956 and 1965. Fathered by Case, Deere, and Massey-Ferguson, companies that previously had not made construction equipment, the new industry was almost completely free of competition from the "big boys," who watched passively from the sidelines as the industry grew. The loader-backhoe was its mainstay, but by the early 1960s it had spread into small bulldozers and track and wheel loaders. Once established, the companies would inevitably develop their product lines upward and create new competition in the profitable mid-range size classes for older, established companies.

Three new products were to have a pervasive influence on the industry during the decade. First, Demag's 1954 introduction of the hydraulic excavator revolutionized the European earthmoving equipment industry during the decade. Poclain and other European manufacturers were quick to follow Demag, and by 1965 excavators were edging out track loaders in popularity there. The technology soon spread to Japan. Hitachi built its first machine, the UH03, in 1965. By the early 1970s the product had received overwhelming Japanese acceptance. Although a number of U.S. manufacturers including Drott and Koehring were offering the product in the late 1950s, excavator popularity in the United States lagged Europe by about fifteen years.

The second key product was the loader-backhoe, which has had no equal as a utility machine. It is the entry-level machine in North America for nearly every would-be grading contractor and is also owned by the largest contractors as well as most state and local governmental bodies. It is ubiquitous in North America, the United Kingdom, and France and enjoys wide acceptance in all other industrialized countries except Japan, where it has never gained a niche. Worldwide annual sales have exceeded forty thousand units and are seldom less than thirty thousand units, an opportunity approaching $2 billion.

The third milestone was the LeTourneau-Westinghouse Haulpak truck. Coming out of the same North Adams Street factory in Peoria that gave birth to the Tournapull scraper in 1938, the Haulpak was a new departure that forced all competitors to reevaluate their truck designs. By 1965 Haulpak and Unit Rig electric trucks were the choice in big, open-pit metal mines once dominated by Euclid trucks.

Wheel loader articulation also made its appearance. The advantages over rear-wheel steer were so manifest that by 1965 the industry was well on its way to a complete conversion to the new steering system for wheel loaders.

By the end of 1965 interstate highway construction was at a peak. After a little less than ten years of work, 21,185 miles—52 percent of the system—were already open to traffic.[118] The program had been a bonanza to contractors and the construction equipment industry alike, but it was a wasting asset. When it was complete some ten years hence, what would follow?

FIVE

The Industry Matures, 1966–75

In the United States, the decade between 1956 and 1965 was marked by unprecedented prosperity, low inflation, and an absence of domestic strife. The nation, enjoying the fruits of the tranquil Eisenhower years, had been at peace with the world and with itself. Such would not be the case in the succeeding decade. The war in Vietnam would create political turmoil and civil unrest that would tragically divide the country and also plant the seeds for a ruinous inflation that would dog the nation for more than a decade. Perhaps as a by-product of the discontent generated by opposition to the war, the decade also saw the rise of interest groups that would challenge programs whose benefits had long been unquestioned, among these the construction of highways and water projects. Following closely on the U.S. pullout from Vietnam, Watergate added further to the strife and division in the country. From the confident, dynamic, economic and political world leader of the mid-1960s, by 1975 the United States was an uncertain nation racked by inflation and feeling the impact of aggressive foreign competition on its domestic industries.

The Economy

The Johnson administration's decision to have guns as well as butter during the Vietnam War was to have a profound effect on the U.S. economy for the next fifteen years. The Consumer Price Index was 81.4 in 1956 and 97.2 in 1966 (1967 = 100). Following these years of relatively mild inflation, the index took off sharply and rose to 109.8 in 1969. November 1969 saw an end to 105 months of economic expansion as high interest rates and the anti-inflationary tactics of the Nixon administration threw the economy into a lingering recession from which it did not fully recover until 1972. But a strange new phenomenon was that inflation persisted in the midst of recession. By the end of 1971 the CPI stood at 121.3, a greater increase in four years than in the twelve years through 1967.[1]

The Nixon administration jawboned industry and labor in an attempt to minimize price and wage increases but to little avail. With his New Economic Policy, Richard Nixon shook the world in August 1971 by closing the gold window and effectively devaluing the U.S. dollar while at the same time shocking the business community and organized labor by announcing a price and wage freeze. The freeze, passing through four phases in thirty-two months until its end in May 1974, provided a temporary palliative in 1972 when the CPI rose only four points. Overall, however, it was eminently unsuccessful in affecting the root causes of inflation that returned with a vengeance and reached double digits in 1974. From 1970 through 1975 the Producer Price Index for construction equipment rose 60 percent, from 115.9 to 185.2 (1967 = 100).[2]

Compounding the already serious problems of the U.S. economy, the Yom Kippur War in October 1973 triggered the Arab oil boycott and a worldwide oil crisis. Directed primarily at the United States, the boycott was lifted in March 1974 but left a permanent quantum increase in energy costs. That, along with continuing efforts to dampen inflation and a general uncertainty and loss of confidence brought about by Watergate, drove the economy into a steep five-quarter recession from the fourth quarter of 1973 through the first quarter of 1975, the longest of the postwar period.

Overall, although the economy (GDP) grew at a robust average annual rate of 5 percent between 1966 and 1970, through 1975 it managed only a total growth of 11.5 percent, with 1974 and 1975 in negative figures.[3] The Dow Jones Industrial Average had topped 1,000 for the first time in November 1972, but, bombarded by adverse events, it began to drift down steadily and bottomed out at 577.6 in December 1974. Then, signaling an economic recovery, the Dow rose during 1975 and ended the year at 852.4.

Despite the Vietnam War, the Arab oil boycott, rampant inflation, and two recessions, the years from 1966 to 1975 could well be regarded as golden for the U.S. earthmoving equipment industry. In the third decade since World War II, the industry experienced a period of dynamic growth and matured. Domestic competition was intense, but prices were good and there was business for all. The U.S. industry was yet to feel the sting of lower-priced Japanese imports.

The Highway Program

In addition to coping with runaway inflation, other forces and events, new and unexpected, affected the earthmoving equipment industry during the decade. The huge breakthrough represented by the establishment of the Highway Trust Fund in 1956 had led the roads lobby to believe that now, finally, funding for highway construction was absolutely secure. The industry was to be rudely disillusioned when in 1966 President Lyndon Johnson ordered a $1.1 billion cutback in the federal aid highway program for 1967 as a measure of curbing inflation. That took the form of "impoundment" of previously authorized appropriations from the Highway Trust Fund because the money could not be legally diverted to other uses.[4] Impoundments became an ongoing practice during the Johnson and later administrations to the extent that nearly $11 billion had accumulated by 1975.[5] Portions were released when it was thought desirable to "stimulate the economy." Among states, the effect was to instill uncertainty about highway planning; among contractors, impoundments affected equipment purchasing and stretched out the interstate system's completion by an indeterminate number of years.

But impoundments were not the only problem to affect the highway program. Suddenly, it seemed to be the surrogate for the solution of every social issue facing the nation. For example, in 1969 the employment of minorities on highway jobs came under regulation by the Federal Highway Administration. Critics, charging that rights-of-way through cities caused disproportionate displacement of lower-income groups, demanded and received more generous provisions from highway funds for replacement housing. Construction delays from social and environmental objections, rarely encountered in the past, became commonplace. To further bedevil state highway departments, Congress adopted a new tactic—the unfunded congressional mandate—whereby states, under threat of loss of federal matching funds, were required to adhere to a variety of new federal requirements, including government safety standards, highway beautification, and even speed limits.

No doubt the most concerted attack on the sanctity of the Highway Trust Fund came from a new group. The mass transit lobby was composed of politicians and interest groups from large metropolitan areas, and they demanded that a portion of highway-user revenues flowing into the Trust Fund be used for construction of mass transit facilities. The interest groups were generally congruent with those opposing highways on social and environmental grounds. The issue was fought out in Congress over several years. George McGovern's 1972 presidential platform even included a provision for converting the Highway Trust Fund into a "Transportation Trust Fund," something that would occur years later. Mass transit forces achieved a victory in 1973 when President Nixon signed a bill permitting a small portion of the Trust Fund to be dedicated for that purpose.[6] Although the amount made an insignificant dent in highway funding and did not satisfy the mass transit lobby, it was the first successful incursion into the heretofore sacroscant Trust Fund and a stinging defeat for the roads lobby that had swept everything before it for almost two decades.

Although the highway program encountered a variety of new problems during the decade, it was still able to continue relatively unabated. In 1968 the Department of Transportation added 1,500 miles to the interstate system, making it 42,500 miles.[7] By early 1975, 85 percent of the system was open to traffic. At that point, nearly all the "easy," rural portions had been completed, and most of the remainder was made up of more difficult and costly urban sections. The Federal Highway Administration estimated that the remaining 15 percent would absorb 36 percent of the total cost of the system.[8]

Water Projects

Between 1966 and 1970 numerous large dams, begun during the previous decade, were completed. In the United States those included the Oroville, San Luis, John Day, and final mainstem dams on the Missouri, and in Canada the Gardiner, W. A. C. Bennett, and Daniel Johnson, among others. The agreement between the United States and Canada in 1964 on the development of the Upper Columbia triggered construction of Mica, Arrow Lake, and Duncan dams in British Columbia; Libby Dam in Montana was begun in 1966. Between 1966 and 1975 the impetus for dam building in North America shifted to Canada with the 1968 start of the Churchill Falls power project in Labrador and the launch in 1973 of Quebec Hydro's massive James Bay project in remote northern Quebec. When completed in 1986, James Bay Phase I, involving 190 million cubic yards of earthmoving, would add 10,300 megawatts of generating capacity at a cost of $11.2 billion. Huge fleets of heavy equipment were at work on these projects. By 1975 it should have been clear to casual observers that the era of mega-dams in the United States was coming to an end because of a lack of suitable sites and also because of environmental objections, but congressional appropriations for water projects of other types continued unabated.

Emphasis shifted in the late 1960s to small dams through the Department of Agriculture's Small Watershed Program, which subsidized hundreds of soil conservation and flood control dams throughout the country.

In 1972 work began on the 253-mile Tennessee-Tombigbee Waterway connecting the Tennessee River with the Gulf of Mexico. Labeled a boondoggle or a huge pork barrel by opponents, the Corps of Engineers project involved 292 million cubic yards of earthmoving, more than the Panama Canal, but was nevertheless completed after fifteen years of work.[9]

The Trans-Alaska Pipeline

With the discovery of oil on Alaska's inaccessible north slope, a group of eight major oil companies formed a consortium, the Trans-Alaska Pipeline Company (TAP), to construct a pipeline to bring the crude oil south to the port of Valdez on Prince William Sound. The eight-hundred-mile, forty-eight-inch line, originally estimated to cost $900 million, was the largest privately financed construction project in history. The project was expected to begin in 1972, but when the company encountered a blizzard of objections from environmentalists and others, it was forced in December 1971 to return the bids of contractors and await new government authorization.[10] At that point it was not at all certain that the pipeline would ever be built, but the Arab oil boycott convinced Congress to override environmental objections. Work was able to begin in 1974. Meanwhile, the Alyeska Pipeline Company, a new consortium that had succeeded TAP, faced a quadrupling of costs from more than three years of inflation and stringent new construction requirements designed to meet environmental concerns. Nearly 1,500 pieces of heavy construction equipment were at work on the project, which involved eighty-five million cubic yards of earthmoving.[11]

Mining

The decade saw the start of three major North American mining projects: the Highland Valley open-pit copper mine in British Columbia, Anaconda's Twin Buttes copper mine in Arizona, and M. A. Hanna's large Wabush Lake iron ore development on the Quebec-Labrador iron range. At Twin Buttes, two hundred million tons of alluvial material were removed on a crash basis in thirty months to get at a low-grade ore body 460 feet below the surface. In a first for the metals mining industry, overburden removal was accomplished entirely by scrapers and bottom-dumps, a fleet of eighty-one of Caterpillar's large hauling units.[12] Highland Valley, after a modest start, would be one of the world's largest open-pit copper mines by the mid-1980s.

The International Scene

Europe, untouched by the Vietnam War, enjoyed a period of growing economic momentum between 1966 and 1975. Merging the EEC, European Coal and Steel Community, and the European Atomic Energy Commission (Euratom), the European Community (EC) was formed in 1967 and expanded in 1973 with the accession of the United Kingdom, Ireland, and Denmark.

Nixon's 1971 closure of the gold window effectively destroyed the international monetary system established at the Bretton Woods Conference in 1944. Under this system of fixed exchange rates, periodic competitive devaluations by nations with weaker currencies and unwillingness to revalue by nations with stronger currencies had given rise over time to serious distortions among the world's currencies. For example, the yen had remained at 360 to the U.S. dollar since the early 1950s. This created competitive problems for U.S. exports and a growing unfavorable U.S. balance of trade.

In the Smithsonian Agreement of December 1972, the major industrialized nations agreed to a new "controlled float" currency system and to certain adjustments to exchange rates versus the dollar, beginning an eight-year period in which the dollar gradually weakened against the German mark and yen. All these developments were watched warily by multinationals who risked serious exchange losses on their overseas investments, but the overall effect of the agreement on exchange rates was, at least for the short term, beneficial to U.S. exporters. The U.S. earthmoving equipment industry, a major exporter, found itself in a new and more complex international business environment of floating exchange rates.

Construction Projects

The threefold increase in the price of oil triggered by OPEC's 1973–74 boycott brought sudden and undreamed of wealth to major oil producers and launched an era of forced-draft infrastructure development in OPEC countries. At the same time it created a totally unexpected bonanza for the construction equipment industry. During the most intensive period, from the mid-1970s to the mid-1980s, Saudi Arabia, Iraq, Iran, Kuwait, the United Arab Emirates, Libya, and Nigeria together probably absorbed in the range of fifteen to twenty-five thousand pieces of heavy earthmoving equipment annually. The manufacturers were almost stunned by this veritable cornucopia of business. Demand was so overwhelming during the first few years of the boom that price was seldom a matter for discussion. Beginning in the early 1980s, however, such markets became increasingly competitive, and Japanese manufacturers gradually predominated. Certainly, the Mideastern boom of the 1970s and early 1980s was an event the construction equipment industry would never forget.

Meanwhile, in Western Europe, in a climate of rising affluence and soaring motor vehicle registrations, construction was underway on an integrated system of limited-access motorways, autobahns, autoroutes, and autostradas comparable to the U.S. interstate system. Largely in place by the late 1980s, the new highways totally transformed the trucking industry and private travel in the United Kingdom and on the Continent.

In the Indus River Basin, Mangla Dam, an eighty-five-million-cubic-yard structure, was completed in 1967. Tarbela, the second major dam in the system, was started by a consortium of European contractors led by Impregilo, a large Italian firm. When completed in 1976, Tarbela, with a volume of 145 million cubic yards was for a time the world's largest rolled earthfill dam.

Beginning about 1970, Brazil suddenly began to live up to its promise as a major new frontier for development. That year it announced its intention to build the 3,100-mile Trans-Amazonica Highway to open the Amazon rain forest to settlement. Viewed in some quarters as quixotic and in others as an outright disaster to the ecosystem, the project nevertheless went ahead to completion. Also during the 1970s, Brazil began a series of major dams, all of which made it a very active export market for construction equipment. All of the activity, however, provided little opportunity for U.S. or European contractors because a cadre of competent large contractors had grown up in Brazil.

International Mining

In Chile, after agreeing to "co-production" arrangements with the centrist Frei government in the late 1960s, Anaconda Company saw its Chuquicamata and El Salvador mines, and Kennecott Copper its El Teniente mine, nationalized outright in 1971 by the leftist Allende government.[13] About the same time, the Zambian government was taking control of the major mines on its Copper Belt. These were alarming developments for the international copper market because the governments' plans to maximize revenues from newly acquired properties would inevitably depress the world price of copper.

Major new copper developments were Palabora in South Africa, started in 1965, and Bougainville, begun in 1973. The latter, reflecting the trend in hauling unit size, acquired a fifty-two-unit fleet of Euclid R-105s.[14]

After years of restricting development of mineral resources to government entities, Brazil began inviting private development of its huge iron ore reserves in 1965. In 1972 it announced a major find in the northern state of Pará; 1.6 billion tons of 67 percent ore had been proven and were to be developed by a joint venture of the government-owned mining company, the Companhia Vale do Rio Doce, and a subsidiary of US Steel.[15] But in the late 1960s the major play in iron ore was in remote western Australia with the discovery of billions of tons of high-grade ore in the Hammersley, Mt. Newman, and Mt. Goldsworthy ranges.[16] Japanese interests contributed heavily to development costs and tied up most future production with long-term contracts.

The Companies

Between 1956 and 1965 only one U.S. earthmoving equipment maker, Case, had a change in ownership. In the succeeding decade, however, four companies were to change hands: Case and LeTourneau-Westinghouse, both for the second time; Euclid under a federal consent decree; and Allis-Chalmers, which entered a construction equipment joint venture as a minority partner with Fiat. Case and LeTourneau were caught up in the merger and acquisition fever of the time, and Euclid was a special situation. Allis-Chalmers's action reflected the company's need to find a strong partner to buttress its fading construction equipment business.

Caterpillar

The Blackie Era

Caterpillar's policy of mandatory retirement for officers at the age of sixty-six brought a series of changes at the top during the 1966–75 decade. With the retirement of Harmon Eberhard in 1966, William Blackie, fifty-nine, was elected chair and CEO. William H. Franklin, fifty-seven, succeeded Blackie as president. Franklin, in turn, moved up to the CEO job in 1972, with William L. Naumann, sixty-three, taking over in 1975, Caterpillar's third CEO in ten years. After nine years of leadership by men trained in finance, Naumann, who joined the company at seventeen in the machine shop apprentice program, was the first postwar Caterpillar CEO from a purely manufacturing background. Lee L. Morgan, fifty-four, was elected president in 1975, the first from marketing to hold that job. Of this group of executives, the visionary Blackie had by far the greatest role in shaping the company in the postwar period. On his retirement as CEO in 1972 the company was a well-established multinational.[17]

William Blackie (1906–96). A Caterpillar officer for twenty-eight years, the last six as CEO, Blackie led the company's overseas expansion during the 1950s and 1960s. (Courtesy of Caterpillar Inc.)

One Blackie innovation would, however, have unintended consequences for the company in the long term. During the late 1950s, through his influence a new management philosophy was introduced into the staff/line relationship whereby the General Offices staff and the operating units would be "jointly and severally" responsible for corporate results. Becoming deeply embedded over more than two decades, the doctrine blurred accountability and gradually led to a time-consuming process of consensus-seeking between line and staff that slowed decision making. Although it had a tradition of deliberateness, Caterpillar by the mid-1970s was becoming ponderous.

Corporate Growth

During the late 1960s Caterpillar's business outside the United States continued to grow, averaging more than 47 percent of total corporate sales with about 70 percent of the overseas business from U.S. exports. With the U.S. recession in 1970 sales outside the United States reached 52.5 percent of the total, a new high.[18] During this period, management was voicing increasing concern over the growing strength of the dollar, which was putting at risk the company's export business. It was also strenuously resisting efforts by various U.S. interest groups to restrict foreign investment as a means of influencing the balance of payments and to "keep jobs at home." Despite government controls on direct foreign investment, Caterpillar was able to continue expansion of its overseas facilities by borrowing eurodollars. At the end of 1975 the company had $810 million in net assets deployed outside the United States compared to $198 million at the end of 1965.[19]

Corporate growth did indeed occur at Caterpillar between 1966 and 1975. Having crossed the $2 billion mark in 1969, the company passed $3 billion in 1973, reached $4 billion in 1974 despite the recession, and was just short of $5 billion by 1975. Much of the apparent growth, however, came from the price inflation of the early 1970s. The company's strength outside the United States was evident in the 1974–75 recession when foreign sales rose to $2.83 billion (up 38 percent) in 1975 and reached a new record, 57 percent of the total.[20]

The old pattern continued: Periodic "controlled distribution" (a euphemism for product allocation) to dealers when demand was strong was followed by a rapid buildup of factory inventories during downturns. But the cyclical nature of the business was so extreme that attempting to put capacity in place to meet the peaks may have been a dubious investment. Nevertheless, the company tried, each year investing more than the last. Investment in facilities, machinery, and equipment totaled more than $2 billion between 1966 and 1975, with 75 to 80 percent in the United States. A major investment was a new basic engine plant near Peoria that eventually included 2.8 million square feet.[21] To provide space for the manufacture of hydraulic excavators, the Gosselies, Belgium, plant was expanded 50 percent by the addition of nine hundred thousand square feet.[22] Manufacturing space doubled between 1965 and 1975, when it totaled nearly thirty-two million square feet.[23]

Contributing to this frenetic spending on increased capacity was the company's belief in an ever-rising demand for its products. Caterpillar's public utterances of the period always emphasized how the worldwide need for more food, water, housing, transportation, and minerals would assure the company's future growth indefinitely, and its own long-range sales forecasts always confirmed that. With manufacturing floor space well in excess of its needs, Caterpillar eventually became a victim of its own rosy forecasts, but during the early 1970s these extrapolations were an article of faith within the company. To finance this aggressive expansion the company became more leveraged, with long-term debt increasing from only $123 million in 1965 to $851 million in 1975.[24]

The Attempt to Acquire Chicago-Pneumatic

The acquisition of Towmotor in 1965 whetted Blackie's appetite for further growth by acquisition. In mid-1967 Caterpillar and Chicago-Pneumatic Tool Company (C-P) announced that they had reached agreement in principle for a "pooling of interests" involving an exchange of shares. C-P, a diversified manufacturer of large diesel engines, industrial tools, compressors, and drilling equipment, had sales of about $151 million in 1966. The Antitrust Division of the Department of Justice immediately challenged the transaction, and after the companies had responded to its questions for several months the department obtained an injunction against the merger on the grounds that it would reduce competition. Fearing a drawn-out court battle, C-P terminated the merger agreement in early 1968. The incident effectively ended the growth-by-acquisition strategy at Caterpillar.[25] Henceforth, growth, with minor exceptions, would be internally generated.

A Breakthrough in the Soviet Union

In the late 1920s and early 1930s American farm tractor manufacturers had received massive orders from the Soviet Union during its first Five Year Plan when it collectivized agriculture on a crash basis. After that, Western equipment manufacturers had obtained few orders of any kind. The late 1960s marked the beginning of another crash program in the Soviet Union, this time to develop its huge resources of petroleum and natural gas. It planned a 3,125-mile pipeline to bring natural gas from Siberia, and, recognizing that it did not produce the kinds of heavy equipment needed for the job, it turned to the West. The Mannesman Company of West Germany was to provide the pipe and procure the equipment needed for constructing the line and placed a $40 million order with Caterpillar for 100 D9 tractors and 240 large pipelayers.[26] Two years later the Soviet Union was again buying, and this time a $40 million tractor order went to International Harvester.[27] Caterpillar, however, obtained a later $68 million order for 550 tractors and pipelayers.[28] Dispensing with an intermediary, the Russians negotiated these orders directly, as they would all future machinery business. In 1973 Caterpillar and International Harvester were given permission to open offices in Moscow.

Through the rest of the 1970s Caterpillar and International Harvester continued to receive large orders from the Soviet Union. Caterpillar obtained the bulk of the tracked equipment orders while Harvester received several for large wheel loaders. During this period of political détente, U.S. earthmoving equipment manufacturers obtained almost all of the Soviet Union's business to the near complete exclusion of Japan.

Caterpillar and Hydraulic Excavators

After several years of development, in 1972 Caterpillar introduced its Model 225 hydraulic excavator, the first of a four-model line. Each year thereafter through 1975 an additional model was added. Full production facilities were provided at both Gosselies, Belgium, and Aurora, Illinois. The line, ranging from the ninety-horsepower, eighteen-metric-ton 215 through the 325-horsepower, fifty-eight-metric-ton 245, was state-of-the-art and had a high-pressure, variable flow hydraulic system, pilot-operated controls, oil disc brakes, and track-type tractor undercarriages.[29] The machines came none to soon for the European Caterpillar dealers, who were being hard-

The Caterpillar 225 hydraulic excavator. (Courtesy of Caterpillar Inc.)

pressed by Poclain, Liebherr, O&K, Akermans, and others. In North America the machines were greeted with only mild enthusiasm because excavators had not yet gained the degree of acceptance they enjoyed in Europe and Japan.

Other Product Developments

Caterpillar had transitioned away from its traditional agricultural market since the 1930s to concentrate on the construction market opportunity. The mining market had always been of peripheral interest to the company. It did well supplying tractors and motor graders to miners, but those products, as auxiliary equipment, made up a small fraction of industry purchases concentrated on production equipment, off-highway trucks, and shovels. The introduction of the thirty-five-ton 769 truck in 1963 did little to change that because the unit was too small to be of interest to large mining operations.

Recognizing the opportunity, Caterpillar began a large truck development program in the early 1960s. At the 1965 Mining Show the company broke a long-standing policy of showing only regular production products by displaying a prototype hundred-ton electric mining truck of an unconventional side-dump design.[30] In the event, the product was never offered, but in late

1967 the 779, a rear-dump electric truck of seventy-five tons, went into production. Following a tradition of highly integrated products, the electrical components were of Caterpillar design and manufacture.[31] The truck was not a success, however. Plagued with a variety of electrical and mechanical problems for which fixes did not appear practical, the unit was discontinued in 1970; the company bought back and scrapped some forty, as well as its electric-drive development program. It was the first bitter taste of failure in the company's history and a serious setback in its efforts to become a major supplier to the mining industry.

But where the 779 failed other new products succeeded. In 1968 Caterpillar brought on the ten-cubic-yard 992 wheel loader that soon dominated its size class. In 1970 the company announced a fifty-ton off-highway truck, the 773, which was also well accepted. And five years after the demise of the 779 Caterpillar reentered the large truck business by introducing the mechanical-drive 777, an eighty-five-ton, off-highway vehicle. Although the 777 was in part a vindication of its earlier unsuccessful efforts with the 779, the company still lagged badly in producing large hauling units for the mining industry.[32]

Probably one of the most successful new product introductions in the company's history was the six-model G-Series family of motor graders brought to market in an eighteen-month period in 1973 and 1974. Although Caterpillar motor graders had been extensively improved over the forty years since the introduction of the Auto Patrol, their basic design had remained unchanged. The G-Series brought a new look to Caterpillar motor graders, with frame articulation, full hydraulic controls, power-shift transmission, oil disc brakes, and integral rollover cabs.[33]

Having abandoned the fifty-horsepower class track-type tractor in 1957 by dropping the D2, Caterpillar watched uneasily as Deere, Case, and Fiat attacked its seventy-five-horsepower D4 from below. In an effort to forestall this erosion, the company decided to again compete in the fifty-to-sixty horsepower class by introducing the D3 track-type tractor, 931 track loader, and 910 wheel loader. Knowing that this size class was extremely price-sensitive, Caterpillar planned to have the machines built in Japan by Caterpillar Mitsubishi, where low labor costs and an undervalued yen would make the products very competitive in the United States and Europe.[34] Unfortunately for the project, in 1972, shortly before the planned introduction, the yen was revalued nearly 15 percent, and that required a like increase in the dollar price. The machines appeared in 1973 but got off to a slow start. Caterpillar dealers were doing quite well selling more profitable, higher-priced products and had by and large lost contact with buyers of that class of machines.

A non-earthmoving expansion effort was concentrated on the truck engine business. In 1960 Caterpillar's Engine Division had introduced a diesel engine targeted at the on-highway truck industry.[35] The company believed that its reputation for the quality and durability of its engines was widely recognized. It was dismayed to learn not only that it was an unknown quantity in the trucking industry but also that its first truck engine did not perform as well in demanding, over-the-road service as did those of the Cummins Engine Company and Detroit Diesel, more experienced in the truck engine business. By the late 1960s Caterpillar had gotten almost nowhere until it reached an agreement with Ford to build a compact V-8 engine for a new line of mid-range trucks.[36] Still, progress was slow to establish its engines in the heavy-duty segment where most of the business was. Despite the commitment of substantial resources, by 1975 Caterpillar's engine business continued to languish at less than 10 percent of total corporate volume.[37]

The Growth in the Dealer Organization

From an average net worth of $2.5 million in 1965, by the end of 1975 the average for U.S. Caterpillar dealers was $6.8 million. The amount for overseas dealers was slightly higher in both years.[38] The Caterpillar account had indeed been profitable over the decade, and dealer financial resources contributed strongly to an already formidable competitive edge.

In 1974 Caterpillar made its North American dealers part of a corporate computerized emergency parts search system.[39] In succeeding years the system grew in sophistication while gradually being expanded to all dealers worldwide. With their ample financial resources, larger dealers had begun purchasing computers in the early 1960s, primarily for parts inventory control, and by the mid-1970s most North American Caterpillar dealers were computerized. The selection of hardware was entirely at the discretion of each dealer, and typically they undertook to write their own software. The result was a veritable kaleidoscope of hardware and software, an absence of compatibility that later proved costly to both dealers and Caterpillar. During the decade, other equipment manufacturers also introduced computerized parts systems, but their dealers, being smaller, were more likely to take guidance from the manufacturers and thus avoid the pitfalls of the early computer age.

Ten Years of Solid Growth

Between 1966 and 1975 Caterpillar more than tripled its business, moving ahead strongly both in the United States and abroad, and profits were good. Manufacturing space more than doubled, and the company continued its almost frenetic capital investment program on a steadily rising curve. Yet sales were still supply-limited through much of the period. As the industry leader in volume and profits, Caterpillar continued to outspend its rivals on research and development. In a major new product initiative, it had entered the fast-growing hydraulic excavator business. Other lines were added or updated, and by 1975 Caterpillar presented an array of products that was intimidating to the competition in its breadth and modernity. Competitors were struggling to keep up.

J. I. Case

Acquisition by Tenneco

Not long after gaining control of Case in 1964, the Kern County Land Company found itself the target of an unfriendly takeover by Armand Hammer's Occidental Petroleum. Kern County found the white knight it was seeking in Tenneco, a pipeline operator and natural resources company, and the deal was closed in August 1967. In the transaction, Tenneco acquired only 56 percent of the shares of Case, the amount owned by KCL. Tenneco's interest in KCL centered on the latter's natural resource assets, and, lacking experience in heavy manufacturing, it regarded Case as more of a "throw in" in the deal. Tenneco at first contemplated spinning off the machinery business, but further study convinced it that construction equipment was a growth industry and Case was worth keeping.[40] Over the next twenty-seven years until it did begin to spin off Case, Tenneco frequently may have wished it had followed its first impulse.

Building the Business

Under its new owner, the Case Construction Equipment Division benefited from a rapid-fire succession of acquisitions. In January 1968 Tenneco acquired the Drott Manufacturing Company of Wausau, Wisconsin, and set it up as a division of Case. Drott, a family-owned concern, had first made its name in the early 1950s with its patented "4-in-1" bucket for track loaders. In 1968 it was building mobile cranes, straddle carriers, 4-in-1 buckets, and, most important, hydraulic excavators. That same year, Tenneco bankrolled the acquisition of the Davis Manufacturing Company of Wichita, Kansas, which made small trenchers, tilt trailers, and cable-laying attachments, and it also became a division of Case.[41]

In 1969 Tenneco purchased the Beloit line of log-skidders and the Uni-Loader line of small skid-steer loaders. The skid-steer loader had become a popular utility machine and complemented Case's strong line of loader-backhoes.[42] Continuing its largesse, in 1970 Tenneco acquired Losenhausen Machinenbau AG of West Germany, which provided Case with a good line of vibratory compactors.[43] Clearly, the emphasis was on construction equipment, and Tenneco's purse seemed bottomless. In 1969, for the first time, construction equipment accounted for more than half of Case's sales.[44]

The construction equipment business was prospering, but Case's agricultural equipment was steadily losing ground and ranked sixth in North American market share in 1970 at about 4 percent after Deere, International Harvester, Massey-Ferguson, Allis-Chalmers, and Ford. Its agricultural sales outside North America were insignificant.[45] In 1970 Case made the momentous decision to withdraw from its loss-making implement lines and concentrate on the manufacture of higher-profit agricultural tractors. When its combine line was discontinued in 1972, Case, a pioneer in grain threshing, was no longer a long-line farm equipment manufacturer. In the realignment of facilities brought on by this decision, Case closed the Rockford, Illinois, plant, where it had been since 1928 when it acquired the agricultural line of Emerson-Brantingham.[46]

Management Changes: Reorganization

Wishing to have its own employee heading the Case operation, Tenneco named as chairman Nelson W. Freeman, who replaced Merritt D. Hill. The job of president and CEO went to James Ketelson, formerly of Price Waterhouse, who in thirteen years with Case had become vice president of operations. Recognizing that the staid old company needed fresh thinking, he brought in several top executives from the outside. For the first time the Construction Equipment Division became a separate operating division that had its own marketing and plants.[47] Ketelson, when he later became CEO of Tenneco, was always a loyal champion of J. I. Case. Recognizing that Tenneco, which had only 56 percent control of Case, might not be willing to provide the financial support Case would need, Ketelson convinced Tenneco's CEO, Gardiner Symonds, to acquire total control, which happened in 1969–70.[48]

In 1972 Ketelson received the call to join Tenneco's corporate staff in Houston as executive vice president of finance. His replacement as Case's CEO was Thomas J. Guendel, whom Ketelson had brought in from WABCO in 1969 to run the Construction Equipment Division.[49]

Overseas Expansion

With the backing of Tenneco, Case moved to strengthen its overseas business, which in 1967 had accounted for only 11 percent of sales.[50] With other American and national manufacturers already battling for a share of the European farm market, Case realized that it, a late-comer with no line of implements, would have little chance and so decided to concentrate in Europe on construction equipment. The Vierzon, France, plant had been building loader-backhoes since 1962 and by the early 1970s was the largest producer on the Continent. Case also had the Vibromax plant in West Germany, and crawler tractors were being assembled at the Leeds, U.K., farm tractor plant. In 1972 the company acquired a 50 percent interest in CALSA, Spain's leading manufacturer of wheel loaders, which employed 350 and had a 147,000-square-foot plant in Zaragoza.[51] The next year Case acquired control, enlarged the plant, and rationalized its wheel loaders with the U.S. product.[52] Overall, by the early 1970s Case had established a strong construction equipment presence in Western Europe.

To strengthen its strategy of being a tractor-only manufacturer in the agricultural market, in 1972 Case paid $19 million to acquire David Brown, Ltd., a British farm tractor manufacturer that had sales of $80 million during 1971. David Brown was to manufacture models under one hundred horsepower while Racine built the larger sizes.[53]

Construction and agricultural equipment plants were established in Brazil, and a construction equipment plant was added in Australia in the early 1970s.[54]

Product Development

Case, which had entered the decade as a producer only of light construction equipment, by 1975 had grown its line well into the medium range. The three-cubic-yard W26B topped the six-model wheel loader line with a 180-horsepower Case engine, and the 1150 remained the largest bulldozer and track loader in the line. In 1971 the improved B-Series Construction King loader-backhoes were introduced.[55] By 1975 Case was offering seven models of small and mid-range hydraulic excavators under the Case and Drott names.[56] Most impressive was the increased breadth of line, which included compaction equipment, log-skidders, forklifts, ditchers, skid-steer loaders, and mobile cranes. In 1975 Case unified the differing paint schemes of its construction equipment divisions under a common color scheme, "Power Yellow" with black accents, and a common logo.[57]

Case: Third-Largest in Construction Equipment

Although the Kern County Land Company acquisition no doubt saved Case from bankruptcy in 1964, it was Tenneco's deep pockets that built the Case Construction Equipment Division, which by 1975 accounted for more than 60 percent of Case's business. Between 1966 and 1975 Case surpassed Allis-Chalmers to become the third-largest U.S. producer of construction equipment. It was close on the heels of International Harvester, the second-ranked producer.[58] Case's numerous acquisitions had helped it outstrip its rival, Deere, which had entered the light construction equipment business at about the same time. By 1975 the company was firmly established as the world leader in loader-backhoes, the mainstay of its construction equipment product line that contributed nearly half of the division's revenues. Case continued its dual distribution system but with increasing emphasis on company-owned stores, which numbered about 150 in 1975.[59] With the funds available to it from its parent, Case expanded its overseas business to 29 percent of the total by 1975. Most of the increase came from construction equipment.[60]

In the early 1970s, after twenty years of either outright losses or very small profits, the decision to exit its unprofitable farm implement business and increases in volume from construction equipment began to create profits for Case. Net operating revenue topped $1 billion for the first time in 1974, with an operating profit of $103 million.[61] But would Tenneco, now a high-flying conglomerate, be satisfied with the return on its steadily mounting investment? The next decade would be a time when Case would have to prove itself to its patient parent.

Deere & Company

Ending the 1956–65 decade with sales of $866 million, Deere topped the billion-dollar mark for the first time during the next year but then saw sales stagnate throughout the late 1960s and reach only $1.137 billion in 1970.[62] During this period U.S. farm equipment demand was in one of its cyclical slumps, but Deere had experienced those before. What was alarming to Deere's top management, however, were the losses from overseas operations, primarily the Deere-Lanz Company in Germany. In the ten years since it was acquired it had never turned a profit, and losses during the late 1960s began to threaten Deere's health. For example, 1967 operating losses from overseas operations totaled $32.8 million on sales of $151 million.[63]

One possible solution to the seemingly intractable problem of losses in Europe was to form a joint venture with a European farm equipment manufacturer. Discussions took place in 1966 and again in 1970 with Klockner-Humboldt-Deutz, the leading German producer, but foundered on Deutz's demand that the joint venture have rights to sell in North America, something to which Deere would never agree.[64] Still seeking a way to stop the bleeding overseas, in 1971 Deere began negotiations with Fiat on a 50-50 joint venture that would pool not only their farm but also their construction equipment operations in Europe, South Africa, and South America. At this point Deere's European construction equipment business was tiny; Fiat was Italy's leading construction equipment producer but had a smaller presence in other countries of the EC. Perhaps there would have been synergy, but after more than a year of deep negotiations Deere backed away and ended its search for an overseas partner.[65]

In the late 1950s and through the 1960s, when a window of opportunity existed for launching its construction equipment in Europe, Deere's preoccupation with its loss-making farm equipment business absorbed its full attention. Deere's construction equipment never really got off the ground in Europe.

Growth in North America

The years between 1966 and 1975 were full of remarkable accomplishment for Deere construction equipment in North America. Entering the period with just two small crawler bulldozer/loaders, a line of loader-backhoes, and a small elevating scraper, over the next ten years the company regularly updated those products and broadened its line to include log-skidders, wheel loaders, a motor grader, a hydraulic excavator, and rough-terrain lift trucks. The new Deere industrial machines were utilitarian, sturdy, and cheap to manufacture, gaining economies of scale wherever possible by using components from the agriculture line.

Demonstrating that its industrial products were not just converted farm machines, in 1967 Deere introduced the JD570 motor grader. It was the world's first grader with frame articulation and led Caterpillar's articulated models by six years. Consistent with Deere's other products, the eighty-three-horsepower JD570 was targeted at light construction equipment buyers even though the big market for graders was in 115-horsepower and larger sizes.[66] The next year the JD544 wheel loader was introduced, followed a year later by the JD644. The two models, with articulation, inboard-mounted wet-disc brakes, planetary final drives, and front-mounted lift arms, were state-of-the-art in their size classes. The JD644 was in the 2.5-cubic-yard mid-range and put the industry on notice that Deere would not be satisfied building only low-end products. Further proof came the same year with the introduction of 131-horsepower JD690 hydraulic excavator. Although the JD690 lagged European excavators in hydraulic sophistication, it was well targeted to the U.S. market of the day. In perhaps its most ambitious product move, Deere announced the JD860, a 215-horsepower, fifteen-cubic-yard, elevating scraper of overhung design to go with the smaller JD760-A, a three-axle machine.[67]

Deere and Its Distribution Organization

From the early days when it targeted rural conservation contractors with its converted farm equipment, Deere, like Case, was now aiming its line of integrated earthmoving products squarely at the small- and medium-sized contractor engaged in site development, sewer and water work, landscaping, and residential streets without neglecting those conservation contractors; in addition, it was building a strong position with pulpwood loggers.

Unlike Case, which resorted to company-owned stores, Deere was building a distribution organization solely of privately owned dealers. To accommodate its broader line, in 1970 Deere designated construction dealers, utility dealers, and forestry dealers, which allowed increased specialization.[68] It also permitted Deere to appoint more dealers who, with responsibility for only a part of the Deere line, could be started up with a smaller capital investment. The ones that succeeded could then be given responsibility for additional products. But starting an industrial dealer organization from scratch was not easy. Drawing on years of experience with small farm equipment dealers, Deere knew there would be few qualified candidates that had adequate capital, and thinly capitalized dealerships tended to fail during recessions. In the early years of establishing its industrial dealer organization, its approach was more like the practices of the farm equipment industry than the earthmoving equipment industry in areas of dealer administration, payment terms, financing, and inventories. In John Deere Credit it had an aggressive and flexible financing organization that contributed heavily to Deere's success in building a dealer organization.

ERA III

Industrial sales rose from $157 million in 1966 to $217 million in 1970 and more than doubled to $465 million by 1974.[69] In 1973 Deere announced the construction of a five-hundred-thousand-square-foot industrial components plant in Davenport to supplement Dubuque.[70] A year later it announced that it was adding 750,000 square feet at Davenport and 822,000 square feet at Dubuque.[71] Along with these expansions of its earthmoving equipment manufacturing capacity, Deere held a worldwide sales meeting in Moline to announce an ambitious product plan for what it called "ERA III," the next five years. With unusual openness for a traditionally secretive industry, Deere made no bones about having plans to push further into the mid-range class by adding several larger machines—an excavator, four motor graders, a wheel loader, and two models of hydrostatic crawler bulldozer/loaders.[72]

Gains in North America, Weakness in Europe

Although the U.S. recession of 1974–75 brought a downtick in 1975's industrial sales at $411 million, Deere's total sales overall of $2.95 billion had more than doubled since 1970 and more than tripled since 1965.[73] After twenty years as CEO, William Hewitt could be proud of his accomplishments. North American industrial sales had surpassed those of Allis-Chalmers—making Deere the fourth-largest after Caterpillar, International Harvester, and Case—but industrial sales remained only about one-sixth of Deere volume compared to more than 60 percent for Case.[74] Deere's overseas business accounted for less than 20 percent of total sales during the mid-1970s but was at last profitable.[75] The company had made little headway in developing overseas industrial business, however. Europe was full of competitors building industrial machines in Deere's product range. To focus on making the European farm equipment business profitable meant that the company had not made the investments necessary to mount a real effort in the industrial business. It was probably too late now.

Unlike Case, Deere's earthmoving product line was entirely internally generated. The conservative Deere management had shunned acquisitions as a shortcut to growing its industrial business. Thus it presented a more uniform and integrated product line, albeit at the price of slower growth. Also unlike Case, Deere avoided company-owned stores, slowly building an independent dealer organization but one with better profitability. It was a policy that would pay dividends in the future.

Allis-Chalmers

After years of stagnation it appeared that Allis-Chalmers, under the leadership of its CEO, Robert S. Stevenson, had finally turned the corner in 1966 with record sales of $860 million and a profit of $26.1 million. Of total sales, 28 percent (about $240 million) was contributed by earthmoving equipment, 30 percent by farm equipment, and the balance by industrial and electrical products. The company had twenty-seven plants, thirty-five thousand employees, and an incredible one thousand products.[76] But the highly diversified and asset-rich old-line company, with a reputation for being an underperformer, was a natural for takeover. A-C's nightmare began in 1967 as Wall Street speculation built that the company was "in play."

A-C as a Takeover Target

In August 1967 James Ling, CEO of Ling-Temco-Vought and regarded as perhaps the top takeover artist of the day, announced a $250 million tender offer for control of A-C's common and preferred stock subject to no opposition from A-C's board. At $45 per share, the offer was certainly attractive to A-C stockholders, but the board, with total holdings of only 0.3 percent of the stock, chose to fight the takeover. Giving as a reason that A-C had held prior talks with General Dynamics on a proposed merger and wished to pursue that avenue, Stevenson rejected LTV's offer.[77]

Two days later, LTV raised its offer to $590 million for 100 percent of A-C's stock, at the time the largest tender offer ever made. Ling claimed that the offer was worth $55 to $60 per share, but again the A-C board rejected it. Two days later it was withdrawn, and LTV ceased its effort to acquire A-C. Within two weeks, negotiations for a friendly merger with General Dynamics were terminated when that company would offer no more than $32 per share for A-C common stock.[78]

These events were merely the beginning of a series of crises for A-C that would extend into 1971. Continuously during this time the company was either seeking a friendly merger or being subjected to further unfriendly takeover attempts. Names figuring in the saga included Kleiner, Bell and Company, Signal Oil and Gas, City Investing Company, and Gulf and Western. Finally, White Consolidated Industries came to own 31 percent of A-C's common shares in 1968. Believing it needed an executive with more savvy in the rough-and-tumble of the merger and acquisition game, in mid-1968 the A-C board hired David C. Scott, fifty-two, an executive vice president of Colt Industries, as president. Six months later Stevenson, sixty-two, apparently overwhelmed by events, opted for early retirement, and Scott succeeded him.

Scott's first problem was dealing with a proxy fight by White for control of the board. The showdown was to be the 1969 annual meeting, but before that took place the Federal Trade Commission announced that it would issue a complaint against White to prevent its takeover of A-C. That led to drawn-out legal maneuverings that reached the U.S. Supreme Court and to repeated postponements of the annual meeting. Ultimately, White was enjoined from voting its shares, and after eighteen postponements the 1969 annual meeting was held in January 1970. In 1971 White disposed of its A-C stock and booked a loss of $63.2 million. Allis-Chalmers had dodged the bullet.[79]

The Struggle for Profits

The battle to remain independent had not been without its costs in diversion of management resources and damaged corporate morale. In the midst of fighting a takeover, the company was hit by the 1970–71 recession. A-C was in serious trouble.[80]

Year	Sales (millions)	Profit (millions)	Profit (percent)
1967	$ 822	$ 5	0.6
1968	777	(54)	—
1969	805	18	2.3
1970	870	15	1.7
1971	889	5	0.6
1972	960	9	0.9
1973	1,166	16	1.4

In seven years the company had netted only $14 million in profits on $6.28 billion in sales. In hindsight, those results made LTV's $55 per share tender offer of 1967 look extremely attractive. A-C's Construction Machinery Division continued to produce 25 to 30 percent of the company's sales during this period but had become a loss-making operation. With minuscule profits, the company could not begin to meet its five divisions' needs for capital and research and development.

With the minimal funds available to it, the Construction Machinery Division tried valiantly to keep the line competitive, but it was steadily losing ground. In the heavy machinery segment it could not keep up with Caterpillar. Now a powerful new competitor, Komatsu, loomed while Deere and Case were pushing aggressively into the light and mid-range segments. A-C lacked hydraulic excavators, which were grabbing a growing portion of the construction equipment pie, and funding internal development of them was out of the question. A-C's position in the construction equipment business was becoming untenable. Something had to be done to get the business off A-C's books, but the company's delicate financial condition would not support heavy write-downs. Yet who would pay even book value for the fifth-ranked U.S. construction equipment producer that was losing money and market share?

A Joint Venture with Fiat

Incredibly, David Scott found a solution. In July 1973 A-C announced that it was pooling its construction equipment business with that of Fiat S.p.A. in a joint venture, Fiat-Allis. For a 35 percent interest in the venture, A-C would not only get a loss-making business off its books but would also receive a much needed $47 million in cash and notes from Fiat in a balancing of A-C's share of the assets contributed. These included plants in

Springfield and Deerfield, Illinois, in Essendine, U.K., and in Brazil. The deal was effective in January 1974.[81]

Fiat, a $3.6 billion corporation, had an estimated $140 million compared to A-C's $198 million in construction equipment sales in 1972.[82] In a highly fragmented Italian industry, Fiat was the largest producer, building small and medium track-type tractors and track loaders. It needed A-C's more advanced technology and larger models to become a major player in Europe, but Fiat could contribute nothing in products or technology to strengthen the venture's North American operations.

With a new, powerful partner, the former Allis-Chalmers North American operation gained renewed confidence, but aside from the name on the products nothing else really changed. At ConExpo '75 Fiat products were incorporated with the Allis-Chalmers line in the Fiat-Allis display.

A New Partnership

The decade had been very difficult for Allis-Chalmers. It was a near miracle that the struggling company had survived as an independent entity, and perhaps stockholders' interests would have been better served by a merger. But it had successfully spun off its money-losing earthmoving equipment business. Once one of the "Big Three" of the earthmoving equipment industry, the Allis-Chalmers brand had now disappeared, supplanted by the new name: Fiat-Allis. Would the resources of the big Italian company create a new, rejuvenated competitor, or had Allis-Chalmers's construction equipment business already lost too much ground to be redeemed? The industry watched.

International Harvester

Between 1966 and 1975 Harvester was able to double its sales, reaching $5.25 billion in 1975, but its chief rivals, Deere in farm equipment and Caterpillar in construction equipment, grew faster. Their sales tripled, Deere's to $2.96 billion and Caterpillar's to $4.96 billion. CEO Harry Bercher hoped that the record $109.7 million profit in 1966 signaled a turnaround in Harvester's abysmal profitability, but instead the slack farm market in the late 1960s and the 1970–71 recession drove profits down. They bottomed out in 1971 at $45.2 million, only 1.54 percent on sales of $2.93 billion.[83]

That same year, Bercher retired after nine frustrating years of trying to stimulate the lethargic giant. His replacement, Brooks McCormick, fifty-four, brought new and much needed vitality to the office of CEO. He also brought a patrician background in the farm machinery business as the great-grandson of Cyrus McCormick's younger brother William and the son of Marion Deering McCormick, granddaughter of William Deering. But he had served his apprenticeship at Harvester, starting in 1940 after his graduation from Yale University. Working his way up through a variety of positions in manufacturing and marketing, both overseas and in the United States, he joined the board in 1958 and was named president and chief operating officer in 1968. After a twenty-year hiatus a McCormick was again running the Old Lady of North Michigan Avenue.

While top management at Harvester had for years commiserated over consistent losses from some of the company's operations, Brooks McCormick was prepared to do something about it. Wisconsin Steel was put up for sale in the early 1970s, but it would be several years before a buyer was found. McCormick also took IH out of the loss-making pickup truck business in 1975. With production of only eighty thousand units per year, Harvester was not able to compete with Detroit.[84] By the mid-1970s McCormick faced the fact that the company would never realize a decent return from the assets employed in its construction equipment business, but getting out presented big problems. Finding a buyer for an also-ran construction equipment business would not be easy, and the business, accounting for about 15 percent of Harvester's volume, was too large to write off. Also to be considered were the division's unfunded pension liabilities and its loyal dealers. Unable to find a buyer, IH was not able to rid itself of its construction equipment incubus during the 1970s.[85]

Soon after taking over, Brooks McCormick began pushing to obtain changes in Harvester's UAW contract. The company had believed for some time that its competitors had more favorable UAW contracts than Harvester, one reason for its higher costs. During 1973 contract negotiations, a strike occurred principally over the issue of compulsory overtime and took out 40,500 UAW members at twenty-five IH plants in eleven states. Harvester had bargained this away during the 1950s while its competitors had retained the right to require overtime. After fifteen days, management caved in and gained only a meaningless token concession from the union.[86] No further efforts would be made on this front until the disastrous strike of 1979–80.

Product Development

Throughout the period between 1966 and 1975 Harvester did a creditable job of keeping its product line current; every model received at least one update. By the end of the decade, the strong Hough wheel loader line consisted of eight articulated models and three small straight-frame machines. Hough was just beginning to replace the H-prefix wheel loaders with the much improved 500-Series, with the 7.5-cubic-yard 560 and the big twenty-two-cubic-yard 580 already in the line. A line of loader-backhoes had been introduced in the early 1970s but were not doing particularly well against Case, Deere, and Massey-Ferguson. The wheel tractor-scraper line had been reworked into a five-model line of two conventional and three elevating models, from the 150-horsepower Model 412 through the Model 433, which was tandem-powered and had 495 horsepower and twenty-one cubic yards. Off-highway trucks had also been improved and now formed a 300-Series, three-model line that ranged from thirty-six to fifty tons.[87] Seeing the trend to hydraulic excavators but unwilling to fund internal development, the company entered the business by acquiring a small French

A Hough 580 wheel-loader. The 500–Series included the top-of-the-line, twenty-two-cubic-yard, 1,075-horsepower model 580. (State Historical Society of Wisconsin negative no. WHi[X3]51371)

excavator manufacturer, Yumbo, in 1970. Yumbo ran a weak fourth in France to Poclain, then the largest European excavator manufacturer; Liebherr; and Richier, which made excavators, wheel loaders, and compaction equipment.[88]

With a myriad of European excavator manufacturers in the 1970s producing increasingly sophisticated machines, Harvester's small excavator operation never had a chance in the EC. In 1975 two small Yumbo excavators were being marketed in the United States, but as the dollar weakened throughout the 1970s Harvester, like other European producers trying to sell in the United States, found the going tough indeed. The company had more success in Europe building Hough wheel loaders in a plant at Heidelburg, Germany, and mid-range track-type tractors and loaders in Doncaster, England.

In a cost-cutting move, Harvester finally merged the Hough and Construction Equipment divisions to form a new Payline Division in 1974.[89]

A Glimmer of Hope

After the 1970–71 recession the U.S. construction equipment industry entered a three-year boom. Boosted by large orders from the Soviet Union, the IH Construction Equipment Division had its most profitable years ever in 1974 and 1975. Sales went from $448 million in 1971 to $887 million in 1975, when the division's share of corporate sales peaked at 17.9 percent. But hopes were quickly dashed the next year when sales, with the slow recovery of the construction industry from the 1975 downturn, fell 25 percent and the division again lost money. The 1975 peak was not topped until 1979, and after 1975 division sales each year accounted for only around 12 percent of the corporate total.[90]

Deepening Profit Problems

With the exception of 1966, International Harvester's profitability on sales never exceeded 3 percent between 1966 and 1975. As volume rose the profit-starved company had no choice but to increase borrowings, and its ratio of debt to total capitalization grew from 27 percent in 1971 to 41 percent in 1975. That year Standard and Poor lowered its rating on Harvester's senior debt, increasing the company's already high interest expense and further exacerbating its cash problems. Still, the early 1970s had seen a strong resurgence in Harvester's more profitable farm equipment business, even exceeding recession-dampened truck sales in 1975 for the first time in twenty years. That year Brooks McCormick publicly discussed Harvester's intention to overtake Deere.[91] It seemed that he had the venerable old company finally moving in the right direction. Unlike his predecessors, McCormick was prepared to rid the company of its losers, but first he had to find buyers for them. That was proving difficult.

Branded a loser and starved of product development funds, in the mid-1970s the IH construction equipment business marked time and watched the gap widen between it and its more profitable rivals.

The LeTourneau-Westinghouse Division of WABCO

Acquisition by American Standard

Fifteen years after the acquisition of LeTourneau by the Westinghouse Airbrake Company, the parent became the object of a takeover battle when American Standard Inc. and the Crane Company fought for control of WABCO. Believing the terms of the American Standard offer to be more favorable, the WABCO board supported that company in the bitter fight even though Crane had acquired 30 percent of WABCO's stock. After Crane's attempt to enjoin the merger was denied, the merger was consummated on June 7, 1968, and the construction equipment business became one step further removed from corporate top management. Thirty-eight percent of WABCO's 1967 sales of $305 million had been by the LeTourneau-Westinghouse Division, and American Standard's sales in 1967 were $600 million. Lewis J. Burger was named vice president of American Standard's Industrial and Construction Products Division. The LeTourneau name was suppressed, and products took on the acronym WABCO.[92]

Diversification Efforts

Although LeTourneau-Westinghouse had made a good diversification with its Haulpak off-highway trucks, it was still handicapped in competing with full-line competitors. In a step to correct that in 1967 it acquired a small manufacturer of wheel loaders, the Scoopmobile Company of Portland, Oregon, which had sales of about $5.5 million.[93] The move got the company nowhere against the powerful competitors already established in the wheel loader business. Scoopmobile remained a fractional player.

A more surprising but no more effective effort at diversification was a

1967 agreement with Komatsu to market its full line of track-type equipment in the United States.[94] As its first attempt to crack the U.S. market, the agreement was likely even more crucial to Komatsu than L-W. At the time, Komatsu's name was not well known in the United States, and imported construction equipment in general had not achieved acceptance with American customers. But L-W dealers were not overly receptive to having a line of Japanese products suddenly imposed on them, with all the training costs and investment in parts inventory and service tools that entailed. The effort was unsuccessful. Many of the few machines that were sold received less than adequate dealer parts and service support, which created a negative image of Komatsu products in the United States that the company would struggle to overcome. After four or five years the agreement was quietly wound up. Although the effort was probably counterproductive as a means of introducing Komatsu products to the United States, Komatsu undoubtedly benefited by the experience of doing business in the U.S. machinery market. It would put that experience to good use later when it began building its own North American dealer organization.

Product Development

Under American Standard ownership, WABCO continued to concentrate on its Haulpak line of off-highway trucks, developing ever-larger models, and its revenues from sales to the mining industry began to exceed substantially its construction industry business. It moved from the 120A, a 105-ton off-highway truck of 1965, to the 120B, which was rated from 100 to 130 tons on 30.00-51 tires. By 1970 it offered a 150-ton model, and by 1975 the 170C. All were electric-drive, two-axle units. In 1970 WABCO began testing its mammoth 3200, a three-axle, two-thousand-horsepower unit on ten 33.00-51 tires.[95] The largest off-highway truck then in series production, the 3200's initial 200-ton rating was quickly raised to 235 tons. (The later 3200B model was rated at 250 tons.) At this point, WABCO and Unit Rig Lectra-Haul were the principal competitors for the business of the large open-pit mines.

On the construction equipment side, the motor grader line was upgraded throughout the 1960s, offering a nine-model range of power-shift and direct-drive options topped by the 230-horsepower, 41,000-pound Model 888.[96] The introduction of the articulated Deere and Caterpillar graders, however, established a standard that WABCO, with its rigid-frame machines, never chose to match. As a result, it steadily lost ground in the motor grader business.

A WABCO 3200 off-highway truck. (Komatsu Mining Systems)

During the early 1960s L-W had entered the elevating scraper business and introduced its small Model D with a Hancock scraper. Soon it extended this upward to the Model C and then applied the principle to its largest Model B. By the mid-1960s, in the apparent belief that it could gain competitive advantage with elevating scrapers over conventional models, it was emphasizing those models. In 1969 it introduced the BT333F, a thirty-four-cubic-yard, tandem-powered scraper that evolved into the 353FT; at 1,025 horsepower it was the ultimate in size and horsepower in elevating scrapers.[97] Although the elevating scraper, because of the cost and weight of its elevating mechanism, never threatened conventional push-loaded scrapers for mass earthmoving, the elevator had an important niche. WABCO's strong push into this type of machine forced other manufacturers to meet its initiative.

A Poor Payoff for American Standard

WABCO construction and mining equipment initially was grouped with pneumatic and drilling equipment and the power and controls group to form the Industrial and Construction Products Division of American Standard. In 1972 the LeRoi pneumatic equipment line was sold off to Dresser Industries and the drilling equipment was also disposed of, the two lines having accounted for $28 million in sales in 1971.

From $131 million in 1966, sales of construction and mining equipment (including LeRoi and drilling) grew rather slowly and reached $197 million in 1971. With the sell-off, sales fell to $161 million in 1972 and then reached $216 million in 1974 and a record $268 million in 1975. The division's contribution to American Standard sales ranged from 10 to 14 percent until 1975, when it jumped to 17 percent. Operating profits of the Industrial and Construction Products Division were generally mediocre throughout the period, ranging from 4 to 8 percent and peaking at 11 percent in 1975.[98]

One could logically ask what a bathroom fixture company inexperienced in capital goods was doing in the off-highway truck business, but such were frequently the results of the merger and acquisition mania. In any case, WABCO construction and mining equipment did little to enhance the overall profitability of American Standard, nor did being a small part of a larger, diversified company make WABCO any more successful in its chosen industries.

The Clark Equipment Company

New Lines

Clark continued to grow and profit between 1966 and 1975 and more than tripled its volume, but its Michigan-brand construction equipment business suffered from lack of breadth. To correct this weakness the company made three acquisitions: Hancock Scraper, the Melrose Company, and Baldwin-Lima-Hamilton (BLH). Hancock, a pioneer in elevating scrapers, was acquired in 1966. Melrose, a private company with sales of about $24 million, pioneered the development of the small skid-steer loader under the brand name Melroe Bobcat. Acquired in 1969, the Bobcats rounded out the lower end of Clark's wheel loader line.[99]

With BLH, acquired in 1971, came the Lima line of power shovels, draglines, and cranes; a line of wheel loaders that Clark discontinued; and the Austin-Western line of motor graders and road rollers. BLH had fallen prey to an acquisition by Armor and Company in 1965 and as a division of Armor had sales of $64.7 million in 1970.[100] A very old name, the Austin-Western motor grader had unique features of mechanical all-wheel drive and the ability to steer the rear wheels and front wheels independently, but weak marketing kept market share low. The acquisition did little to change that, nor did it have a significant strengthening effect for the Michigan product line.

Product Development: The Big Loader

During the mid-1960s Clark entered the wheel log-skidder business with its line of Ranger-brand products. During the late 1960s Clark introduced its articulated Series III loaders, bringing the product line up to date. During the decade, large wheel loaders gradually won acceptance in rock applications in both construction and mining. In construction, growth in haul-unit size called for larger loading equipment, but power shovels of appropriate size were impractical to move from job to job. Wheel loaders filled the bill and finally put an end to power shovels in construction. Miners also liked large wheel loaders for their mobility and as backup for production loading equipment. Clark had pioneered the large wheel loader business with its 375 and

The industry's largest machine when introduced, the Michigan 675 had two engines totaling 1,316 horsepower and weighed 194 tons on 67.00-51 tires. (Historical Construction Equipment Association)

475 models, and in 1975 it took a quantum leap with the twenty-four-cubic-yard 675, which was aimed squarely at the mining industry.[101] Perhaps a bit ahead of its time, the lumbering 675 was not well accepted by the mining fraternity.

The Move South

Needing more space for its growing construction equipment business, in 1975 Clark announced that it would build a 309,000-square-foot plant in Asheville, North Carolina, thus becoming the first construction equipment company to move south in search of lower-cost labor. Others would emulate Clark in the coming years. The 1- to 2.5-cubic-yard Michigan loaders were moved to Asheville, and the remainder of the line continued at Benton Harbor.[102]

Clark, a Wheel Loader Specialist

Clark broke the billion-dollar mark in sales in 1973 and reached more than $1.4 billion in 1975. Profits between 1970 and 1975 were steady if unspectacular, ranging from $29 million in the 1971 recession year to $55 million and averaging $40 to $45 million. The company had become a multinational and had plants in the United Kingdom, France, West Germany, Brazil, Argentina, and Australia, with construction equipment usually sharing manufacturing facilities with lift trucks.[103] As a wheel loader specialist, Clark-Michigan was particularly effective with the rock products industry but continued to be handicapped by its rather narrow product line when competing in the construction market. Efforts to diversify its construction equipment line had not been successful. The coming decade would put that weakness to the test.

Massey-Ferguson

Massey-Ferguson began the 1966–75 decade with worldwide sales of $932 million. Deere, with sales of $1.06 billion, had grown faster during the previous ten years and was now a shade ahead of M-F, but M-F claimed world leadership in unit sales of farm tractors. With 42 percent of its volume in North America, it was third in North American farm sales behind Deere and International Harvester. In an effort to strengthen its image in the U.S. farm equipment industry, M-F moved the headquarters of its North

American operations in 1966, along with some implement production from Toronto, to the heart of the Corn Belt: Des Moines, Iowa.[104] Slower off the mark in establishing its industrial and construction equipment business (the ICM line) than Case and Deere, M-F's industrial sales in 1966 were about $75 million compared to $157 million for Deere and slightly more for Case.[105] Sales came mainly from loader-backhoes. But M-F liked the construction equipment business and had aggressive plans to expand it.

Construction Equipment Expansion

With Landini already building small crawlers, M-F chose Italy for its first new construction equipment plant. It announced in 1966 that it would build a 350,000-square-foot manufacturing facility in Aprilia, south of Rome, to produce construction equipment in the EEC.[106] The line, launched in 1968, consisted of the MF300 and MF500, small-to-mid-range track-type tractors and track loaders, and the MF33, MF44, and MF55, which were 1.25- to 2.5-cubic-yard wheel loaders. Also introduced were two small track excavators.[107] In 1969 came the construction of a five-hundred-thousand-square-foot plant in Manchester, England, primarily for the production of loader-backhoes that drew on engines from Perkins at Peterborough and components from M-F's large farm tractor plant at Coventry.[108] In 1970 M-F purchased the Lorain wheel loader line from Koehring, which consisted of three models from three to six cubic yards.[109]

The Hanomag Acquisition

Perhaps impatient with the slow progress of its ICM line, in 1974 M-F snapped at the opportunity to acquire (for $45.2 million cash) the West German firm Hanomag AG, which made small to mid-range track-type tractors, track loaders, and wheel loaders.[110] Hanomag, an old-line farm tractor manufacturer with antecedents dating back to 1835, had entered the construction equipment business after World War II and had withdrawn from the farm tractor business in 1971.[111] Earlier, the company was acquired by Rheinstahl AG, a steel maker that had become financially troubled and wished to dispose of the reportedly unprofitable equipment business. Hanomag, with a three-million-square-foot plant in Hannover, had highly integrated products, including its own diesel engines, which, considering its relatively low volumes, almost assured Hanomag of being a high-cost producer. With the acquisition, M-F gained a reservoir of customer loyalty in

Germany; Hanomag had an estimated 25 to 30 percent share in the lines in which it competed. Elsewhere in the EEC, however, it had little standing, and it was totally unknown in North America. Hanomag's 1974 sales were about $94 million.[112]

M-F announced a plan to market Hanomag products worldwide and followed it up at ConExpo '75 by showing, under the M-F logo, three Hanomag wheel loaders, 2.8- to 5- cubic yards; two track-type tractors, 144 and 180 horsepower; and a 2.4-cubic-yard track loader.[113] Surprisingly, M-F, experienced multinational that it was, failed to reckon on the steadily weakening dollar in relation to the strengthening German mark, which soon complicated any plans it had for Hanomag sales in North America. Unable to gain improved economies of scale in an already high-cost producer, M-F was left with the same unsatisfactory situation that existed under Rheinstahl ownership. It had purchased a loss-making operation that brought with it some market share in Germany but little else.

Slow Progress in Construction Equipment

Despite these large expenditures, M-F's push into the construction equipment business made a very small impression on the North American industry. Outside North America, the loader-backhoe business proved to be the most successful aspect, eventually achieving respectable market shares of as much as 22 percent in Germany, 18 percent in France, and 11 percent in the United Kingdom. The North American market share, however, against strong competition in a large, twenty-to-thirty-thousand-unit industry, was smaller—in the 5 to 7 percent range.[114]

That M-F was able to achieve at least modest success with its loader-backhoes but much less with its crawlers, wheel loaders, and excavators illustrates the much higher standard required of the distribution organization to market heavier types of construction equipment successfully. Case handled the problem by using company stores. Deere's construction equipment product line evolved more slowly, which allowed for a more gradual development of its dealers' capabilities. M-F entered the field late and tried to leap-frog into mid-sized products with a dealer organization that did not have the financial resources and marketing capabilities to sell and support a new line of more costly and sophisticated products. In addition, the products themselves offered little if any differentiation in a marketplace where customer brand loyalties were already well established. The company, with little experience in the construction equipment industry, had set itself a very difficult task.

Still, progress was made. Sales of the ICM Division reached a respectable $355 million in 1975, 14 percent of corporate total.[115] Although that was 86 percent of Deere's 1975 industrial sales volume, Deere's share of the $5 billion North American market, at 7 to 8 percent, was likely about double that of Massey-Ferguson's.

Poor Profitability

Riding up on the boom of the 1970s, M-F's farm equipment business grew dramatically. Aided by the growth in ICM and Perkins engines sales, corporate volume reached $2.5 billion in 1975. But Massey-Ferguson, like International Harvester, underperformed in profits. And again like International Harvester, M-F would soon have to decide how much longer it could afford a loss-making construction equipment business.

The Euclid Division of General Motors

The Euclid Divestiture

After more than eight years of litigation with the Department of Justice's Antitrust Division, General Motors, in a consent decree, agreed to divest the portion of its earthmoving product line acquired in 1953 from the Euclid Road Machinery Company: off-highway trucks and bottom-dumps. Paying $24 million cash, the White Motor Company took over on July 1, 1968. It acquired the Euclid name, the old Euclid plant in Cleveland, and the rights to sell the products through the fifty dealers composing the North American GM/Euclid dealer organization. Dealers would continue to sell the GM earthmoving products not affected by the decree: scrapers, wheel loaders, and track-type tractors. For a time, GM continued to build Euclid products from its Motherwell, Scotland, plant.[116]

The Birth of Terex

Having lost the name *Euclid* in the United States, General Motors renamed its earthmoving business the "Terex Division" and retained its "Hi-lite Green" color. Knowing that divestiture of its trucks would be a likely outcome, GM had spent little on them since the government brought suit in 1959 but had concentrated instead on other products. Four new wheel loaders were introduced in 1966 under a new nomenclature, the 7200-Series. The models were updated, and the ten-cubic-yard 72-81 was added in 1969. From its original two-model line of track-type tractors, the TC-12 and C-6, it added two models and adopted a new nomenclature. The line became the 82-30, 82-30T, 82-40, and 82-80. Scrapers received updates and had no change in nomenclature.[117]

Terex and the Off-Highway Truck Business

In 1973 Terex reentered the already crowded off-highway truck business and introduced a new line that by 1975 had reached five models that ranged from the 33-05 at twenty-eight tons to the 33-15 at 150 tons.[118] Incorporating modern frame, body, and suspension designs, the units were superior to the old line purchased by White.

The Terex 3300-Series line included this fifty-five-ton 33-09, but Terex was never able to regain the dominant position once held by Euclid in the off-highway truck business. (Historical Construction Equipment Association)

Terex: A Disappointing Venture for GM

In 1975, sixteen years after the Justice Department filed suit, General Motors had come full circle. Its Terex Division seemed more competitive than ever with a broader and updated product line that included new off-highway trucks, but the promise of the 1950s had never materialized. Emphasis continued to be on mid-range and larger machines, and thus Terex focused on medium- and large-sized earthmoving contractors and open-pit mines, a fairly narrow audience. Its scrapers had numerous loyal partisans among earthmoving contractors, although it lost considerable ground in the mining industry when it allowed its truck line to become obsolete during the government suit and then was out of the business for five years. Although Terex did build track-type tractors and wheel loaders, the company remained a hauling unit specialist in the eyes of most equipment buyers. By 1975, twenty-two years after entering the earthmoving equipment business, it is doubtful that the venture had measured up to the hopes of the General Motors top management.

The White Motor Company

Until it acquired the Oliver, Minneapolis-Moline, and Cockshutt farm equipment companies in the early 1960s, White had remained within its specialty of building heavy on-highway trucks. Although its share of the truck market was declining, in 1968 it still claimed 21 percent of that business in the United States.[119] After the Euclid acquisition in that same year, White took on a similarity to International Harvester in that each had trucks and farm and earthmoving equipment. The two companies were similar in another way as well. Neither was very profitable.

White and Its Problems

At the time of its acquisition of Euclid, White projected 1969 sales of its new earthmoving equipment line at $45 million.[120] It had acquired a not-so-modern line of off-highway trucks topped by the unique articulated Euclid R-X, renamed the R-105. White now had to begin the process of working through and updating the line, which took several years. In the meantime, the company was hemorrhaging from its earlier ill-advised farm equipment acquisitions. It is puzzling to view in retrospect White's acquisition of the three weak farm equipment companies and consider just what White management thought it could bring to the equation. What it did produce were the high costs of rationalizing the lines, plant closures and realignments, and funding pension costs, but there was little offsetting gain in increased sales or market share. In 1969, on total sales of $950 million, White made only $12.4 million.[121]

A White-White Merger

Management believed that a merger would be the answer to the company's declining fortunes. The suitor was none other than White Consolidated Industries, the lineal descendant of the White Sewing Machine Company, the father of the White Motor Company. White Consolidated's CEO Edward S. Reddig was a leading corporate raider who had just finished an unsuccessful attempt on Allis-Chalmers, and White Consolidated still owned 31 percent of A-C's common stock. Considering that the White Motor Company also competed in the farm equipment business, White Consolidated's ownership of the A-C stock was enough, by itself, to bring down the Justice Department on the proposal. Under government pressure, the merger of the two Cleveland-based companies was called off in early 1971. In the meantime, White Motors lost $42 million on its farm equipment business in 1970 and ended the year with a net loss of $19 million on $810 million in corporate sales.[122] No dividends would be paid on White's common stock for 1970 through 1973.

A New CEO

The losses along with the collapse of the proposed merger called for new management, and the White board, looking for a high-profile executive who could reassure the company's restive bankers, in early 1971 brought in Semon E. (Bunkie) Knudsen, son of a former GM president, himself a former GM executive and a recently resigned president of Ford. Later that year Knudsen assured the investing community that White intended to stay in the farm equipment business.[123] A major problem for Knudsen was an ill-conceived engine plant that White had built but not completed in Canton, Ohio, using $50 million in industrial revenue bonds guaranteed by the city. Although paying the interest on the bonds, White not only lacked the capital to complete the tooling but was also having second thoughts about the viability of the entire project. Ultimately, White got out from under the burden when Massey-Ferguson's Perkins acquired the plant in 1975.[124] Although Knudsen could not work miracles, his presence did bring a measure of stability to White.

Product Development

In 1971 White began field-testing on the Mesabi Range the R-210, a large gas-turbine, electric-drive, off-highway truck expected to sell for $500,000, an unheard of sum at the time for a single piece of equipment.[125] In the event, due to the turbine's insatiable appetite for fuel, the truck never went into production. Still, White did modernize the Euclid truck line and gradually introduced new models. By 1975 it was offering an updated R-35 and R-50, a new R-85, the R-105, and a new R-170 electric-drive unit.[126] Although bringing nothing new to the art, the line was quite competitive. In addition to the United States, Euclid was building trucks in Canada, Belgium, South Africa, and Australia.

White's Precarious Position

With the reentry of Terex into the off-highway truck business in 1973, Euclid was faced with the need to find new North American dealers. Doing so was not critical, however, because its principal source of business, the mining industry, was accustomed to dealing directly with the manufacturer. As a small portion of White's volume, likely on the order of 5 percent to 10 percent, Euclid neither contributed nor detracted greatly from the shaky profitability of its struggling parent. The real question was how long the parent would survive its steady losses in farm equipment and the poor profitability of its truck business.

Dresser Industries

Founded in 1880 and incorporated as the S. R. Dresser Manufacturing Company in 1905, the company was taken public in 1928 by the investment banking firm of W. A. Harriman and Company, Inc. Prescott S. Bush, a Harriman partner, became closely associated with Dresser and served on its board from 1930 until being elected to the U.S. Senate in 1952. His son, George W. Bush, worked briefly for Dresser after World War II before making his fortune as an independent oilman. The company became Dresser Industries in 1944.[127]

In its early years, the business was based largely on Solomon Dresser's invention, the Dresser coupling, patented in 1888, which made possible the gas transmission pipeline. Throughout its existence the company has been heavily involved in equipment for the oil and gas industry. Beginning in the early 1930s and shortly after going public, Dresser established a pattern of growth by acquisition that still continues and has involved more than thirty major acquisitions.[128]

Dresser and the Earthmoving Equipment Business

In the early 1970s Dresser displayed a growing interest in the mining industry through two acquisitions, LeRoi and the Jeffrey Galion Company, the first of several that would take the company not only into the mining industry but also deep into the construction industry. In 1972 it purchased from American Standard (WABCO) its Pneumatic Equipment Division for $6.6 million, gaining the LeRoi brand of air compressors and air tools used in construction and mining.[129] But that was small potatoes compared to what came next.

With heavy dependence on the oil and gas industry, Dresser began looking at a different part of the energy sector, the coal industry, as a possible growth opportunity, and the Arab oil boycott affirmed its attractiveness. On May 31, 1974, Dresser acquired the Jeffrey Galion Company, a firm based in Columbus, Ohio, and owned by the Jeffrey family, for $120 million in cash and about $19 million in stock. Jeffrey Galion had three major enterprises: underground coal mining machinery, which was what had initially attracted Dresser; Hewitt-Robins material-handling products for the mining industry; and Galion motor graders, hydraulic cranes, and static road rollers. Jeffrey Galion sales in 1973 were $223.5 million, and Dresser topped $1 billion for the first time that year.[130]

The Galion products took Dresser squarely into the construction equipment industry, a field in which it had no previous experience. Galion, an old-line road machinery manufacturer founded in 1907 in Galion, Ohio, had been acquired by the Jeffrey family in 1928.[131] After the war, the Galion motor grader, never highly regarded by contractors, was successful as a public bid item with states, counties, and local governmental bodies. Lacking a grader in their line, International Harvester dealers frequently handled Galion products.

Also in 1974, Dresser entered the diesel and gas engine business through the acquisition of Waukesha Motor Company from Bangor Punta Corporation for $20.1 million in cash. Waukesha, with sales of about $65 million, directly competed through most of its engine size range with Caterpillar's industrial engines.[132] Suddenly, Dresser and Caterpillar had become competitors in two product areas, motor graders and diesel and gas engines. There would be substantially more areas of competition in the future.

Plans for More Earthmoving Equipment Acquisitions

With its aggressive acquisition policy and astute management of its earlier-acquired businesses, Dresser was a fast-growing enterprise. Sales doubled from 1973 to 1975 and topped $2 billion. Profits were nearly $124 million.[133] That provided fuel for further acquisitions in the construction and mining equipment industries, where Dresser would become a major player in the coming decade.

Komatsu

Under the dynamic leadership of Ryoichi Kawai, Komatsu experienced steady growth between 1966 and 1975. The formation of the Caterpillar-Mitsubishi joint venture in 1963 had presented a serious challenge to Komatsu's domination of the home market and galvanized the company into action. Recognizing that to compete with Western technology in world markets it would need to shorten its learning curve, Komatsu had formed joint ventures with Bucyrus-Erie in 1963 to gain hydraulic excavator technology and International Harvester in 1965 for wheel loader technology.[134] Production of wheel loaders closely modeled after Hough machines began almost immediately. The more complex excavators took longer, beginning production in 1968.[135] Thus Komatsu quickly entered the two fastest-growing product lines of the construction equipment industry.

Competition from Caterpillar Mitsubishi

Beginning in 1965, Caterpillar Mitsubishi (CM) took six years to fill out its planned ten-model line of bulldozers and track and wheel loaders through the mid-range, giving Komatsu a breathing spell in which to strengthen its product line and domestic distribution organization. In the event, CM's domestic market share topped out at little more than what Mitsubishi Heavy Industries had before the joint venture. Once a distribution organization was in place, CM had modest success importing the heavier Caterpillar machines it did not build in Japan. But through 1975 CM had not been able to shake Komatsu's grip on the Japanese domestic market.

Overseas Expansion

Believing that its products were now capable of competing on even terms with U.S. and European machines, Komatsu began to address the need for a distribution system outside Japan. In 1967 it set up N.V. Komatsu Europe S.A. in Belgium, a marketing company and Komatsu's first foreign subsidiary.[136] Also in 1967, LeTourneau-Westinghouse had agreed to market Komatsu track-type products in the United States. With the failure of that effort, however, Komatsu set up a U.S. marketing subsidiary, Komatsu America Corp., in 1970. The company had a long, tough battle ahead to establish independent dealers in Europe and North America where the Komatsu name was not well known, and Japanese construction equipment in general had not been accepted by the marketplace.

Komatsu chose Brazil for its first overseas manufacturing operation and began production of a mid-sized bulldozer there in 1975.[137]

The Undervauled Yen and an Obsession with Quality

Throughout the decade, Komatsu's earthmoving sales grew steadily; by 1975 they reached close to $1 billion, more than 60 percent in the Japanese home market.[138] At that point, Komatsu was already in second place behind Caterpillar on a worldwide basis and in fourth place after Caterpillar, International Harvester, and Case outside Japan. Quality had become a obsession with Komatsu, and the company's Total Quality Control Program was years ahead of anything Western manufacturers were doing to systematically improve quality. The company's fledgling export business was no doubt aided by the undervalued yen—360 per U.S. dollar into 1971 and still averaging 305 in 1975. There is no better evidence that Caterpillar was beginning to notice Komatsu than a statement in Caterpillar's 1970 annual report: The Japanese "were not entitled to obtain extraordinary competitive advantage on the basis of outmoded foreign exchange rates."

Industry Product Development

The 1966–75 decade was marked by growing sophistication in the field of hydraulics, the leading example being the hydraulic excavator. The trend away from cable actuation in favor of hydraulics continued, and by 1975 the cable control was virtually extinct. More powerful engines and larger tires made possible impressive growth in the size of wheel loaders and off-highway trucks, and the largest machines in both categories roughly doubled in capacity during the period. Tractors, motor graders, and scrapers, although not growing significantly in size, received a variety of refinements. Increased emphasis was placed on operator safety and comfort, with roll-over protection structures becoming a statutory requirement in the United States. In Europe, increasingly elaborate cabs were becoming a marketing necessity, and manufacturers had to meet steadily more stringent limitations on operator and spectator sound levels.

The Hydraulic Excavator

Without question, the outstanding development of the decade was the boom in hydraulic excavators. In impact on the earthmoving equipment industry it ranked with Holt's track-type tractor, the Auto Patrol motor

The Demag H485 was the industry's first successful super-large hydraulic front shovel. This model, an enhanced 485SE weighing 750 short tons and having a forty-six-cubic-yard bucket, became the H485SP. Rope shovels of equivalent capacity weigh 1,150 to 1,250 tons. (DemagKomatsu GmbH)

grader, the Tournapull scraper, and the Hough wheel loader. Beginning in the late 1950s, the hydraulic excavator had grown from insignificance to the second-largest single product group in value terms (after wheel loaders) in the worldwide earthmoving equipment. Hydraulic excavators ranged in size from the one-ton mini to the 680-metric-ton Demag H485SP.

A European innovation, the excavator was quicker to gain acceptance there and in Japan than in North America. Europeans and the Japanese recognized the machine's advantages as an earth excavator, whereas Americans initially regarded it primarily as a trenching machine. The Europeans and Japanese also liked the 360-degree swing, perhaps because of tighter urban working conditions. The great popularity of the loader-backhoe in North America probably slowed acceptance of the small hydraulic excavator, however the loader-backhoe, a utility tool, could not compete with the excavator's bucket and stick forces, reach, digging depth, and 360-degree swing. In Europe and Japan, the track-type loader, once the preeminent contractor tool for excavating and loading bank material, in a matter of less than ten years lost its position to the excavator. Track loader sales plummeted. Within a few years a similar thing occurred in North America, although to a lesser degree.

In the early postwar years, the United States had numerous power shovel manufacturers, many of which also built cable-operated backhoes ("pullshovels" or "back-actors") used almost exclusively for trenching, but after being exposed during the late 1950s to the superiority of the hydraulic excavator, there was a virtual stampede to abandon the cable pull-shovel in favor of hydraulics. The clearest evidence lay in the change from the 1963 Road Show, when few hydraulic excavators were displayed, to ConExpo '69, when numerous companies showed hydraulic excavators, including Koehring, Lorain, Northwest, Bucyrus-Erie, Link-Belt, Hein-Werner, P&H, Insley, Unit, Drott, Massey-Ferguson, and Deere.

Excavators, the predominant product at ConExpo '75, were displayed by nearly all the companies that had shown them in 1969 as well as by Caterpillar, International Harvester (Yumbo), and Case. With non-U.S. manufacturers permitted to display for the first time, Poclain, Demag, O&K, and Akermans added their excavators to the array. In total, at least eighteen brands of excavators were shown. No other product, not even the wheel loader, had proliferated so rapidly. Clearly, the field had become very crowded, and the next decade would witness a thinning out of competitors.

The Elevating Scraper

Appearing during the mid-1950s, early elevating scraper mechanisms were mechanically driven by a power take-off shaft from the tractor, an awkward arrangement that kept the scraper small. LeTourneau-Westinghouse, with electrical controls, was able to circumvent that handicap by driving the elevator mechanism electrically. By 1961 it was offering its twenty-cubic-yard Model C wheel tractor-scraper in an elevating version. Advances in hydraulics enabled others to join the trend, using a hydraulic motor to drive the elevator, and by 1970 every manufacturer of wheel tractor-scrapers offered one or more sizes of elevating scrapers, some with rear-engine tandem power.[139]

Tire Development

No history of earthmoving equipment would be complete without at least a brief discussion of the vital role played by the pneumatic tire. In contrast with the early days, when the industry was essentially built around the track-type tractor, after World War II the balance shifted to products mounted on rubber tires. The wheel tractor-scraper, off-highway truck, and wheel loader drove the trend. Thus, the U.S. equipment industry was forced to rely on the Akron tire makers to provide a product suitable for a variety of applications as well as to support the trend to heavier machines by the timely development of new and larger sizes. The tire industry's challenge was twofold: to provide large, low-pressure single tires for off-road use on wheel tractor-scrapers, bottom-dumps, and wheel loaders and to provide high-pressure dual-type tires for off-highway trucks.

The 1930s: The Developing Need for Off-Highway Tires

As the pioneer in developing rubber-tired earthmoving equipment in the early 1930s, R. G. LeTourneau was the first to grapple with the inadequacies of then-available tires for heavy-duty, off-road service. After an unsuccessful experiment with balloon-type aircraft tires, he equipped his 1934 Model B Carryall scraper with six 13.5-20 truck tires.[140] He mounted duals on the rear to provide adequate load-carrying capacity. Dual tires in scraper work was a less than satisfactory solution but one LeTourneau used frequently on his crawler-drawn scrapers, even after adequate single tires were available, probably for cost reasons. Two smaller, mass-produced tires were cheaper than one large, specialized single tire.

A major breakthrough occurred in 1934 when Firestone made available the first prototype 18.00-24 tires for off-road service, and they quickly went into production. Four years later, Firestone introduced the 24.00-32, which was followed in quick succession by the 30.00-40 in 1939 and the mammoth (for the day) 36.00-40 in 1940. The first Tournapull, built in 1938, used 18.00-24s, but as prewar Tournapulls escalated in size LeTourneau installed larger tires, reaching 30.00-40 on his forty-two-cubic-yard, heaped capacity A3 model in 1940.[141] Although designed for earthmoving service, the tires were not low-pressure. Mounted on flat rims, they required relatively high inflation pressures (upward of seventy pounds per square inch) to avoid the tire bead's movement (creep) around the rim. To correct that tendency, R. G. LeTourneau invented a five-degree, tapered-bead rim assembly that allowed lower inflation pressures and opened the way for the later development of the wide-base tire. He received a patent on the device in 1945.[142]

The Wide-Base Tire

In working with LeTourneau, Caterpillar, and others during the early 1950s, Akron developed a wide-base tire for use on scrapers and, as they became available, large wheel loaders. Thus, for example, the 24.00-29 conventional scraper tire evolved into the 29.5-29 wide-base tire. The wide-base tire operated at a lower pressure (thirty to thirty-five pounds per square inch) and had a larger footprint that gave improved flotation, but at the equivalent ply rating it had slightly less load-carrying capacity. The wide-base tire was regarded as a major advance and became standard equipment on most scrapers in the mid-1950s.

As experience with large single earthmoving tires increased, equipment owners began demanding improved resistance to sudden failures from rock cuts and punctures. That led Akron to add tread rubber and adopt a squarer profile than the previous rounded one. By the late 1950s the increased rubber in the tires was leading to a new problem. Bigger loads and higher speeds were causing increased sidewall flexing, which caused heat buildup, particularly in wide-base tires working in high ambient temperatures. The heat buildup was such that the tire tread could separate from the plies, resulting in sudden total and irreparable failure. Thus, scraper manufacturers were placed in a position in which their products frequently could not deliver full-rated capacity due to tire heat limitations. Customers were not happy, but a solution was slow in coming from Akron.

When Caterpillar introduced its 600-Series scrapers in 1962 it attempted to resolve the problem by offering an optional, slimmer, rounded tire with less tread rubber for high-speed use on good roads, but that approach was not successful. Contractors were not willing to invest in two sets of tires for their fleets, so high-speed tires were widely misapplied and were quickly withdrawn. During the 1950s tubeless tires were perfected and came into general use in earthmoving tires.

Growth in Truck Tire Sizes

High-pressure dual tires shared the problem of heat buildup with large single tires but to a lesser extent because the high-pressure tire was less subject to sidewall flexing. Still, slow development of larger high-pressure tires was frustrating the introduction of much-sought-after larger trucks. In the 1950s truck manufacturers tried to circumvent the problem by putting more wheels under their vehicles through the use of tandem rear axles and fifth-wheel semi-trailers. Both solutions had serious drawbacks, but with no alternative the mining industry, as the primary consumer of large rear-dumps, bought them anyway. Gradually, Akron made larger sizes available. The successive introduction of 21.00-49, 24.00-49, and 27.00-49 tires that began in the early 1960s was the breakthrough needed to make it possible for two-axle truck sizes to escalate to more than a hundred tons. Tire sizes have continued to increase. The 44.00-57, in use on the largest trucks, exceeds twelve feet in outside diameter.

The Radial Tire

The solution to the industry's heat problems with tires was at hand, but Akron was reluctant to adopt it. It was the radial tire, which the French company Michelin had introduced in 1947. Instead of plies of cotton, rayon, or nylon fiber set at an angle or bias across the conventional tire, radial tires used steel wires set at 90 degrees to the tread. The stronger wire required less material in the tire carcass, resulting in cooler running among other advantages. But the radial produced a stiffer ride, something that would have required Detroit automakers to redesign their suspension systems. Despite the manifest advantages of the radial, the U.S. tire industry stayed with the bias-ply and bias-belted tires. Until Akron converted to radials for its automotive tires there was little chance that it would produce radials for the earthmoving equipment industry.

As American motorists gradually learned of the advantages of the radial and Akron began to lose significant replacement tire business, the U.S. tire industry read the handwriting and in the early 1970s began converting to radials.[143] Meanwhile, Michelin had already begun to make them available in sizes the earthmoving industry needed, and equipment manufacturers offered them as options. Typically, radials are standard on today's earthmoving equipment; bias-ply tires, if offered at all, are optional.

The Beadless Tire

Caterpillar, as the industry's largest consumer of earthmoving tires, became seriously disaffected by what it viewed as Akron's poor response to the industry's tire problems of the late 1950s and early 1960s and resolved to start its own tire development program. After several years of work in the company's research department, Caterpillar made public the development of what it called the "beadless" tire in 1970. While the conventional tire had a horseshoelike cross-section, the beadless tire was oval in cross-section, forming a torus ring that was helically and circumferentially wound with wire filaments. A replaceable tread belt could be mounted to the basic carcass. It was a revolutionary new concept that the company hoped had commercial possibilities beyond use on its own equipment.

The trend to replace power shovels with wheel loaders for truck loading in quarries and other rock applications has already been discussed. Although the loader had the muscle to do the work, owners were not satisfied with tire life in this demanding environment. Caterpillar, believing it had a solution to the problem, in 1973 offered the 992B, a ten-cubic-yard wheel loader on beadless tires with a circumferential belt fitted with replaceable steel shoes. The package later was also offered on its seven-cubic-yard 988B wheel loader.[144] The product successfully reduced tire operating costs, but it did so at a substantial premium in initial price. In the end, the high initial cost of the beadless tire defeated it. It was never applied to any other Caterpillar vehicles, and the company was unsuccessful in gaining the interest of other equipment manufacturers in the product.

The beadless tire with a replaceable belt of steel shoes on a Caterpillar 992 lowered wheel loader tire operating costs in severe conditions, but high initial cost kept demand low. (Courtesy of Caterpillar Inc.)

ConExpo '69

Recognizing that the Road Show attracted the interest of a much broader audience than just the road-building segment of the construction industry, after 1963 manufacturers agreed to change the event's name officially to the "Construction Exposition" (ConExpo). Again held at Chicago's International Ampitheater, the show was remarkable in that it featured a great number of hydraulic excavators. New large wheel loaders were also prominent, including the Hough H-400B, Michigan 475, Caterpillar 992, and Terex 72-81—all in the nine-to-twelve-cubic-yard range. After displaying a prototype of the world's largest crawler tractor, the five-hundred-plus-horsepower HD-41, in 1963 but not putting it into production, Allis-Chalmers again showed the tractor—this time promising 1971 delivery. Deere was there with its new JD690 excavator, JD644 wheel loader, and JD860 scraper, and Massey-Ferguson introduced its new line of construction equipment. The timing was ideal for Terex to introduce its new name to the industry and also show off the new 7200-Series wheel loaders and 8200-Series track-type tractors. Aside from the 992, Caterpillar showed no major new machines but displayed a variety of refinements and updates to existing products.

The show was attracting more international attention, with twelve thousand from overseas among the 125,000 registrants. Foreign manufacturers, however, were not yet permitted membership in the Construction Industry Manufacturers Association. Undaunted, Poclain rented outdoor space across the street and showed its HC-300, a 2.5-cubic-yard hydraulic excavator.[145]

ConExpo '75

Outgrowing Chicago's International Amphitheater, the 1975 show was split between that venue and the new McCormick Place exhibition hall. Again, hydraulic excavators were ubiquitous. This time Caterpillar showed its four-model line that included the new 245 with front shovel. With foreign manufacturers now admitted to CIMA membership, Poclain, Demag, O&K, and Akermans showed excavators, and O&K stole the show with the RH60, a 130-ton, 12.5-cubic-yard front shovel. It was a stunning demonstration of how far ahead the Europeans were in large excavator design. Other outsized products included the Michigan 675 wheel loader at twenty-four cubic yards, the Hough 580 at twenty-one cubic yards, and the Haulpak 170C and White-Euclid R-170 rear-dump trucks.

Replacing its aging D8H with the first series change since 1958, Caterpillar displayed its new D8K and replaced the D9G with a D9H. Horsepower increased about 10 percent on both models, and new sealed and lubricated track was standard. Caterpillar also showed off its new 777, an eighty-five-ton off-highway truck. Fiat-Allis showed a prototype HD-31 intended to compete head-on with the Caterpillar D9. Deere introduced the JD750, its first hydrostatic crawler, and the JD755 track loader as well as larger motor graders. Massey-Ferguson displayed wheel loaders and crawlers from its new acquisition, Hanomag.

Attendance was a record 128,000, with twenty thousand from overseas. Although the show was an apparent success, it would be the last one for Chicago, its traditional postwar venue. Differences with unions over exhibit set-ups drove manufacturers to seek another location.[146]

Summary, 1966–75

Manufacturers' sales of earthmoving equipment in the United States had increased about two and one half times since 1965 and reached about $5 billion in 1975, but the price of machinery had nearly doubled over the decade, making real growth less impressive. Still, the decade was good to the industry as a whole, although strains had begun to appear in two of the old-line producers. Allis-Chalmers had not been able to grow its business with the industry and opted for a joint venture with Fiat. International Harvester, by the end of the decade, was looking for a buyer for its unprofitable Payline Division. Their places were being filled by the relative newcomers, Case and Deere, who by 1975 were well into the mid-range product sizes. Caterpillar, with about one-third of the U.S. business, dominated an industry in which its nearest competitor, International Harvester, had an estimated 10 percent.

Outside North America, the earthmoving equipment business had grown even more rapidly during the decade, fed by the burgeoning European and Japanese economies and the boom in OPEC countries. In the developing world, major infrastructure projects and increased activity in the extractive industries had further fueled demand. Komatsu's nearly $1 billion in worldwide earthmoving sales during 1975 was now second only to Caterpillar in heavy equipment. After an abortive effort to enter the U.S. market via the WABCO distribution organization, Komatsu had drawn back and was building its own North American dealer system. It would succeed in doing so with surprising speed.

The hydraulic excavator joined the wheel loader as the two most significant postwar product developments. To be a major player in 1975 required strong lines of both products because track-type tractor and track loaders took a diminishing slice of the pie.

Although the U.S. interstate highway program was nearing an end, new

sources of business had come from the boom in the Mideast and from Brazil and Southeastern Asia. At the end of 1975 the worldwide construction
equipment industry had every reason to believe that the next ten years would
be an extension of the past thirty years of remarkable expansion. Well before the next decade was out, however, it would be terribly disillusioned.

SIX

The Pinnacle and the Fall, 1976–85

After a short downtick during the mid-1970s, earthmoving equipment sales rose steadily through the next four years and reached a postwar peak in 1979, when every U.S. manufacturer with the exception of strike-affected Caterpillar had record sales. But the industry was unaware at the end of 1979 that it was standing on a pinnacle from which it would fall with terrible speed. The drop was so sudden and savage that despite desperate efforts to downsize none of the major U.S. and European earthmoving equipment manufacturers escaped without serious operating losses. By 1985, as the industry emerged from the turmoil, smaller and weaker companies, with few exceptions, had either exited the business or been forced to form new combinations while stronger companies found that their markets had been invaded in force by Japanese competitors. The 1976–85 decade was truly a unique period in the history of the industry.

The Nation

The Economy

Taking root in the late 1960s, inflation continued to bedevil the U.S. economy throughout the 1970s. Even the long and fairly severe 1974–75 recession could only squeeze inflation down to 5.8 percent in 1976. It quickly renewed its upward trend and reached double digits in 1979, 1980, and 1981, with an appalling 13.5 percent peak in 1980.[1] Consumer prices rose 68 percent between 1975 and 1981, but machinery prices outstripped the CPI, rising 73 percent in the same period.[2] Because all U.S. equipment manufacturers were subject to similar labor agreements and materials costs, prices went up in lockstep across the board.

Triggered by events in Iran surrounding the overthrow of the Shah, the second world oil shock of 1979–80 injected another strong shot of inflation into the world economies as the price of oil temporarily reached a multiple of nineteen times what it had been only ten years earlier. The prime rate, which had been rising since 1977, spurted to a high of 20 percent in March 1980.[3]

In mid-1980 the OECD warned of a global slowdown from high interest rates and oil prices and urged members to hold to restrictive policies to fight inflation. Taking office six months later, the Reagan administration, grimly determined to roll back inflation, was quick to adopt such policies. The seeds of a worldwide recession had already been sown and were beginning to germinate. By mid-year the U.S. economy was diving, which triggered a domino effect, and thus the world entered the longest and deepest recession since the Great Depression.

Between 1979 and 1983 the U.S. economy grew only 2.7 percent in real terms.[4] The deep slump decimated the housing industry—at the 1982 low, residential construction was only 60 percent of the 1979 level.[5] The recession-led contraction in the construction industry was exacerbated by a highway program that had been slowing since the mid-1970s.

The Highway Program

The slowdown in interstate construction activity is illustrated by the fact that in 1976, after twenty years of work, 38,000 miles of the 42,500-mile system were open to traffic but only an additional 2,250 miles had been opened five years later.[6] The remaining portions were primarily in urban areas, the most difficult, costly, and often controversial sections. But another less obvious factor was at work to reduce highway construction. The federal tax on motor fuel, the source of funds for the Highway Trust Fund, had been set at 4 cents per gallon in 1959 and was still at that level in 1981 despite the huge amount of inflation that had occurred over the intervening twenty-two years. A dollar of spending in 1981 was only buying perhaps a third the amount of construction it had bought in 1959, which had a heavy impact on equipment buying.

Aside from inflation, another factor squeezing state funding for roads was the rapidly escalating cost of maintaining the interstates. The Federal Highway Administration estimated that highway maintenance expense had risen 328 percent between 1967 and 1979.[7] Although the 1956 Federal-Aid Highway Act had generously provided 90 percent federal funding for construction of the interstate system, the states had retained their traditional responsibility for maintaining all federal aid highways within their borders. The earliest parts of the system were now more than twenty years old, and the added mileage of the high-standard interstates in addition to the effects of inflation had overwhelmed state highway maintenance budgets despite increases in motor fuel taxes by many states. By the early 1980s, after all the billions spent over the preceding twenty-five years on the world's largest construction project, the highways and bridges of the federal aid system were beginning to fall apart.

Reacting to pressures from the states and stimulated by an unemployment rate of more than 10 percent, Congress acted in 1982 to relieve the situation. Funded by a 5 cent increase in the federal motor fuel tax, a $32.9 billion program was enacted to provide states with about $5.5 billion annually for five years for highway maintenance. The program was expected to create 320,000 jobs. For the first time in the history of the federal aid program, states would receive federal aid for maintenance.[8] The program brought about a huge reorientation of the American roads industry. It went from new construction, which is highly machinery-intensive, to repair, resurfacing, and reconstruction, which are costly but much less machinery-intensive. Equipment sales mirrored this shift. The highway program would never again generate the massive sales of heavy construction equipment it once did.

Water Projects

Although the day of the mega-dam was over in North America, Congress in the late 1970s continued generous funding of its favorite water projects over the strong opposition of the Carter administration and environmentalists. A classic example was the Central Arizona Project (CAP). First authorized in 1968, the $3.8 billion water project was the most expensive ever authorized by Congress and would carry Colorado River water through 330 miles of concrete-lined canals and tunnels, up 1,200 feet to Phoenix and then on to Tucson. Despite periodic efforts to kill it, the Central Arizona Project took on a life of its own and was eventually completed after more than twenty years of work.[9]

Other Construction

The Trans-Alaska Pipeline was completed in 1977 after three years of work at a cost of $7.7 billion, nearly three times the estimate when work was restarted in 1974. It was the costliest privately financed engineering project in history. The construction equipment fleet was auctioned off (including 719 track-type units), and although the general-purpose machines were absorbed with surprisingly little impact on new equipment sales, the many used pipelayers glutted the market for a decade.[10]

The International Scene

Fifteen years of rampant inflation and the Reagan administration's efforts to stifle it had triggered one of the most dramatic swings in exchange rates the world's major trading currencies had ever experienced. With the closure of the gold window in 1971, the dollar started a ten-year decline against the D-mark and other low-inflation currencies. From a rate of $0.295 in August 1971, the mark peaked at $0.551 in January 1979. Meanwhile, under pressure from its trading partners, Japan was forced to permit the yen to strengthen, and it went from 300 in January 1975 to 203 in January 1981—a 32 percent swing.[11]

Still, with U.S. inflation of almost 70 percent in the same period, imported Japanese equipment was even more competitive in the United States in 1981 than it had been in 1975. In the OPEC countries, where the machinery business was booming, U.S. manufacturers were fortunate that the price of oil was denominated in dollars but still had to face growing competition from Japan. Overall, due to high inflation U.S. equipment exporters gained very little in competitiveness from the dollar's slide, whereas low-cost Japanese manufacturers were becoming more competitive worldwide. Clearly, the U.S. position of dominance in earthmoving equipment was becoming steadily more vulnerable. By 1981, had it not been for their less-developed dealer distribution system, Japanese manufacturers would have been making even deeper inroads in North America and elsewhere.

Meanwhile, the non-oil-producing nations of Latin America and Africa had been enjoying boom years through the late 1970s as the money center banks recycled petrodollars into their economies in the form of easy loans, raising the nations' dollar indebtedness sharply. Ostensibly to support needed infrastructure development, too often these funds enriched corrupt politicians or were dissipated in consumer spending. As the worldwide slump deepened in 1982, these nations took a double hit of higher oil prices and loss of export markets for their commodities. Their fragile economies fell into steep recessions accompanied by disastrous currency devaluations. Less-developed, non-OPEC countries had bought record amounts of earthmoving equipment as late as 1981, and then their purchases plummeted to almost nothing.

Major International Projects

The focus of mega-projects had definitely shifted to the less-developed world, with South America in the forefront. The joint Brazil-Paraguay 12,600-megawatt Itaipu hydroelectric power project on the Parana River, begun in 1976 and completed in 1983, involved twenty-six million cubic yards of excavation and 14.4 million cubic yards of concrete. Six hundred machines worked on the $9.5 billion project.[12] But from an earthmoving standpoint, Brazil's 7,260-megawatt Tucururi hydro project on the Tocantins River was even larger. Completed in 1984, it involved an earth and rock fill dam of 111 million cubic yards. A joint hydroelectric project on the Parana River between Argentina and Paraguay, the 106-million-cubic-yard Yacyreta Dam was begun in 1984. And in Venezuela, the Guri Dam on the Caroni River, ninety-three million cubic yards, was underway. The 10,300-megawatt hydroelectric project would be completed in 1986. These projects absorbed thousands of pieces of heavy earthmoving equipment.

Not all the mega-projects of the decade were in South America. Started in 1985, the 110-million-cubic-yard Ataturk Dam on the headwaters of the Euphrates River in Turkey would be the world's eighth-largest earth fill dam when completed in 1992.[13] About four hundred Caterpillar machines were at work on the project.[14]

In the Middle East, Saudi Arabia projected spending a staggering $132.5 billion between 1981 and 1985 on construction, including the building of three new cities: Jubail on the Persian Gulf, Yanbu on the Red Sea, and King Khalid Military City in the north.[15] Equipment buying in the Middle East reached a fever pitch in the early 1980s.

The Soviet Union built 8,400 miles of oil pipelines and 19,500 miles of gas lines in the five years through 1980.[16] It did so largely with American equipment, but after 1981 the U.S. embargo would shut out American suppliers.

International Mining

In the state of Pará, Brazil, where eighteen billion tons of 67 percent iron ore had been outlined, the Grand Carajas iron ore project started up, which involved opening the mine and constructing 555 miles of railroad to the port.[17] It would eventually be the world's largest iron mine.

The increase in the price of oil brought on by the 1979–80 oil shock heightened interest in the potential of the huge Canadian oil sands ("tar sands") deposit near Ft. McMurray, Alberta. The deposit, containing billions of barrels of bitumen locked in the sands, had been known for decades, but the costs of extraction had always exceeded the world price of crude oil. With oil prices at an all-time high, a consortium of oil companies began negotiations with the Alberta and Canadian governments to exploit the sands. Knowing that a very large-scale operation would be required and fully aware of the volatility of oil prices, the consortium was understandably cautious of the huge initial capital investment. With assurances from the Canadian government and financial support from the provincial government, however, the project went ahead. By 1984 Syncrude, the principal producer, already had a daily capacity of 109,000 barrels.[18] In terms of annual tonnage moved, the project would eventually be one of the largest mining operations in the world. By 1992 the Syncrude tailings pile contained an estimated 540 million cubic meters of processed oil sands.

A Strengthening Dollar

In early 1981, after ten years of downward drift, the dollar suddenly turned, triggered by the manifest intentions of the Reagan administration to bring inflation under control. In a drastic revaluation, by early 1985 the dollar had actually returned to the 1971 rate with respect to the mark; the yen had weakened to 260, near its 1972 rate of 300.[19] In Europe, to maintain competitiveness in local currencies, American equipment manufacturers were forced to lower dollar prices and could not hope to obtain U.S. price levels when competing against European and Japanese manufacturers in developing countries. And in North America, just as the equipment market was recovering from the deep 1981–82 recession, U.S. manufacturers had to meet the greatest price disadvantage they had ever faced from imported equipment. It was a matter of "cut prices or don't sell." Manufacturer and dealer profits nosedived.

Between 1981 and 1985 American manufacturers wondered whether things could get any worse. The decade had produced extremes in the business environment the likes of which they had never experienced. There had been six years of galloping inflation through 1981; two recessions, the second of which was the deepest and longest since the depression; record-high interest rates; and four years of unfavorable exchange rates.

The Companies

For the earthmoving equipment industry, the 1976–85 decade was divided into two distinct periods. During the five or six years through 1980 or 1981 the companies generally followed past patterns of growth and profitability. In the ensuing years through 1985 they experienced unprecedented losses, retrenchment, and, in some cases, failure. The decade, more than any other, reshaped the face of the industry. Companies will be discussed in two categories: survivors and victims.

The Survivors

Caterpillar

The 1976–81 Period   After nearing the $5 billion mark in 1975, Caterpillar broke through in 1976 and reached $5.04 billion. An early 1976 *Wall Street Journal* feature article on the company was entitled "What Recession?" The title was a reference to the company's performance when it literally blew through the 1974–75 recession, setting new sales and profit records in 1975.[20] Caterpillar, according to the article, could double sales and profits in the next five years, a prediction that proved to be overly bullish, but nevertheless sales and profits did grow about 70 percent by 1980. That same year the company seemed recession-proof when results appeared unaffected by the brief economic downturn in the first half. Although by the third quarter of 1981 the economy had dropped into another recession, for the year the company flirted with the $10 billion mark—$9.15 billion in sales and a record $579 million profit.[21]

Despite a highly inflationary environment during the period, the company was able to maintain an average profit on sales of 7 percent by following its traditional price leadership policy of aggressive increases.[22] For example, the company said that fully 40 percent of its 1978 sales increase over 1977 was due to price inflation, which worked out to an average across-the-board price increase of 9.4 percent for the full year.[23] U.S. competitors were more than happy to remain under the Caterpillar price umbrella, moving their prices in tandem with the price leader. The steadily weakening dollar helped prices on the company's business outside the United States, which averaged 54 percent of total sales over the six years.[24]

It was the golden era of OPEC business for Caterpillar. Its sales in Africa and the Middle East, mostly of large, U.S.-built, high-profit machines at full margins, rose each year and reached almost $1.9 billion in 1981, 21 percent of the corporate total. In Europe, where about half of Caterpillar's sales came from its European plants, competition from locally built products was intense. But there, too, the weak dollar helped the company hold its prices near U.S. levels. Caterpillar sales in Europe averaged about $1 billion annually during the period.[25] It was with some disquiet, however, that the company noted the turn in February 1981 when the dollar reversed its ten-year downward trend.

A New High in Capital Spending   Despite $2 billion in capital spending between 1966 and 1975, Caterpillar continued to have frequent periods when it was supply-limited. In 1973 it had announced a $1.6 billion spending program for 1975 through 1977, but that was only the beginning of an even larger expansion that followed. Between 1976 and 1981 capital spending totaled more than $3.8 billion. Major expansions were completed at Davenport, Iowa; Joliet, Illinois; Leicester, U.K.; and Piricicaba, Brazil. A 1.8-million-square-foot addition to the Morton, Illinois, parts distribution facility was announced that would nearly double its size, and three major green field projects for new plants were started at LaFayette, Indiana; Brampton, Ontario; and Beloit, Wisconsin.

Apparently frustrated by its inability to expand existing plants and complete new plants fast enough to meet its perceived needs, the company began buying up vacant industrial buildings that totaled more than 2.2 million square feet of space in Wisconsin, Iowa, Illinois, California, and Mississippi. Major expansions were quickly announced for the Pontiac, Illinois, and Burlington, Iowa, sites. Manufacturing space increased by one-third, from thirty-two million square feet in 1975 to more than forty-two million square feet in 1981.[26] The company was pulling out all the stops in an effort to provide facilities to meet its long-range sales forecasts.

The Morgan Era   On the retirement of William Naumann in late 1977, Lee Morgan, fifty-seven, was elected chair and CEO. Morgan, an Illinois farm boy and University of Illinois graduate who joined Caterpillar in 1946, was another of the company's many "home-grown" CEOs, a characteristic that seemed to bemuse Wall Street. The idealistic Morgan believed that Caterpillar was an enterprise of "high purpose" derived from the putative benefits to humanity made possible by earthmoving equipment, and he sought, not altogether successfully, to imbue the company with that spirit.

During the first four years of Morgan's tenure, the company continued to follow the formula that had been so successful. Sales grew by 56 percent, and the profit rate, while trending down, was still good. The frenetic expansion program begun by his predecessors was accelerated during these years, piling on fixed charges and steadily raising the break-even point, which, in view of seemingly perpetual sales and profit growth, gave no one cause for concern. But Morgan and Caterpillar's marketing management and dealers did feel growing unease about justifying substantial price premiums over Komatsu. Clearly, Komatsu had a significant product cost advantage over Caterpillar that went far deeper than exchange rates or the differential in wages and benefits, and at that point Komatsu's product quality was probably superior to Caterpillar's. Caterpillar's costs and quality were out of control, and top management in 1981 had no inkling of the radical changes that would be necessary in structure and manufacturing practices before the company could regain its competitive edge.

The Acquisition of Solar   Caterpillar, like several other manufacturers, was caught up in the gas turbine vogue of the late 1950s and early 1960s. Even after it was clear that the turbine would not displace the diesel engine in mobile equipment, the company continued its turbine development program as an extension of its line of industrial engines. As vice president of the Industrial Division in the early 1960s, Lee Morgan became the chief advocate within the company of the gas turbine. In 1965 Caterpillar marketed an internally developed turbine-generator set, but it proved inadequate and was quickly withdrawn. Morgan later bought the rights to a Boeing turbine, but it, too, proved to be less than state of the art and was never put into production.

After spending millions on turbine development over a twenty-year period Caterpillar still had nothing to show for its efforts, but 1981 brought a new opportunity to enter the business. Hard-pressed by creditors, International Harvester was putting its Solar Division up for sale. The division, purchased by Harvester in 1960 for about $12 million, was a $344 million business in 1980. Determined not to be outbid, Morgan offered $505 million cash, and Harvester, dazzled by the size of the bid, snapped it up. At the time of the sales agreement in May 1981 the thirty-two million outstanding IH common shares were quoted at $17.50, putting a market valuation on the entire company of only $560 million.[27] Later, Morgan parried suggestions by some analysts that Caterpillar had paid too much, pointing to Solar's potential.[28] Still, Caterpillar's 1981 annual report had to reflect the $146 million amount paid over book value, but the company was, at last, in the gas turbine engine business.

The 1982–85 Period   Despite the deepening recession in the latter half of 1981, Caterpillar predicted a modest sales increase for 1982 with an economic recovery after mid-year. Instead, sales fell steadily, with operating losses beginning in the third quarter. Fourth-quarter sales were only 42 percent of the previous year, producing a loss of $204 million. Full-year results showed sales down 29 percent for a loss of $180 million, the first since 1932. Caterpillar labeled it "the worst business downturn in fifty years." Production schedules were cut drastically, with attendant massive layoffs. By year end, 24,600 people had lost their jobs, and corporate employment was down almost 30 percent. Management was now trying desperately to stop the capital spending flywheel but succeeded only in reducing it to $534 million from a planned $750 million for 1982.[29]

But the worst was yet to come. Sales in 1983 dropped another 16 percent to $5.4 billion, with the loss reaching $345 million. The corporate expansion program was not only halted but also thrown into reverse with the announcement of the closure of six plants: Mentor, Ohio (lift trucks); Newcastle, England; San Leandro; Milwaukee; Burlington; and Edgerton, Wisconsin. More than five million square feet of manufacturing space was involved. The closure of San Leandro severed the company's last manufacturing connection with its California origins. Caterpillar said those steps were necessary "to reduce excess capacity, lower overhead costs and consolidate manufacturing operations" and took a $112 million charge against 1983 results.

Although still very low, Caterpillar's U.S. sales in 1983 did rise 13 percent from 1982, but that was more than offset by a 32 percent decline overseas.[30] The company was not getting the countercyclical effect it had always enjoyed from its business outside the United States. The whole world was in a slump, sharply reducing business everywhere. The growing strength of the dollar added to Caterpillar's problems. In Europe the company was forced to reduce its dollar prices to dealers to hold market share by maintaining dealer selling prices in local currencies at competitive levels; some models reached as low as 50 to 60 percent of U.S. price levels. Production costs of these European-built models, when translated into dollars, also declined but not enough to offset the price reductions.

The large price differential between European and U.S. dollar prices for the same models set in motion a grey market wherein new and near-new European-built Caterpillar machines began flowing through "irregular" channels (brokers and used equipment dealers) to the United States, absorbing a portion of U.S. demand. The company estimated that up to three thousand of its machines flowed through the grey market between 1981 and 1985. Similarly, a grey market developed between Japan and Southeast Asia that caused major disruptions to markets in Thailand, Malaysia, Singapore, and Indonesia.

Meanwhile, after Komatsu had struggled to build a North American dealer organization through the late 1970s, lower costs and a favorable exchange rate created big price differentials that suddenly made the Komatsu account very attractive to dealers handling other brands, and many signed on. Transaction price differences of 20 to 30 percent and sometimes more became the norm between Komatsu and competitive U.S.–built equivalent models.[31] Having been forced to lower prices in Europe and Southeast Asia, Caterpillar had hoped to maintain a "price island" in North America, where equipment prices traditionally had been higher. But Komatsu and other Japanese manufacturers were putting increasingly heavy pressure on Caterpillar's U.S. prices at the same time the recession was affecting its volume, which gave the company's profitability a double hit. Under these intense pressures, to protect market share Caterpillar was forced also to lower dealer net prices in the United States and to discount.

Thus, despite retrenchment, 1984 showed an operating loss, which, when compounded by a further special charge of $226 million for reductions and consolidations of manufacturing space, produced a net loss of $428 million. No new plant closures were announced, but buildings were closed at several U.S. locations, and it was decided not to complete the 1.8-million-square-foot expansion of the Morton parts distribution facility.[32] The uncompleted steelwork stood for eight years as a stark reminder of the folly of overexpansion.

A Return to Profit, a New CEO   Although sales were up only 2 percent in 1985, Caterpillar's retrenchment measures over the preceding three years had the desired effect: The company was profitable on operations but only broke even after interest expense and special charges. A one-time gain on an asset sale plus other income created a profit of $198 million. In early 1985 Morgan reached retirement age and was succeeded by George A. Schaefer, fifty-six. A somewhat chastened Morgan, who had the misfortune of having the worst recession since the Great Depression occur on his watch, left a company that in real terms was substantially smaller than when he took over in 1977. Schaefer, with a financial and manufacturing background, had become an executive vice president only four years earlier, but his appointment as vice chairman in 1984 over the heads of more senior executives had made him the heir-apparent. He took steps to further reduce employment, which had crept up in 1984, and ended 1985 with a net reduction of eight thousand people. From a high of 89,400 in 1979, employment was now 53,600. After losses that totaled almost $1 billion from 1982 through 1984 it appeared that operations were stabilized at a profitable level.[33]

Problems with Quality   Caterpillar, long dominant in large machines and with a very strong position in the mid-range, was finding itself challenged on its home ground as never before. Reluctant to break with its long-standing policy of not discounting private business, the company first attempted to meet Komatsu's price competition by offering non-price inducements such as extended warranties and special parts availability guarantees. But the company soon learned to its chagrin that customers were now demanding these extra assurances anyway because of a perceived slippage in Caterpillar's vaunted reputation for quality.

A combination of factors had, over time, unquestionably eroded Caterpillar product reliability. The company had acquired a reputation for poor early reliability of its new models until they were "debugged" after a year or so, something that did not reflect well on its product development program. The increasing technical sophistication of the machinery had put new demands on manufacturing, and the years of product allocation had also taken their toll. When production schedules here high and dealers were pleading for machines it was tempting for the shop to let testing and inspection standards slip and "let the dealer fix it." Habits acquired under these conditions were not easy to break when conditions changed.

An example of how oblivious the company had become to the slippage in quality was illustrated by the decision in 1979 to change the color of its machines. The traditional "Hi-way Yellow" had been closely identified with Caterpillar for almost fifty years, but because of the paint's high lead content the Occupational Safety and Health Administration ruled that Hi-way Yellow could no longer be used without an extensive revamp of factory painting facilities. In a manufacturing-driven decision, the company chose to switch to "Caterpillar Yellow."[34] That drab, brownish-yellow resulted in such a marked deterioration in the appearance of the machines that some dealers at their own expense routinely repainted the machines when received from the factory.

Establishing Cat Finance   While the rest of the industry had long since been participating in the retail finance business through captive credit corporations, Caterpillar had avoided that business, believing it could obtain a better return from its manufacturing activities. Caterpillar Credit Corporation remained small, mainly helping a few dealers finance inventories while retail financing was left entirely to dealers to arrange. The growing interest among some customers in leasing prompted the company to establish Caterpillar Leasing Company in 1981, and that evolved into Caterpillar Financial Services Corporation (CFSC) in 1983, absorbing the small credit corporation. At that point the company made a cautious commitment to the retail financing business, although at year end CFSC's portfolio totaled only $190 million.[35]

Business with the Soviet Union   Beginning in the late 1960s, Caterpillar had enjoyed a succession of large deals with the Soviet Union involving thousands of machines for pipeline construction and the Siberian pulpwood logging industry, but all that began to change in 1980. The Soviet invasion of Afghanistan brought an end to détente and prompted the Carter administration to take a tough line on the export of any products that could be regarded as having strategic value to the USSR. After the declaration of martial law in Poland in December 1981, the Reagan administration imposed an outright embargo on the export of strategic materials to the USSR. It was during this period that the Soviets were planning a 3,600-mile line to bring natural gas to Western Europe, a move strongly opposed on strategic grounds by the Reagan administration, which was doing everything it could to block it.

Meanwhile, Caterpillar was in the midst of negotiating sales of pipelayers to the USSR, but in each case obtaining the necessary U.S. government approval was highly uncertain. Finally, after closing a $90 million deal for two hundred Model 594 pipelayers, the largest built by the company, and on-again, off-again approval by the government, shipment of the order was disapproved.[36] The company was saddled with fifty completed machines and material for an additional fifty. Worse, the Russians labeled Caterpillar an "unreliable supplier," opening the door to Komatsu. During the early 1980s, when it desperately needed the business, Caterpillar watched from the sidelines while Komatsu supplanted it as the Soviet's favored supplier of heavy machinery.[37] After more than four years of being shut out, Caterpillar was again able to obtain an order from the Russians in late 1985. In the meantime, Komatsu products had proven themselves an acceptable alternative.

The Loader-Backhoe Business   The most important new products of the decade for Caterpillar came in 1985 with the introduction of a line of loader-backhoes, signaling a major shift in strategy for the company. In the twenty-eight years since Case had displayed its first loader-backhoe at the 1957 Road Show, Caterpillar had watched passively as Case, Deere, Massey-Ferguson, JCB, and others had preempted that entry-level machine and built preference for their brands with fledgling contractors, steadily extending their product lines up into the mid-range. The new Caterpillar loader-backhoes meant that the company could carry the fight back to its tormentors and challenge them for the loyalties of this huge group of utility machine users.

Caterpillar had studied the loader-backhoe in the 1960s and 1970s but could never meet cost targets by using company-built components, and there was no willingness to make an exception to that time-honored policy. A new study in the early 1980s showed that the products could be built competitively by using purchased components, and, in a more flexible corporate climate, the project was approved. In the event, a five-model line built from purchased components was introduced between 1985 and 1988 and assembled in Leicester, England.[38] Dealer reaction was mixed. Many had lost touch with that segment of buyers and found it difficult to reestablish contact. The new Cat Finance organization played a key role in helping the company push into the market for loader-backhoes.

The choice of the United Kingdom as sole source proved unlucky for the U.S. market because 1985 marked a turn in exchange rates from a strengthening to a weakening dollar. Market share grew very slowly, but Caterpillar had the staying power to persevere.

The Elevated Sprocket   The accepted industry norm for undercarriage design since Benjamin Holt's track-type tractor of 1904 had been an arrangement in which the track passed around a rear driving sprocket and a front idler wheel, forming an oval. In 1978 Caterpillar made a dramatic departure when it introduced the elevated sprocket on its massive new D10 ("hidrive") tractor, at the same time reclaiming the title as the world's largest crawler at seven hundred horsepower and ninety tons, equipped. Raising the sprocket and adding a rear idler enabled the track to move around three points, forming a triangle. The new design isolated the driving sprocket from potentially damaging ground impacts and radically improved service accessibility to the drive train. In addition, track rollers were flexibly mounted in a modified bogie arrangement, improving ground contact and ride.

It was a gutsy move for Caterpillar, considering that its conventional machines already dominated the large tractor business. The elevated-sprocket design was gradually extended and by 1985 covered the D9, D8, and D7 models.[39] Although it had some early reliability problems, the new concept gradually won acceptance. It was a costly development program for Caterpillar that entailed some risks, but the longer-term effect was to

The seven-hundred-horsepower D10 appeared in 1978. By the mid-1980s all Caterpillar mid-range and larger tractors were hi-drive. (Courtesy of Caterpillar Inc.)

strengthen its position in track-type tractors, particularly in the larger sizes. No competitor has yet chosen to emulate the elevated sprocket.

Hydrostatic Track Loaders   In another major departure from tradition, the company introduced four new hydrostatic track-type loaders between 1980 and 1983 to replace its line of conventional mechanical-drive Traxcavators. Although Deere had already introduced two hydrostatic track loaders, the new Caterpillar machines were more unconventional and had rear-mounted engines and more sophisticated hydraulic drive systems. Production facilities were provided for the complete line in the United States, France, and Japan.[40] In view of the sharp decline that had been occurring for a decade in worldwide demand for track loaders because of the growing popularity of hydraulic excavators, the heavy investment in development and production facilities for these models was dubious, especially because Caterpillar was already the market leader with its conventional line. Satisfied owners of older Caterpillar and other brands of conventional track loaders were slow to accept the 25 to 30 percent more costly new models.

Still pushing for a larger share of the mining truck business, in 1985 Caterpillar introduced the 130-ton, mechanical-drive, off-highway model 785.[41] Unit Rig and WABCO electric-drive trucks of similar and larger capacities had been the established standard in the mining industry since about 1965. Caterpillar, a very late market entry, had a difficult challenge in gaining acceptance for the 785, although it proved a good performer and gradually became an accepted alternative.

The Branding Program   Throughout its history, Caterpillar had jealously guarded its trademark, applying it only to products of its own design and manufacture, but in 1984, in the greatest departure ever from its traditions, the company adopted a program of applying its brand to other manufacturers' products. Perhaps partially driven by the tough years of the early 1980s, the company believed the program represented a profit opportunity as well as a means of quickly adding several much-needed product lines that would be difficult and costly to generate internally in a timely way. The company would purchase such products from the manufacturers for resale through its powerful distribution system in the expectation that the additional volume thus created would lower manufacturing costs sufficiently to offset the markup taken by Caterpillar. CMI paving products, CMI-owned Raygo and Albaret vibratory compaction equipment, and German-built Eder small hydraulic excavators were followed in 1985 by British-built DJB articulated dumpers.[42] The company was astute in selecting paving and compaction equipment, wheel excavators, and dumpers as product lines in which it needed to be, but branding was something entirely new for Caterpillar and its dealers. In the coming decade the concept would be put to the test.

A Plant with a Future   Before the recession of the early 1980s Caterpillar had spent billions on expansion, pouring money into additional floor space and new tooling to increase manufacturing capacity. Although top management believed that it was modernizing facilities through these investments, factory modernization as it is now understood was not occurring. Little attention was paid during these years to reexamining long-accepted factory practices in areas of material flow, in-process inventories, just-in-time supplier deliveries, and other areas where the potential for cost reductions was relatively untapped. The serious reverses between 1982 and 1984 forced a rethinking, and management came to realize that it could lower costs and operate with much reduced manufacturing space provided that operations were radically modernized to use facilities more efficiently. Thus was born the Plant with a Future (PWAF) program, which involved new tooling and a massive rearrangement of factories within existing space and was to be carried out over six years at a cost of about $2.1 billion, including $700 million in normal replacement costs. Unlike previous lavish capital spending, the program focused on cost reduction and proved to be the wisest capital investment the company ever made.[43] Indeed, it may well have been the salvation of Caterpillar.

Downsizing: A New Experience for Caterpillar   After more than thirty-five years of uninterrupted expansion of manufacturing facilities, the pivotal year of 1982 marked the point at which Caterpillar was forced to retrench for the first time in its history. Between 1983 and 1985 it closed about 20 percent of its manufacturing space and stopped construction on additional space. A *Wall Street Journal* article in late 1984 reported that Caterpillar had 70 percent more manufacturing space than in 1974 for 12 percent lower production.[44] But with the 1985 birth of PWAF, the company embarked on a new course that would pay huge dividends.

From a product standpoint, the three most significant events of the decade for Caterpillar were entry into the loader-backhoe and paving products businesses and the development of a new mining truck. The first two were product lines that a few years earlier the company would have judged unlikely candidates for entry. Loader-backhoes brought Caterpillar and its dealers into contact with a large group of buyers that previously had not regarded the company as a potential supplier. As highway spending shifted from new construction into resurfacing and reconstruction, paving products gave continued access to those dollars. With the new truck, Caterpillar was positioning itself to become a source of production equipment to large mines.

Unlike several companies in the industry, Caterpillar entered the perilous decade between 1976 and 1985 with a strong financial base that allowed it to survive where others had failed. But the company would never again be the same. Based on the Producer Price Index for Construction Equipment, in constant dollars Caterpillar at the end of 1985 was only 70 percent the size it had been in 1975. It had glimpsed its mortality and in the process gained a measure of much needed humility. Important changes had already occurred, and more would come.

Komatsu

At the start of the decade between 1976 and 1985 Komatsu's total earthmoving sales were about $900 million, nearly 20 percent of Caterpillar's worldwide total, but their sales to world markets outside Japan were only about 8 percent of Caterpillar's. That did not deter Ryoichi Kawai, Komatsu's president, from setting a goal to overtake Caterpillar and become number one worldwide. Komatsu workers took management exhortations toward the goal seriously, and slogans to that effect were regularly worn on headbands in the shop. While North American workers were periodically on strike for more paid time off among other things, Japanese workers took their "vacations" working in the shop and strikes in the North American sense were unheard of. These and other differences began to show during the 1970s. The Komatsu product line expanded rapidly and quality improved. Komatsu export prices were low, and although American critics attributed that to Japan's policy of maintaining a cheap yen, the Caterpillar Mitsubishi operation in Japan could not match Komatsu's costs.

New Products   Throughout the 1970s Komatsu pursued a goal of matching Caterpillar's product line. With its D155A already challenging Caterpillar's popular D8 tractor, Komatsu introduced the D355A and then the D375A to compete with the D9 and the D455A and D475A to compete with the D10, and pipelayer versions were made available. A line of scrapers was added along with articulated motor graders. In 1982 Komatsu purchased International Harvester's half of their joint venture wheel loader company, Kimco, which opened the way for the sale of wheel loaders by Komatsu in North America.[45] The line was quickly redesigned and made much more competitive. Off-highway trucks were added to compete model for model with Caterpillar until Komatsu jumped ahead during the late 1970s by introducing the HD-1200, a 132-ton mechanical-drive unit. Caterpillar would not have an equivalent unit until 1985.

It seemed at times that Komatsu's goal, at almost any cost, was to demonstrate to the world that its technology was as good or better than Caterpillar's. When Caterpillar introduced its four-model line of sophisticated hydrostatic track loaders between 1980 and 1983, for example, Komatsu followed with a single model as if only to show that "yes, we can do it too." By 1986 the Komatsu product line included:

Bulldozers	Sixteen models, through the 650-horsepower D455A
Hydraulic excavators	Eight models, through the 175-ton PC1500
Wheel loaders	Seventeen models, through the 7.1-cubic-yard WA600
Motor graders	Eleven models, through the 200-horsepower GD705A
Off-highway trucks	Five models, through the 176-ton HD1600M[46]

The impressive number of models of each product type reflected Komatsu's strategy: use one or two derivatives of each basic model to flood the product line and narrow the spacing between models to offer customers more than one choice in each size class. This, in addition to the lowest costs in the industry and aggressive pricing, caused major disruptions in the product and pricing strategies of U.S. competitors.

Inevitably, Komatsu would have to challenge Caterpillar for the world's largest crawler, which it did at ConExpo '81 when it displayed a prototype D555A, which at one thousand horsepower and 132 tons outclassed Caterpillar's D10 in size.[47] The scaled-up conventional machine was clearly not ready for production, and it would be the late 1980s before Komatsu would tentatively offer it for sale. By then Caterpillar had ten years' experience with

the D10 and had introduced the D11. Komatsu also displayed the prototype HD-1600, a 176-ton off-highway truck, at ConExpo '81, and the
company's capabilities seemed unlimited.

Breakthroughs in the Soviet Union and Middle East   Beginning in the late
1960s, when the USSR began to accelerate development of its petroleum and
mining industries through the purchase of imported equipment, U.S. manufacturers were the preferred source. Caterpillar, International Harvester, and
Fiat-Allis obtained most of the large tractor, pipelayer, and wheel loader
business, and Unit Rig, WABCO, and others obtained orders for large mining trucks. But Komatsu was not shut out altogether. After it developed the
HD-1200 Komatsu was able to compete for the truck business, and in 1979
it obtained a $30 million order for twenty units.[48] Komatsu was also the
main beneficiary of U.S. sanctions that arose from the invasion of Afghanistan and events in Poland and effectively ended American heavy equipment
sales to the USSR. Beginning in 1982 and for several years thereafter, Caterpillar and other U.S. manufacturers had to watch enviously as Komatsu
negotiated orders for literally thousands of big machines with the Russians.

In the Mideast, U.S. manufacturers labored under increasing handicaps.
When the Shah of Iran's forced-draft modernization program went into high
gear after the first oil crisis of 1973–74, American equipment suppliers
obtained the lion's share of some very large purchases of equipment by the
Iranian government. That ended abruptly with the 1979 downfall of the
Shah and the ensuing hostage crisis; after 1980 it became virtually impossible for American firms to do business in Iran. Japan, as Iran's largest petroleum customer, offered the obvious alternative, and Japanese equipment
manufacturers, Komatsu and others, again became the preferred suppliers.

Iraq had nationalized private equipment dealers during the 1970s, effectively forcing almost all equipment and parts sales through a quasi-govern-
ment agency that acted as a "dealer." Forced to deal direct, U.S. manufacturers were usually unable to operate under the prevailing Iraqi business
practices without breaking the U.S. Foreign Corrupt Practices Act. Less
squeamish Japanese and European manufacturers took the business, but
again the more aggressive and lower-priced Japanese predominated. Both
sides during the eight-year Iran-Iraq war purchased thousands of machines,
but U.S. manufacturers obtained little of the business.

Anti-boycott regulations designed to prevent recognition of the Arab
boycott of Israel provided a further handicap to U.S. manufacturers' Middle
East sales during this period. Of the large Arab OPEC oil producers, Saudi

Arabia, Kuwait, and the United Arab Emirates did remain open to most U.S. manufacturers, but the strong dollar of the early 1980s made obtaining business in these countries increasingly difficult against the Japanese.

All in all, U.S. foreign policy and self-imposed standards of business conduct combined with unfavorable dollar-yen exchange rates to raise barriers to U.S. manufacturers. Komatsu became the principal beneficiary in markets where previously it had not been the major supplier. It obtained thousands of orders, in many cases almost uncontested, built a volume base, and made its products all the more competitive in the open Western markets. Yet even if U.S. manufacturers had not been handicapped, Komatsu's up-to-date product line and aggressive marketing would still have won the company an important share of the USSR and Middle Eastern markets.

Overseas Expansion   Komatsu had established marketing subsidiaries in Belgium in 1967 and in the United States in 1970 but had no overseas manufacturing until it began production of a mid-sized bulldozer in Brazil in 1975. The next year it began assembling large bulldozers in Mexico in a joint venture with Dina, a Mexican government manufacturing entity. Another marketing subsidiary was established in Germany in 1981, and in 1983 Komatsu began a manufacturing joint venture in Indonesia. Finally, in 1985 the company moved to challenge its chief rival, Caterpillar, on Caterpillar's home grounds when Komatsu America Manufacturing Corporation was established, investing $24 million in a 650,000-square-foot former Lorain crane plant in Chattanooga, Tennessee.[49] Japanese-built machines were shipped to Chattanooga for installation of U.S. content, which, although minimal, allowed Komatsu to advertise as a U.S. manufacturer.

In 1985 the European Community charged Japanese excavator manufacturers with dumping and slapped on stiff countervailing duties of as much as 30 percent. Komatsu realized that it had to establish manufacturing in the EC or forget about competing there. In an ironic twist, at the end of 1985 Komatsu purchased the 744,000-square-foot former Caterpillar Birtley plant in Newcastle, U.K., as the base for its EC manufacturing operation.[50] To some, it was more evidence that the leader was shrinking while its Japanese rival was growing.

Increasing Success in North America   By 1980 Komatsu had dealers in all major metropolitan areas of the United States and Canada, and although in some areas sales coverage was sketchy, Komatsu had a presence where most business was located. Despite Komatsu's lower prices, Caterpillar was fairly successful in defending its market share. Komatsu's gains came primarily at the expense of weaker competitors, but there is little doubt that it was able to seriously affect Caterpillar's profitability. For 1983 Komatsu stated that it had exported $130 million (likely valued at inter-company prices) in construction equipment to the United States and claimed a 7.5 percent share of the year's recession-shrunken market. It expected to double the export figure in 1984.[51]

Closing the Gap   In 1985 Komatsu had an estimated $3 billion in worldwide earthmoving equipment sales, of which nearly $1.2 billion were outside Japan compared to Caterpillar's $5.2 billion and Caterpillar-Mitsubishi's $675 million.[52] From only 20 percent in 1976, Komatsu's sales were now more than 50 percent of its rival's and Komatsu was number two to Caterpillar outside Japan. With Caterpillar in the midst of the worst reverses in its history, it appeared that Komatsu might someday achieve its goal of becoming number one. The company never had a losing year throughout the equipment business's deep recession during the early 1980s. Although by Western standards Komatsu's announced profits were never impressive, such things were measured by a different standard in Japan. Looking out on the world of the early 1980s from their bastion in Tokyo, Komatsu's leaders had every reason to be optimistic as they viewed the shrinking sales, red ink, and business failures of Western competitors.

The J. I. Case Division of Tenneco

For Case, like most other companies in the North American farm and construction equipment industries, the 1970s were years of growth and prosperity. From $598 million in 1972, Case sales quadrupled to $2.4 billion in 1979.[53] Beginning the 1970s at a 50-50 split between agricultural and construction equipment, by 1979 two-thirds of Case's sales were in construction equipment, making it the third-largest worldwide after Caterpillar and Komatsu.[54] But Case's sales came entirely from light and mid-range equipment. In 1982, the twenty-fifth year of loader-backhoe production, Case built its two-hundred-thousandth unit.[55]

The Poclain Acquisition   After a spurt of Tenneco-financed acquisitions in the late 1960s and early 1970s to broaden its construction equipment product line, Case concentrated for the next few years on consolidating its organization, upgrading the product line, and increasing sales. But in 1977 a new expansion opportunity appeared. Poclain, the loss-making French manufacturer of hydraulic excavators, was in serious financial difficulty. In the 1950s the company had pioneered hydraulic excavators and by 1977 it was still the world excavator sales leader, but overexpansion and increasingly stiff competition from German manufacturers and Caterpillar in Europe had put the closely held company in extremis.

With more than fifteen years of manufacturing experience in France and confident that it knew the ropes in that country, Tenneco-Case wanted to buy Poclain outright but failed to reckon on the highly sensitive political aspects involved in the sale of a French company to American interests. Although no French investors came forward to rescue Poclain, in the end Case was restricted to a 40 percent interest in the French parent and full ownership of Poclain's overseas marketing facilities—all for $65 million.[56] It was a temporary reprieve but Poclain continued to lose money, and Case ownership edged up 44 percent after a second bailout in 1984.[57]

Although the Poclain acquisition strengthened Case's position in Europe, it did nothing for market share in North America, where the Poclain brand had little recognition.

The Consolidated Diesel Corporation   Through the years, the Construction Equipment Division had made do with diesel engines designed for Case farm tractors in the years before the company was even in the construction equipment business. Limited in horsepower, the engines restricted the size of both farm and industrial machines produced by Case, but the cost of developing a new engine line from scratch was more than even Tenneco was willing to subsidize. In one of its more astute moves, Case resolved the problem in 1978 when it formed a 50-50 joint venture with Cummins Engine Company to build a line of mid-range diesels. The venture, Consolidated Diesel Corporation (CDC), also filled a need for Cummins, which led the market in diesel truck engines but lacked strong products in the range of less than 250 horsepower. CDC was soon producing new, low-cost diesels from a modern plant in North Carolina.[58]

Tenneco's Burden   Acquiring Case in 1967 as part of the Kern County land deal, Tenneco had invested $727 million in the business in the ensuing eleven years but was still awaiting a dividend.[59] The parent, now a conglomerate with sales of $8 billion, was becoming restive. Even Tenneco president James Kettelson, who always had a soft spot for Case, was becoming impatient with the lack of return. In the late 1970s, after years of allowing Case almost complete autonomy, corporate headquarters began applying tighter oversight and quickly generated friction between Houston and Racine. Thomas J. Guendel, Case's chair and CEO, resigned during a blowup in late 1979, citing "differences in management philosophy." Although he had led Case through seven years of growth, he had been unable to generate a satisfactory return for Tenneco. Guendel's replacement was president Jerome K. Green, forty-three, who had a background in finance.[60]

Hard Times   Case sales peaked in 1979 at about $2.4 billion. It would be 1985, after it had acquired the International Harvester farm equipment business, before it would top that level and even longer before it would see an operating profit. The company began to feel the six-year slump in U.S. farm sales in 1980, which was followed in 1981 by a worldwide downturn in construction equipment. Case operating revenue bottomed out in 1984 at $1.7 billion with an operating loss of $105 million.[61] In an effort to maintain volume, Green returned to the practice of heavy discounting, which deepened the profitability problem.[62] Emphasis continued on company-owned retail outlets, which grew to about 250. During these years it was rumored that Tenneco, despairing of ever turning the company around, wanted to divest Case but was unable to find a buyer.[63] It seemed that Tenneco was stuck with the perennial underperformer.

The Acquisition of International Harvester Farm Equipment   Because Case had quit the implement business in 1972, the company's farm tractors accounted for only 4.6 percent of the worldwide farm equipment market in 1984, which made Case one of the smaller players.[64] Kettelson, now Tenneco's CEO, believed that Case had a clear choice—either get deeper into farm equipment or get out altogether. So in 1984, when Harvester was forced to sell its farm equipment business, he bit the bullet and took Tenneco-Case deeper. Tenneco paid $260 million in cash and $170 million in preference stock in addition to the assumption of certain liabilities (including up to $75 million in unfunded pension obligations) for the business. At the time, Harvester had 15 percent of the worldwide market, second to Deere's 32 percent. Case had come full circle since 1972 and was again a long-line farm equipment manufacturer, as Case International. It was a controversial move. Many on Wall Street thought Tenneco was throwing good money after bad.[65]

   With the addition of the Harvester volume, Case's 1985 sales jumped to $2.7 billion, but charges for plant closures, the costs of integrating the two companies, and continuing weak farm markets brought the biggest operating loss yet—$214 million. Construction equipment now accounted for less than half the business.[66]

Tenneco's Gamble   Between 1976 and 1985 Case kept its construction equipment products competitive with periodic updates, but aside from the Poclain venture it refrained from entering major new product lines. Its loader-backhoe line continued to lead the market worldwide and contributed nearly half of Construction Equipment Division's revenues.[67]

Despite pouring in more than $1 billion in seventeen years, Tenneco's generosity had not been able to make Case profitable. Successfully transforming itself from mainly a farm equipment company to the third-largest construction equipment company, Case, after the Harvester purchase, had reverted to being about 60 percent farm and 40 percent construction. Going deeper into farm equipment was a gamble, but if successful, doing so would make Case stronger and help its Construction Equipment Division. It would take almost another decade for the scenario to play itself out.

Deere & Company

The years between 1976 and 1981 were golden ones for Deere's construction equipment business; sales more than doubled to just under $1 billion. The new products promised for ERA III also appeared on schedule; in fact, Deere led the industry with its seemingly endless succession of innovative new machines. In 1979, a peak year for construction equipment sales for both companies, Deere's—at $997 million—were about 60 percent of Case's, although the two companies were fairly close if loader-backhoe sales were excluded. Deere had pushed more aggressively into pulpwood logging equipment with derivative machines from the construction equipment line, whereas Case was far stronger in Europe. Deere was 60 percent of Caterpillar in total sales but only 10 percent in construction equipment sales in 1981, the last good year before the slump. But what differentiated Deere and Caterpillar from the rest of farm and earthmoving equipment companies was that neither company had experienced a losing year since the early 1930s.[68]

Facilities Expansion   At the start of the 1976–85 decade Deere was in the midst of a six-year, $1 billion expansion program, a significant portion of which was directed at its two construction equipment plants, Davenport and Dubuque. In 1978 a 440,000-square-foot expansion was announced for the

Davenport plant to bring it up to about two million square feet, about the size of the Dubuque facility.[69] Manufacturing space had increased by 70 percent when the program was completed in 1979, and Deere announced that it would spend another $2 billion on facilities through 1985.[70] More space was badly needed all through the late 1970s because Deere could not keep up with farm equipment demand; its construction equipment business was growing even faster.

In fact, things were going so well with its construction equipment business that in 1978 Deere announced its target of becoming number three in the worldwide industry (presumably after Caterpillar and Komatsu) by 1990 and number two by 2000.[71] It was an audacious goal to say the least, considering that Deere was fifth in 1979 and far behind the leaders.[72] But the company made no bones about its near-term plans to move from mid-range into large equipment, which is what would be required to be number three or number two. Before these plans could be set in motion, however, the disastrous six-year farm equipment downturn intervened and was paralleled by the construction equipment recession of the early 1980s. Quietly, Deere was forced to cancel its ambitious plans.

The Down Years   With little overseas construction equipment business as a cushion, Deere felt the 1980 U.S. recession immediately on the construction equipment side, and layoffs began in April at Davenport and Dubuque. More followed, and the plants were temporarily closed in the fall to reduce inventories. Still, business held up remarkably well for the year and almost equaled the 1979 record. But 1981 saw a 20 percent drop that created a $38 million operating loss followed by a 26 percent slide in 1982. Construction equipment sales were now only 60 percent of the 1979 peak. Because of its strong farm equipment position Deere was slower than its competitors to feel the full effects of the downturn in that segment, but by 1982 it, too, was suffering. The company generated $193 million in operating losses before tax credits on its farm and construction equipment between 1982 and 1984 but was able to show a small net profit each year because of tax credits and the income from its financing and insurance businesses. From a peak of more than 65,000 in 1979, employment at the end of 1985 was 40,500.[73]

Although its North American construction equipment business had shown gratifying growth since 1975, the same had not been true for Deere in Europe. What had been all along a weak construction equipment effort was dealt double blows during the early 1980s by the recession in the EC and the strong U.S. dollar, which made importing Deere machines from the

United States impractical. Deere called it quits for construction equipment in Europe and withdrew its manufacturing and marketing effort.

New Products   Soon after the 1974 announcement of its product plans for ERA III (1975–79), Deere began a rapid-fire series of new product introductions. From ConExpo '75 through ConExpo '81 it added four crawler bulldozers and matching loaders topped by the JD750-755; two additional wheel loaders, including the five-cubic-yard JD844; two larger motor graders; the JD890 hydraulic excavator; and several new products for the logging industry. In addition, all existing models were updated or upgraded at least once. In 1975 Deere claimed another technological first with the JD750 hydrostatic bulldozer and matching loader, which used Sundstrand hydrostatic components, and later added the 650 and 850, which had the same feature. Hydrostatic front-wheel assist on motor graders was another first. All in all, it was a very impressive performance. At ConExpo '81 Deere changed the nomenclature on its industrial products, dropping the JD prefix.

Despite the shrinkage in volume and profits in the early 1980s, Deere's product program continued. The 990 hydraulic excavator was added in 1982, along with a wheel version of the 690 excavator. But a climate of pessimism brought on by operating losses and intense Japanese competition caused Deere to still face a substantial investment to fill out its excavator line.[74]

Recognizing that Japan had state-of-the-art excavator technology and that Japanese manufacturers were low-cost producers, in 1983 Deere entered into a manufacturing relationship with Hitachi on hydraulic excavators. Only the 690 would continue to be built in Davenport. The remainder of a broadened line would be Hitachi-built machines manufactured in Japan and shipped less engines to a plant in North Carolina. There, Deere engines would be installed, final assembly completed, and Deere decals and paint applied.[75] Although Deere was able to take advantage of Hitachi's low costs and economies of scale, the company risked potentially unfavorable dollar-yen exchange relationships by going offshore for an important part of its product line.

In 1981 Deere had a total of 440 industrial dealers in North America spread across the construction, utility, and/or logging categories. Another 234 were overseas, although many of them were joint agricultural-industrial dealers.[76] Although the large number of North American dealers gave Deere good geographic coverage, it also made for small sales opportunities for many dealers. The recession of the early 1980s in construction equipment created serious financial problems for many of the company's small dealers. To avoid massive dealer failures, Deere was forced to provide extended terms on dealer receivables of up to eighteen months and in some cases twenty-seven months beyond original due dates. Some interest was waived completely. Between 1982 and 1984 such measures cost Deere more than $80 million in foregone interest.[77]

Problems with Sanctions   Deere joined Caterpillar, Dresser, Fiat-Allis, and other companies caught up in the sanctions applied by the Reagan administration against the USSR. In 1982 Deere negotiated a technology deal with the Soviets on a 150-horsepower farm tractor, but the administration denied approval. The loss of the contract would cost the company $150 to $200 million in revenues.[78]

Changing the Guard   After twenty-seven years as CEO of Deere & Company, William Hewitt, sixty-seven, stepped down in August 1982, having been nominated ambassador to Jamaica. Robert A. Hanson, fifty-seven, president and COO since 1979, was named CEO and became chairman when Hewitt's nomination was confirmed.[79] When Hewitt succeeded his father-in-law, Charles Deere Wiman, in 1955, Deere was second to Harvester in the farm equipment business and had not yet entered the construction equipment business. At the end of Hewitt's tenure Deere was far and away the world's leader in farm equipment and the third-largest U.S. manufacturer of construction equipment, a truly outstanding record of leadership. Deere never had a losing year under Hewitt.

A Formidable Competitor for the Mid-1980s   Deere's construction equipment sales began rebounding in 1984, nearing 1979–80 peak levels of more than $900 million in 1985. But farm equipment sales were not yet out of the trough and dropped to $2.5 billion, a ten-year low.[80] Notwithstanding the seemingly endless farm recession, Deere emerged from the 1976–85 decade a more formidable competitor in the U.S. construction equipment market. In some product categories its North American market share was in the 20 to 30 percent range—even higher in small elevating scrapers. Where its product lines competed head to head with Case, with the exception of loader-backhoes, Deere's North American market share was generally higher, but Case still had more worldwide sales. The fact that Deere's construction equipment business was concentrated in North America put it at the mercy of the U.S. business cycle, with little countercyclical potential from overseas.

Overall, Deere had managed its construction equipment business astutely. Although there had been some operating losses, the company came out of 1985 well positioned as one of the major players in the game.

Dresser Industries

After acquiring the Jeffrey Galion Company in 1974, Dresser continued to push into construction and mining equipment with the purchase of the Marion Power Shovel Company in 1977, paying $126 million in cash and securities for the closely held company based in Marion, Ohio. Although results were not made public, Marion, at estimated sales of $350 to $400 million, was the second-largest power shovel maker after Bucyrus-Erie. At the time of its acquisition by Dresser, Marion's principal business, which still continues, was the manufacture of large walking draglines for coal stripping, mining shovels for truck loading, and large-diameter blast hole drills.[81]

The Acquisition of the Payline Division   From $2 billion in sales in 1975, Dresser grew steadily through the late 1970s and had reached $4 billion by 1980. The company's profits also doubled in the same period to $261 million, continuing to stoke an appetite for acquisitions. From 1978 through 1982 the Mining and Construction Equipment Division of Dresser generated a consistent $550 to $600 million in sales, including Galion, Marion, LeRoi air equipment, and the Jeffrey underground coal mining line.[82]

For years Dresser was rumored to be a likely buyer of International Harvester's construction equipment business. With Dresser's affinity for growth by acquisition and its evident interest in the construction and mining equipment industry, it seemed a natural combination. Unable to strike a deal, Dresser waited until Harvester's financial position forced it to unload the unprofitable business at almost any price. When the deal was closed in November 1982 Dresser had paid $82 million in cash, about 25 percent of book value. The parts and new machine inventories alone were probably worth more than the price paid. Included were plants at Libertyville, Illinois; Candiac, Quebec; Heidelberg, Germany; and a parts facility at Broadview, Illinois. The rights to the names "International" and "Hough" were also included. Harvester's construction equipment sales in 1981 had been $743 million, but the deep slump had brought 1982 sales down to only $433 million.[83]

What did Dresser get for its money? The most valuable asset was the 500-Series, a well-integrated, eight-model wheel loader line that featured Z-bar linkage and oil disc brakes on most models. The remainder of the line, although basically sound, was less than state of the art and had suffered from weak marketing. In their respective size classes, the track-type tractor and track loader models were at or near the bottom in market share, as was the scraper line. There were no excavators, loader-backhoes, or trucks.

At the price, it appeared Dresser had made a very good buy. Still, it had purchased a business that since the mid-1960s had rarely made an operating profit, a business that had been starved of capital, and one that, once the second-largest in the world industry, was now no better than sixth. It would be child's play to make money by selling off the heavily written down inventory, and consolidation measures that Harvester had taken before the sale would probably help profitability, but, in the long term, making money from this fading construction equipment business would be a challenge. Regardless, Dresser was now deeply committed to the earthmoving equipment industry.

The Acquisition of WABCO   In 1984 Dresser saw an opportunity to round out its construction and mining equipment lines when the WABCO Division of American Standard became available. The off-highway truck line would complement its newly acquired International-Hough line as well as the Marion shovels. Dresser would be unique in being able to offer the open-pit mining industry a package of loading and hauling equipment from one manufacturer. It picked up WABCO for a bargain price of $66.3 million, effective June 1, 1984.[84] WABCO, along with International-Hough, Marion, and Jeffrey Galion, were consolidated into the Mining and Construction Equipment Division.

For fiscal 1984 Dresser reported sales for the division of $852 million (including five months of WABCO) and an operating profit of a meager $25.5 million. With a full year of WABCO sales and a recovery in construction, 1985 sales jumped to $1.02 billion.[85]

Dresser: A Full-Line Competitor   With the acquisition of Marion, the Payline Division, and WABCO, along with the Galion and LeRoi lines purchased earlier, Dresser had put together a line of products that was formidable in its breadth and exceeded in some respects the two other full-line producers, Caterpillar and Komatsu. The Payline Division had been capital-starved, however, and the several years of uncertainty over Harvester's future in the construction equipment business had made customers leery of buying the products. Also, the various acquisitions had resulted in a totally nonintegrated distribution system that was very weak outside North America. Dresser faced the difficult tasks of rebuilding International-Hough's standing and constructing a coherent worldwide dealer organization. Ironically, Dresser chose a moment when the earthmoving equipment industry was seeing numerous retrenchments, divestitures, and outright failures to move deeper into the business. During the next decade the company's almost infallible record of success with its many acquisitions would be put to the test by its earthmoving equipment business.

The Clark Equipment Company

Coming out of 1975 at a little over $1.4 billion in sales, Clark had a modest two-year dip before seeing new growth that took the company to a record $1.7 billion in sales and a profit of $106 million in 1979.[86] But it was downhill from there. Clark's automotive, material handling, and construction equipment businesses were all hard-hit by the recessions of the early 1980s.

Once the market leader in lift trucks, Clark was being devastated by low-priced Japanese imports. Recognizing that its efforts to diversify its construction equipment line had failed, the company began scaling back to its core wheel loader line. The motor grader plant (formerly Austin-Western) in Aurora, Illinois, was closed in 1978, and production moved to the Lubbock, Texas, scraper plant.[87] But that was short-lived. In early 1981 Clark announced the closure of Lubbock and complete withdrawal from the scraper and motor grader business.[88] The Lima, Ohio, crane plant was also closed and sold.[89] Thus, the descendants of three more old and respected names in the earthmoving equipment business—Lima, Austin-Western, and Hancock —became extinct.

Leaving Michigan   From a peak in 1979, Clark's 1982 volume was off 40 percent, to $1 billion, about one-third of which was construction equipment. In a drastic retrenchment later that year Clark announced that it was leaving Michigan, closing its four plants there (in Benton Harbor, Jackson, Battle Creek, and Buchanan), and taking a $139 million charge for reorganization. Loss for the year was $154.5 million, the first since 1933. Remaining plants were in Asheville, Statesville, and Rockingham, North Carolina, and Georgetown, Kentucky (lift trucks). After some sixty years of close identification with the Michigan-based automotive industry, Clark was seeking a friendlier labor climate.[90]

At this point Clark's construction equipment consisted of the recently updated Michigan line of eight Series-C wheel loaders, from the 1.5-cubic-yard 35C to the 12-cubic-yard 475C, and the Melroe Bobcat line.[91] Of Clark's construction equipment acquisitions, only Melroe remained.

Euclid and the Formation of VME   In what was clearly a positioning move, in January 1984 Clark bought Euclid from Daimler-Benz for between $34 and $39 million.[92] Daimler-Benz had acquired Euclid from White Motor in 1977 for about $70 million, but after only seven years it apparently had its fill of the off-highway truck business. Euclid was now in the hands of its fifth owner since 1953.

The following April, Clark and Volvo BM, a subsidiary of AB Volvo of Sweden, announced a 10 percent stock swap as a first step to combining their construction equipment businesses. In January 1985 a full merger of the businesses was consummated, to be known as VME. Each company contributed $100 million in net assets. Headquarters would be in the Nether-

The Volvo BM DR631 was the first commercially successful overhung articulated dumper. The excavator-dumper earthmoving system was popular in Europe twenty years before it began to gain acceptance in North America. (Volvo Construction Equipment North America Inc.)

Volvo popularized the concept of the wheel loader as a versatile tool-carrier and forced other manufacturers to offer derivative models with similar features. This 4300 demonstrates the Volvo parallel lift feature. (Volvo Construction Equipment North America Inc.)

lands. Combined sales for 1985 were projected at about $800 million, with slightly more than half from Michigan-Euclid.[93]

The merger seemed a good fit. More than 70 percent of Volvo's business was in Europe, whereas 70 percent of Michigan-Euclid's was in North America. Volvo BM had its origins in an old-line Swedish manufacturer of farm tractors, Bollinder-Munktell, which had been acquired by AB Volvo, the parent. At the time of the merger with Clark, the Volvo BM product line consisted of five models of wheel loaders through 4.5 cubic yards in capacity and a line of articulated all-wheel-drive dumpers up to twenty-five tons.

There was redundancy in the Michigan-Volvo wheel loader lines, but the plan was to phase out the small Michigan models in favor of the Volvo units.

It is not clear who actually invented the articulated dumper, but without question Volvo BM was the first to successfully exploit the concept commercially. Beginning in 1966, it introduced the DR631, a 4-by-4 articulated model that had a capacity of ten metric tons. By the mid-1980s it had built ten thousand dumpers and claimed, probably correctly, to be the world's largest producer of off-road hauling units, albeit small ones.[94]

Volvo BM completely dominated the Swedish wheel loader market and was extremely strong in the rest of Scandinavia. Although there was nothing unique about the basic Volvo wheel loader, the company had led the industry in providing an elaborate cab filled with operator amenities. In fact, it had become well-nigh impossible in Sweden to sell a wheel loader that lacked these features. Volvo also led the way with a wide variety of front-end attachments for its wheel loaders along with a hydraulic "quick coupler" that permitted rapid change from one attachment to another without leaving the cab. The loader lift linkage provided "parallel lift," which allowed the raising of pallet loads like a lift truck. Volvo wheel loaders were the first of what would become known as "tool-carriers."

The acquisition of Euclid by Clark just before the joint venture was a move to add a line of rear-dump off-highway trucks with rigid frames to the impending combination. But the venture lacked hydraulic excavators, products that had become absolutely essential to a well-rounded line. VME searched vainly for several years to find a suitable partner that would fill this need.

A New Force in the Industry   The Michigan wheel loaders, introduced in the mid- to late 1950s, were the first truly modern machines of their kind and temporarily outstripped their rival, Hough, in bringing innovations to the industry and forcing the pace of early wheel loader development. But by the late 1960s Michigan no longer had a technological lead and was soon contesting with Hough for second place behind the leader, Caterpillar.

The 1985 merger of three fairly small players put VME in a class with Dresser and Deere in the $1 billion range in earthmoving equipment sales. The Volvo BM business had not been profitable for AB Volvo, and, likewise, the Michigan construction equipment line had lost money in the early 1980s. It was a marriage of convenience for both parents, effectively divesting themselves of unwanted businesses. With the formation of VME, the Clark Equipment Company ceased direct involvement in heavy construction equipment, retaining only the Bobcat line, a consistent profit-producer. The industry wondered, Would the combination of three specialized short-line players make a viable new competitor?

Fiat-Allis

When the joint venture was formed in 1974 it established two companies. Fiat-Allis Inc., headquartered in Carol Stream, Illinois, would handle North America, and Fiat-Allis B.V., headquartered in the Netherlands, would cover Europe. Ownership of each company split 65-35 Fiat/Allis-Chalmers. At the outset, the North American operation continued essentially unchanged from when it was wholly owned by Allis-Chalmers except that it now had the deep pockets of Fiat behind it. Manufacturing continued at Deerfield and Springfield, Illinois, with corporate offices and a parts warehouse at Carol Stream.

The narrow Fiat product line of small and medium bulldozers and track loaders was largely redundant to the Allis product line, so Fiat products did little to strengthen the combination in North America. Perhaps with a premonition of things to come, Fiat insisted that the product line be repowered with Fiat engines. But the Fiat name worked no magic with North American buyers, and the operation, with a stagnant or declining market share, continued to make losses. Volume of the venture peaked in 1980–81 at $849 million, with the North American operation contributing just over half.[95]

Business with the Soviets   The North American operation quickly felt the effects of the 1980 U.S. recession. At mid-year it announced job cuts and the relocation of some production from Deerfield to Springfield, and in December all manufacturing was consolidated in Springfield. Deerfield closed altogether.[96] What may have kept the Fiat-Allis doors open in North America during this period were some large tractor orders from the Soviet Union, where Fiat's connections were probably the best of any Western industrial corporation. In early 1981 an $84 million order for three hundred tractors was obtained, followed late that year by a $25 million, 107-tractor order. Two more orders were brought in early 1982, totaling $80 million for 270 tractors. To avoid potential sanctions, the later orders would be supplied from Italy, but the Reagan administration vetoed a technology transfer deal with the USSR for $110 million. The denial of that license brought a threat from Fiat-Allis to close its North American operations, with a loss of 2,100 jobs, but it later backed off that stance. Still, it complained bitterly that the deal had involved a commitment from the USSR to buy 60 percent of its construction equipment needs from F-A and would have led to later sales of $600 million.[97]

Dissolution of the Partnership   Meanwhile, despite the Soviet business, losses continued to mount. From the beginning of 1977 through 1982 they totaled $183 million in the North American operation.[98] New capital infusions had been required, but with Allis-Chalmers unwilling to contribute, its share of the enterprise had shrunk from 35 percent to 12 percent. In September, Fiat-Allis announced that lack of orders was forcing it to close Springfield indefinitely. Ten days later, Allis-Chalmers filed suit to liquidate the joint venture. Fiat, it stated, had "increasingly controlled the joint venture partnership so as to further Fiat's own interests without regard to the interests of Allis-Chalmers."[99] The litigation dragged on for three years and ended in late 1985, when Fiat purchased Allis-Chalmers's remaining interest for $10.7 million. The company was renamed Fiatallis.[100] With that, Allis-Chalmers, after fifty-seven years in the business, severed its last tenuous connection with earthmoving equipment.

By 1983 the worldwide slump in construction equipment had brought Fiatallis sales down to $511 million, of which only $206 million was contributed by Fiat-Allis North America. After a modest sales recovery in 1984, the uncertainties aroused by the difficulties between the two partners began to have an impact on North American customers, whose purchases steadily dwindled.[101]

Fiat-Allis in Europe   In Europe there was some synergism from the addition of A-C products, allowing F-A to increasingly dominate the Italian market, where the name Fiat was omnipresent. Preferential government-subsidized financing for Italian-made products helped. A small Italian manufacturer of hydraulic excavators was acquired to round out the line. North of the Alps, however, Fiat-Allis distribution continued to be weak, forcing the company to form distribution subsidiaries in the larger countries. By 1985 Fiatallis remained a small player in Europe north of the Alps. Total sales outside North America totaled $354 million in 1985.[102]

Fiat Alone   Once one of the "Big Three" of the U.S. earthmoving equipment industry, Allis-Chalmers was a classic example of a company that could not decide what business it was in. Perhaps as late as the 1950s, had A-C chosen to concentrate on farm and earthmoving equipment it might have been able to carve out a strong position. By the 1960s, however, it was too late. Its more profitable, more specialized rivals were by then unassailable to A-C. The joint venture with Fiat merely postponed the inevitable.

Unlike Allis-Chalmers, Fiat had the deep pockets to persevere in a business that composed a tiny portion of its volume, analogous to General Motors's experience with Euclid/Terex. Fiat also had a reasonably well-assured volume base in Italy from which to work. After the dissolution of the partnership it planned to go it alone in North America with imported products, although skeptics wondered how long that would last.

The Victims

International Harvester

Since taking over as CEO in 1971 Brooks McCormick had a growing conviction that Harvester badly needed a complete reorganization. But he believed that his ideas, to carry credibility with entrenched management, required an objective study by an outside organization. The consulting firm of Booz, Allen, and Hamilton was commissioned in late 1975 and about a year later brought in recommendations that dutifully ratified McCormick's ideas. As implemented in 1977, the company went from three functional North American divisions and an overseas division to five international business groups that would be autonomous and entrepreneurial: Truck, Agricultural Equipment, Payline, Solar, and Components. Although the reorganization had its positive aspects, the company found that as its financial difficulties mounted it could no longer support decentralized decision making. In 1981 the organization was recentralized into three groups.[103]

The McCardell Era   Influenced by examples of miracle turn-arounds accomplished at a number of large companies by dynamic executives, McCormick became convinced that along with reorganization Harvester needed such a leader, and he was prepared to step aside if that person could be found. Thus began the McCardell era at International Harvester. Archie R. McCardell, fifty-one, was president and chief operating officer of Xerox when recruited as president and CEO by McCormick in December 1977. McCormick retained the job of chairman. McCardell had begun his career at Ford as one of Robert McNamara's "whiz kids" and moved to Xerox in 1966.

He had a reputation as a tough cost-cutter. To get him, McCormick offered not only a generous salary but also an unusual inducement that later proved controversial. Harvester would loan McCardell $1.8 million to buy sixty thousand shares of Harvester common stock, the loan to be repaid over seven years, but the loan would be forgiven if McCardell could bring Harvester's financial performance ratios up to the average of its major competitors.[104]

Profits in 1977 had reached an all-time high of $202.8 million, but in 1978, despite an 11 percent sales increase, profits dropped back to $186.7, only 2.8 percent on sales. In an interview at the end of 1978 McCardell said he had identified, and planned to eliminate, $600 million of "excess costs" within Harvester. Earlier, he had announced an $82 million increase in capital spending for 1979 to $362 million, the highest in Harvester's history.[105] Frequently quoted in the financial press, McCardell was always bullish about the future of the company. Brooks McCormick and the board were impressed enough to elevate McCardell to the chairmanship in mid-1979; McCormick would remain on the board to chair the executive committee.

McCardell and the UAW   Results for 1979 gave solid reason to believe that McCardell was in fact a miracle worker who was well on his way to turning the old company around. Sales jumped 26 percent, but profit rose an eye-popping 98 percent to $370 million ($12.01 per share).[106] It was incredible, but more perceptive observers knew that in preparation for negotiations for a new contract with the UAW in late 1979 Harvester had built up dealer inventories, pulling business from 1980. Still, the results were the best ever for Harvester, and with that success in hand McCardell was ready to take on the UAW. There is no doubt that Harvester had a less favorable UAW contract than the Big Three auto makers, Caterpillar, and Deere because of unwise concessions Harvester had made to buy labor peace during the 1950s and 1960s. That was where McCardell hoped to find some of that $600 million in excess costs. The company's demands centered on two issues—compulsory overtime and a limit to job transfers—but the union was in no mood for give-backs. Thirty-five thousand UAW workers walked out on November 1, 1979, the first day of Harvester's fiscal 1980.[107]

Although Pat Greathouse, the UAW International chief negotiator, made efforts at conciliation, the locals were recalcitrant and the strike dragged on for 172 days. After two quarters of losses totaling $579 million, the company blinked first and signed a contract containing almost none of the concessions it had been seeking. McCardell attempted to put a bold face on it by claiming that the increase in productivity from the new contract would reduce needed capital investment by as much as $500 million over the next decade. But no one was fooled. It was a costly defeat for Harvester.[108]

The Beginning of the End   By mid-summer 1980 it was clear that a global slowdown was underway. In the United States the farm economy led the way. The hoped-for rebuilding of Harvester farm and construction equipment dealer inventories did not occur, and the company lost $397 million for the year. Despite the loss and a sharp increase in Harvester's debt, McCardell called it a temporary setback and remained bullish on the future, although some financial analysts called McCardell's optimism "a facade." Rating agencies were not taken in by McCardell's projections. Moody's reduced IH Credit Corporation's commercial paper rating from Prime 2 to Prime 3, effectively taking the company out of commercial paper as a financing source. Finally, after a history of regular dividend increases even when results did not justify them, the board cut the annual rate from $2.50 to $1.20.[109]

In the face of this gloom, the board rocked the financial community by announcing that it was forgiving McCardell's $1.8 million loan based on Harvester's 1979 financial performance ratios, which, according to the board's reading, had exceeded the average of the competition. Shortly thereafter, a $973,000 loan made on a similar basis to Warren Hayford, president, was also forgiven. It appeared to Harvester's creditors that the company was not facing up to the seriousness of its financial condition.[110]

After a further loss of $96 million in the fiscal quarter ending January 31, 1981, the company made the first public recognition of its financial problems at the February annual meeting, announcing the omission of the common dividend for the first time since 1918 and the planned sale of its Solar Division. There was also talk of a financial restructuring into a master agreement with the 225 lending institutions holding its $3.4 billion in short-term debt, which, with the prime rate near 20 percent, was assuming crisis proportions. Subsequently, Harvester set a target of May 1 to complete the restructuring, but that proved wildly unrealistic.

In the event, the final agreement with the banks was not signed until December 22. Exceeding in size the government-backed $1.5 billion Chrysler bailout of 1979, the $4.15 billion package gave Harvester a two-year breathing period. It was a classic example of the "too-big-to-fail" syndrome at work when Harvester's major banks browbeat the smaller lenders into line. Financial analysts said the agreement fell short of solving the company's fundamental problems: the lack of profitability and the need to be scaled down.[111]

Selling Solar   Meanwhile, the Solar Division had been sold to Caterpillar for $505 million cash, to take effect August 1, 1981. With a book value of $220 million, Solar had a 1980 profit of $11 million, the only profitable Harvester division that year. Harvester gleefully accepted the windfall and booked a gain of $243 million, but it refused to disclose to creditors how it used the $505 million. That lead to speculation that Harvester was preparing for a Chapter 11 filing.[112]

Despite McCardell's earlier rosy projections, Harvester reported an operating loss of $636 million for 1981, which, when netted out with extraordinary gains, resulted in a loss for the year of $393 million on sales of $7 billion.[113] That same year marked the 150th anniversary of Cyrus McCormick's invention of the reaper. It had been the worst year in the company's history, but even worse lay ahead in 1982.

The Sale of the Construction Equipment Business   In 1979 the Payline Division's sales had topped $1 billion for the first time with a small $53 million operating profit, but sales fell 24 percent during the 1980 recession to generate an operating loss of $154 million.[114] That year Harvester discontinued its line of loader-backhoes, which over about eight years had made almost no impression on the market.[115] Although Brooks MCormick had discontinued capital spending in the Payline Division, McCardell had reversed that policy, hoping to make the business more attractive to a buyer. But in the midst of deepening financial troubles in early 1981 the company said it would invest no more in construction equipment.[116] It was urgent that the cash drain of the non-core construction equipment business be stopped. The year 1981 was spent desperately seeking a buyer while trying to stanch the losses. Layoffs and temporary plant closures held Payline's 1981 operating loss to $63 million.[117]

In early 1982 it was apparent that Harvester was preparing for the divestiture of its construction equipment business. In February it announced the sale of its 50 percent interest in Kimco, a joint venture with Komatsu, to Komatsu for $51 million and booked a $30 million gain.[118] Also in February, Harvester announced the consolidation of its Payline Division at the Libertyville plant, leaving Melrose Park with diesel engine production only.[119]

In August it became public that IBH Holding, the aggressive new German construction equipment concern, was negotiating to buy Harvester's construction equipment business, but that arrangement quickly died. Harvester was desperate for cash, and IBH had very little of that commodity.[120]

The long-awaited announcement finally came in September. The Payline Division would be sold to Dresser Industries, effective November l. Including the write-down on assets, additional pension costs, and severance pay, Harvester took a charge against 1982 results of $366 million to exit the business. That, when added to the $17 million Payline operating loss in 1982, brought the year's total loss to $383 million from construction equipment. The company booked after-tax cash proceeds from the transaction of $67 million in its 1983 fiscal year and took an additional charge of $6 million.[121] Earlier in 1982, the French Yumbo excavator business (with $34 million in 1981 sales) had been sold to a group of Yumbo executives, and the Payhauler line of off-highway trucks was also sold to employees. Neither transaction generated significant cash flow.[122]

Thus ended International Harvester's fifty-four-year involvement with earthmoving equipment, beginning in 1928 with its first crawler tractor. From 1944, when it organized the Construction Equipment Division, the company was engaged in a serious effort to challenge Caterpillar for the number-one position, a challenge that became more quixotic as the years went by. By the late 1960s Komatsu had taken over the number-two position; by the late 1970s Case was number three; and by the time of the sale Harvester was seventh after Caterpillar, Komatsu, Case, IBH, Deere, and Fiat-Allis.

The Breakup of the Company   Five months after the financial restructuring of December 1981 the company was already in technical default on its agreement with the banks when its net worth dropped below $1 billion. Another restructuring had become necessary. At this point the bankers were tired of McCardell's optimistic projections that were never achieved and he was ousted, replaced as CEO by Louis Menk, sixty-four and a board member. Donald Lennox, sixty-three, became president, and a drastic retrenchment was begun.[123] Two truck plants including Ft. Wayne, as well as five agricultural equipment plants and two foundries, were closed and operations consolidated at remaining plants. Including the $383 million for the construction equipment business, 1982 special charges totaled $906 million. That, when added to the operating loss, produced a net loss for the year of $1.738 billion, the largest to that time for an American industrial corporation. The company ended the year with a long-term debt of $2 billion and net assets of only $145 million.[124]

But the pain was not yet over. The company continued to hemorrhage on the farm equipment side from the deep slump in agriculture and lost another $485 million in 1983 and then $55 million in 1984. On November 26, 1984, an agreement was reached for the sale of the agricultural equipment business to Tenneco.[125] Because Tenneco purchased only selected physical assets of Harvester's farm equipment operations, further write-downs were necessary in 1985, producing a net loss of $364 million. But the five-year nightmare was finally over. The company was reorganized into Navistar International Corporation, the surviving truck business. From International Harvester's peak of $8.4 billion in sales and some 98,000 employees in 1979, Navistar was a $3.5 billion corporation with 16,800 employees in 1985. It had, however, survived.[126]

A Failure of Management   The last five years of International Harvester were the inevitable outcome of the preceding fifty years of consistently poor profitability. The 1979–80 strike followed by a recession set the company on a final slippery slope from which it never recovered. Some blame Archie McCardell, but although he may have allowed the strike to go on too long he was not responsible for the deep-seated complacency that permeated Harvester management or the wrong-headed policies of the preceding five decades. Entrenched management, steeped in past glories, believed that the company was bulletproof, whereas the board, through unwarranted dividend increases, had failed to conserve desperately needed capital.

Analysts said the company had too many businesses but, excepting steel, any of them, if run separately and managed well, likely could have been made profitable. The failure of management to act decisively and improve profitability as far back as the early 1950s led ultimately to the tragic breakup of one of the oldest and most respected industrial corporations in America.

The sale of Harvester's agricultural equipment business to a competitor resulted in a healthy net decrease in North America's excess farm tractor manufacturing capacity, but unfortunately the same was not so with Dresser's purchase of the construction equipment business. That capacity, after years of neglect by Harvester, was given another life. Would the profitable Dresser company breathe new vitality into it? The next decade would reveal the answer to that question.

The White Motor Company

After a disastrous loss of $69.4 million on $1.23 billion in sales in 1975, the directors of White Motor again sought a merger with White Consolidated, encouraged by Edward S. Reddig, Consolidated's chair and CEO.

Reddig was sure that he could turn White Motors around. This time, on the basis of the "failing company" doctrine, the Justice Department approved the combination, but Consolidated's board, wary of the money-losing record of Motors, backed out at the last minute. Differences between the board and Reddig, who favored the merger, led to the resignation of Reddig, the longtime head of White Consolidated.[127]

The Struggle for Survival   With the immediate possibility of a merger closed off, White Motors management, knowing it was nearing the end of the string, began selling non-core assets to raise cash. Its unprofitable farm equipment business, with sales of $341 million in 1975, would be difficult to sell, so White turned to the assets in the Industrial and Construction Equipment Division, its one profitable operation. Between July and October 1976 it gained about $85 million by selling in quick succession the Superior diesel engine and gas compressor business, Alco Diesel, and White Engines Inc. (the former Hercules Diesel), along with a small materials-handling business.[128] Finally, it was reported in October that the Euclid off-highway truck business would be sold to Daimler-Benz. When finalized the following May, Daimler-Benz paid about $70 million for a business that had 1976 sales of $140.3 million and an operating profit of $6.3 million. The sale included an antiquated 443,700-square-foot plant in Cleveland.[129]

Thus, after a brief nine years under the White Motor banner, the Euclid name changed hands again, the fourth owner in twenty-four years. Daimler-Benz had earlier toyed with the idea of acquiring White's on-highway truck business but settled for the off-highway trucks, a business in which it had no experience whatever. It would soon find the business was not to its taste.

Bankruptcy   The sale of assets gave White Motor some breathing space, but it continued to bleed from its on-highway truck and farm equipment businesses. In early 1980, after nine painful years as White Motors CEO, Bunkie Knudsen retired, thus avoiding having to preside over the death of the company.[130] After an earlier financial restructuring had not resolved its problems, the company was headed for a second restructuring when one of its banks froze White's deposits. It was the final blow. The next day, September 4, 1980, White petitioned for bankruptcy. In November the White–New Idea farm equipment assets were sold to TIC Corporation. In December the Western Star truck operation was sold to Canadian investors, and the following September the company was wound up when the core White truck business was sold to AB Volvo for $70 million, roughly half book value.[131]

Farm Equipment and White   Probably the leading cause of White's ultimate demise was the very unwise acquisition of three weak farm equipment companies in the 1960s: Oliver, Cockshutt, and Minneapolis-Moline. Over the next fifteen years White spent precious capital consolidating and modernizing that business in a fruitless pursuit of profitability in an industry with large excess capacity and several rivals with deeper pockets. The money would have been better spent strengthening its core heavy truck business, where it had a major market position, ranking second behind International Harvester. But short of funds for needed modernization of its facilities, the truck business was only marginally profitable. The acquisition of Euclid in 1968, although a questionable diversification for a company already unable to meet its capital needs, had little effect, either positive or negative, on the fortunes of White Motor Company.

Massey-Ferguson

In 1976 Massey-Ferguson sales reached a new high of $2.77 billion, almost tripling since 1970, while profits had more than doubled to $118 million. To the casual observer it appeared that the multinational company, the world leader in farm tractor unit sales, was thriving. Despite these seemingly positive results, however, financial analysts were becoming concerned over the company's growing debt.[132] After the 1974 acquisition of Hanomag, M-F's Industrial and Construction Machinery (ICM) Division sales had spurted, reaching a respectable $380 million in 1976, which, with parts sales, was already about two-thirds of Deere's industrial volume.[133] But there was one problem—ICM was losing money in construction equipment.

Retrenchment in Construction   Hanomag, M-F's main construction equipment operation, had not been profitable under its previous owner, but M-F was sure it could turn the company around by expanding sales to North America. M-F's plans were frustrated by an underdeveloped North American dealer organization and the steady depreciation of the dollar versus the mark—20 percent between July 1974 when it acquired Hanomag and early 1978. Hanomag, a high-cost producer, was a loser from day one for M-F.

Although 1977 corporate sales hit $2.8 billion, construction equipment losses and high interest expense conspired to cut profits to only $32.7 million. M-F's debt was out of control, and some analysts estimated interest expense as high as $193 million for the year. At the annual meeting in February 1978 the company announced that the common dividend would be omitted and admitted that it had not been able to turn Hanomag around.[134] In March, M-F discontinued the sale of Hanomag products in North America, and it seemed likely that the money-loser would be divested. That was confirmed when M-F took a $116 million write-down of its construction equipment assets against 1978 results. When added to a $90.9 million exchange loss and an operating loss of $49 million on construction equipment, the total net loss for the year was $256.7 million on sales of $2.92 billion.[135]

Although the investing community knew M-F was in trouble, no one expected a loss of this magnitude. In July 1978 the Argus Corporation, the Canadian holding company that had effective control of M-F, installed Conrad Black as chairman. The thirty-five-year-old Black, a member of the family that controlled Argus, was regarded as something of a boy wonder in Toronto investing circles. He said the M-F board meetings were "a farce."[136] But in 1980 Black resigned as chair to avoid the appearance of seeking public funds to bail out the Argus holdings after M-F, in an effort to stave off bankruptcy, began negotiating Canadian government financial support. Soon after, Argus donated its M-F stockholdings to M-F's underfunded pension funds and ended its fifty-year involvement in the company's affairs.[137]

M-F and the Construction Equipment Business   It was clear that M-F was cutting its losses in construction equipment when in December 1978 it closed its Akron, Ohio, plant, its main U.S. source for construction equipment. The production of loader-backhoes was continued at Des Moines and Manchester, England.[138]

An early 1979 *Wall Street Journal* article described M-F as having "a chaotic international management and manufacturing structure." Although still holding the number-three position worldwide in farm tractors, it now had only 15 percent of the rich North American tractor market. M-F had bet borrowed money on large-scale expansion and diversification around the world, but the bet had not paid off. Too many of its seventeen wholly or partially owned plants were either unprofitable or only marginally profitable.[139]

In March, A. A. Thornbrough, longtime president and CEO who had presided over M-F's headlong expansion since the mid-1950s, resigned. His replacement was Victor Rice, president since 1978, who had come to M-F from Perkins.[140]

In November it was announced that effective February 1, 1980, Hanomag, the loss-plagued construction machinery operation, would be sold to IBH Holding AG, the rising German construction equipment firm. Price was not disclosed, but it appeared that capital-short IBH somehow paid cash.[141] After taking the $116 million write-down in 1978 largely against its Hanomag construction equipment assets and an operating loss of $49 million, M-F was probably delighted to get the loser off its books at any price. The decision to acquire Hanomag in 1974 had been a costly mistake.

M-F had introduced its first heavy construction equipment in 1968 and was totally out of the business by early 1980. Although its loader-backhoe business may have been profitable during that period, it is unlikely that heavy equipment was ever in the black during the twelve-year experience. Unlike Deere with a very healthy farm equipment business and Case with the deep pockets of Tenneco behind it, M-F did not have the financial staying power to support its losses.

The End of Massey-Ferguson   But the pain was not yet over for Massey-Ferguson. The loss for 1980 was $225 million after a whopping interest expense of $230 million and an additional $25.5 million adjustment to the final selling price of Hanomag. After losses totaling $995 million from 1980 through 1985 and three financial restructurings, the company reorganized as Varity Corporation in 1986 and began diversifying into automotive parts and components. Sales climbed back from a low of $1.3 billion in 1985 to $3.1 billion in 1991, with automotive products accounting for 43 percent, more than farm and industrial equipment.[142] Landini was sold in 1989 for $25 to $30 million. In late 1992 Varity severed its last connection with the earthmoving equipment business when it sold off its loader-backhoe business based in Manchester, England, for $18 million in a management buy out. The business had produced only 1,600 loader-backhoes and $84 million in sales in 1991.[143]

That year, the hundredth anniversary of the founding of the Massey-Harris Company, Varity abandoned Canada and became a Delaware corporation. The once premier multinational corporation of Canada no longer had operations there. Into the early 1990s Varity's Massey-Ferguson farm equipment business was still producing more than $1 billion in sales but was a continuing drag on earnings. Varity sold the business to AGCO for $328 million in April 1994 and ceased all connection with farm equipment.[144]

IBH Holding AG

In the annals of construction equipment there is no other story like that of IBH and its founder, Horst-Dieter Esch. For pure entrepreneurial boldness Esch has no equal in the history of the business. Born in Germany in 1943, he grew up there, completing his education with an M.B.A. from University of Southern California in 1967. Returning to Europe, his first job was with Duomat, a German manufacturer of bituminous rollers, and by 1969 he was back in North America in Toronto to head a Duomat–Blackwood Hodge joint venture. At the time, Blackwood Hodge, a publicly owned British corporation, was the world's largest distributor of construction equipment and had dealerships throughout the British Commonwealth and elsewhere that sold chiefly Euclid and later Terex products. By 1974 Esch was in charge of Blackwood Hodge's European operations.[145]

Forming IBH Holding   In 1975, believing he now had a good knowledge of the construction equipment business, the thirty-two-year-old Esch resigned from Blackwood Hodge and with $550,000 in capital from Blackwood Hodge stock options formed IBH Holding AG in Mainz, West Germany.

Esch knew that a large number of very weak construction equipment manufacturers in Europe could be purchased at bargain prices. These companies, generally small and privately held with narrow, specialized product lines, had been established to serve specific national markets under varying economic conditions from those that obtained in Europe in 1975. Typically short of capital, they had not been able to expand distribution to take advantage of the broader market created by the EEC and were being crushed by the larger, better-financed firms doing business throughout the EEC. By the late 1970s many small firms were in financial difficulty and their owners were desperate to get out, but draconian social laws made bankruptcy and liquidation an unpalatable solution because of government-mandated severance pay, redundancy costs, and pension expenses. That is where Esch came in.

Beginning with minimal capital in 1975, he began to pick up small companies, offering equity in IBH in exchange for the assets. Little if any cash changed hands, but Esch was a godsend to the owners of the failing companies. They received equity in IBH, but Esch retained the voting rights. By that means, through 1979, IBH had acquired seven small construction equipment companies with sales of $103 million. Throughout its existence, IBH profit figures were never made public.[146]

Acquiring Hanomag and Terex   IBH was now beginning to be noticed in the trade press, and Esch was taking on the aura of a genius. But even bigger things lay ahead. In early 1980 the industry was rocked when in quick succession IBH took over Hanomag; Hymac, the largest British hydraulic excavator manufacturer; and gained a 50 percent interest in Wibau, a German manufacturer of asphalt plants and concrete pumps. Esch even persuaded Schroeder, Muenchmeyer, Hengst and Company (SMH), a Frankfurt private bank and owner of Wibau, to make a capital contribution, and the bank took a 10 percent equity position in IBH. Major German banks were not interested in backing the fledgling company and regarded Esch as something of an upstart, but after the Wibau transaction the fates of IBH and SMH were to become closely intertwined. With these three additions, IBH sales in the first half of 1980 were projected at about $350 million.[147]

To this point all acquisitions had been in Europe, but Esch was looking longingly at the huge U.S. construction equipment market that no European producer had yet been able to crack. But he understood, as some European manufacturers before him had not, that distribution was the key to success in the North American market. In the first half of 1980 IBH began buying shares of Pettibone Corporation on the open market and by midyear had acquired about 13 percent for $8 million. Pettibone, a U.S. manufacturer of materials-handling equipment, had forty company-owned branches, which were the attraction. Esch said he planned to acquire up to 25 percent, giving him effective control.

But before the plan was carried to fruition IBH's North American distribution problem was resolved in Esch's biggest coup. General Motors announced on September 30 that it was selling its Terex Divison to IBH, effective January 1, 1981. The division, which some financial analysts estimated to be worth up to $350 million, had sales of about $500 million. General Motors appeared to be headed for its first loss in sixty years and had been disposing of what it regarded as non-core assets to concentrate on its stumbling car business. A GM vice president was quoted as saying that Terex had been non-viable since the 1968 consent decree forced the sale of its off-highway truck line. Again, the specifics were not made public. Obviously, Terex was worth several times the value of IBH, but in a startling development GM not only transferred ownership of Terex to IBH but also invested $22.2 million for a 13.6 percent stake in Esch's company. It almost appeared that GM was paying Esch to take the unwanted division off its hands, accepting IBH notes in payment. Only the U.S. Terex operation was involved, but later in a separate transaction IBH also acquired the U.K. Terex plant at Motherwell, Scotland. General Motors took no voting rights in IBH through these transactions.[148]

The Struggle for New Capital   Esch quickly put together a display of his varied product line for ConExpo '81 in Houston at the end of January. Of IBH's eleven companies, the Terex name was the only one familiar to most attendees, so the Terex nameplate and color were applied to everything. The addition of Terex doubled sales in 1981, and IBH reached $1.03 billion. Only Caterpillar, Komatsu, and Case were larger. No profit figures were given, but Esch said that IBH "broke even" for the year and interest expense was $48 million. At this point IBH's capital totaled $85.8 million, an extremely narrow base for a billion-dollar company.[149]

More capital was vital to support such a large sales base. In May 1981, GM, to protect its shaky investment, agreed to take half of a $27.1 million capital increase, bringing its share to 19.8 percent and making it the largest stockholder. Other major stockholders were Powell Duffryn Ltd., a British concern, at 19 percent, SMH Bank at 11 percent, and Esch at 16.6 percent. The remainder was spread among the former owners of the numerous small companies acquired by IBH. Esch continued to control voting rights.[150]

By now plaudits for Esch were rising to a crescendo in the European trade press, and even the *Wall Street Journal* had some flattering comments. He was labeled a wunderkind and the savior of the EC's earthmoving equipment industry, which before IBH had never had a company that could compete with the U.S. giants. The aura of confidence Esch exuded was indeed convincing, but there continued to be skeptics based on the finances of IBH, which, as a closely held private corporation, remained murky.

In May 1982 Esch was able to ease the pressure somewhat by finding a new investor, Dallah Establishment of Jeddah, Saudi Arabia, which put in $38.6 million in new capital for a 17.9 percent stake. GM, maintaining its position as the largest stockholder, added $8.6 million. Esch now controlled 11.6 percent of the equity and 56 percent of the voting rights. IBH added another investor in July when Babcock International, a British engineering firm, sold its construction equipment business to IBH, Babcock taking a 10.1 percent stake. These investments implied that IBH now had a nominal capital of about $240 million.

In mid-1982 International Harvester approached the always receptive Esch, hoping to unload its construction equipment business; some considered IBH to be the most likely purchaser. But unlike General Motors when it sold Terex, Harvester was looking for cash rather than notes. Esch bowed out and said they could not agree on pensions and other commercial terms.[151]

The Collapse   Despite all these seemingly positive developments, things were not going well for IBH in 1982. The worldwide slump in construction equipment was hitting the entire industry, and IBH was not immune. But IBH, a privately held company, did not have to make public the full dimensions of its problems. Esch admitted to a loss of some $40 million for the year.

As the slump deepened in 1983 there were no new acquisitions, and Esch became abnormally quiet. That quiet was broken, however, by an explosion on November 7, when the press broke the story that IBH Holding AG had filed for protection from its creditors under German bankruptcy laws. As the story unfolded, it was revealed that what had triggered the IBH action was the near collapse of SMH Bank, which needed $230 million to keep its doors open, bringing on a crisis in German banking circles. The big German banks stepped in to rescue SMH, and when bank regulators saw the size of SMH loans to IBH they pulled the plug. It was all over for IBH. SMH, a small private bank, had an exposure with IBH of between $334 and $372 million. The whole edifice came crashing down with the failure of the IBH holding company, and all the companies filed for bankruptcy, including Terex in the United States.[152]

Not surprisingly, it appeared several firms that had sold their construction equipment businesses to IBH were owed large sums—Babcock International as much as $32 million and General Motors at least $80 million. It was also learned that GM had written off $37 million of its IBH debt in 1982 and would have been asked to write off another $48 million for 1983, amounts owing from the 1980 IBH acquisition of Terex.[153] To protect its position GM took steps to reacquire both the U.S. and Scottish Terex operations only three years after it had divested those unwanted properties.

As the receiver delved deeper, the IBH loss for 1982 was found to have been $181 million rather than the $40 million stated by Esch. It was also revealed that beginning in 1982 some IBH companies engaged in phony intercompany sales; equipment never left the yard but receivables were sold for cash. The holding company faced claims totaling more than $533 million.[154]

In another development, the IBH receiver, claiming that in lieu of promised cash infusions GM's capital contributions had only been in the form of offsets to debt and other in-kind credits, demanded reimbursement of $46.5 million from GM. All in all it was a very messy affair for the American giant.[155]

The Aftermath   When the collapse occurred, there was speculation that one positive aspect of the debacle would be a much needed reduction in industry capacity, but such was not the case. With two or three minor exceptions all the companies continued in business, usually back in the hands of the former owner, who promptly began looking for another buyer. Massey-Ferguson wisely had taken its full lumps when it sold Hanomag to IBH and so had no interest in either company. With no parent, Hanomag was near liquidation when the state of Lower Saxony and the city of Hannover came to the rescue with financing to save the 2,500 jobs. Like a phoenix, Hanomag rose from the ashes, awaiting another buyer.[156]

Resigning shortly after the collapse, Esch was taken into custody by West German officials. In late 1984 he was sentenced to 3½ years in prison for fraud.[157] And so ended the saga of IBH and Horst-Dieter Esch. As an entrepreneur Esch had few equals during his IBH days, but he dared too much. Perhaps without the deep slump of the early 1980s he might have pulled it off.

The WABCO Division of American Standard Inc.

The foregoing companies were victims in the sense that they either failed completely or survived only in drastically altered form, but in any case they disappeared entirely from the earthmoving equipment industry. American Standard Inc. is a victim in the sense that it found it necessary to reduce drastically its earthmoving product lines and exit the earthmoving equipment business altogether. The key Haulpak product line endures, however, and thus is not considered a victim.

Between 1976 and 1980 WABCO Division sales grew from $249 million to $316 million, which, when inflation is considered, represented an actual shrinkage in size. Operating profits trended steadily down from $39 million in 1976 to $2 million in 1980. More and more the fortunes of WABCO were dependent on off-highway truck sales as its scrapers and graders lost share in a shrinking market. WABCO scraper and grader sales totaled only $46 million in 1979, 15 percent of the division, and the next year the decision was taken to discontinue the product lines. The Toccoa, Georgia, plant that R. G. LeTourneau had established in 1939 was closed, and the company took an $11 million charge.[158] Thus, the lineal descendant of the LeTourneau company that invented the wheel tractor-scraper in 1938 ceased manufacturing scrapers, and the motor grader line begun by J. D. Adams in 1885 became extinct. Only Caterpillar, Komatsu, and Terex remained in the large scraper business.

WABCO sales were flat at $310 million during 1981 but began a free-fall with the onset of worldwide recession. They dropped to $194 million in 1981, with an $8 million operating loss; 1983 was even worse at $173 million in sales and an operating loss of $15 million. A drastic downsizing was carried out in 1982. The Brazilian plant was sold, the Australian plant closed, and employment was reduced 40 percent. Since 1976 American Standard had put little capital into WABCO—a total of only about $40 million over eight years. Product upgrades had been made, but only one new truck had been introduced, a 120-ton mechanical-drive unit.[159]

The Sale to Dresser   At the end of 1983, after fifteen years, American Standard concluded that off-highway trucks did not fit with bathroom fixtures and began looking for a buyer for WABCO. After its 1982 purchase of International Harvester's construction equipment business, Dresser Industries opted to add WABCO off-highway trucks to its Construction and Mining Equipment Division and paid $66.3 million, effective June 1, 1984. American Standard took a charge of $22 million.[160] With that, WABCO passed into the hands of its third owner since R. G. LeTourneau sold out to Westinghouse Airbrake in 1953. With the sale to Dresser went the Peoria North Adams Street plant founded by LeTourneau in 1935.

An Expensive Experience for American Standard   WABCO never accounted for more than one-sixth of American Standard's business and often as little as 10 percent. In its zeal to become a conglomerate, American Standard fought a bitter, litigious battle in 1968 with Crane for control of WABCO, a business wildly divergent from American Standard's core interests, only to find it had entered a competitive, capital-intensive industry in which it was one of the smaller players. By the early 1980s the industry was no place for small, specialized manufacturers like WABCO, and American Standard folded its cards.

Industry Product Development

The Proliferation of Hydrostatic Drives

Hydrostatics were particularly well suited to slow-speed, creeping-type applications and so were adapted early on into pavers and bituminous rollers and later into subgrade trimmers and pavement profilers-cold planers as they were developed in the 1960s and early 1970s. After the rapid evolution of the hydraulic excavator in the previous decade, hydrostatics underwent substantial refinement between 1976 and 1985; as know-how proliferated the hydrostatic drive system spread to new applications. Hydrostatic drive could provide stepless travel speeds in track-type tractors and track loaders, in contrast to the power-shift transmission as well as independent control of each track, enabling power turns and eliminating steering clutches. But it did have a disadvantage—it was less efficient in transferring flywheel horsepower to the ground across the full spectrum of ground speeds. Still, hydrostatics promised to open a new era of precise controlability and ease of operation of tracked vehicles. Deere was first in 1975–76 with its 750 bulldozer and 755 track loader, followed later by the larger 850 model. Between 1981 and 1983 Caterpillar introduced its four-model line of hydrostatic track loaders, but the company was not persuaded that hydrostatics were appropriate for bulldozers and preferred to stay with the "hard drive," as did Komatsu.

Liebherr, a privately held German manufacturer of hydraulic excavators, began developing a line of fully hydrostatic rear-engine loaders during the 1980s, both track-type and wheel-type, with emphasis on controls that were literally finger-tip and used joysticks, buttons, and switches.

As hydrostatic pumps and motors became more compact, efficient, and cheaper, hydrostatic drive became almost the standard in Europe on small utility machines. Case, Caterpillar, Deere, and the British JCB Company, however, firms accounting for the bulk of the loader-backhoe market, stayed with the proven and cost-effective mechanical drive.

Electronics Arrive

Hydrostatic drive was not necessarily the answer for every type of vehicle, but it helped emphasize that improved controlability and ease of operation had become primary sales features, and fast-developing chip technology appeared to offer equipment manufacturers a way to enhance those features in their machines. Electronic systems to monitor the vital signs of equipment had replaced gauges by the end of the decade, and manufacturers had developed diagnostic service tools that worked in conjunction with on-board electronics.

Electronics began to appear in hydraulic excavators to allow operators to optimize the hydraulic system to digging conditions. And development even began toward putting the excavator cycle on a programmable micro-processor that would control repetitive digging and loading functions with minimal operator intervention. Similarly, work was going ahead on an electronic system for the continuous monitoring of a production equipment fleet in, say, a large open-pit mine. Data on payloads, travel speeds, and cycle times would be transmitted from production units in real time to a central computer for storage and analysis. In addition, equipment vital signs could be continuously monitored and tied into the operation's overall equipment maintenance program, which would, of course, be fully computerized. With the speed at which microprocessor technology was advancing, the practical application of these concepts would be near at hand by the end of the decade.

Articulated Dumpers

The articulated dumper, popularized by Volvo BM in Europe, filled a niche that scrapers and on- and off-highway trucks could not reach. With all-wheel drive and large single tires, the dumper did not require established haul roads like trucks. Being top-loaded, dumpers could handle materials not suitable for scrapers. Normally matched with hydraulic excavators, dumpers were well suited to the prevailing wet conditions of Northern Europe and the United Kingdom. Between 1976 and 1985 the dumper-excavator combination established itself in Europe as the preferred system for off-road earthmoving. By 1984, when an estimated 1,300 dumpers were sold worldwide, North American manufacturers could no longer ignore the product, even though few had been sold there to date. At that point the principal competitors were Volvo BM, the leader, followed by the British DJB Company and Moxy, a small Norwegian firm. Dumper size had also drifted upward, and the twenty-two- to twenty-five-ton sizes became popular. DJB, using Caterpillar drive-train components, had the largest range (from twenty-five- to fifty-five-ton capacity), but the market for larger than twenty-five tons was quite small. The rather lightweight dumper bodies did not lend themselves to heavy rock work.

Caterpillar entered the business in 1985, when it branded the DJB line. Terex introduced a twenty-three-ton model, the 2366, and VME added its 5350, a twenty-five-ton unit.[161] The entry of Caterpillar and Terex and the formation of VME gave the dumper new impetus in North America, where it began to gain acceptance.

The Mini Excavator

The mini excavator, officially classified as less than six metric tons in weight, began to appear in quantity in Japan and Europe during the early 1980s. Although it is not clear where this small utility tool was first developed, there is no doubt that the Japanese were the first to commercialize it successfully on a large scale. Gaining production experience on a huge home market volume base of as many as thirty to forty thousand units annually, the Japanese quickly invaded Europe with the product.[162] The EC common external tariff, however, allowed some European production to coexist with the Japanese. The mini effectively put an end to hand labor on small excavating and trenching jobs. It filled a niche below the loader-backhoe in price, but in North America, where the loader-backhoe was well established as the accepted utility tool, the mini initially was regarded as something of a toy and was slow in gaining acceptance.

Other Developments

The decade saw a somewhat slower rate in the scaling up of machines than had taken place in previous years. The need to move construction equipment from place to place imposed a practical limit in size that generally had been reached in the 1960s, however large open-pit mines were relatively free of such limitations. In its constant drive to lower unit costs the mining industry had moved into the 170- to 190-ton truck size and was poised in 1985 to move to the next generation of 240 to 250 tons. Dresser-Haulpak was already there with its 3200B, and other manufacturers were busy developing their entries.

The most important development of the decade in loading equipment was the emergence of large hydraulic front shovels to compete with rope shovels, long the entrenched truck loading tool in open-pit mines. Poclain led the way in 1971 with the 136-metric-ton EC1000, followed by the 161-ton 1000CK in 1975. Demag followed with its 310-metric-ton H241 in 1978, topped the next year by O&K's massive 549-metric-ton RH 300. The industry may have overreached with these huge machines because initially few were sold. The Poclain machines were failures and were withdrawn, and only three RH 300s were built. O&K persevered with the much more successful 243-metric-ton RH 120 in 1983. Liebherr joined the battle in 1985 with the R994, competitive to the RH 120.[163]

U.S. rope shovel manufacturers, Bucyrus-Erie, Marion, and P&H, had dominated the business since the inception of open-pit mining around the turn of the century but now found themselves challenged by European hydraulic machines. Continuing to develop larger rope shovels, the U.S. manufacturers also introduced hydraulic machines that met with less success than their European counterparts.

Wanting to minimize time under the shovel, the mining industry began to move to the three-pass truck-shovel match as optimum, which meant that the next generation of 240- to 250-ton trucks would call for fifty-cubic-yard shovel equipment.

ConExpo '81

After five postwar shows in Chicago, CIMA selected the Houston Astrodome to host ConExpo '81. Although all the economic signs were pointing down, a nervous industry still turned out in force. The show was billed as one-third larger than 1975, but there was little that was exciting. Non-U.S. manufacturers, which had first participated in 1975, increased in 1981. Exhibiting for the first time ever, Komatsu made a splash with prototypes of its monster thousand-horsepower D555A track-type tractor and the HD-1600, a 175-ton off-highway truck. Hitachi, with hydraulic excavators, and Kobelco, with hydraulic excavators and wheel loaders, were other first-time Japanese exhibitors. IBH was there with a potpourri of equipment under its newly acquired Terex banner, and Liebherr was another new excavator participant. Aside from Caterpillar's new hydrostatic track loaders, the U.S. industry, with little that was completely new, emphasized updated products.[164]

In a sign of the times, ConExpo was beginning to feel competition from European machinery trade shows, the largest of which, Bauma Fair, was held every three years in Munich. Large manufacturers were also increasingly restive over the high costs of the never-ending trade shows and beginning to question their cost-effectiveness.

Summary, 1976–85

Although the U.S. economy suffered from persistent inflation throughout the 1970s, the earthmoving equipment industry grew and profited steadily. After a series of year-on-year increases through the latter half of the 1970s, U.S. earthmoving equipment sales peaked in 1979 at about $8 billion, an all-time high in physical volume even allowing for the 38 percent inflation in equipment prices since 1975. From the peak, the industry entered a shallow downturn in 1980 that became a precipitous drop in 1981 and was triggered by the record high interest rates that brought construction activity and equipment purchasing to a near standstill. At the bottom of the trough in 1982, U.S. industry sales were down about one-third from the 1979 peak in nominal dollars and even more in physical volume, and every manufacturer had dropped below break-even point. Canada's economy moved in tandem with the United States, and Europe, the non-OPEC countries of Africa and the Middle East, and all of Latin America shared the deep slump by 1982.

As losses mounted amid an atmosphere of gloom in an industry with substantial excess capacity worldwide, U.S. and European equipment manufacturers were forced to reassess their positions, and a major shakeout took place among the weaker competitors. Those with deep commitments to the earthmoving equipment business hunkered down and awaited better times.

Meanwhile, through the first half of the 1980s the Japanese equipment manufacturers appeared to thrive while their Western competitors retrenched, divested, or failed. Komatsu grew steadily and became a clear number two worldwide with never a losing year. During the decade several large Japanese industrial conglomerates entered export markets with construction equipment: Kawasaki and Furukawa produced wheel loaders; Kobelco (Kobe Steel) made wheel loaders and excavators; and Hitachi, Sumitomo, Kato, JSW, and Mitsubishi Heavy Industry built excavators. By 1985 the world leader in hydraulic excavators was indisputably Japan.

As the industry shrank in the early 1980s, cumulative corporate losses in the earthmoving equipment industry reached into the billions. U.S. manufacturer profits were dealt a further blow by the revaluation of the dollar that began in 1981 and forced dollar selling prices down worldwide. Over the course of the decade, the nature of the U.S. heavy construction industry changed dramatically as, for all practical purposes, the interstate program was completed. Emphasis shifted to repair, resurfacing, and reconstruction of existing roads and bridges. Henceforth, the manufacturers would rely increasingly on the mining industry as the principal consumer of large equipment.

With the economic recovery beginning in 1983, the industry's survivors emerged from their storm cellars to survey the wreckage. In the United States, 1985 industry sales in nominal dollars climbed back to near the 1979 level, but physical volume was less than 70 percent of the 1979 peak from price inflation of more than 40 percent.

The decade had been a roller-coaster ride for the survivors. There had been a severe shakeout, but at the end of 1985 six players still had more or less comprehensive product lines: Caterpillar, Komatsu, Case, Dresser, Deere, and Fiatallis. Each had sufficient resources and the evident determination to persevere in the business. Of companies with less than full lines, a weakened Terex, back under GM ownership, was a question mark. VME had unique strengths in both the EC and the United States, and Hitachi had become the leading producer in the highly fragmented world excavator business. Liebherr had become stronger in the EC, and JCB was a solid competitor in the world's loader-backhoe business.

At the end of 1985 more uncertainties faced the earthmoving equipment industry than at any previous time. Had the industry topped out, or would real growth resume? How many players could survive in a mature industry? Were Western manufacturers capable of matching or beating Japanese costs? Could the Japanese juggernaut be stopped or was Japanese domination of the industry inevitable? The next decade would provide some surprising answers to these questions.

SEVEN

Recovery and Renewal, 1986–95

Compared to the extreme dislocations of the previous decade, the period from 1986 to 1995 was one of high growth in a relatively stable economic environment. The embattled earthmoving equipment industry was able to take advantage of these quieter times to rebuild on more solid foundations. But the decade would be remembered most for its earthshaking political events—the breakup of the Soviet Union and the opening of the People's Republic of China—which were to have a major impact on the industry.

The Nation

Coming out of the 1981–82 recession, the U.S. economy entered a seven-year expansion exceeded in duration only by the nine years of the 1960s. But unlike previous expansionary periods, inflation was kept in reasonable check through the mid-1990s. After the devastating double-digit increases of 1979–81, the Consumer Price Index, slowed by the recession, increased only 1.9 percent in 1986, the lowest increase in more than twenty years.[1] A combination of excess industry capacity, Japanese competition, and the generally lower inflation rate also brought the Producer Price Index for construction equipment under control after the galloping price escalation of the 1970s. The index rose 30 percent from 1985 through 1995 compared to an increase of 96 percent for the ten years through 1985.[2]

Realigning Exchange Rates

After ten years of steady devaluation beginning in 1971 that were followed by four years of runaway revaluation, in September 1985 the dollar's rise was reversed when the United States and its major trading partners agreed to cooperate in realigning exchange rates. The accord succeeded perhaps too well and triggered a slide in the dollar that, except for a brief uptick in 1989–90, continued for ten years. From a high of 263 in February 1985, the dollar-to-yen rate broke through 100 in early 1994 in a free-fall that took it as low as 80 in 1995.[3] In a period of price restraint by U.S. equipment manufacturers this swing turned the tables on Japanese manufacturers in world markets. For the first time, Japanese equipment exporters found themselves hard-pressed to compete with U.S.-sourced earthmoving equipment for dollar-denominated export business. Although Japan had achieved leadership in hydraulic excavators, the threat of complete Japanese domination of the worldwide earthmoving equipment industry seemed to be over.

Recovery

Housing starts were a strong driver in the recovery of the U.S. construction equipment industry. Record high interest rates had knocked the bottom out of the housing industry, cutting starts from more than two million in 1978 to just over a million in 1981. Pent-up demand and lower rates brought a resurgence, the industry averaging more than 1.7 million starts between 1983 and 1987.[4] With a clientele largely composed of urban development contractors, Deere and Case were the principal beneficiaries of the housing mini-boom. Caterpillar, more dependent on heavy construction, benefited less. Deere's 1985 construction equipment sales were almost back to the company's 1979 pre-recession record while Caterpillar's 1985 sales languished at only 73 percent of its 1981 peak and did not top that level until 1988.[5]

The Highway Program

The watershed Highway Act of 1982 had changed the basis of federal aid to states by providing funds for the first time for highway maintenance, causing a fundamental shift in the balance of highway spending and with it a change in the nature of demand for heavy equipment. When new congressional action was required in 1987, the interstate system, authorized in 1956 and originally targeted for completion in 1970, was 98 percent complete. Over the years about 2,500 miles had been added to the original forty-one-thousand-mile system. Acutely aware of the continuing public support for highways, Congress provided $87.9 billion for the next five years, but more than 20 percent of that was earmarked for mass transit, reflecting the strong political influence of the major metro areas. Emphasis for the next five years would continue on highway repair, resurfacing, and reconstruction. The federal tax on motor fuels was increased by 5 cents per gallon, bringing it to 14 cents.[6]

In 1991, when highways next received congressional attention, a record six-year $151 billion bill was passed, again with about 20 percent earmarked for mass transit. A new 155,000-mile national highway system was also authorized that would incorporate the interstate system with key portions of the federal primary system, triggering a long-range upgrading program of the latter. After thirty-five years, the cost-sharing formula was changed from 90-10 to 80-20 federal-state. As a part of the 1992 tax increase, the federal tax on motor fuel was raised 4.3 cents, bringing it to 18.3 cents per gallon compared to the 3 cents of 1956. This time, however, the 4.3 cent increase was not earmarked for the Highway Trust Fund.[7]

Thus, despite a shift away from the massive earthmoving of the 1960s and 1970s to build the interstate system, highways in the 1980s and 1990s continued to be the primary engine that drove the heavy construction industry in the United States, albeit with somewhat different types of equipment.

The Denver International Airport

Since the opening of the Dallas–Fort Worth airport in 1974 no major new airports had been built in the United States until 1990, when Denver International was started. The controversial $2.3 billion project was the largest U.S. earthmoving job of the decade, involving more than eighty million cubic yards of excavation. The huge quantities of earthmoving called for large fleets of scrapers and bottom-dumps reminiscent of the bygone era of massive earthfill dams.[8] But with many scrapers sitting idle since the wind-down of interstate construction, few new ones were sold for the Denver job.

The International Scene

Formation of the European Union

Since the signing of the Treaty of Rome in 1957 the nations of Western Europe had pursued the dream of a single European market. Progress toward that objective accelerated between 1986 and 1995 with the ratification by the twelve-member nations of the Single European Act in 1987 and the Maastricht Treaty in 1993, the latter creating the European Union. Full economic union could not be a reality, however, until a single unified currency existed. Since 1972, when members had linked their currencies by creating the "snake," the EEC had strived toward monetary union but was consistently baffled by the seemingly insuperable differences between the economies of the strongest and the weakest members. The Maastricht Treaty set a goal of 1999 for establishing irrevocably the parities of currencies among members and the takeover by a European central bank of monetary policy.[9] These developments will likely have minimal effect on the earthmoving equipment industry because almost all major competitors already have a base within the EU.

The Breakup of the Soviet Union

Ironically, at the same time Western Europe was taking the final moves toward economic union, the Soviet Union, in the political event of the century, stunned the world by disintegrating into an uncoordinated group of independent national entities. During the perestroika and glasnost periods preceding the breakup, the former Comecon nations of Eastern Europe had already begun political and economic reform, with the reunification of Germany the key event.

Western and Japanese manufacturers of earthmoving equipment had been doing business with the Soviet Union for more than twenty years but always through monolithic central purchasing organizations. Now all that suddenly changed. With economic reform it was possible to conduct business with those who actually used the equipment, primarily in the extractive industries, and even to set up independent and quasi-independent dealers in some of the new states of the former Soviet Union and in the countries of Eastern Europe. Manufacturers rushed to establish marketing and product support organizations and joint ventures to cover these emerging markets. The beginnings of economic reform strengthened demand for equipment by industries able to earn hard currency—for example, petroleum, natural gas, and precious metals—but a private construction industry on the model of that in the West would take many years to develop.

The Opening of China

Economic reform was also occurring in the People's Republic of China, although at a more deliberate pace. As economic growth in China began to accelerate during the mid-1980s, the need for heavy equipment in the extractive industries was filled by large purchases of Western and Japanese equipment by government agencies. Joint ventures between Chinese state manufacturing entities and foreign equipment manufacturers multiplied along with technology-sharing agreements as companies scrambled for position in the potentially huge market. A further liberalization in the early 1990s made it possible to establish privately owned earthmoving equipment dealerships. But the position of U.S. equipment manufacturers doing business in China would remain tenuous as long as China's most favored nation status and the issue of human rights continued to be linked in political debate in the United States.

International Free Trade

With the completion of the Uruguay Round of the General Agreement on Tariffs and Trade (GATT) in 1993, the outlook brightened for increased world trade. An agreement had been reached that would lead to eventual elimination of tariffs on most types of earthmoving machines, leveling the playing field for all participants worldwide. With the world moving inexorably into three large trading blocs of the Americas, the European Union, and Japan, the agreement could prove vital to continued growth in international sales of earthmoving equipment.

Major International Projects

The world's largest earthmoving project during the decade was Japan's Kansai International Airport. Begun in 1987, the seven-year, $7.7 billion project required the placement of 239 million cubic yards of fill to create an island.[10]

Having completed the $11.2 billion James Bay Phase I in 1986, Quebec Hydro announced that it would begin construction of Phase II in late 1989. Again centered on the La Grande River in northern Quebec, this phase, at a cost of $5.8 billion, would add another 2,400 megawatts to the 10,300 already installed in Phase I and would be the largest civil engineering project then underway in North America.[11]

An area of friction in U.S.-Chinese relations was the recalcitrant attitude of the United States with regard to the Three Gorges Dam project on the Yangtze River. The massive $10.5 billion project, entailing a concrete gravity dam 574 feet high and 6,600 feet long, would generate 17,680 megawatts of power and make navigation on the Upper Yangtze possible while providing flood control on the lower river.[12] Bowing to the objections of environmentalists and human rights activists, the Clinton administration denied U.S. Export-Import Bank support to manufacturers of equipment for the project.[13] Given the clear determination of China to proceed with an undertaking it considers vital to economic development, the government's action was a severe competitive handicap to U.S. equipment suppliers.

Caterpillar

After losses totaling almost $1 billion between 1982 and 1984, Caterpillar's 1985 profit on operations had only sufficed to cover interest expense and special charges. It was still not clear whether the plant closures and consolidations taken between 1983 and 1985 were going to be enough to put the company back on a profitable basis under existing business conditions. When 1986 results showed operating profit down from 1985 despite a 9 percent increase in sales, it was apparent that not enough had been done. Another round of plant closures was announced. The 2.4-million-square-foot Davenport, Iowa, plant, the company's newest major facility; the 1.1-million-square-foot Glasgow, Scotland, plant, the company's first major overseas facility; and the three-hundred-thousand-square-foot Dallas, Oregon, lift-truck plant would be closed. The company would take a charge against 1986 results of $112 million. After-tax profit for the year was a meager $76 million on $7.32 billion in sales.[14]

The events surrounding the closure of the Glasgow plant were particularly unpleasant. Caterpillar had announced earlier that the facility would be updated under the company's Plant with a Future Program and had received a grant from the U.K. government. News of the planned closure culminated in the occupation of the plant by militant union members for about three months, which created a public relations nightmare.[15]

A Name Change and a Poison Pill

At the 1986 annual meeting a change in name was approved. The words *Tractor Company* would be eliminated, and the company would become "Caterpillar Inc." The company said the word *tractor* no longer accurately described its product line. At the same time, the state of incorporation was changed to Delaware, ending Caterpillar's historical association with California. Following the popular trend among American corporations, Caterpillar also classified its board and eliminated cumulative voting for the election of directors.[16] Later that year, a shareholders' rights ("poison pill") plan was adopted, designed to make an unfriendly takeover virtually impossible.[17]

With these actions Caterpillar, like many other large corporations, protected itself against the wave of takeovers rampaging through Wall Street while further entrenching management. In 1991 it replaced Navistar (the successor to International Harvester) as one of the thirty companies making up the Dow Jones Industrial Average.

Intensifying Cost Problems

Caterpillar's sales increased every year from 1984 through 1990, reflecting the steady recovery in the worldwide market for earthmoving equipment. With the weakening dollar helping prices, profits hit $350 million in 1987 and zoomed to a record $616 million in 1988. It seemed that happy days were here again, but profits unexpectedly dropped to $497 million in 1989 and to only $210 million in 1990 on record revenues of $11.4 billion. With no special or non-recurring charges and after several years of intensive cost-reduction efforts, how could Caterpillar net only 1.8 percent on sales of more than $11 billion? Gross margin, after improving to 21.9 percent in 1988, had drifted to 17 percent in 1990. Although the company was experiencing heavy losses in Brazil from a devaluation and government controls, Caterpillar's costs were still too high.[18]

Fites and Reorganization

In mid-1990 George Schaefer, chair and CEO since 1985, retired, and Donald V. Fites who had been president and COO since 1989, was elected to succeed him. Fites, fifty-six, whose background was primarily marketing, was another of Caterpillar's home-grown executives and had joined the company directly from Valparaiso University in 1956.[19] No other incoming CEO in the sixty-five-year history of the company had faced the challenges confronting Fites: implementing a complex corporate reorganization, handling upcoming negotiations with the UAW that gave every indication of being the toughest in years, and dealing with the critical cost problems that continued to dog the company.

After several years of study, in January 1990 Caterpillar had announced its intention to reorganize the company, but it fell to Fites to handle the specifics as one of his first acts as CEO. In July 1990 the company decentralized into seventeen divisions—thirteen profit-center business units along product or geographic lines and four central service groups, each division headed by a vice president reporting to one of three group presidents reporting to the CEO.[20] (This was later expanded to seventeen business units and five service divisions under four group presidents.) The ponderous, bureau-

Becoming chairman and CEO of Caterpillar in 1990, Donald V. Fites ably led the company through some difficult times into a sustained period of record growth and profits. (Courtesy of Caterpillar Inc.)

cratic General Offices organization, dating back to the 1950s, was dismantled. Its $250 million in general corporate expenses largely pushed into the business units, where profit pressures would force a reevaluation of these costs.[21] The reorganization met the target date of being nominally in place by January 1, 1991.

The labor negotiations resulted in a strike (see the appendix to this volume) that began on November 7, 1990, although the company said it had negligible effect on 1990's results. The $2.1 billion plant modernization program, hailed as the panacea for the company's cost problems, was now 80 percent complete, but the company was still not able to produce profits through the entire business cycle, as events would soon demonstrate.

A Return to Red Figures

Proof of this came with the recession that began in the second half of 1990 and bottomed out in the second quarter of 1991. With 1991 sales down 11 percent to $9.8 billion, Caterpillar took a loss of $404 million, including $268 million in after-tax, nonrecurring charges for still more plant closures and consolidations. Of the remaining $136 million loss, more than half came from Brazil.[22] Slated for closure this time were the York, Pennsylvania, parts manufacturing operation and the nine-year-old Brampton, Ontario, plant.[23] At the end of 1991, despite plant closures, consolidations, and modernizations over the preceding nine years, Caterpillar's break-even point was more than $10 billion.

That was borne out when 1992 produced a before-tax loss of $373 million on machinery and engine operations on sales that were flat from 1991. The one bright spot of the year was a $53 million gain from the sale of 80 percent of its lift-truck business to a joint venture with Mitsubishi Heavy Industries, effectively extracting Caterpillar from that unhappy business after twenty-seven trying years. Caterpillar chose 1992 to recognize "Employers' Accounting for Postretirement Benefits Other Than Pensions" (SFAS 106) and two other smaller accounting changes, resulting in a non-cash charge of $2.2 billion and a net loss of more than $2.4 billion.[24]

Although corporations tend to minimize the importance of the effect of non-cash accounting changes, they are nevertheless a charge against profits and stockholders' equity and reduce total capitalization. In Caterpillar's case, the ratio of debt to total capitalization at the end of 1992 skyrocketed to 78 percent for the consolidated company (including Cat Financial Services Corporation) and 67 percent for machinery and engines. Those ratios affected the company's ability to borrow and made it vital that Caterpillar quickly return to healthy profitability.

Better Times

With a worldwide recovery from the recession, 1993 sales increased $1.4 billion to $11.2 billion. That 13 percent increase produced a $703 million swing in operating results from 1992's $124 million loss (before special charges) to a $579 million profit, indicating sharply improving costs.[25] Despite record sales, average employment was the lowest in recent corporate history at 50,443. And, in a huge windfall, Caterpillar received a federal tax credit of $134 million plus $251 million in interest for overpayments from 1979 through 1987, bringing net profit for the year to $652 million, the highest the company had ever recorded.[26] The strong sales recovery put most popular models on allocation to dealers.

On booming worldwide sales, Caterpillar revenues topped $14 billion in 1994, with profit jumping 46 percent to $955 million. Machine sales reached more than $10 billion for the first time. With business conditions continuing to improve, 1995 profit increased to $1.14 billion on revenues of $16.1 billion. The United States contributed 48 percent of the $11.3 billion in earthmoving machine sales. The results were all the more remarkable for the fact that in the last half of 1994 and all of 1995 most of the company's U.S. plants were operating with a temporary work force due to the UAW strike.[27] They also indicated clearly that Caterpillar, at these volume levels, would be extremely profitable.

Caterpillar's engine business was becoming a large enterprise in its own right, with sales reaching $4.1 billion in 1995. Although a great deal of emphasis was placed on the North American OEM truck engine market, the fact was that 53 percent of 1995 engine sales were outside the United States, essentially all U.S.-produced engines sold by dealers.[28] Meanwhile, financial products were growing even faster. Cat Finance's portfolio increased from $3.3 billion in 1993 to about $5 billion in 1995, when it contributed $88 million in operating profit.[29]

Product Development

Although Caterpillar's profitability in the first seven years of the 1986–95 decade was less than impressive, the company did not stint on its product development program, and it accelerated the flow of new products and updated the technology in its existing line.

The New Japanese Joint Venture

After introduction of its four-model line of 200-Series hydraulic excavators in the early 1970s, Caterpillar R&D emphasis shifted to other product families. Although excavators had received numerous improvements over the years, by the mid-1980s Caterpillar found itself badly behind the curve in excavator technology. The company's position was further complicated by the lack of an excavator presence in Japan. There, Japanese competitors were producing upward of sixty thousand excavators per year (not including minis), with 75 percent sold in the home market. In a major lapse by Caterpillar in reading the trends, the 1963 joint venture agreement with Mitsubishi made no provision for excavators. Both companies subsequently entered the business independently, Caterpillar more successfully than MHI, but the Caterpillar Mitsubishi joint venture, lacking an excavator product line, was hamstrung when competing in the large Japanese home market that was 40 percent excavators.

In a development of great significance to the product line, in 1987 Caterpillar and Mitsubishi Heavy Industries reorganized their CM joint venture into a new company, Shin Caterpillar Mitsubishi (SCM), to include hydraulic excavators.[30] Recognizing that cutting-edge technology on excavators resided in Japan, Caterpillar agreed with MHI to set up a joint Japanese-American SCM design team in Japan to create a new line of excavators to replace the obsolescent 200-Series line. The new venture was soon producing a line of interim models based on updated MHI machines equipped with Caterpillar engines. Offered for sale worldwide, these models complemented the Caterpillar 200-Series line still being produced in the United States and Europe. In 1991 the design team's first product appeared, a state-of-the-art, twenty-five-metric-ton machine, followed over the next three years by six additional models until the 200-Series and interim models were completely phased out. The new line was produced in Japan, Europe, and the United States.[31] With the addition of excavators, SCM sales more than doubled from about 150 billion yen in 1987 to more than 350 billion in 1991.[32]

New Track-Type Tractors

The conversion of the mid-sized track-type tractor line to the elevated sprocket was completed in 1985–86 with the introduction of the H-Series D4 through D7. In an astute piece of product strategy, Caterpillar redesigned the seven-hundred-horsepower D10 with a new engine and other changes into the 770-horsepower D11N. The D9L and D8L were similarly upgraded, and a new D8N at 285 horsepower was inserted in the line. The D8N came standard with controlled differential steering allowing continuous power to both tracks in variable radius turns, a feature of Cletrac crawler tractors for fifty years. Liebherr and Deere hydrostatic drive crawlers also had that

Introduced in 1986, D11N was the largest in Caterpillar's second generation of elevated-sprocket tractors. (Courtesy of Caterpillar Inc.)

capability, but the Caterpillar system retained the three-speed powershift transmission with steering and speed changes effected through a new tiller bar controlled by the operator's left hand. The feature was later added to the D6H and D7H.[33] With the sophisticated H- and N-Series machines Caterpillar reclaimed a clear technological leadership position in crawler tractors.

A Reentry into Agricultural Tractors

With the discontinuance of the D2 tractor in 1957, Caterpillar's interest in the agricultural tillage market waned. The company continued to sell a few industrial-type crawlers for agricultural service in large-scale irrigated operations of California and Arizona and later began offering mid-range "Special Application" crawlers modified for agricultural tillage, but only a handful of Caterpillar dealers worldwide participated in the market. As the market evolved into larger and larger agricultural wheel tractors, Caterpillar's interest was rekindled, but other priorities intervened after considerable development work on a proposed line. The project was killed in the late 1970s.

At about this point, as an outgrowth of its work with the beadless tire, the company developed what came to be called the "Mobil-trac system." That involved a rubber track belt wound with high-tensile steel wire and mounted under tension around a rear-drive wheel and front idler with a flexible bogie system. It gave rise to the idea of marrying the work previously done on the agricultural wheel tractor with Mobil-trac, and in 1987 Caterpillar introduced the Challenger 65, a 270-horsepower, thirty-one-thousand-pound, agricultural crawler tractor. With differential steering controlled by a conventional steering wheel and Mobil-trac, the machine could travel over the road at up to eighteen miles per hour, overcoming one of the principal objections to steel track machines in agriculture.[34]

The machine was quick to gain acceptance from large operators already using conventional crawler tractors, but the premium price over a wheel tractor slowed acceptance in the midwestern farm belt. Still, Caterpillar persevered and introduced a larger model and an improved 65B in 1991.[35] These machines competed only for the very small top end of the market, however. To reach the larger portion of the market, in 1994 the company began introducing three smaller, row-crop versions.[36] With the Mobil-trac's low ground pressure as the principal selling feature of the Challenger, Caterpillar had returned to the same concept for the agricultural market that

The first of an eventual six-model line, the Cat Challenger 65 offered farmers a powerful tractor with minimal soil compaction. (Courtesy of Caterpillar Inc.)

motivated Benjamin Holt when he installed tracks on a steam traction engine in 1904. After years of declining interest in the market, Caterpillar had reentered it and was a serious contender for the tractor business.

The Mining Vehicle Center

In a move to accelerate development of large vehicles for the mining industry, in 1987 the Mining Vehicle Center was set up at the Decatur, Illinois, plant and had its own staff of engineers to centralize development of all types of large machines for the industry.[37] The center topped out the three-model line when it introduced the 240-ton 793 off-highway truck in 1991.[38] These were mechanical-drive units in an industry overwhelmingly electric drive in the larger sizes. In a span of six years Caterpillar had closed the gap in truck capacity with industry leaders, but competitors were already working on the next generation of more than three hundred tons.

In 1990 the center introduced the massive twenty-three-cubic-yard-capacity 994 wheel loader that weighed 188 tons, fifty tons heavier than the largest competitive wheel loader then available.[39] Although the 994 had a substantially higher price, it quickly took market leadership but was soon challenged by the new LeTourneau L-1400 and later the even larger L-1800.[40]

With three models in the 150- to 240-ton range, Caterpillar mining trucks were exclusively mechanical-drive. (Courtesy of Caterpillar Inc.)

Under a contract design arrangement with a European group, in record development time the center brought out a three-model line of large hydraulic front shovels topped by the 5230, which had twenty-two cubic yards and 347 tons. Caterpillar could now compete with Hitachi, O&K, Demag, Liebherr, and P&H in the three- to four-hundred-ton range of hydraulic front shovels for truck loading.

Reining in the Branding Program

Begun in 1984, the branding program had quickly put Caterpillar into paving products, compaction equipment, small excavators, and articulated dumpers, but the company and its dealers found there was also a downside to branding other manufacturers' products. To avoid stocking thousands of new parts in its own warehouses, Caterpillar had hoped to rely on manufacturers to ship parts directly to dealers. The dealers, however, soon learned that the level of parts service was not up to the standards they had come to expect routinely from Caterpillar. Parts books were not uniform and varied in detail, and service literature was sometimes sketchy. It was also becoming clear that some branded products, notably asphalt plants and concrete paving equipment, did not fit well with the remainder of the product line. These problems, compounded by the uneven quality of the products themselves, were bringing a rising chorus of complaints from dealers and customers.

That led Caterpillar to put an end to the program for earthmoving products through a series of agreements with the various manufacturers, either to gain outright control of the design and manufacture of the products or establish contract manufacturing relationships under Caterpillar design control. Concrete equipment and asphalt plants were not included in the new arrangements. Although the experiment with branding had created a certain amount of trauma, the program did put the company into the asphalt paver, vibratory compactor, and dumper businesses with its own product lines.

But Caterpillar made little headway with its slowly developing line of asphalt pavers until 1991, when it acquired the Barber-Greene Company from Astec Industries. Barber-Greene, one of the oldest and most respected names in asphalt pavers, had fallen on hard times and was near bankruptcy. Caterpillar purchased the business for $25 million and continued to sell the pavers under the Barber-Greene name from a plant in DeKalb, Illinois.[41]

Changing Product Strategy

Although less spectacular than the big machines, small and mid-range products generated the majority of industry sales dollars and profits. It was in these segments that competition was strongest and product differentiation the most difficult. To stay competitive, each model had to be upgraded at least every three or four years, with the industry trending to ever-increasing frequency. Following a policy of installing incremental improvements as they became available, Caterpillar was slow to make model (series) changes. For example, the mid-range 950 wheel loader, first introduced in 1964, did not receive a Series B designation until 1981, although the machine had received numerous major improvements in the interim.[42] This conservative policy was intended to assure customers that a series change meant they would be receiving a significantly improved model, but it also denied the marketing organization the promotional value derived from periodic model changes and reflected a certain complacency. Meanwhile, competition was making fewer interim changes and benefiting from more frequent series changes. Recognizing the disadvantages of its approach, in the late 1980s Caterpillar's product strategy began to target more timely series changes, and as product business units were established in 1991 they assumed responsibility for implementing the new strategy.

With the reorganization, loader-backhoes along with other products in the less-than-one-hundred-horsepower range came under the control of the Building Construction Products business unit, which moved to a new plant in Clayton, North Carolina.[43] A revamped loader-backhoe line was introduced in 1993.[44] This time it appeared that the company had hit the target. Market share finally began to move up, with Caterpillar moving into the number-two position in the United States, behind Case and ahead of Deere.[45]

Transforming Caterpillar

The increasingly aggressive product program between 1986 and 1995 left Caterpillar at the end of 1995 with a formidable, state-of-the-art product line across the board. Beginning about 1992 that began to be reflected in increased worldwide market share and, coupled with a solid recovery in demand for equipment, resulted in profits totaling more than $2 billion for 1994–95. That accomplishment was all the more remarkable because the company was in the throes of an intense struggle with the UAW between 1992 and 1995.

Between 1990 and the end of 1995 Caterpillar was transformed. From a company with serious cost problems in the late 1980s, by the end of 1995 Caterpillar gave all the signs of an enterprise that could be profitable through the entire business cycle. Although it would take another recession to demonstrate that, there was no doubt that Caterpillar had made fundamental changes in the way it operated: drastic downsizing from the 1983 peak of 45.7 million square feet to about 33 million square feet of utilized space; the $2.1 billion plant modernization program; a total reorganization of the company; rigid control of employment; judicious outsourcing; and transfer of some operations to lower-cost locations. Finally, the combination of these factors put the company in a position to operate successfully through a four-year battle with the UAW and break the pattern bargaining lock. Although the union did not concede victory, the company clearly won the first round of what was likely to be a continuing battle.

Although the downsizing and plant modernization were begun before Fites's accession to the CEO job, the other actions were largely or entirely carried out under his leadership. That was emphatically so with reorganization as well as the struggle with the UAW. The reorganization, launched in 1991, was conducted during a recession in which the company lost more than $600 million and thus required steadfastness of purpose and confidence in the outcome. Likewise, the four-year battle with the powerful UAW took steely nerves. Fites had indeed proven himself a worthy CEO.

Overall, with the quality and breadth of its product line, the strength of its dealer organization, and the financial resources at its disposal, at the end of 1995 Caterpillar had never been stronger. It had faced down the Komatsu challenge, and the appearance of another major challenger seemed highly unlikely.

Komatsu

The turn in exchange rates that began in 1985 from a strengthening to a weakening dollar marked a critical turning point for Komatsu's earthmoving equipment business. As the yen's value rose from 200 to the dollar in 1985 (in year-end figures) to 121 in 1987, Komatsu's export business from Japan came under intense cost pressure. The company had by then recognized that it could no longer hope to compete solely from Japan. In 1987 Komatsu had wholly owned plants in Chattanooga, Tennessee, and Newcastle, England, as well as in Brazil, with Chattanooga and Newcastle just starting up and joint ventures in Mexico and Indonesia. The value of production from these operations in 1987 totaled only about $100 million, but in 1988 that figure more than tripled.[46]

Komatsu Dresser

In a move that surprised the industry, Komatsu and Dresser Industries announced that effective September 1, 1988, they would pool their respective construction equipment businesses in the Western Hemisphere to form a 50-50 joint venture: Komatsu Dresser Company. Included would be Dresser's Construction and Mining Equipment Division, not including Marion, Jeffrey, and the air tools business. Komatsu would contribute its Chattanooga plant and its Brazilian operation. Manufacturing space totaled 3.5 million square feet, and assets were in excess of $1 billion. Headquarters would be in Libertyville, Illinois. Both companies would account for their interests in the venture on an equity basis.[47]

What was difficult to understand was that the Komatsu and Dresser competing product lines would continue to be manufactured as before and would be marketed by their respective dealers as if no combination had been formed. The arrangement was so full of potential conflicts that to outside observers it seemed unlikely that it could long endure.

In 1989, the first full year, Komatsu Dresser sales totaled $1.36 billion, and Dresser products probably contributed slightly more than half. (Dresser's construction and mining sales for 1988 included $710 million attributable to operations transferred to Komatsu Dresser.) Operations of the venture in 1989 produced a $9.6 million loss after tax, not an impressive start. The venture lost $46 million on flat sales in 1990. Then the 1991 recession dropped sales 25 percent to $1.01 billion, bringing a loss of about $100 million before a $23 million gain to the venture from the sale of its unprofitable Brazilian operations back to Komatsu. After that, Komatsu Dresser's area of operations was limited to North America. To cut costs, the Cambridge, Quebec, plant and one of two Ohio Galion plants were closed.[48]

Control of Komatsu Dresser

On August 1, 1992, Dresser severed its connection with the construction equipment business by spinning off its 50 percent interest in Komatsu Dresser—along with Marion, Jeffrey, and the air tools business—into a new corporation: Indresco.[49] Without the deep pockets of Dresser supporting it, Indresco had to absorb a $54 million loss from Komatsu Dresser in 1992.[50] Perhaps foreseeing more losses in the future, in September 1993 Indresco sold 31 percent of K-D to Komatsu for $60 million, which gave Komatsu 81 percent with an option to buy the remainder. A year later Komatsu picked up the option and became the sole owner.[51] On acquiring control, Komatsu closed the plant in Libertyville, where Frank G. Hough had started his wheel loader business nearly fifty years earlier.[52] In January 1996 the name of the wholly owned subsidiary was changed from Komatsu Dresser to Komatsu America International Company.[53]

What motivated Komatsu to throw in with Dresser, a company whose earthmoving business was a declining force in the industry? In the late 1980s the stronger yen was forcing Komatsu to increase offshore manufacturing operations, and the grossly underused Payline manufacturing space made Dresser an attractive partner. Also, with its North American market share

At 320 tons and 2,500 horsepower, the Komatsu 930E was the first off-highway truck of more than three hundred tons to reach successful series production. (Komatsu Mining Systems)

stalling during the late 1980s, Komatsu felt the need for stronger identification as a North American manufacturer.

Despite the North American tie-in, Komatsu gained little in market share and nothing in profits from its six-year joint venture with Dresser/Indresco. When the venture wound down, however, Komatsu was left with about 2.3 million square feet of North American manufacturing space (for which it paid very little) producing Komatsu-brand products from plants in Peoria, Illinois, Chattanooga, Tennessee, Galion, Ohio, and Candiac, Quebec, not including the idle million-square-foot Libertyville plant. The jewels of the acquired assets were the 1.2-million-square-foot Peoria plant and the Haulpak line of off-highway trucks that came with it.[54] Komatsu's own line of Japanese-built off-highway trucks, topped by the HD-1600, a 176-ton unit, had never been highly regarded in the mining trade, but Haulpak allowed it to become a major player in the international mining market. The strategy was soon evident when in 1995 Komatsu announced what was then the world's largest mining truck, the 320-ton 930E, to be built in Peoria.[55] Later that year Komatsu formed a 50-50 joint venture with Mannesman Demag AG of Dusseldorf, Germany, to manufacture and distribute large hydraulic excavators and front shovels.[56]

Expansion in Europe

The European Community accounted for nearly one-third of the world excavator opportunity, second after Japan in size but with almost as many excavator manufacturers. As a result, a number of high-cost manufacturers produced relatively low volumes there. Europe was a tempting target for the low-cost Japanese producers, and they began to penetrate with imports in the early 1980s, much to the consternation of local producers. While Komatsu may have already been planning a European excavator source, the imposition of countervailing duties by the EC in 1985 no doubt accelerated those plans. By 1990 Komatsu was producing about $120 million in excavators in its Newcastle, England, plant for the European market.[57] The first major Japanese competitor to establish manufacturing in the EC, it was soon followed by others. In 1989 the EC removed the countervailing duties.[58]

Also in 1989, Komatsu established a license agreement and contract manufacturing arrangement with FAI S.p.A. of Italy for the supply of mini-excavators for the EC. Komatsu later took a 37 percent equity position in FAI, converting the arrangement to a joint venture.[59]

Having firmed up its excavator supply for the EC, in 1990 it did the same with wheel loaders when it acquired a 24.9 percent interest in Hanomag.[60] Terms were not announced, but no doubt the perennially financially troubled company viewed Komatsu as a godsend. Komatsu later raised its share of Hanomag to 64.1 percent.[61] Hanomag still had the same plant in Hannover that it had under Rheinstahl, IBH, and Massey-Ferguson ownership. In 1993 it produced $225 million in equipment and had 1,300 employees.[62]

To fill out its line for the EC, Komatsu needed an articulated dumper, and in 1991 it took an equity position in Moxy AS, a small Norwegian manufacturer that had survived through government subsidies. The Komatsu brand was applied to the four-model Moxy line of dumpers, twenty-five to thirty-five metric tons. With these arrangements, Komatsu had secured its position as a major competitor in the EC.

The Rest of the World

Komatsu set up its first overseas manufacturing operation in 1973 in Brazil and, like Caterpillar and others, had to weather difficult times there. By the 1990s Komatsu of Brazil was building excavators, bulldozers, and motor graders in 480,000 square feet of space with about a thousand employees.[63]

Over the years Komatsu set up numerous license and technology sharing agreements, beginning as early as 1958 with Bharat Earth Movers Ltd. in India for crawler bulldozers. Since the mid-1980s Komatsu has stepped up its joint venture and licensing activities, with emphasis on the Pacific Rim. Joint ventures operate in Indonesia, Thailand, and Vietnam, and Komatsu has several license agreements with various entities of the People's Republic of China and one with Samsung Ltd. in South Korea. These ventures and licenses cover a variety of machines and engines.[64]

In 1993 Komatsu and Cummins Engine Company formed two ventures under a cross-licensing arrangement whereby certain Cummins engines would be built in Japan for use in Komatsu equipment and for sale, and certain Komatsu industrial engines would be built and sold by Cummins in the United States.[65] The agreement was critical for Komatsu because its engines could not meet impending emission regulations in California.

The Home Market

Meanwhile, between 1989 and 1993 Komatsu's sales of construction equipment in Japan had stagnated, averaging about 340 billion yen within a fairly narrow range.[66] With a home market that was 40 percent excavators, Komatsu was hard-pressed to hold market share against the many other Japanese excavator manufacturers ranged against it. It seemed that everyone was in the business and had state-of-the-art machines, including Hitachi, Kobelco, MDI-Yutani, Sumitomo, IHI, Kato, Takeuchi, and the new Caterpillar Mitsubishi. Excavator production in Japan, not including minis, hit an astronomical eighty thousand units in 1990. There was tough competition, especially from Hitachi, which had excellent technology, and Caterpillar Mitsubishi, which, next to Komatsu, had the most extensive distribution system in Japan. As the Japanese economy slumped during the early 1990s Komatsu's home market construction equipment sales fell from 386 billion yen in 1991 to 313 billion in 1993, accounting for only 36 percent of corporate sales (the lowest share in company history) compared to 42 percent as recently as 1989.[67]

Struggling to hold market share in the home market and facing up to the hard reality that it was making no headway in efforts to overtake Caterpillar, Komatsu stepped up its diversification from earthmoving equipment. The figure dropped from more than 75 percent in the early 1980s to 63 percent by 1993.[68] During the early 1990s the company conceded that it no longer expected to supplant Caterpillar as number one.

Product Development: Marketing

Having filled in its line between 1976 and 1985, between 1986 and 1995 the company concentrated on keeping its wheel loaders and excavators, representing about 70 percent of the world opportunity, on the cutting edge of technology. The Vanguard Series introduced in the mid-1980s were for several years the best small and mid-range wheel loaders on the market, with inboard-mounted, wet-disc brakes, Z-bar linkage, and advanced cabs. In 1989 Komatsu introduced its six-model Explorer-series hydraulic excavators, which had extremely sophisticated hydraulics the equal of anything then on the market. Until it began introducing its 300-Series in 1992 Caterpillar could not match the Komatsu excavator line. In 1994 Komatsu introduced a new six-model line of small to mid-range Avance Dash 6-Series excavators to North America: the PC120-6 through the PC250-6. All but the PC120 were U.S.-made. The machines offered the latest in load-sensing hydraulics and mode selection.[69]

Track-type machines, motor graders, trucks, and scrapers received periodic updates but did not keep pace with Caterpillar, which opened a clear technological lead in these product families. Komatsu showed the D555A track-type tractor prototype at ConExpo '81 but did not bring it to market until 1991 as the D575A-2 at 145 tons and 1,050 horsepower.[70] It enjoyed only modest commercial success, however. Caterpillar's N-Series elevated-sprocket machines had only strengthened that company's already dominant position in big tractors. In the eight years to 1994 Caterpillar sold a thousand D11N tractors.[71]

Although Komatsu's wheel loaders and excavators were maintained at state-of-the-art levels, during the course of the decade the remainder of the line lost ground to Caterpillar, which enjoyed extraordinary advances during the period and would win any spending contest on research and development.

Through a continuing effort, Komatsu built a distribution network of privately owned dealers throughout the world. In North America, Komatsu at the end of 1995 had about fifty dealers with 155 locations.[72] It also had a relatively sophisticated worldwide parts distribution system ("P-WINS") in warehouses at strategic locations. The company had often pursued large sales in the less-developed world in partnership with Japanese trading companies, allowing local dealers little or no participation. Haulpak also pursued large mining sales on a direct factory basis.

A Solid Number Two

In 1989, after twenty-five years as CEO, Ryoichi Kawai was succeeded as president by Tetsuya Katada, although Kawai continued as chairman.[73] In the modern era of the earthmoving equipment industry only William Hewitt of Deere had a longer tenure. Under Kawai the company grew in size in yen terms by a factor of more than twenty while setting new standards for quality, an impressive record of leadership. Kawai relinquished the chairmanship to Katada in 1995.[74]

Komatsu's worldwide construction equipment sales were up 15 percent in 1995, totaling $7.1 billion, 53 percent of which was in Japan (conversion rate of 87 yen per dollar on March 31, 1996). Komatsu Dresser contributed $1.25 billion. The Construction Equipment Division accounted for 67 percent of the corporate total.[75]

In the mid-1990s Komatsu, always a tightly managed company, employed only ten thousand people in its Japanese earthmoving equipment production facilities, which consisted of about 10.8 million square feet of manufacturing space.[76] Following the standard Japanese practice, the company relied heavily on outsourcing. With the yen reaching all-time highs through the early 1990s, strong cost pressures forced a restructuring of Komatsu's Japanese manufacturing operations, bringing a charge against operations of $172 million and a reduction in employment by a thousand.[77] The company took the necessary steps to secure its position in North America and Europe with local manufacturing, however. It was a sign of the times when Komatsu announced in mid-1995 that it would begin pricing exports in yen, an acknowledgment that it could no longer continue to raise prices on dollar-based deals.[78]

Komatsu, in a comfortable number-two position in the worldwide earthmoving equipment industry at the end of 1995, would continue to challenge Caterpillar wherever there was business to be had. As of the late 1990s no candidate was likely to unseat Komatsu from its position behind Caterpillar.

Dresser Industries

In 1983, the first full year of operations with Payline products, Dresser reported revenues from construction equipment of $458 million, of which $358 million was produced by Payline and the remainder by Galion and the air tools business. As the industry recovered from the slump of the early 1980s, Dresser construction equipment revenues (excluding Marion) for 1984–87 averaged $535 million. After the 1984 acquisition of WABCO, total construction and mining equipment annual sales were in the $900 million-plus range for 1985–87. That figure was undoubtedly well below Dresser management's expectations when one considers that Payline and WABCO, as late as 1981, had combined sales of more than $1 billion.[79] The Mining and Construction Equipment Division produced modest operating profits in five of the years between 1983 and 1988 and had an $18 million loss in 1987.[80]

The Joint Venture

With these disappointing operating results in hand, in 1988 Dresser management opted to join Komatsu. At the outset it appeared that Dresser management regarded the joint venture as a means to spark their laggard equipment business, but they were quickly disillusioned. Between 1989 and 1991, when Dresser held a 50 percent share, the venture lost money every

year. Dresser's share of the losses amounted to $79 million, and additional
capital contributions required from Dresser were $77 million.[81] Dresser
began looking for a way out. In 1989 it had divested its European construction equipment operation, a vestige of the Harvester business, to Furukawa.
That left Dresser with only about $45 million of construction equipment
exports outside the Western Hemisphere not covered by the joint venture.[82]

Forming Indresco

Dresser found its way out in 1992 with the spin-off of all its unwanted
businesses—Marion, Jeffrey, air tools, its 50 percent interest in Komatsu
Dresser, and an unrelated minerals and refractory products business,
Harbison-Walker, which was acquired in 1967. A new corporation, Indresco,
was formed to own these businesses, and all shares distributed to Dresser
stockholders at a ratio of one share of Indresco per five shares of Dresser.
Dresser took a charge against stockholders' equity of $414 million in the
transaction but was free of all the construction and mining equipment businesses it had so avidly acquired beginning with Jeffrey Galion in 1974.[83]

The unhappy outcome of Indresco's two-year involvement in Komatsu
Dresser has been described previously. Indresco had small operating profits
in 1992 and 1993, but accounting changes produced net losses totaling $106
million on sales that averaged $550 million. The company was profitable
in 1994 and 1995. On October 31, 1995, Indresco became Global Industrial Technologies, Inc. when the latter was set up as a holding company for
Indresco. The new company continued to operate the Marion, Jeffrey, and
refractory businesses as before.[84]

Before the acquisition of Harvester's Payline Division, Dresser had a small
but profitable equipment operation in Marion and Jeffrey Galion. The wisdom of adding the moribund Payline business is certainly open to question,
but Dresser management believed that it could effect a turnaround based
on its track record of success with acquisitions. When the anticipated sales
volumes and profits did not materialize, Dresser sought to remedy its problems by entering into a joint venture with Komatsu. That decision cost
Dresser more than $150 million in losses and additional capital contribu-
tions in three years. In the end, Dresser stockholders paid for this string of
decisions to the tune of $414 million in return for shares in a small spin-off
company, Indresco.

Deere & Company

Deere's construction equipment sales recovered quickly from the 1982 trough, but such was not the case with farm equipment, which continued the downward trend begun in 1982. The company's agricultural sales bottomed out in 1986 at $1.9 billion from a peak of more than $4 billion in 1981. During the deep recession of the early 1980s, construction equipment sales had diminished to only 12 percent of the corporate total, but after the slide in agricultural sales it accounted for 25 percent in 1986. Meanwhile, sales of Deere's fastest-growing division—Lawn, Grounds Care, and Consumer Products—were $750 million in 1986 and jumped to $915 million in 1987, when they topped construction equipment sales by $4 million.[85]

First Losses

Although Deere had operating losses on equipment operations between 1982 and 1985, income from finance operations had let the company avoid red figures. In 1986, however, the continuing deterioration in the agricultural market finally caught up with it. In a desperate effort to reduce inventories the company had cut farm equipment production schedules to the bone and lost money through the first three quarters. To add to its problems, a strike began August 23 at all UAW locations, lasted 162 days, a Deere record, and brought a fourth-quarter loss of $140 million. Farm equipment's disastrous operating loss of $392 million brought a net loss of $229 million for 1986, Deere's first since the early 1930s. Construction equipment eked out an operating profit of $4 million on $868 million in sales.[86]

Deere said the strike was about controlling costs, and the work stoppage did help the company reduce inventories. After a further loss of $193 million in the first fiscal quarter the strike ended on February 1, 1987, but weak earnings through the rest of the year brought another net loss, $99 million for 1987, the company's 150th anniversary.[87]

Restructuring and a Return to Profitability

Although layoffs beginning in 1981 had reduced the direct labor payroll, Deere was slow to restructure in the face of declining markets. Finally, for the years from 1985 to 1987 the company took a total of $186 million in charges to close 3.3 million square feet of farm equipment manufacturing space, restructure operations, and permanently reduce employment, including $82.6 million against construction equipment. Capital spending from 1986 through 1990 trended upward but averaged only about $200 million, by no means enough to effect major changes in manufacturing operations at a company of Deere's size. At the end of 1987 the company said it had lowered its break-even point by half since 1981, although results at the bottom of the next business cycle did not bear that out.[88]

With little in construction equipment sales outside North America, Deere was heavily reliant on the vagaries of the North American housing market and thus, indirectly, on mortgage interest rates. Clientele was composed largely of small and medium-sized contractors involved in urban housing and commercial construction markets, and Deere had gained a leading position in the logging industry, which changes in housing demand also impacted. On the strength of exceptionally high U.S. housing starts through the mid-1980s, Deere construction equipment sales rebounded from the recession. They reached $911 million in 1987 and in 1988 topped $1 billion for the first time, exceeding the previous high of $996 million set in 1979. With the farm equipment inventory problem resolved, a recovery in the market brought an astonishing 45 percent jump in 1988 sales. An important segment was again profitable, and the company made $315 million, its highest profit ever.[89]

Diversification

In 1985 a wholly owned subsidiary, Heritage National Healthplan, was established to handle Deere's internal health-care program. Healthplan, later opened to other organizations, became a significant business in its own right. Premium revenues from health care as well as those from earlier established insurance operations generated revenues in excess of $700 million in 1995. The credit corporation, set up in 1958, became the largest captive retail finance organization in the equipment industry, with $5.9 billion in assets. Growing revenues from Deere's non-equipment operations provided the company with a comparatively secure buffer against the ups and downs of the equipment industry. Credit, insurance, and health care combined produced a greater operating profit in 1995 than either industrial equipment or lawn and grounds care equipment.[90]

During the 1980s Deere explored ways of expanding its engine business through sales to original equipment manufacturers. A short-lived engine marketing joint venture with GM's Detroit Diesel Division was announced in 1986 but fell through in early 1987 when Deere backed out.[91] In June 1989 Deere acquired Funk Transmissions from Cooper Industries.[92] Later that year it established the Deere Power Systems Group to pull together its OEM engine and components sales activities.[93] The group, a part of the Industrial Equipment Division, made steady progress and reported 1993 sales of thirty-five thousand engines in the 20- to 375-horsepower range, with estimated revenues of $80 to $100 million.[94]

Deere purchased the rights to the Wankel rotary engine from Curtiss-Wright in 1984 but never commercialized the product successfully.[95] In 1986 Deere made overtures to acquire financially troubled Versatile, a manufacturer of large, four-wheel-drive farm tractors and based in Winnipeg, Canada, but the deal did not go through.[96] Ultimately, Versatile ended up in the hands of Ford–New Holland.

Recession and More Losses

Construction equipment sales continued rising in 1989 and 1990 and reached $1.35 billion. Surprisingly, however, operating profit in 1990 dropped 39 percent to only $63 million, an indication that the earlier restructuring had not been deep enough. As another recession began during the second half of 1990 and sales tumbled, it was apparent that Deere's rosy projections of a break-even point had not been accurate. As the recession deepened, Deere construction equipment had operating losses in both 1991 and 1992. The 1993 recovery brought sales back to 1990 levels and generated a meager $20 million in operating profit after $16 million in special charges. But that year the company elected to take non-cash charges of $1.1 billion for changes in accounting standards (SFAS 106), which brought a corporate net loss of $921 million. At the end of 1993 Deere's ratio of consolidated debt to capitalization (including Deere Credit) rose to 70 percent; that for equipment operations alone was 47 percent. Such levels would have been unthinkable at conservative Deere not too many years earlier.[97]

In a booming U.S. market, construction equipment sales jumped to a record $1.64 billion in 1994 (up 22 percent), with an operating profit of $132 million. Strong demand carried over into 1995, and sales rose another 14 percent to $1.875 billion while operating profit surged an amazing 50 percent to $198 million. Total corporate revenues topped $10 billion for the first time, including $1.3 billion in non-equipment income. Employment in equipment operations was down to thirty-two thousand from a peak of more than sixty-five thousand at the end of 1979.[98]

Deere construction equipment operations since 1985 had made a meager contribution to corporate profits—until 1994 and 1995. Despite restructurings in the early 1990s, at the end of the decade it appeared that Deere needed sales in the range of $1.4 to $1.5 billion to make an acceptable operating profit on construction equipment.

The Joint Venture with Hitachi

The contract manufacturing arrangement on excavators set up in 1983 with Hitachi became a 50-50 joint venture in mid-1988 and included small wheel loaders and track-type tractors. In addition to excavators, Hitachi would supply Deere's three smallest wheel loaders from Japan and market them as well as Deere track-type machines under the Hitachi brand in Asia. Final assembly of the Japanese-built excavators for the North American market would take place at a new, jointly owned plant in Kernersville, North Carolina.[99]

Relying on an off-shore source for a major part of the product line was a risky move in 1983 and even riskier in 1988. As the yen dropped below 100 in 1995, Deere may have had reason to doubt the wisdom of the decision; its product costs in dollar terms were then likely lower than Hitachi's. That was borne out when in 1995 Deere announced that beginning in 1996 a Deere-Hitachi operation in Mexico would build excavator models of less than twenty metric tons to shorten delivery times and reduce currency exposure.[100]

In November 1991 Fiat announced that Deere would join the Italian-based Fiatallis-Hitachi hydraulic excavator combination in a new three-way venture targeted at Europe. Deere would contribute technology on loader-backhoes, track-type tractors, and track loaders.[101] The arrangement seemed logical in view of Deere's long-standing relationship with Hitachi, but the announcement proved premature when a few months later Deere closed the door on its participation.[102] For the second time in twenty years Deere backed away from a venture with Fiat.

Product Development

After the recession of the early 1980s caused Deere to abandon plans to move beyond the mid-range into heavier equipment, the company's product strategy was one of filling in models within its established horsepower ranges and giving the line frequent updates. Between 1986 and 1995 no industry company executed its product strategy any more successfully than Deere. By the end of 1995 the Deere earthmoving product families had received as many as three series changes. Fresh, updated products had been provided with a remarkable frequency, and gaps had been filled.

At the close of the decade Deere had a solid array of state-of-the-art small and mid-range products in seven families; loader-backhoes, track-type tractors, track loaders, wheel loaders, excavators, motor graders, and elevating scrapers. Product families were well integrated, and models within families were closely spaced, giving Deere coverage of more than 70 percent of the total earthmoving equipment unit opportunity. In addition, the company had an excellent line of forestry machines. In 1995 the company reported that virtually the entire construction equipment product line would be replaced by new models by 1998.[103]

With inboard-mounted planetary final drives, wet-disc brakes, and Z-bar loader linkage, the Deere 544H wheel-loader was state-of-the art. (Deere & Company)

Marketing: Distribution

Between 1971 and 1995, as Deere's product line expanded and became more competitive, the dealer organization prospered. Starting in the early 1970s with more than four hundred small industrial dealers in North America spread across the construction, utility, and logging categories, Deere began a process of identifying the stronger ones and winnowing out the weaker ones. By the mid-1990s the number had been reduced to about 125 full-line industrial dealers and four hundred locations.[104] Beginning with a large number of mostly weak, undercapitalized dealers whose very existence was periodically threatened by every new recession, Deere did an outstanding job of building a distribution organization composed of substantial businesses that had adequate resources to compete effectively in the industry.

Both Deere and Case followed a practice of selling factory-direct to large national rental services such as the Hertz Equipment Rental Corporation, something Caterpillar had never been willing to do. After their rental service, these machines were then disposed of on the open market, absorbing a portion of retail demand and denying dealers any part of the revenue stream created from rental income and used equipment sales. The direct sales policy had been adopted years earlier as a means of participating in the short-term rental business (rent-to-rent), apparently in the belief that dealer organizations would not or could not successfully compete in that growing segment of the business. In 1995 Deere went even further when it initiated direct participation in the business by acquiring an interest in a regional equipment rental concern, a move some could interpret as competing with one's own dealers.[105]

Changes at the Top

On June 1, 1990, Robert A. Hanson retired as chairman of Deere and was succeeded by Hans Becherer. Becherer had been groomed to succeed Hanson, having been named executive vice president in 1986, president and COO a year later, and CEO in 1989.[106] Since taking over from William Hewitt in 1981 Hanson had had the challenging task of leading Deere through the toughest years in its history and presiding over the company's first losses since 1933. Although he took restructuring actions during the late 1980s, it fell to Becherer to take sterner steps in 1991 and 1992. Still, Hanson gets credit for building the company's insurance business and taking Deere into health care. After a dynamic period of product development in the 1980s he handed off an industrial product line that was in excellent shape.

A Pattern of Astute Management

As it watched its traditional farm equipment competitors fall into disarray, dissolution, or divestiture, Deere steadily tightened its grip on worldwide leadership. Of the seven long-line companies that existed in 1930, only Deere and Case remain, with International Harvester, Allis-Chalmers, Massey-Harris, Oliver, and Minneapolis-Moline having disappeared as independent companies. In the mid-1990s Deere enjoyed a worldwide position in the farm equipment business similar to that of Caterpillar in earth-moving equipment. On the base of its solidly profitable farm equipment business, Deere nursed a fledgling construction equipment business into viability. Never overreaching, the company brought the business along gradually and deliberately, internally generating the products one by one and never resorting to company-owned stores. It was a pattern of astute management.

In 1978, when Deere set an objective of becoming number three worldwide in construction equipment by 1990 and number two by 2000, it had not, of course, foreseen the deep recession of the early 1980s that forced it to lower those goals and drop plans to move into heavier equipment. It is ironic that by 1995 Deere had achieved the number-two position in North America after Caterpillar yet had never moved beyond mid-range construction equipment. Largely on the strength of its position in North America, in 1995 Deere held the number-five spot worldwide behind Caterpillar, Komatsu, Case, and Volvo.

Traditionally, Deere's principal construction equipment weakness has been a weak market presence in Europe, and it seems unlikely that the company will be able to change that materially in the face of well-established competition from producers there. In this regard, Case is stronger than Deere. Thus Deere's hold on the number-five position is heavily dependent on movements in the North American market with respect to the rest of the world.

The J. I. Case Division of Tenneco

Between its 1967 acquisition of Case and its 1984 acquisition of International Harvester's farm equipment business Tenneco had poured about

$1 billion into Case, but at the start of 1985 Tenneco was blissfully unaware that amount was only a down payment on what lay ahead. Having swallowed a farm equipment business larger than the one it owned, Tenneco found the digestive process costly, investing an additional $1 billion between 1985 and 1987 in losses, restructuring, plant closings, and product development.[107] And this was at a time when the farm market was at low ebb and produced anemic sales and cash flow.

In the mid-1980s Tenneco was beginning to change from one of Wall Street's high-flyers to an underperformer. Revenues in 1985 were more than $15 billion on assets of $20 billion, but profit was only $172 million. The company had a series of major reverses from investments gone bad—the Great Plains coal gasification project, Cathedral Bluffs oil shale project, and a polyvinyl chloride business.[108] Although Case had never contributed significantly to parent company profits, Tenneco was no longer in a position to comfortably absorb Case's perennial operating losses.

Continued Operating Losses

After breaking even in 1982 Case had operating losses before interest and taxes every year through 1988 that totaled $789 million on sales that had gone from $2 billion to $4.3 billion.[109] Even James Kettelson, Tenneco chair and a longtime Case supporter, became exasperated and stated in 1988 that Tenneco would consider selling Case if the subsidiary remained a drag on earnings.[110] But the old question remained, Who would buy?

In November 1987 Jerome Green, Case's CEO since 1979, was fired in a blowup over the late introduction of a new line of agricultural tractors. Green had put through a fairly deep restructuring in 1986 and 1987, closing nine plants in the United States and Europe and reducing employment, but he stayed with the old Case strategy of trying to fight through downturns by emphasizing market share, keeping up production schedules, loading the distribution system with inventory, and discounting heavily. His replacement was James K. Ashford, brought over from Tenneco's automotive components business.[111]

Although Case sales rose 18 percent in 1988 to $4.3 billion on the rebound in the agricultural market, the company was still paying for restructuring and consolidations and had an operating loss before interest and taxes of $142 million. With those costs behind him, in 1989 Ashford finally produced an operating profit of $228 million on a continuing rise in volume to more than $5 billion. That swing in profitability of $370 million in one year brought jubilation in Racine and Houston, and it seemed that at last Case's problems were behind it. But it was not to be. Case's costs were still too high and its margins too low. Despite another rise in sales to $5.4 billion in 1990, operating profit fell to $186 million and a frustrated Ashford resigned.[112]

A First Restructuring

Ashford's replacement, Robert J. Carlson, a former Deere senior vice president and an old friend of Ketelson, was not in place until July 1991.[113] Meanwhile, the economy had entered another recession, and with sales diving it was obvious that Case was in for a big loss in 1991. At this point Tenneco recognized that previous Case restructurings had not been deep enough. In September the 1991 restructuring plan was announced, involving charges of $461 million, which, when added to a large operating loss, brought Case's after-tax loss for 1991 to $985 million and threw the parent company into a loss of $748 million.[114] In August a discouraged James Ketelson had announced his retirement, effective May 1992. His replacement, Michael H. Walsh, chair of Union Pacific, was brought on board October 1 as president and COO.[115]

With Ketelson's retirement in May 1992, Walsh, who had become Tenneco's CEO on January 1, became chairman, and Dana G. Mead, fifty-six, was recruited from International Paper as president and COO.[116] During 1992 Walsh and Mead concluded that Case did not fit their vision for a future Tenneco and resolved to spin Case off, but they knew their money-losing subsidiary would first have to be made attractive to investors. With the task of carrying out their plan for Case, Mead became CEO of Case in September 1992 in addition to his role at the parent.[117]

A Second Restructuring

Case's 150th anniversary was marked in 1992, but there was little cause to celebrate. On sales of $3.8 billion, the company had a before-tax loss and special charges of $322 million. Then, in March 1993, the restructuring program was adopted in preparation for the spin-off and involved a huge pre-tax charge of $920 million against Case's 1992 results. That brought a $1.33 billion after-tax loss for the year on top of 1991's $985 million. By anyone's definition it was all adding up to real money. Tenneco took a $1.3 billion loss, including $699 million for SFAS 106 ($223 million charged to Case).[118]

The objective of the second program was to effect fundamental changes at Case that previous tentative and piecemeal restructurings had failed to address: eliminate excess manufacturing capacity; increase outsourcing; discontinue unprofitable, highly proliferated products; and convert to an entirely independently owned dealer organization by disposing of the 250 company-owned stores.[119] Mead kindled the enthusiasm of Racine management by making it clear that the program was preliminary to spinning off Case as an independent company.[120]

Although Case's 1993 sales were flat, the downsizing and other measures effected since 1991 began to bite, and the company produced a $39 million profit. Employment had been reduced to 17,100 from 30,300 in July 1990.[121] Throughout this period Tenneco had contributed another $800 million in capital to Case but now believed the company to be ready for spin-off. On June 24, 1994, in an initial public offering at $19 per share, 29 percent of Case's seventy million common shares were sold to investors, netting $380 million to Tenneco.[122] Additional offerings followed, and at the end of 1995 Tenneco's stake was down to 21 percent. In February 1996 Tenneco filed with the Securities and Exchange Commission to sell off the remainder of its holdings.[123] Total proceeds of its sales of Case stock yielded Tenneco about $2 billion before tax.[124] The funds were to be used in the plan to redeploy assets into more profitable enterprises but were woefully short of the sums invested and the losses incurred in almost thirty years of struggling with its underperforming subsidiary.

A Return to Profitability

Mead's drastic restructuring worked wonders at Case. On a 14 percent sales increase to $4.3 billion, profit jumped to $131 million in 1994. Clearly, the break-even point had been dramatically lowered, and Wall Street responded by bidding Case shares up into the $45 range in 1995. Mead succeeded Michael Walsh as chair and CEO of Tenneco in May 1994 on the death of the latter. On April 1, 1994, he relinquished the CEO job at Case to Jean-Pierre Rosso, fifty-three, a former Honeywell executive who had been hand-picked to run Case after the spin-off.[125]

Proof of the wonders of the restructuring came in 1995 when profits reached $337 million on sales of $4.9 million. Never in the previous fifty years had the company had profitability at anything even approaching that rate. Gross margin was 23.5 percent for both 1994 and 1995, and 1995 net profit on sales was 6.8 percent.[126] These ratios put Case in a league with Deere and Caterpillar.

The Construction Equipment Business

After the acquisition of the International Harvester farm equipment business, the share of Case sales from construction equipment dropped from more than 60 percent to the low 40s, the percentage fluctuating depending on the relative strengths of the two markets from year to year. Case's worldwide construction equipment sales (including parts) rose from about $1.3 billion in 1986 to a peak of more than $2 billion in 1990, fell to about $1.7 billion between 1992 and 1994, and rose to nearly $2 billion in 1995. Loader-backhoes continued to generate about 40 percent of construction equipment revenues.[127]

Although Drott built some of the first North American hydraulic excavators, none of the Case-Drott excavator models ever gained a strong share of the U.S. marketplace. Well into the 1980s Case marketed small and mid-

The Case 9050B hydraulic excavator. The 9000-Series improved Case's position in the North American market for excavators. (Courtesy of Case Corporation)

The Case 590 Turbo Super L. Although not as dominant as it once was, the Case loader-backhoe line continued to lead the world industry. (Courtesy of Case Corporation)

sized excavators under both the Case and Drott brands and in 1986 augmented these models by introducing its Delta line of larger, French-built Poclain machines: the 125B, 170B, and 220B. They were marketed in North America under the Case-Poclain label, a ploy that made little headway in market share. The Case distribution organization could effectively market the small and mid-sized machines but was less capable of handling the larger Poclain machines. Customers for these sizes generally looked elsewhere.

In March 1987 Tenneco issued $80 million in preferred stock for an additional 23 percent of Poclain, gaining control with 67 percent.[128] Later that year Poclain was rolled into the French Case operation, bringing the Case-Tenneco share to 93 percent.[129]

In 1992, as a part of the restructuring, Case contracted with Sumitomo Construction Machinery Company for the latter to supply excavators under the Case brand for North America. A six-model line of Japanese-built units through the 98,500-pound Model 9060 was introduced, and Case ceased building excavators in North America.[130] Equipped with Consolidated Diesel Corporation engines, these machines were more competitive than any excavators Case had previously offered in North America.

In 1995, Case-Poclain built a seven-model excavator line in France for the European market supplemented by eight mini models supplied by Kubota and MacMotor. That year 22 percent of Case's construction equipment revenues came from excavators, with an estimated two-thirds coming from Europe.[131]

Case's five-model W-prefix wheel loader line of the mid-1980s was at least a generation behind the industry and survived chiefly on low-margin governmental business. Beginning in 1988, Case introduced a new four-model line through the five-cubic-yard 921 as well as two derivative XT tool-carriers. With Z-bar linkage and other features, the machines were competitive.[132]

After Caterpillar's entry into the loader-backhoe business in 1985 both Case and Deere took steps to defend market share by introducing updated models. Case retained market leadership in North America with an estimated 35 percent market share despite gains by Caterpillar.[133] Case, Caterpillar, and Deere accounted for more than 80 percent of North American loader-backhoe sales.[134] In Europe, Case was building two modified versions of its U.S. loader-backhoe models and was a close second to JCB.

Case's track-type tractor line was restructured from seven to four models, and Case exited the track loader business altogether. In 1995 bulldozers contributed only 5 percent of the company's construction equipment sales.[135]

The product strategy growing out of the restructuring—the elimination of unprofitable models, outside sourcing of excavators, and frequent product updates—had by the end of 1995 substantially strengthened the Case construction equipment line. Products were being presented in well-integrated families of closely spaced models within the ranges in which Case had chosen to compete. Although not as comprehensive as the Deere line, Case offered the products most commonly needed by small to medium-sized urban development contractors in the North American market. Its principal vulnerability lay in a heavy dependence on loader-backhoes. Although for more than thirty years Deere tried with little success to make inroads into Case's loader-backhoe business, the Caterpillar models of the 1990s presented a serious challenge to Case and surpassed Deere in market share.

A New Case

By 1991 Case's losses had become so severe that they threatened the financial health of Tenneco. To their credit, Walsh and Mead realized it was vital that Case be divested, and they took the tough and costly decisions that made possible the eventual spin-off. After twenty-eight years as a Tenneco subsidiary Case had come full circle, independent again. The restructuring likely would have produced improved results even under the continuing ownership of Tenneco, but a newly independent Case showed just how well an enterprise can perform once freed of "guidance" from a remote parent. The spin-off was a win-win situation for both companies.

On the farm equipment side, a revitalized Case-International was likely to be a cause for concern at Deere. On the construction equipment side, although the elimination of company stores could cause some short-term market share loss it could also yield an almost immediate improvement in gross margins. By the end of 1995 only sixty-eight company-owned stores remained.[136] Case's success as a viable, long-term competitor in earthmoving equipment would depend on the quality of the entrepreneurs chosen to replace company stores, how well those dealers were developed and supported, and a continuing flow of fresh, competitive products.

The VME Group

When VME was organized in the spring of 1985, AB Volvo and Clark, each with an initial investment of $100 million in assets, held equal cross-ownership in the shares of VME Holding Sweden (VMEHS) and VME Americas Inc. (VMEA), a Delaware corporation.[137] VMEHS had its main plant at Eskilstuna, Sweden, in addition to several smaller facilities also in Sweden. VMEA had Euclid plants in Guelph, Ontario, and Euclid, Ohio, and wheel loader plants in St. Thomas, Ontario, Asheville, North Carolina, Strasbourg, France, and Brazil. Clark's Strasbourg plant was later closed as was the Euclid, Ohio, operation, leaving Guelph as the sole source for Euclid trucks.

Product Line

The year after the formation of the company, VME eliminated the redundancy in the Volvo-Michigan product lines when it introduced the Swedish-built Volvo "Allrounder" line of five wheel loaders to the United States. From 1.5 to 4.5 cubic yards, they replaced the Michigan machines of similar sizes. Allrounders hit the North American market at about the same time Caterpillar was introducing its response, "IT" tool-carriers. The remaining portion of the former Michigan wheel loader line consisted of five models topped by the twelve-cubic-yard 475C, which gave VME a total of ten models. The Euclid truck line remained essentially unchanged at eight models, from twenty-five tons through the electric-drive R-190 at 190 tons. Of the Swedish-built Volvo articulated dumper line, initially only the twenty-five-ton unit in 4-by-4 and 6-by-6 configurations was introduced to the North American market.[138] Michigan also brought the Ranger line of log-skidders to VME; however, those products were divested in 1990.[139]

Sorely needing excavators to round out its line, VME confirmed rumors that it was seeking an excavator partner when in 1988 it acquired a 4.5 percent interest in the Swedish firm of Akermans Verkstad AB. Akermans, a smallish, closely held company, had a six-model line of track excavators through the fifty-six-metric-ton H25C in addition to three wheel models.[140] Although it had a good reputation in Europe for sturdiness, Akermans was nearly unknown in North America. In an effort to gain access to the North American market, it had purchased the small Hein-Werner excavator manufacturing company in the United States in 1981, but that move did not produce the desired results.[141]

Equipped with forks, this Volvo L90C wheel loader is a versatile, utilitarian tool-carrier. (Volvo Construction Equipment North America Inc.)

The Volvo A25C dumper. Long dominant in Europe, in recent years the Volvo articulated dumper has gained acceptance in North America and now leads that market as well. (Volvo Construction Equipment North America Inc.)

To strengthen its position in Europe, in 1990 VME acquired 25.1 percent of Zettelmeyer Baumaschinen GmbH, a German manufacturer of small wheel loaders and utility machines.[142] Zettelmeyer was a fugitive from the IBH debacle, having been acquired by that ill-starred company in the late 1970s. Since the breakup of IBH, Zettelmeyer had struggled as an independent. In 1991 VME completed its acquisition of Akermans and raised its stake in Zettelmeyer to 70 percent, the total purchase price for the two acquisitions amounting to $172 million.[143] VME acquired the remainder of Zettelmeyer in 1994 for $39.9 million.[144]

During 1993 VME and the Hitachi Construction Machinery Company formed an off-highway truck joint venture, Euclid-Hitachi Heavy Equipment, Inc., under which Hitachi would market Euclid trucks in Asia. That would allow Hitachi, lacking hauling units in its line, to package the Euclid rear-dumps with its large hydraulic front shovels for sale to the mining industry.

Profit Problems

From the outset, the VME Group made very little money. With the acquisitions of Zettelmeyer and Akermans, 1991 European sales spurted to 3.5 times those in North America. But in North America, where prices were better, sales stagnated. After losses in the 1991–92 recession totaling $138 million, retained earnings were in a deficit of $64 million and shareholders' equity was down to $155 million from a 1990 high of $310 million. At the end of 1991 the company was in a financial crisis. Its ratio of debt to total capitalization was 65 percent, and with the expectation of another bad year in 1992 the parent companies were forced to contribute additional capital of $15 million each and provide subordinated loans of $35 million each to keep VME afloat. Despite these actions, the ratio worsened to 71 percent at the end of 1992, and the survival of the company was in serious jeopardy unless VME could quickly become profitable.[145]

In 1991 and 1992 a restructuring of manufacturing operations cost about $23 million. A plant at Landskrona, Sweden, and the St. Thomas plant were closed and their operations consolidated at Eskilstuna and Asheville, respectively.[146] The company's recovery efforts received a major assist when in 1992 the Swedish government allowed the krona to float freely. It immediately weakened, which improved the competitive position of Swedish products in Europe and North America.

Although 1993 sales of $1.24 billion were down 9 percent from 1992, the restructuring and better price realization generated a profit of $30 million. With the economic recovery in Europe and North America, 1994 sales jumped 26 percent to a record $1.57 billion with a healthy 8.4 percent profit of $132 million, the best yet for VME. European sales topped $1 billion, and those for North America reached $430 million.[147] It seemed that VME had successfully weathered the crisis.

Clark and Restructuring

After the spin-off of its Michigan construction equipment business to VME in 1985, Clark was left with its lift-truck subsidiary, the Clark Material Handling Company; the Melrose Company; the automotive components business; and the 50 percent interest in VME accounted for on an equity basis. In a diversification move, for $152 million in 1990 Clark acquired Hurth Axle S.p.A., an Italian manufacturer of off-road transmissions and axles.[148]

Clark's volume in 1990 was $1.5 billion, of which the lift-truck business accounted for $634 million. But with the advent during the 1970s of low-priced Japanese competition, the lift truck had almost become a fungible product and the business had ceased to be profitable for high-cost U.S. producers. Clark's 1990 operating profit from that segment was a tiny $9.6 million.[149] The 1990–91 recession drove the business into a $40.7 million operating loss, and Clark, resolving to divest it, sold the business, effective July 31, 1992, to Terex Corporation for $90 million, booking a gain of $8.5 million.[150] Thus, Clark, credited with inventing the lift truck in 1928 and with more than sixty years in the business, ended its connection with that industry.

Clark was so anxious to divest its lift-truck business that it was willing to retain contingent liabilities for $40 million in guarantees and $220 million in recourse on product financing in order to consummate the sale to Terex, which was experiencing losses and was undercapitalized.[151] There was serious question about whether Terex would escape bankruptcy, although the company was able to remain viable. By 1995 most of the liabilities had been liquidated.

Continuing its restructuring of the company, in 1994 Clark sold its Clark Automotive Products Company subsidiary in an initial public offering for $103 million with a gain of $33 million. It was now completely out of the automotive components business. That same year, Blaw-Knox, an old-line manufacturer of asphalt paving equipment, was acquired from White Consolidated Industries for $145 million. Blaw-Knox's 1994 full-year sales were $104 million.[152]

Selling Out to Volvo

At this point Clark had exited three of its traditional businesses—lift trucks, automotive components, and earthmoving equipment—except for its 50 percent equity interest in VME. Of its earlier acquisitions, only Melroe remained. Clark was less than satisfied with the results VME had produced in its ten-year existence. Although VME had generated a good profit in 1994, its overall record of profitability had been poor, and losses totaled $138 million in 1991–92. Also, it was an extremely cyclical business, something Clark was trying to escape in its restructuring, and the lack of control inherent in a joint venture was not appealing to management. Thus, after Clark threatened to take public its share of the venture, in March 1995 Volvo agreed to buy Clark's share of VME for $573 million, netting Clark about $430 million after taxes and putting an end to its forty-year involvement with the wheel loader business.[153]

Clark had hardly finished counting its cash when it was hit with a tender offer by Ingersoll-Rand for 100 percent of its shares. With a show of reluctance, the Clark board was able to push the offer to a generous $86 per share, and for a price of $1.5 billion the Clark Equipment Company ceased to exist.[154]

Volvo on Its Own

Following the 1995 buy out of Clark's share, VME was renamed the Volvo Construction Equipment Group. That year, sales reached a new record of $1.9 billion. Since its formation in 1985 VME had done well in Europe and nearly tripled its business, which included the addition of Zettelmeyer and Akermans. The record in North America, however, was less impressive. North American sales, about $480 million in 1995, were 25 percent of the corporate total compared to about 55 percent in Europe.[155] Volvo growth in North America had come largely from articulated dumpers, where the company led during the mid-1990s; it had battled with Komatsu for third place behind Caterpillar and Deere in wheel loaders.[156] The company had virtually no North American presence in the vital hydraulic excavator field. Still, the Volvo Construction Equipment Group came out of the decade a much stronger company. With the resources of AB Volvo it was positioned to remain a factor in the worldwide earthmoving equipment business.

Terex Corporation

Assembling a New Competitor

The deep recession of the early 1980s in the worldwide equipment business fatally wounded a number of companies and financially weakened every company. Of the survivors, the short-line companies found the postrecession environment particularly difficult in an industry with 30 to 40 percent excess capacity. The situation was made to order for Randolph W. Lenz, an entrepreneur and turnaround specialist who targeted financially troubled heavy equipment companies. Beginning in 1983, in a series of acquisitions reminiscent of Dieter Esch's IBH, Lenz collected a string of old and respected companies that were in financial difficulty. At thirty-six, Lenz was four years older than Esch when Esch formed IBH, but Lenz, unlike Esch, eventually took his company public.[157]

In 1983 the Northwest Engineering Company of Green Bay, Wisconsin, an old-line power shovel manufacturer founded in 1925, was near liquidation. The company, with an excellent reputation for building a sturdy rock machine, had never expanded its shovel line above four-cubic-yard capacity and was unable to compete for the business of large, open-pit mines. An effort to enter the hydraulic excavator business had not been successful. Its sales had fallen to only $10 million. Incredibly, Lenz was able to acquire Northwest out of bankruptcy for a personal investment of only $1,200 cash.

Eighteen months later Lenz acquired Bucyrus-Erie's $20 million construction equipment business for $8 million. Bucyrus-Erie had also fallen on hard times and was selling assets to raise cash. Primarily a replacement parts business for non-current Bucyrus-Erie construction products, the purchase also included the rights to the Dynahoe loader-backhoe. No longer in production, the Dynahoe was an extra-heavy-duty niche machine that had enjoyed some successes in the northeastern United States. Lenz later restarted production.

Still doing business as the Northwest Engineering Company, Lenz began to attract notice when in late 1986 he acquired Terex USA from General Motors for $19 million. After the IBH bankruptcy of 1983, Terex had reverted to General Motors in two entities, Terex USA and Terex Equipment Ltd. (TEL) of Scotland. From about $500 million in sales as a GM division in 1979, Terex's 1986 sales were about $150 million, with slightly more than half from the U.S. company. With the acquisition, Lenz took an option to purchase TEL that was exercised in June 1987 for $19 million. The U.S. Terex company was operated for a short time from the leased Hudson, Ohio, plant, but with the acquisition of TEL and its seven-hundred-thousand-square-foot Motherwell, Scotland, plant all U.S. manufacturing was discontinued and production transferred to Scotland.

Between the two Terex acquisitions, Lenz picked up the Koehring Crane and Excavator Company, a division of AMCA International Ltd. For $22 million net he received the respected Koehring line of hydraulic excavators and Lorain hydraulic cranes, as well as a 380,000-square-foot facility in Waverly, Iowa. Koehring had started in the concrete mixer business in Milwaukee in 1906 and entered the shovel and dragline business in 1922. The company was a pioneer U.S. manufacturer of hydraulic excavators in the late 1950s, and for a period during the 1960s and 1970s its large units were market leaders in the sewer and water segment. Beginning in the 1960s, Koehring went on an indiscriminate acquisition binge and bought, among others, the Thew Shovel Company, Schield-Bantam Excavators, and the Buffalo-Springfield Roller Company. Indeed, it became something of a construction equipment conglomerate with a large stable of brands. Koehring sales peaked in 1979 at $477 million, and it was acquired by AMCA in 1980.[158] Terex consolidated Koehring, Lorain, and Northwest manufacturing operations at Waverly.

Lenz was not finished. In 1988 he picked up Unit Rig Equipment Company out of bankruptcy for $21.8 million. The company, a leader in the large mining truck business, was viable and had sales of $75 million, but its parent, Kendavis Industries, had reverses in the oil business and had gone bankrupt in 1985 owing creditors more than $500 million.[159] In 1984 Unit Rig had purchased the Dart line of mechanical-drive off-highway trucks to complement its electric-drive units. With the Unit Rig purchase, Lenz acquired a 325,000-square-foot plant in Tulsa, Oklahoma.

In 1988 the Northwest Engineering Company turned itself inside out in a downstream merger and become Terex Corporation, with Northwest becoming a division of Terex. The company went public in 1988 with a NASDAQ listing, but Lenz retained control. Sales in 1988 were $343 million.

In 1989 Lenz made his biggest move to date when he acquired Fruehauf Trailer for $231 million. This time he may have overreached. Terex sales jumped from $343 million in 1988 (without Fruehauf) to $1.023 billion in 1990 (with Fruehauf), and Terex recorded a $45 million profit for the year. But the recession hit the trailer business hard, and it began generating operating losses in 1991. That year Terex took Fruehauf public, retaining 42 percent, but still lost $33 million on sales of $784 million.[160]

Undeterred by his first loss since entering the equipment business and the already high debt of Terex, in 1992 Lenz acquired the Clark Materials Handling Company, a lift-truck business, for $90 million in notes. Clark Materials Handling brought $500 to $600 million in sales but was not a money-maker, having generated a $40 million operating loss in 1991. For thinly capitalized Terex the question was whether it could turn Clark around quickly enough. The answer seemed to be that it could not, because Terex lost $61 million in 1992 on sales that with the addition of Clark jumped back to $1 billion. That was followed by a $65 million loss in 1993 as sales slumped to $670 million. The continued existence of Terex was shaky indeed. A Price Waterhouse audit that year stated that there was "substantial doubt about the Company's ability to continue as a going concern."[161]

Product Line

Before acquisition by Terex, Koehring had established an arrangement with IHI of Japan for supply of a line of small to mid-range hydraulic excavators for sale under the Koehring brand in North America. The mid-to-large range was covered by five U.S.-built Koehring 66-Series excavators. Although heavier Koehring excavators still had some following among sewer and water contractors, overall the company was a very small player and unviable in the North American industry and practically unknown outside North America. When losses in the early 1990s forced a restructuring, Terex discontinued the Koehring excavator line but retained three models in scrap-handler configurations. At the same time the antiquated Northwest line was discontinued, as was the Dynahoe loader-backhoe.[162]

During the mid-1990s Terex continued to offer a line of five conventional scrapers topped by the TS-46C from its Motherwell, Scotland, plant and competed with Komatsu for the 20 percent of the worldwide conventional scraper business not controlled by Caterpillar. The plant also produced two Terex wheel loaders, articulated dumpers, and off-highway trucks. Its wheel loaders, at 5.5- and 8.0-cubic-yard capacity, were not significant competitors in that industry other than perhaps in the United Kingdom. Beginning in the mid-1980s with a twenty-five-ton unit, the Terex dumper line was expanded to four models of 6-by-6 machines through forty tons.

Terex's most comprehensive line and strongest market position was in the off-highway truck business. The line, originally developed under General Motors ownership after the 1968 divestiture of Euclid, consisted of seven models, 30 through 120 tons, when Lenz acquired it in 1987. A year later the purchase of Unit Rig brought a four-model line of electric-drive trucks, from the 120-ton Mark 30 through the 205-ton MT2050.

Unit Rig also built a three-model line of Dart mechanical-drive trucks, from 85 through 130 tons, which created an overlap with the Terex line. That line was subsequently rationalized and upgraded and by 1995 consisted of five models from thirty-four through ninety-four tons, with the newer models equipped with oil-disc brakes. Dart units filled the 100- to 130-ton mechanical-drive segment, although few were sold. In the meantime, Unit Rig added the MT4000 and was introducing the MT4400, a 262-ton unit.

The original Unit Rig Equipment Company electric-drive truck concept was based on technology drawn from the oilfield business. The diesel engine–DC drive had been used to power drilling rigs. A prototype was built in 1960 and followed in 1963 by production of the revolutionary Mark 85,

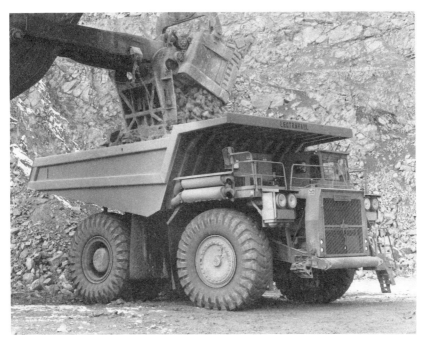

The Unit Rig MT-4000 240-ton truck is representative of the electric-drive mining trucks available in this size class. Unit Rig launched the electric-drive truck era in 1963 with the M-85. (Terex Mining)

the first commercially successful electric-drive truck.[163] Throughout the late 1960s and early 1970s Unit Rig was the leader in the large electric mining truck business, but gradually, as the technology proliferated, the field became more crowded and no one company was able to dominate.

Dart had a long history in the mining truck business. In the 1950s and early 1960s it had led the way as the industry moved into the sixty-five-ton and larger sizes and was a leader in the mining truck business. In 1967 it was building a 120-ton model, the largest commercially available mechanical-drive unit at the time. As the mining industry moved strongly to electric drive, Dart's mechanical-drive trucks steadily lost market share. Unsuccessful in its efforts with electric drive, the company gradually receded to the position of a minor truck supplier. The company also entered the large wheel loader business and introduced the D600 in 1967, a seven-hundred-horse-power, fifteen-cubic-yard mechanical loader targeted at the mining industry. It was then the industry's largest conventional wheel loader but has since been outclassed in size by several competitive machines.[164]

A Tenuous Existence

After losing about $150 million from 1991 through 1993, in 1994 the sale of $30 million in assets, mainly Fruehauf shares, allowed Terex to eke out a $461,000 profit on sales of $787 million. Heavy equipment made up 29 percent of the business ($226 million), 60 percent was material-handling, and the remainder was cranes. Despite these meager results, in 1995 Terex made yet another acquisition and bought the French PPM crane company for $59 million. Year-end results brought a loss of $35 million on sales, which, with the PPM acquisition, reached $1.03 billion. Earthmoving products accounted for $250 million.[165]

In connection with the PPM transaction, Terex underwent a $250 million refinancing that management claimed put the company back on a sound financial footing. Shortly thereafter Lenz retired, to be succeeded as CEO by Ronald M. DeFeo. During twelve years as CEO Lenz had miraculously kept the company afloat, acquiring additional loss-making or marginally profitable companies while closing down losers acquired earlier. In strong worldwide demand conditions Terex earthmoving product lines should generate profits, although they accounted for only about 25 percent of the company's business in 1995 whereas the low-margin lift-truck business contributed more than 50 percent of sales. The future of Terex may well hinge on a successful turnaround or divestiture of the low-margin Clark Materials Handling.

Fiatallis

With the 1985 split from Allis-Chalmers, Fiatallis no longer had a strong incentive to continue manufacturing operations in the United States The strong dollar had made U.S.-built products less competitive in world markets, and its U.S. source had done little to stem Fiatallis's deteriorating position in North America. Further complicating the situation was Libya's 15 percent ownership in Fiat, which created a serious public relations problem for Fiat in the United States.[166] (Later, Fiat bought back Libya's holdings at a substantial profit to that country.) With a plan to supply North America with imports from Italy and Brazil, Fiatallis closed its 1.6-million-square-foot Springfield, Illinois, plant in early 1986, although an office and parts operation in Carol Stream, Illinois, remained open. Track-type tractors and track and wheel loaders were moved to Lecce, Italy, and motor grader and scraper production went to Brazil.[167]

That only aggravated Fiatallis's already anemic market position in North America. By 1990 North American sales, almost all imports, were only $123 million, and wholesale defections had decimated the dealer organization. In 1991 Fiatallis announced that it was discontinuing machine marketing operations in North America.[168]

European Operations

Following closely on the divorce from Allis-Chalmers, in late 1986 Fiat announced the formation of a joint venture on hydraulic excavators with Hitachi that would fill a need for both companies. With a weak line of excavators, Fiatallis recognized that it could not compete with the more technologically advanced products being built north of the Alps. Hitachi, whose imports were blocked by the countervailing duties imposed by the EC, sought a base for entry into the European market. The original ownership split was Fiat, 51 percent; Hitachi, 45 percent; and Sumitomo, 4 percent. Manufacturing facilities were provided in Fiatallis's former excavator plant in Turin, Italy, where imported Hitachi components would be married with Iveco engines and other Italian content for sale in Europe, Africa, and the Middle East by Fiatallis and Hitachi distribution organizations.[169] At the outset other European excavator manufacturers watched the venture narrowly to assure that it was achieving the 60 percent European content required by the EC under its anti-dumping regulations.

A Joint Venture with Ford

With the success of Fiat-Hitachi, Fiat sought further strategic alliances. In 1991 it formed a major joint venture with Ford-New Holland, merging the two companies' farm and construction equipment businesses in a holding company, NH Geotech N.V., based in the Netherlands. Fiat was the majority partner with 80 percent. Ford's construction equipment was essentially its loader-backhoe business while Fiat contributed Fiatallis.[170] Fiat-Hitachi remained independent, but Geotech became the owner of Fiat's majority share of the F-H venture. Two years later Ford, which appeared to be using the venture merely as a means of exiting the machinery business, sold its share of NH Geotech to Fiat.[171] With that, Ford ended its seventy-five-year association with the farm equipment industry begun during World War I when Henry Ford introduced his revolutionary, light-weight farm tractor. The formation of NH Geotech measurably strengthened Fiat's worldwide standing in the farm equipment business and brought it a distant number-three position in North America behind Deere and Case-International, where previously Fiat was a nonentity. Similarly, Ford successfully competed in the loader-backhoe business in North America and Europe. While Ford was fifth worldwide behind Case, JCB, Caterpillar, and Deere, Fiatallis was almost unknown in the field outside Italy.

The Purchase of Benati

In early 1990 Fiat-Hitachi paid $28 million to acquire Benati S.p.A., a small Italian manufacturer of excavators, loader-backhoes, and wheel and track loaders. In the highly fragmented Italian industry, Benati, with 1989 sales of $96 million, was likely the second-largest equipment manufacturer after the Fiat interests. The Benati line was almost totally redundant to the Fiatallis and Fiat-Hitachi lines, but it was rumored that the acquisition was intended to deny Benati to Sumitomo Construction Equipment, which was seeking an independent foothold in the EC.[172]

The Consolidation of Fiatallis and Fiat-Hitachi

After the abortive effort to bring Deere into the venture, NH Geotech decided to roll Fiatallis into Fiat-Hitachi, bringing Fiat's share to 80 percent. Unable to graft on Deere's track-type tractor and wheel and track loader technologies, New Holland N.V. (formerly Geotech) needed a means to strengthen its weak product line in these sectors, which was still drawing on old Fiat-Allis designs. In late 1994 NH announced that TCM, a Japanese wheel loader manufacturer, would become a 5 percent partner in the Fiat-Hitachi venture to develop new wheel loaders at the Fiatallis plant in Lecce, Italy.[173] TCM originally had entered the wheel loader field years earlier through a license from Clark-Michigan.

Reentry into North America

In 1994 Fiat-Hitachi announced that it was reentering the North American market after an absence of about two years, when only a parts operation had been sustained. The products would be marketed under the Fiatallis brand. Because the former Fiatallis dealer organization had almost totally disintegrated, Fiat-Hitachi planned to effect the reentry through five independent master distributors who would act as dealers in their own right and appoint new sub-dealers, gradually covering the Continent. A seven-model line of track excavators through the thirty-three-metric-ton FH330.3 would come from Italy, as would track-type tractors through the 340-horsepower FD30C and track loaders. Small to mid-sized wheel loaders would come from Italy and Brazil, and a full line of motor graders would be supplied from Brazil.[174] Fiatallis's reentry into North America brought three brands of Hitachi-designed excavators into competition in one marketplace: Deere, Hitachi, and Fiat-Hitachi.

Having only recently abandoned the North American arena, the reentry of Fiat-Hitachi cum Fiatallis took on a somewhat quixotic aspect considering the firm's already minuscule market share when it left, not to mention the deeply entrenched North American competition from almost entirely local sources fortified by well-established dealer organizations. Add to that a product line that brought no new technology to the market. One can only assume that the operation was predicated on the expectation of a price advantage from the historically weak lira and Brazilian real.

The Perseverance of Fiat

From the formation of its joint venture with Allis-Chalmers in 1973 through the present, Fiat must be credited with perseverance if nothing else in its earthmoving equipment enterprise. In a situation analogous to General Motors with Euclid/Terex, Fiat's earthmoving equipment business made only a small contribution to the Agnelli empire. Unlike GM, however, Fiat never gave up in the face of considerable adversity. Sales of the parent, New Holland N.V., were $5 billion in 1995, of which Fiatallis contributed $587 million from manufacturing operations in Italy and Brazil. That made Fiatallis a rather small player in the world market for earthmoving equipment.[175] The company continued to be the market leader in Italy but had little presence in North America and was a non-participant Japan, the latter two markets together accounting for nearly 60 percent of the world opportunity.

The gaining of Hitachi technology secured a seat for Fiat-Hitachi at the excavator table in Europe, while TCM will almost certainly provide a major upgrade to the obsolescent wheel loader line, an equally important product sector there. Italy has traditionally benefited from the weak lira with respect to its major trading partners, yet the push by the European Union toward a single currency may reduce or eliminate that advantage.

An improving product line backed by the deep pockets of Fiat should assure the survival of Fiatallis in the EU, and Fiat's long-standing connections in Eastern Europe and Russia will also be advantageous. Overall, although Fiat demonstrated its staying power in the earthmoving equipment industry, its chief rivals in Europe (Caterpillar, Komatsu, Liebherr, and Volvo) also have the necessary resources and determination to maintain or improve their positions. Thus, it is doubtful that Fiat will be able to effect a change in its ranking.

Liebherr

Founded in 1949 by Hans Liebherr, the company remains a family-owned concern headquartered in Switzerland and with earthmoving equipment manufacturing facilities in Germany, Austria, and France. Initially a builder of tower cranes, the company continues to offer a comprehensive lines of tower and mobile cranes. Liebherr moved early into hydraulic excavators and expanded into track-type tractors and wheel loaders during the 1980s. The company has also diversified into real estate, hotels, household appliances, machine tools, and aircraft components. In 1995 worldwide sales of excavators, tractors, and track and wheel loaders amounted to $1.09 billion, about 30 percent of the corporate total.

Products

Liebherr keeps plants small and locates them in stable, rural communities where the work ethic is high. It is the company's philosophy that this has paid off in high quality and productivity. In 1983 a Swiss holding company was established to control the nearly fifty Liebherr subsidiaries, and at about the same time a plant was built in Bulle, Switzerland, to manufacture diesel engines and hydraulic pumps and motors. The Deutz and Mercedes engines Liebherr had used have largely been supplanted by Liebherr engines with Cummins engines in larger machines. The manufacture of its own engines in 4, 6, and V-8 configurations has met Liebherr's objective of full quality control over the components of its products, however comparatively low production quantities must make those engines costly.

Liebherr has built its reputation on a line of hydraulic excavators composed of twelve state-of-the-art track models ranging from a fourteen-metric-ton unit through the massive twenty-eight-cubic-meter-capacity, 530-metric-ton R996 front shovel (introduced in 1995) in addition to five wheel models. The R996 is a clear challenge to Demag's leadership in super-large hydraulic mining shovels, however Demag's H485SP at 680 metric tons remains the world's largest hydraulic shovel. In a departure from a tradition of developing its own products, Liebherr coupled the introduction of the R996 with the purchase of the Wiseda Company, a small independent manufacturer of mining trucks in Baxter Springs, Kansas. A new company, Liebherr Mining Truck Inc., would continue to build Wiseda's 190- to 215-short-ton and 240-short-ton electric-drive trucks at the Kansas plant.

Although closely identified with Germany, Liebherr manufactures only a small portion of its earthmoving equipment there. Most track excavators are built in Colmar, France, while bulldozers and track and wheel loaders are sourced from two small plants in Austria.

Liebherr heavily promoted its "Litronic" management system of electronic load-sensing and control of excavator functions, but sophistication in this area is by no means exclusive to Liebherr. Having built a leadership position in hydrostatic technology through excavator development, Liebherr elected to extend that know-how into bulldozers and track and wheel loaders. The company is unique in that its entire earthmoving line is hydrostatically driven. With the objective of increased ease of operation and controllability through the use of buttons, switches, and joysticks, the company has successfully grafted its excavator control technology onto bulldozers and loaders. Liebherr's 1995 track-type tractor line consisted of five models through the 330-horsepower PR 751, and all but the PR751 had a track-loader counterpart. The eight-model wheel loader line ranged from 0.7 cubic meters through 5 cubic meters (the L561).

Meanwhile, competitors have also made advances in ease of operation and controlability. Overall, despite its technical virtuosity, Liebherr has been hard-pressed to demonstrate a productivity advantage from hydrostatic drive versus the mechanical-drive trains other manufacturers use in track-type machines and mid-sized-to-large wheel loaders.

Marketing: Distribution

Using a combination of factory outlets and dealers, Liebherr has focused marketing efforts on the EU and has achieved a certain success there, especially in countries where it has a manufacturing presence: Austria, Germany, and France. Liebherr, like Caterpillar, emphasizes quality and high technology and appeals to more sophisticated buyers.

In 1970 Liebherr established a presence in North America with a small plant in Newport News, Virginia, to assemble and add U.S. content to imported excavators, but that effort was abandoned in 1982 and the plant became a distribution center. In twenty-five years of trying, Liebherr failed to raise its penetration of the North American excavator market beyond low-single-digit levels and had little success with its other earthmoving products. With full or near-full lines and established distribution systems, Caterpillar, Komatsu, Deere, and Case had the North American opportunity well covered and set a difficult task for Liebherr. Although the company's North American subsidiary has worked hard to enhance its image as an excavator specialist with a high-quality product line, Leibherr, one of fifteen or so brands fighting for excavator market share, is unlikely to move beyond single digits. The remainder of its product line is not well known in North America.

In view of Caterpillar's entry into the large mining-shovel business, the Komatsu-Haulpak tie-in with Mannesman-Demag, and the Volvo Construction Equipment (Euclid) joint venture with Hitachi, Liebherr believed it was imperative to find a means to package its large shovels along with mining trucks. The acquisition of Wiseda gave it that ability and strengthened it as a supplier to the mining industry. But these companies and ventures can offer only a hydraulic front shovel, which limits the attractiveness of their truck-shovel packages with some larger mines.

A Unique European Union Competitor

In the hands of Hans Liebherr's heirs, Liebherr in the mid-1990s continued to be a closely held enterprise, and thus it is difficult to gauge the profitability of its earthmoving equipment business. Judging by Liebherr's perseverance in the field, however, one can assume that this segment of its business has been profitable over the long term.

With its full line of excavators and good representative lines of track-type tractors, track loaders, and wheel loaders and the addition of mining trucks, Liebherr is unique as the only EU-based competitor that has a nearly full line and is positioned to pursue a high percentage of the unit opportunity in construction and mining. Given its first-rate technology, the company's ability to make serious market-share gains hinges almost entirely on improving the effectiveness of its distribution system. This will be a difficult and time-consuming task.[176]

JCB

JCB is by no means the world's largest manufacturer of earthmoving equipment, but it is unique in being the only one whose CEO has been knighted. Sir Anthony Bamford, son of the founder Joseph C. Bamford, gained that distinction as the head of the sole remaining British-owned competitor of any significance in the earthmoving equipment industry.

It all began in 1945, when Joe Bamford started a company to make agricultural trailers. The venture met with little success until Bamford hit upon the idea of a loader-backhoe, which he introduced in 1954. Based on that, JCB claims to have invented the concept, but whether or not Joe Bamford was the first to mount a backhoe on the rear of a farm tractor there is little doubt that his company was the first to commercialize the product successfully in Europe just as Case was first in North America. It is remarkable that despite not having a farm tractor base upon which to draw for high-volume, low-cost components, JCB was able to compete successfully through the years with its rivals.

Although the company diversified into other types of earthmoving equipment, the loader-backhoe has always been its primary revenue source. In 1995 four basic models were offered in a variety of configurations to suit the European and North American markets. With the exception of excavators built by a joint venture, JCB has focused exclusively on the less-than-one-hundred-horsepower segment of the market and drawn heavily on components from its core loader–backhoe line for use in its other products. All manufacturing takes place in the United Kingdom. Perkins engines are used almost exclusively.

Diversification

Diversification began in the 1960s and 1970s when JCB attempted unsuccessfully to enter the track-type tractor business and did introduce a limited line of hydraulic excavators. Although JCB was not able to compete with higher-technology excavator manufacturers on the Continent, it was able to hold a niche within the United Kingdom for more than two decades, although even that was threatened when Komatsu began producing superior excavators there in 1986 and forced JCB into action to maintain its position. Sumitomo Construction Machinery found in JCB the European Union entry it had been seeking, and a joint venture was formed in 1991 to manufacture excavators in the United Kingdom.

By 1995 the venture was producing six models from thirteen to thirty metric tons in the United Kingdom, with seven-ton and forty-two-ton models built by Sumitomo in Japan. All were for sale under the JCB brand in the EU, Africa, and the Middle East. The company's most successful products after loader-backhoes were rough-terrain forklift trucks and rough-terrain telescopic boom units, all targeted at the construction industry.

JCB entered the wheel loader business in 1968 through the acquisition of Chaseside, a near-defunct British manufacturer. Initially, lack of heavier components limited the JCB wheel loader line to the low end of the industry range, but this is a likely area for expansion.

After abandoning a brief joint venture with Kubota on mini-excavators, JCB entered that business with its own line in 1989. Skid-steer loaders, another addition to the construction equipment product line, were introduced in 1993.

Marketing

JCB has always been strongly marketing-oriented, and as the only British success story in the construction equipment industry the company receives strong reinforcement from the British trade press. Worldwide sales in 1994 totaled $863 million on shipments of eighteen thousand units. After allowing for parts shipments, that produced an estimated average unit value of $40,000 to $45,000, reflecting the company's focus on light construction machinery. In 1994 about 35 percent of volume was in the United Kingdom, 30 percent in the rest of Europe, 15 percent in North America, and the balance distributed throughout the rest of the world.

The company's distributor-dealer organization covers the United Kingdom intensively, and distribution subsidiaries sell through dealers in most major countries on the Continent. It claimed about 35 percent of the 1994 European loader-backhoe market and a 16 percent overall market share in units for Europe, but in value terms JCB accounted for less than 8 percent of the EU market for earthmoving equipment in 1994.

JCB established a presence in the United States in 1971 with a small assembly operation in White Marsh, Maryland. At the outset the company attempted to sell European-style sideshift loader-backhoes rather than the center-pivot configuration preferred in North America; as a result, it made little headway. After providing a modified design for the North American market, loader-backhoe sales began to progress and peaked at about 9 percent market share in the late 1980s. North American share has since stabilized at about 6 percent; the company has comprehensive coverage of the North American market through a network of independent dealers.

JCB has had success in North America with its rough-terrain material-handling products but has sold only a few wheel loaders. In the mid-1990s it began introducing mini-excavators and skid-steer loaders to an already crowded North American market. Because of Sumitomo's prior commitments to Case the JCB-Sumitomo venture will not be able to market excavators in North America.

A Well-Focused Enterprise

A tightly managed family-owned concern, JCB is a quick-reacting, dynamic company that has a record of consistent profitability. Anthony Bamford, fifty in 1995, had provided strong leadership while keeping corporate goals in line with financial capabilities. With about 65 percent of its business outside the United Kingdom, JCB has had reasonably good countercyclical protection. Originally a loader-backhoe specialist, for some years the company has successfully pursued a strategy of supplying all types of the higher-volume construction machines in the less-than-one-hundred-horsepower segment and became a strong and growing force in that chosen niche.[177]

The Shovel Manufacturers

In chapter 2 three pioneer American shovel manufacturers—Bucyrus-Erie, Marion, and Harnischfeger (P&H)—were described as being the only companies to survive in the cable-operated ("rope") shovel business into the mid-1990s. Because they have focused only on a specialized segment of the earthmoving equipment business, there has been no subsequent discussion of them. In view of their unique contributions over the years, however, particularly in the mining industry, it is appropriate that a brief overview of their stories since World War II be included here.

The Loss of the Construction Market

The rapid evolution of track and wheel loaders and the development of the hydraulic excavator began eroding the market for smaller sizes of power shovels soon after the war. By the mid-1950s it was clear that the heyday of the small power shovel for construction was past. To continue to partici-

pate in the market would require that shovel manufacturers build hydraulic excavators. Bucyrus-Erie and P&H entered the hydraulic excavator business in the 1960s with machines sized for construction, but those offerings
made little impression on the market. Neither company had a distribution
system capable of effectively marketing the products to contractors, and the
machines were not technologically advanced. Eventually, the two companies exited the hydraulic excavator business. But with growing competition
from European-built hydraulic front shovels for mining industry business,
all three companies entered that field during the late 1970s and early 1980s.
Bucyrus-Erie and Marion subsequently withdrew, but P&H persevered and
introduced its largest model, the 375-ton 2250, in 1990.[178]

Although unsuccessful in the construction market for hydraulic excavators, P&H was a major player in the construction crane business after the
war with a comprehensive line of hydraulic and lattice boom models. When
the company was restructured during the 1980s the decision was made to
get out of cranes, and the last interest in that business was sold off in 1991.[179]

From 1935 on, Bucyrus-Erie had produced bulldozer blades, controls,
and crawler-drawn scrapers for the construction industry and supplied such
items to International Harvester until IH bought the rights to the products
in 1953.[180] Still casting about for a viable entry into the construction market, in 1971 Bucyrus-Erie purchased the Hy-Dynamic Company of Lake
Bluff, Illinois, maker of the Dynahoe heavy-duty loader-backhoe.[181]

Meanwhile, a very conservative Marion continued to concentrate on the
shovel and dragline business. The conservative nature of the company is illustrated by the fact that its name remained the Marion *Steam* Shovel Company until after World War II, when "Steam" was changed to "Power."[182]
In a misreading of the trends, in 1955 Marion purchased the Osgood Company, an old-line manufacturer of small power shovels for the construction
market.[183]

Mining Opportunities

Fading opportunity in the construction market left shovel manufacturers no alternative but to concentrate more intensively on the mining market. The steady escalation in off-highway truck sizes that began during the
1950s and took off during the 1960s proved a bonanza. When a mine purchased larger trucks it would almost always upgrade its shovels. Marion
introduced its 191-M, a ten-cubic-yard machine, in 1951, soon followed by

The Bucyrus 495-B can load a 240-ton truck in three passes. (Bucyrus International Inc.)

the similarly sized Bucyrus-Erie 195-B. P&H was building its nine-cubic-yard 1800 in 1961.[184]

P&H led the move into the next generation when in 1969 it introduced the twenty-five-cubic-yard 2800. Bucyrus-Erie followed in 1972 with the 295-B, and Marion in 1974 with the 201-M.[185]

As the mining industry demanded ever-larger loading tools, the shovel manufacturers clearly had no choice but to match competitors' offerings. With the mining industry seeking to load 240-ton trucks in three shovel passes, rope shovel manufacturers offered the Marion 301-M, the Bucyrus-Erie 495-B, and the P&H 4100. All weigh 1,200 to 1,300 short tons and have a capacity of eighty to ninety tons per pass (approximately fifty cubic yards, depending on the material). In preparation for the next generation of trucks of more than three hundred tons, P&H introduced its 5700 model in 1990–91. In its 5700XPA version the machine carries a nominal bucket rating of seventy cubic yards and has a capacity per pass of 120 tons.[186]

The postwar trend to increased open-pit coal mining also paid dividends to shovel manufacturers. From the 1950s on, the desire to mine ever-deeper coal seams drove the development of larger and larger stripping shovels and draglines. Beginning with the thirty-six-cubic-yard Bucyrus-Erie 1050-B stripping shovel introduced in 1941, the growth of such machines culminated in the Marion 6360, a 180-cubic-yard, fourteen-thousand-ton unit introduced in 1965.[187] P&H never participated in the giant stripping shovel race and focused instead on loading shovels. But the era of the stripping shovel was short-lived, displaced by the walking dragline that could dig deeper and cast further. Large draglines have predominated since the 1960s and been produced by Bucyrus-Erie, Marion, and Page Engineering, the latter company being credited with the invention of the dragline in 1903. In 1987 P&H entered the mammoth dragline business through the purchase of Page.[188]

The size of the machines reached an apex with the Bucyrus-Erie 4250-W, which weighed fourteen thousand tons and had a 220-cubic-yard bucket. Put in service in 1969, only one was ever built.[189] Unlike loading shovels, which are replaced periodically as mines upgrade to larger trucks, large

The Bucyrus-Erie 4250-W was the largest dragline ever built. (Bucyrus International Inc.)

draglines often work for the life of the mine and are never replaced. Thus very few are sold, so under existing competitive conditions each sale represents a major plum for the lucky company. For example, a 1993 contract P&H received for a Model 9020 120-cubic-yard walking dragline was valued at $45 million.[190]

The mining industry's move into ammonium nitrate as a blasting agent created the need for large blasthole drills, and in 1953 Bucyrus-Erie began introducing its successful R-Series rotary drills, crawler-mounted and with integral compressors, in diameters up to fifteen inches. Marion also competes in this business with its M-Series, and P&H entered in 1991 through the purchase of the Gardner-Denver line from Cooper Industries.[191]

Hard Times in the 1980s

After the war and through the 1970s the three shovel companies prospered by doing business with the mining industry. The oil shock of the early 1970s was a stimulus to the coal industry, and shovel manufacturers benefited. But they were hard-hit by the recessions of 1980–82. The bottom fell out of copper prices, causing two of the largest producers, Kennecott and Anaconda, to disappear as independent companies. The coal industry also was forced to retrench. Bucyrus-Erie's sales topped out in 1982 at $687 million with a modest $25.7 million profit.[192] Sales for 1983 dropped 20 percent, however, and charges of $135 million for downsizing brought a loss of $133 million.[193]

Losses in the early 1980s put Harnischfeger in severe financial straits. It had been in technical default on its debt by 1982 and barely escaped bankruptcy after a loss of $76.5 million in 1983. After three generations with a Harnischfeger as CEO, Henry Harnischfeger, grandson of the founder, stepped down in 1984, and an outsider, William W. Goessel, was brought in to run the company.[194] Marion, however, as a wholly owned subsidiary in Dresser's Mining and Construction Equipment Division, was able to ride through the difficult times of the early 1980s. The division posted operating losses of only $10 million in 1981 and 1982 on sales of about $570 million.[195]

Bucyrus-Erie and Harnischfeger were extensively restructured during the 1980s. To raise funds and refocus the company on its mining business, Bucyrus-Erie sold off its Construction Equipment Division (Dynahoe and parts) in 1985 to Northwest Engineering (later Terex), and a precision gear business was sold in 1988. A leveraged buy out by management was effected in 1988, but the large debt thus created brought crushing interest expenses. After losses every year from 1988 through 1993 on sales ranging from $139 million to $249 million, the company took bankruptcy in early 1994. It emerged after a financial restructuring as Bucyrus International, Inc., but continued to experience losses in 1994 and 1995.[196]

Harnischfeger's new management chose to reorient the company and entered the paper-making machinery business in 1986 with the purchase of the Beloit Corporation, an activity that began to account for more than half of the company's volume. Mining Equipment Division sales of $255 million, consisting entirely of shovels and draglines, made up only 17 percent of the corporate total in 1989. But a series of acquisitions, including Page Engineering in 1987 and Gardner-Denver in 1991, changed the balance back in favor of mining equipment. In 1994, in a major move, Joy Technologies Inc. was also acquired, putting Harnischfeger into underground mining equipment; that was followed by the 1995 acquisition of Dobson Park, a British manufacturer of underground coal mining equipment. The acquisitions were expected to push the Mining Equipment Division's contribution to more than half the company's volume; corporate sales in 1995 were $2.15 billion.[197] Meanwhile Marion, its two competitors in turmoil, quietly continued to build shovels, draglines, and drills.

The Future: A Crowded Field

What of the future for these three companies, each more than a hundred years old? With competition from no less than five well-established manufacturers of large hydraulic front shovels making serious inroads into the loading shovel business, growth prospects for the rope shovel must be viewed as somewhat less than favorable. But a reservoir of preference for the rope shovel still exists in the mining industry, and it does not seem likely that the hydraulic machine will overtake the rope machine in size. Meanwhile, the large dragline, not threatened by other methods, appears secure. The question would seem to be whether three manufacturers can continue in the rope shovel business while dividing a shrinking pie.

Industry Product Development

Since the late 1960s, when the physical size of machines used for construction began to level off, manufacturers have concentrated on differentiating products and enhancing machine productivity through refinements that focused on increased horsepower, improved controls, ease of operation, and operator safety, comfort, and convenience. Having somewhat tentatively introduced electronics in the previous decade, between 1986 and 1995 manufacturers embraced them wholeheartedly; by 1995 there were few machines that did not use electronics to enhance controls and monitoring systems. Excavators led the way, and those without sophisticated load-sensing and mode selection were not players in the hydraulic excavator business.

Unlike construction equipment, mining equipment continued to grow in size, moving from the 170- to 190-ton to the 240-ton truck, with the more than three hundred tons in the offing. Six manufacturers—Komatsu (Haulpak), Terex (Unit Rig), Caterpillar, Liebherr Mining Truck (Wiseda), Volvo Construction Group (Euclid), and LeTourneau—were contesting for the large mining truck business. Shovel equipment moved in tandem with truck size, and large hydraulic front shovels gained acceptance among miners.

In addition to old-line rope shovel manufacturers (Bucyrus-Erie, Marion, and P&H), the large mining-shovel business was being contested by several brands of hydraulic front shovels of more than three hundred metric tons, including Demag (with Komatsu), O&K, Liebherr, Hitachi, P&H, and Caterpillar. Even more so than on construction equipment, chip technology, on-board microprocessors, and other electronics were essential components of mining equipment.

The Japanese Excavator

Beginning in the early 1980s, excellent technology and quality combined with the production experience and economies of scale from a huge home market were giving the Japanese excavator industry a nearly unbeatable edge in the business worldwide. North American and European manufacturers were soon being forced to face up to one of two unpleasant realities. First, Japanese costs were so far below their own that it was more profitable to discontinue manufacturing excavators and contract for Japanese-built excavators for resale (Deere, Case, Koehring, and Link Belt are examples), or, second, lower costs and improved excavator performance could be achieved by obtaining a strong injection of Japanese design and manufacturing know-how for their own excavator brand (as with Caterpillar, Fiat, and JCB). As a result, by 1995 more than 80 percent of worldwide excavator production was being built in Japan, being built by a joint venture outside Japan to a Japanese design, or being built outside Japan but with a predominant Japanese influence in design.[198] That overwhelming influence created a design convergence and made product differentiation increasingly difficult.

The Korean Construction Equipment Industry

Beginning during the previous decade, South Korea began developing a construction equipment industry that matured between 1986 and 1995. Centered in the three industrial conglomerates of Daewoo, Samsung, and Hyundai, emphasis was on hydraulic excavators based on Japanese technology, and with favorable costs the Koreans have even become component suppliers to the Japanese. Each company produced wheel loaders, and Samsung built one crawler tractor model. Through the mid-1990s manufacturing operations were confined to Korea, but the companies were exporting to the European and North American markets and developing distribution organizations there. Korean machines, as completely undifferentiated products, brought nothing unique to the market and with sketchy distribution were unlikely to exceed low single-digit market shares outside Korea.

ConExpo '87

Since ConExpo '81 the industry had gone through trying times indeed, but 1987 found manufacturers once again optimistic as they gathered at a new location, Las Vegas, for what would be the last CIMA-sponsored construction equipment show with industrywide participation. Caterpillar, after several years of losses and a reported slippage in quality, reasserted its leadership position by dominating the show with a massive market-oriented display. New products included loader-backhoes and N- and H-Series elevated-sprocket tractors. Even more impressive was the increased breadth of line demonstrated by the array of newly added products under Caterpillar's branding program. Komatsu, Case, and Deere also had impressive displays.[199]

Before the next ConExpo scheduled for 1993 Caterpillar, Case, Deere, Komatsu, and most of the other heavy equipment manufacturers had withdrawn from the CIMA in a dispute over governance of that organization. As a result, ConExpo '93 lacked the pulling power provided by the big construction equipment, and the show appeared destined to become much smaller or disappear altogether.[200] In a move to forestall its demise, in 1995

ConExpo announced a merger with the Construction/Aggregate Show (CON/ AGG) to conduct the new ConExpo-CON/AGG '96 show in Las Vegas.

Meanwhile, the Bauma Fair, held in Munich every three years, had steadily grown in importance to rival—and after 1987 displace—ConExpo. Bauma 95, targeted at the construction and mining industries, proved to be the largest machinery show ever held, with attendance totaling 350,000 and 4.3 million square feet of exhibits from 1,450 companies.[201]

Summary, 1986–95

The earthmoving equipment industry has experienced a recovery and renewal since the dark days of the early 1980s. At the close of 1995 the $30 billion worldwide industry had never been more robust.[202] Despite the doomsayers' predictions over the previous decade that growing completion of world infrastructures would make earthmoving equipment a declining industry, it was showing remarkable vitality. It was clear, however, that in North America, Europe, and Japan it was at best a replacement rather than a growth industry. Price realization in 1995 was the best it had been since before the recession of the early 1980s, and corporate profits were at an all-time high. Along with strong demand, strategic downsizing had made a major contribution to improved profits. Employment in 1995 at U.S. companies was typically 50 to 60 percent of its peak. Japanese and European companies, more constrained in their ability to reduce employment, had also pared head counts. Downsizing, joint ventures, mergers, and acquisitions since 1985 had eliminated some excess industry capacity, although excavator capacity may have increased during the decade through the addition of Korean producers.

Along with downsizing, the formation of strategic alliances and joint ventures had been a prominent characteristic of the decade. The long list includes Volvo-Michigan, Euclid-Hitachi, Deere-Hitachi, Fiat-Hitachi, Komatsu-Dresser, Komatsu-Demag, Komatsu-Cummins, and JCB-Sumitomo, not to mention the ventures formed by numerous companies with entities of the former Soviet Union, People's Republic of China, and in the rapidly growing countries of Southeast Asia. In a significant move, Caterpillar and Mitsubishi Heavy Industries also reorganized their venture to include excavators. The wave of joint ventures reflected the harsh realities of the marketplace of the 1980s and 1990s, that is, the prohibitive investments and high risks involved in going it alone into major upgrades and new technologies and the pressures to avoid being shut out of important markets. Companies clearly were positioning themselves for the long pull.

Since 1985 no development had more impact on the industry than the weakening of the dollar, which was at 80 yen per dollar in 1995 as opposed to 260 ten years earlier. In addition, by starting from a higher base U.S. manufacturers were able to make relatively greater cost reductions during the decade through downsizing and modernization than the already lean Japanese. If such a shift had occurred the other way, U.S. manufacturers would have been totally devastated, yet, remarkably, the resourceful Japanese adjusted.

Still, a quantum shift had occurred in the competitive balance. What had seemed in 1985 an unstoppable Japanese juggernaut sweeping all before it with low-cost exports had been tamed. To compete in North America, the Japanese were forced to establish real value-added manufacturing operations there. Similarly, unfavorable exchange rates plus the EU common external tariff brought the Japanese to Europe in the late 1980s. For the Japanese, it was a rude awakening from the luxury of being able to export from a secure home market base for all those years. But the wake-up call may have come too late for them to make big gains in market share against entrenched local competitors. In any case, the realignment of currencies brought about a leveling of the playing field in the earthmoving equipment industry although the strong yen to weak dollar is unlikely to be a permanent state of affairs.

EIGHT

Perspectives

It is interesting to reflect on why some companies were successful where others failed during the first fifty years of the modern era of the earthmoving equipment industry. From this narrative, it is clear that of the many companies that have been a part of the industry the most successful have had two salient characteristics:

- a concentration on machinery as the primary if not the sole business of the enterprise
- a deep commitment to building a strong, independent dealer organization as the principal means of distribution.

The Concentration Principle

It is striking that in such a large worldwide industry only three major companies exist whose principal business is earthmoving equipment: Caterpillar, Komatsu, and JCB. Concentration has been their guiding principle from the outset. Caterpillar is nearly 75 percent earthmoving, with most of the remainder in closely related diesel engines. Despite efforts to diversify, Komatsu remains nearly 70 percent earthmoving, and the small, family-owned JCB devotes 100 percent of its efforts to construction equipment. Acquisitions have played a minor role, if any, in the growth of these companies. Diversification has come from expansion of their product lines within the industry. Earthmoving equipment is the lifeblood of these companies, and the top decision makers' attention is riveted on that business.

This account is replete with examples of erstwhile competitors whose earthmoving equipment businesses were never more than secondary corporate interests or sidelines. The most egregious example of corporate dilution was Allis-Chalmers, which at its peak manufactured some thirty distinct product lines. The International Harvester of the 1950s, already stretched by four businesses (trucks, farm equipment, construction equipment, and steel), added yet a another, gas turbines, in 1960. Clark's construction equipment always played second fiddle to its lift-truck business. All eventually found it necessary to exit the earthmoving equipment industry.

Companies entering the industry through acquisition also have, with rare exceptions, chosen or been compelled to leave the business by divestiture, withdrawal, or failure. The list is long and includes some distinguished names: General Motors, American Standard, Dresser, Tenneco, White Motors, IBH, and Daimler-Benz. Their failure follows a consistent thread—a misreading of what it took to compete in the earthmoving equipment industry. Some underestimated the capital-intensive nature of the business and were unprepared or unable to make the outlays necessary to stay competitive. Unable to obtain an acceptable return on its equipment business, even General Motors eventually grew weary of this drain. Companies entering the business through acquisition often did so based on premises that proved faulty. White and Daimler-Benz apparently believed that the off-highway truck business was a natural adjunct to the on-highway truck business. Dresser, with its record of successful acquisitions, was confident that it could turn around a failing Harvester Payline business. Going in, some underestimated the handicap of a short-line participant in attracting good dealers and gaining customer recognition against powerful full-line competitors. Finally, the cyclical nature of the earthmoving equipment business, the relatively long manufacturing lead times, the high unit value of inventories, and the unique marketing demands are all characteristics that require top management who has industry-specific experience and whose attention is not diffused across a variety of unrelated enterprises.

Starting modestly with derivatives of farm tractors, Deere, Case, and Massey-Ferguson were able to bootstrap their way into the construction equipment industry through the synergies in manufacturing between farm and construction equipment. Deere followed the most conservative line and was able, sustained by good profits from its farm equipment business, to stay the course and emerge with a successful secondary business generating about 20 percent of revenues. Case, with a much less profitable farm equipment business, might not have survived in any business had it not been acquired by Tenneco. As one of many unrelated businesses of a profitable conglomerate, Case's consistent losses were subsidized by an incredibly patient and long-suffering parent. But Tenneco's experience with Case again bears out the concentration principle. After the spin-off, an independent Case has demonstrated its vitality.

Massey-Ferguson's failure in the construction equipment business did not result from lack of concentration as much as from an attempt to force the pace of growth through the unwise acquisition of Hanomag, a high-cost source. That plus a dealer organization unprepared to market mid-sized construction equipment generated losses that the overextended, debt-laden farm equipment business could not sustain.

The Volvo and Fiat construction equipment enterprises, subsidiaries of European automotive manufacturers, are seemingly at variance with the principle of concentration although certain similar special conditions apply. Initially, both had relatively secure home-market volume bases and parents willing and able to subsidize years of losses. These factors combined to shelter them while they gained experience in the industry. A series of acquisitions funded by the parent has allowed Volvo to broaden its line and gain a lodgment in North America. With a high degree of autonomy from the parent, Volvo Construction Equipment appears to be doing the right things to compete successfully.

The acquisition of Allis-Chalmers's weak construction equipment business did little to strengthen Fiat. Only its preferential position in Italy and parent company subsidies kept it in business. Carrying the proud name of Italy's largest manufacturer, Fiatallis could not be allowed to fail. An alliance with Hitachi also injected new life into the enterprise. Still, Fiat-Hitachi and Volvo Construction Equipment, as non-core businesses of large parents, could yet fall victim to the concentration principle.

With the exception of Komatsu, the Japanese and Korean earthmoving equipment manufacturers generally are offshoots of large and diversified industrial corporations (Hitachi, Kobe Steel, Furukawa, Kawasaki, IHI, Sumitomo, Hyundai, Daewoo, and Samsung, for example). For the parent, it is just one of many businesses, entered opportunistically within a protected home market and with undifferentiated products that often contain a high percentage of purchased components. Although Hitachi and Kobelco have had a degree of success in international markets, the commitment of other of these diversified parents to the earthmoving equipment industry, absent a significant position outside the home market, may yet also be put to the test.

The Dealers

Throughout the modern era of earthmoving equipment, a convergence in product design has slowly but inexorably occurred and, if anything, accelerated since the mid-1970s. At the same time, among leading manufacturers the critical but largely intangible characteristic of product quality has also converged. One result of these trends has been to enhance the role of the dealer in the balance of price and value in the customer's buying decision. And where differences in features and quality among products of top manufacturers have narrowed, differences among competing dealers have widened.

No history of the industry would be complete without recognizing the immense contribution that dealers have made to the success of both manufacturers and users of earthmoving equipment and describing how the role of dealers has evolved.

The Franchised Dealer

Cyrus H. McCormick, recognizing the vital importance of strong retail distribution, built a network of independent dealers whose first loyalty was to the McCormick brand of farm equipment. It was his franchise agreement, introduced during the 1880s, that set the pattern for retail distribution of farm and later construction equipment to the present day.

By enlisting the capital of the dealer-entrepreneur, manufacturers minimize their investment in distribution facilities. In addition to capital, an independently owned dealer brings familiarity with local culture, business conditions, customers, and sources of financing. Being a dealer means gaining the right to sell and service desirable and presumably profitable products from stipulated locations with the assurance, subject to satisfactory performance, of being the exclusive representative in those locations.

Manufacturers evaluate dealer performance using objective measures such as market share, customer satisfaction, profitability, continuity, and other factors. They are not hesitant to provide a great deal of "advice and counsel" aimed at improving dealer effectiveness. Conversely, in making important marketing decisions manufacturers can benefit hugely by drawing on the collective experience of their independent dealers. Overall, each party has a distinct role, but there is little question that manufacturers hold the whip hand in the relationship.

In North America before World War II, exclusive dealers, full-line selling, and floor planning (the financing of dealer inventory) were already prevalent in the farm equipment industry. Because prewar earthmoving equipment manufacturers still had relatively narrow product lines, their dealers, although exclusive to the major manufacturer, usually carried other noncompeting lines and a range of allied or auxiliary equipment. After the war, as the major manufacturers filled out their lines with their own brands of bulldozers, controls, track and wheel loaders, scrapers, and excavators, their dealers became more "pure," dropped other lines, and relegated auxiliary equipment to filling specialized niches.

Although a good product line is essential, strong, loyal dealer organizations are the result of well-conceived policies toward dealer selection and administration that the manufacturer consistently follows in good times and bad. At bottom, the touchstone of dealer loyalty is long-term profitability. The Caterpillar dealer organization has become the paradigm. Over a span of seventy years Caterpillar created what is generally acknowledged to be the world's finest independently owned distribution organization for industrial products. Other manufacturers with full or near full lines have drawn on the Caterpillar approach to finding, developing, and administering dealers.

Dealers for a second group of limited-line manufacturers, while carrying a flagship brand such as Volvo, Terex, or JCB, typically carry several, sometimes numerous, secondary product lines. That gives rise to certain intractable problems endemic to non-exclusive dealers—competition for attention; investment in inventory, training time, and facilities; and issues involving non-common business procedures, parts systems, and service literature.

No earthmoving equipment manufacturer in North America has been able to survive long-term with a distribution system other than one relying principally if not entirely on independently owned dealers. The independent dealer system for distribution of construction equipment is so deeply implanted in North America that it has acted as a formidable barrier to foreign manufacturers wishing to enter the market. The would-be entrant is presented with a terrible dilemma. No serious penetration can be made or positive cash-flow stream generated until a reasonably comprehensive distribution system is in place. But the up-front costs of building a factory-owned system are prohibitive, and it takes years to find and train enough suitable dealer candidates. Both Deere and Komatsu can attest to the long struggle required to create a credible dealer organization in North America.

In Europe, although the independent dealer is the system of choice for most manufacturers it is less deeply implanted than in North America. European farms before the war were less mechanized than those in North America, and thus the farm equipment industry was not as well developed. The exception was Great Britain, where Ford and Ferguson had become large manufacturers of tractors. Food shortages soon after the war emphasized the necessity of increasing farm productivity, triggering a variety of government schemes to encourage mechanization and stimulating development of the equipment industry. Nearly thirty-two companies produced farm tractors in Germany in 1951, for example, and even into the late 1950s fifteen to twenty manufacturers competed for the farm tractor business in each major continental country.[1]

Manufacturers in that melee were forced to adopt a variety of channels to gain representation at the local level, including factory direct to independent dealer, retail factory branch, factory branch distribution to dealer and sub-dealer, different classes of dealers with different terms, cooperatives, and independent distributor to dealer and sub-dealer. In Germany it was not unusual for dealers to carry several directly competing lines of farm equipment—a kind of smorgasbord from which customers could choose. Wholesale prices often were established in dealer-by-dealer bargaining with the factory.[2]

Thus, as European manufacturers of earthmoving equipment developed after the war, the distribution of machinery was not as strongly tied to a direct factory–independent dealer tradition, and manufacturers were, of necessity, more directly involved in the distribution chain. That frequently took the form of establishing marketing subsidiaries in each major European country. The subsidiaries worked to develop dealers in their areas, provide credit, assemble factory shipments, maintain and distribute inventories to local dealers, and sometimes sell directly. These intermediate marketing organizations, similar in function to farm equipment distributors, were necessary because dealers, often small and financially weak, needed more support than a remote factory was able to provide.

In Japan, Komatsu established a pattern of extremely dense coverage using a mixed system of factory branches and independent dealers and sub-dealers to blanket the country with a high number of retail points and force other manufacturers to emulate that system. Elsewhere in the world, government restrictions, language, and the need for local knowledge and contacts make locally owned independent dealers almost mandatory.

The Evolution of Dealers

In the early years after the war, when machinery was in short supply, dealers usually had a customer order in hand before placing an order on the factory. Discounting to obtain sales was unnecessary. Customers arranged their own financing through third-party lending institutions, and dealers received full payment up front. They rarely rented earthmoving equipment. Nor did most customers, with a mind set to ownership, wish to rent. Used equipment was shunned by dealers. Customers were encouraged to dispose of used machines on the open market, especially if the machines were of another brand. Dealer repair service was slow, labor-intensive, and expensive. Parts sales, then as now, were a lucrative profit source, and the quality of parts service was already a critical differentiator among brands of products.

Under those conditions it is little wonder that equipment dealers, many with only nominal capital and management skills, made a great deal of money in the first decade after the war. But following the Korean War, as pent-up demand was satisfied and competition grew more intense, the level of know-how required to run a successful dealership began to increase sharply. Growing machine populations in the late 1950s and early 1960s forced dealers to become more active in the used equipment business, which called for new skills and additional capital. Competition among aggressive captive finance companies and outside financial institutions brought a liberalization of credit terms, less stringent standards of creditworthiness, and higher risk to dealers. Astute financial and credit management was an increasingly critical factor in dealer operations.

The Advent of Rental

Great Britain pioneered equipment rental after the war when drastic swings in the economy penalized equipment ownership and encouraged the formation of the "plant-hire" industry. Machines were usually rented complete with operator for periods ranging anywhere from a day to the duration of a job, practices that still continue. Many contractors rely heavily if not entirely on plant hire for their equipment needs. That has had a pervasive influence on the equipment business in the United Kingdom in two ways. Large plant-hire operators, as major purchasers of equipment, naturally have discouraged dealers from competing directly in the rental business, and the simplistic parameters used to establish rental rates—such as horsepower and bucket capacity—have favored machinery that is less sophisticated and lower-priced.

Except in very specialized cases, North American machinery buyers remained closely tied to the traditional objective of gaining ownership of equipment, although the concept of lease and rental had begun to take root by the 1960s and would ultimately would bring sweeping changes. Encouraged by finance houses and the more well-heeled and aggressive dealers, rental gradually became an established form of merchandising. Initially, it was nothing more than a disguised installment sale ("rent to sell"). Terms were rigorous, but intensified competition with the passage of time brought an easing in minimum periods and rental payments and an increase in the percent of payments applying to equity. That merchandising approach has continued in wide use, although growing acceptance of the pure rental concept has made it more likely that equipment will be returned at the end of the rental period.

Paralleling the United Kingdom's plant-hire business, a new phenomenon made its appearance in North America during the 1960s: the "rent-to-rent" business in which national chains and local operators rented light construction equipment by the day or week or for longer periods. This was anathema to dealers, and few chose to compete until the severe recession of the early 1980s changed the face of the earthmoving equipment business.

The depth and duration of that recession created widespread financial havoc among contractors who had large fleets of idle equipment. It also brought fundamental change in the attitude of the construction industry toward equipment ownership. The advantages of returning idle rental equipment to the dealer during business downturns took on new attractiveness. During the late 1980s the more perceptive and aggressive dealers who were financially capable began to establish rental fleets across the full spectrum of machine types and sizes. That had major ramifications for the industry: a large upward ratchet to dealer capital requirements and a sharply increased flow of low-hour used equipment into the marketplace. It also created a new hazard—the amount of unsold equipment in users' hands subject to return (the "rental overhang"). In the event of a business downturn, that overhang could potentially flood dealer yards with "near new" used equipment and devastate factory shipments of new machines until rental returns were absorbed. The growth of the rental business brought increased risk. The operation of large rental fleets had clearly become a game in which only the most astute and well-financed dealers could play.

Pure leasing was slower to gain acceptance, but during the late 1970s and early 1980s increasingly sophisticated, more financially attractive leases were developed that began to interest machinery users. Businesses with machinery needs peripheral to their principal business activity were especially attracted to the concept of a full-service lease.

Product Support

Along with sales, the provision of replacement parts and repairs to equipment users, generally referred to as "product support," is the other primary role of a dealer. The two are wholly interdependent. Without sales, the product support opportunity eventually disappears, but without product support, sales cannot be sustained. The quality of product support is unquestionably the number-one industry differentiator, and the dealer, by extension, reflects the degree of emphasis that the manufacturer places on this area.

The Parts Business

Parts sales are critical to dealer profitability. Usually composing up to a third of dealer sales volume, parts can account for 60 to 80 percent of gross profit. During recessions parts sales may be the only source of profit, literally keeping the doors open.

Inventory control is the essence of the parts business and was the first area of equipment dealers' operations to be computerized. Wealthier, more adventurous dealers who purchased computers could create inventory management methods not practical using manual record keeping. The primitive computers of the early 1960s, for example, represented a huge advance from tedious Cardex and other paper systems, and as computers became more affordable through the 1970s and 1980s their use for parts inventory control became general.

Most machinery users regard parts service as the most important element of product support, ahead of mechanical repair service. Other things being equal, the higher the dealer's off-the-shelf delivery ratio, the higher the customer's satisfaction.

All major manufacturers now operate relatively sophisticated parts systems that provide on-line ordering and search service. Using these systems in combination with premium freight and delivery services, even poorly stocked dealers are able to draw upon manufacturer warehouses and provide twenty-four-hour service within North America and Europe for more than 90 percent of items. Although that has somewhat blunted the competitive edge that larger players enjoy, it comes at a cost in terms of lowered customer satisfaction when compared to over-the-counter delivery and reduced dealer profit margins from heavy reliance on emergency-type services.

For a few years after World War II the original equipment manufacturers enjoyed a near-monopoly on parts for their machines, but the rest of the parts industry was growing rapidly, particularly for fast-moving items an owner could easily install such as undercarriage parts, ground engaging tools, and filters. To retain their parts business, larger manufacturers increased proprietary features, but in a remarkably short period the parts competitors were able to offer similar features. Now, for models with significant field population, few parts items are unavailable from non-OEM sources.

The Service Business

In the early postwar years there were three sources for repairs: the machine owner's shop; the independent, third-party shop; and the dealer. During the 1950s and 1960s the increasing sophistication of equipment gradually precluded most independents and shade-tree mechanics from being sources of repairs. Owners performed whatever repairs they could, and more complex jobs went to the dealers. Through the 1970s, owners generally were unamenable to the use of components rebuilt by dealer repair shops, not wanting to inherit "someone else's problems." But the labor-intensive, one-at-a-time dismantling and reassembly of major components in dealers' shops—of engines, transmissions, turbochargers, pumps, and cylinders—became so costly that the concept of off-the-shelf rebuilt components, widely accepted in the automotive industry, gradually began to seem attractive.

Initially, manufacturers began with factory-rebuilt engines while dealers rebuilt other components as they saw the need to do so. Manufacturers' rebuild programs have expanded steadily into a wide range of components and, benefiting from economies of scale, have tended to supplant dealer rebuilds. Rebuilt components have revolutionized repairs by sharply reducing costs and turnaround times. The wide availability of factory- and dealer-rebuilt, fully warranted components has deprived the non-OEM parts industry of access to much of the piece parts business it formerly enjoyed, although numerous independent rebuild houses have come into existence.

An outgrowth of the trend to rebuilt components coupled with improved shop management made possible by computers has been dealers' increased use of flat-rating repair jobs, again mirroring the automotive industry. As opposed to the almost open-ended time-and-material methods of the past, now customers can usually know in advance and within a narrow range what jobs will cost.

In the 1980s, to cope with the growing complexity of their machines, manufacturers began providing built-in diagnostic systems that when coupled to sophisticated diagnostic shop equipment could quickly identify problems. Paralleling this was a movement to computerization of parts and service literature. Thus, immense changes have occurred during the 1980s and 1990s in dealer service shops and in the job description of what used to be called the "mechanic." Well-thumbed, greasy parts books and service manuals have given way to computer terminals that computer-literate service technicians use to look up references on CD-ROM, order parts, and enter service accounting data. High-tech dealer field service vehicles are equipped with the latest in electronic diagnostic tools, laptop computers, and cellular telephones. Although these developments have entailed major dealer investments in equipment and training, it has paid off. As equipment becomes steadily more complex, even operators of large fleets can rarely justify the purchase of the variety of elaborate and expensive diagnostic tools and test benches needed and instead look to dealers to provide those services.

From rough-and-ready days at the end of World War II the business of being an equipment dealer has evolved into one calling for a high degree of management competence in marketing and finance backed up by topnotch technical know-how. With a mid-sized piece of construction equipment costing $150,000 to $200,000, equipment dealerships are not small businesses. Some, now into their third or fourth generation of family ownership, are among the largest privately owned enterprises in their localities or countries. For example, in 1995 Caterpillar's 186 dealers worldwide had a total net worth of $4.99 billion.[3]

The manufacturer-dealer relationship is one of powerful mutuality. The manufacturer's support, consistency, and fair dealings create strong and loyal dealers, who in turn make a huge contribution to the success of the manufacturer.

Fifty Years of Product Trends

Since the end of World War II the products of the earthmoving equipment industry have expanded immensely, both horizontally into many new families of machines and vertically in size and horsepower within families. Coming out of the war, Caterpillar had two families of earthmoving products: crawler tractors and motor graders. By the mid-1990s it had ten, Komatsu and Deere eight, Fiat-Hitachi seven, and Case six. Wheel loaders and hydraulic excavators, which did not exist in 1945, have become the core construction products and account for about 70 percent of world industry's unit volume. Deeper manufacturers also cover, variously, crawler tractors and loaders, motor graders, scrapers, off-highway trucks, dumpers, loader-backhoes, skid-steer loaders, compaction and paving equipment, and a variety of derivative products such as pipelayers, wheel bulldozers, and tool-carriers.

The growth in product size within families has been no less impressive. Unconstrained by the need to move from job to job, equipment for open-pit mining has shown the most spectacular growth. The twenty-two-ton rear-dump truck of 1947 has grown by a multiple of fourteen to 320 tons. In 1946 a six-cubic-yard power shovel was considered large in the metals mining industry. Fifty years later the huge trucks were being loaded by fifty-cubic-yard power shovels. General-purpose construction equipment has also shown impressive growth. At the end of World War II the LeTourneau Super C Tournapull with LP Scraper at fifteen cubic yards heaped was the largest wheel tractor-scraper in series production. By the mid-1960s that had risen to fifty-four cubic yards. The 1946 Caterpillar D8 2U-Series, then the largest crawler tractor in production, is dwarfed by the D11 and the even larger Komatsu D575A-2 at 145 tons and 1,050 horsepower. Perhaps an even greater difference is indicated by contrasting the amount of operator effort required to pull the long-throw levers and stamp on the pedals of the old D8 with the finger-tip controls of most current pieces of earthmoving equipment.

Throughout the 1930s and into World War II, crawler bulldozers, motor graders, towed scrapers, off-highway trucks, and power shovels were the mainstays of the construction industry, but two postwar product developments—the wheel loader and the hydraulic excavator—had the greatest influence on the industry in the modern era. From the early postwar Hough machine of 1.25 cubic yards, the wheel loader developed rapidly and reached six cubic yards in the late 1950s, twelve cubic yards by the late 1960s, and twenty-four cubic yards in the 1970s.

The first fully hydraulic excavator appeared during the mid-1950s, built by the German company Demag and soon followed by Poclain and other European manufacturers. The technology spread quickly to Japan, where the product was especially well adapted to local conditions, and North America. From the modest twelve- to fifteen-metric-ton machines of the mid-1950s, by the early 1970s the industry reached 135 metric tons with the introduction of the Poclain EC1000, the first large mining excavator. From there the industry continued to escalate to 680 metric tons (the Demag H485SP), and even larger machines were under development. With more manufacturers than any other type of earthmoving equipment, the excavator industry has always been intensely competitive. That results in large engineering expenditures to increase the technical sophistication of one's offerings. Certainly, excavators have led the way in using microprocessors in hydraulic load-sensing and control.

Thus have companies increased both the breadth of their lines and the range of products within families. Although it is easy to cite the dramatic increases in product size and horsepower, as the physical size of equipment for construction tended to level off in the late 1960s and early 1970s most increases in productivity came from more horsepower and increased technological sophistication in the less tangible areas of hydraulics, operator comfort, ease of control, visibility, and serviceability. Such innovations have added significantly to the cost of equipment. In addition, government mandates for product safety, reduced noise levels, and emissions have had a large but difficult to quantify impact on cost. However desirable from a social standpoint, they have done little to increase productivity.

The Cost of Moving Earth

Between 1945 and 1960 the U.S. Department of Commerce Producer Price Index (PPI) for Construction Equipment increased by a multiple of about 2.2, much of that occurring immediately after the war as price controls were removed. From 1960 through 1995 the index rose another 4.9 times. Most of that was between 1967 and 1982, the most inflationary fifteen years of the twentieth century, when the index rose 3.4 times. Lowered inflation, intense foreign competition, and strenuous cost control efforts by U.S. manufacturers restrained prices between 1982 and 1995, and the index rose only 36.7 percent. Overall, through 1995 the index had risen by a mind-boggling multiple of 10.8.[4]

The real issue, however, concerned not the price of machinery but the unit cost of moving earth. Have the increases in power and capacity and the myriad improvements, innovations, and refinements over the fifty-year period enhanced productivity sufficiently to offset the escalation in machinery prices? That question is extremely difficult to answer precisely. Heavy earthmoving equipment yields optimum unit costs only in high-volume, mass-excavation conditions where its full capacity can be used. Such conditions prevail in most large open-pit mines but are rarely found on contemporary construction jobs. Therefore, the answer to the question may not be totally clear-cut.

One approach is to examine the trend in the U.S. Federal Highway Administration Index of the cost of common excavation in highway construction. The index can be taken only as a crude indicator because a great many variables influence the cost of moving dirt, not the least of which is the cost of labor in addition to the price of machinery. Thus, the index for the period from 1960 to 1995 has risen by a multiple of 7 compared to an escalation of 4.9 times in PPI machinery prices.[5] That significant gap implies that improved, more powerful machinery alone has not been able to restrain the cost of earthmoving in highway construction. A major portion of this gap can be attributed to the escalation in hourly labor costs since 1960, which contractors, constrained by physical conditions from upgrading to superlarge equipment, have been unable to offset.

Meanwhile, the open-pit mining industry, while experiencing escalation in hourly labor rates comparable to the construction industry, has been able to take full advantage of the growth in equipment size and efficiency and apply it to mass-excavation operations. Although cost per ton is closely held proprietary information in the mining industry, one can infer from the low grades of ore now being mined profitably, particularly in copper and gold, that the industry has been able to hold the line on or even reduce unit costs with the help of equipment manufacturers. It would be out of the question to attempt to mine such grades with 1960 equipment.

Earthmoving Equipment and the Environment

As the conservation movement grew during the first half of the twentieth century, it rarely, if ever, targeted the earthmoving equipment industry for criticism. In fact, one group—soil conservationists—regarded earthmoving equipment as an ally, a valuable tool that enabled farmers to construct ponds and terraces and also practice other conservation techniques. But that view, along with a great many other things, began to change during the 1960s with the rise of the environmental movement. For those in sympathy with the movement and their supporters in the media, it was not long before the word *bulldozer* had become synonymous with the unthinking destruction of ecosystems.

Equipment industry leaders were at first mystified and then shocked by the virulence of the attacks on their companies and the products they built. To them such objections seemed totally irrational. The bulldozer, as an inanimate object, could only do what it was guided to do. At the core of the environmentalists' concern was the fact that construction equipment had advanced enormously since World War II, making feasible assaults on nature that would have been unthinkable with earlier, more primitive equipment. One example concerns the hastily conceived Trans Amazonica Highway of the 1970s that opened the rain forest to subsequent development. Such projects, unhappily, redound to the discredit of the bulldozer.

Although it is not the role of this book to cite good or bad uses of the bulldozer, it is clear that given the power of current earthmoving equipment it is fully appropriate for projects involving major rearrangement of nature to receive long and careful study as to their long-term effects. An example of a project that had a happier outcome is the Trans Alaska Pipeline, which was carefully restudied to address environmental concerns before it proceeded. The outcome, at perhaps triple the original cost estimate, was a project that from an environmental standpoint is considered generally satisfactory.

There is no turning back the clock for earthmoving equipment. It is very large and powerful and likely to become even more so. That means project planners are now more than ever accountable for assuring the wise use of this equipment.

Conclusions

As the first practical piece of mobile farm machinery, Cyrus McCormick's horse-drawn reaper of 1831 launched the American farm machinery industry, and it was from that base that many companies later branched into earthmoving equipment. Handicapped by lack of a suitable power source, earthmoving machinery was slow to develop in the nineteenth century, but steam power made an important contribution in the ladder dredges used to excavate the Suez Canal and in the steam shovel, which by the late 1800s had evolved into an effective tool for moving earth and rock. The combination of the steam shovel and the steam locomotive made possible the mass excavation entailed in large civil works such as the Panama Canal and gave birth to open-pit mining at the turn of the century. The first steam-powered crawler tractor soon followed.

But it was the internal combustion engine, bringing sweeping changes to all of society, that gave real mobility to earthmoving equipment, beginning in the first decade of the twentieth century with the Holt track-type tractor powered by an internal combustion engine. At the same time the automobile was triggering an era of road-building that provided a strong new stimulus to the demand for construction equipment. Thus, over the first four decades of the twentieth century the fledgling industry had what it needed to fuel development: a practical mobile power source and a strong demand for its products. Holt's 1908 crawler tractor marked the point when earth moving equipment began to diverge from its parent farm equipment industry, a process that continued until well after World War II, when Case, Deere, Massey-Ferguson, Ford, Fiat, JCB, Hanomag, and others entered the construction equipment business. Milestones in industry development before World War II were:

1838	The steam shovel (William S. Otis)
1885	The towed leaning-wheel road grader (J. D. Adams)
1901	The steam-powered track-type tractor (Alvin O. Lombard)
1903	The dragline (John W. Page)
1908	The track-type, internal-combustion-engine-powered tractor (Benjamin Holt)
1912	The crawler-mounted power shovel
1913	The walking dragline (Monighan Machine Corporation)
1928	The cable-controlled bulldozer (R. G. LeTourneau)
1931	The track-type, diesel-powered tractor (the Caterpillar Diesel 60)
1931	The integral motor grader (the Caterpillar No. 10 Auto Patrol)
1932	The Carryall scraper (R. G. LeTourneau)
1934	The modern heavy-duty, off-highway truck (Euclid Road Machinery Company)
1935	The wheel tractor, bottom-dump wagon (Euclid Road Machinery Company)
1938	The integral-wheel tractor-scraper, the Tournapull (R. G. LeTourneau)

The end of World War II brought the dawn of the industry's modern era.

With Europe and Japan in shambles, a handful of American companies—Caterpillar, International Harvester, Allis-Chalmers, LeTourneau, Euclid, Cletrac, LaPlante-Choate, shovel makers Bucyrus-Erie, Marion, and P&H, plus a few smaller concerns—were for all practical purposes the entire worldwide industry, which was estimated in 1947 at $500 to $600 million. Pent-up demand in North America and the need to rebuild the shattered economies of Europe and Japan created enormous potential for growth.

By the end of the first postwar decade the world industry had more than doubled, and it appealed to major new players—General Motors, Westinghouse Airbrake, and Clark Equipment—in the United States. At the same time, economic recovery in Europe was attracting numerous new entries there. Meanwhile, Japan was already approaching self-sufficiency in earthmoving equipment, with Komatsu leading the way. Two important new tools, the wheel loader and the hydraulic excavator, had appeared.

The next twenty years were a time of almost uninterrupted growth for the industry, fueled by massive expressway construction in North America, Europe, and Japan; the worldwide need for better housing; huge water projects; and rapid expansion of open-pit coal and metals mining. The period also saw the creation of a new sub-industry, light construction equipment, when Case, Deere, Massey-Ferguson, JCB, Ford, and others entered that business. By 1975 some of these companies had already developed their product lines into the mid-range.

The 1976–85 period saw a peaking of demand in mid-decade followed by a deep recession and five years of revaluation of the dollar, which brought on a severe shakeout and realignment in the United States and left the industry substantially smaller in real terms in 1985 than it was at the peak.

For the survivors, the years between 1986 and 1995 were ones of downsizing, factory modernization, and corporate restructuring as U.S. and European companies struggled to respond to new marketplace realities. Gradually the industry recovered. The opening of the former Soviet Union and the People's Republic of China to sales and investment also brought a quantum increase in industry opportunity, and competitors scrambled to gain a foothold in those new markets.

By the end of the first postwar decade all the major earthmoving product types that still exist had been invented. Product development began to focus on a scaling up in size and increases in technological sophistication, a process that continues. Because each manufacturer believes that its offerings have made a unique contribution to the industry, any listing of key products is bound to be controversial. The following postwar products, however, either had an indisputably strong impact on subsequent designs or were a bold departure from accepted concepts:

1947	Hough rubber-tired wheel loader, hydraulically actuated and engine in the rear.
1947	Allis-Chalmers HD-19 track-type tractor, torque-converter drive in a large tractor.
1947	LeTourneau Model B Tournapull with Tournamatic powershift transmission.
1948	LeTourneau Tournadozer wheel bulldozer.
1949	Euclid 51FDT-15SH "twin-power," powershift wheel tractor-scraper.
1954	Caterpillar D9 track-type tractor with turbocharged engine and a 40 percent increase in tractor size.
1954	Demag B-504 fully hydraulically controlled excavator.
1955	Caterpillar 933, 955, and 977 fully integrated track-type loaders.
1955	International Harvester/Hough with Z-bar loader linkage.
1955	Euclid TS-18 overhung, "twin-power" wheel tractor-scraper.
1957	Case 320 loader-backhoe, complete factory-packaged loader-backhoe. (JCB introduced an attachment loader-backhoe for farm tractors in 1954.)
1958	LeTourneau-Westinghouse Haulpak off-highway truck with a new mainframe concept, suspension system, and body style.
1958	R. G. LeTourneau electric wheel-equipped earthmoving products.
1959	Caterpillar 944 wheel loader, with front-mounted lift arms.
1962	Euclid Division L-20 and L-30, conventional wheel loaders with articulated steering.
1963	Caterpillar 769 truck, oil-disc brakes on earthmoving equipment.
1964	Unit Rig M-85 electric-drive off-highway truck.
1966	Volvo BM DR 631 articulated dumper with power to rear wheels.

1967	Deere JD-570 articulated motor grader.
1971	Poclain EC1000 large hydraulic front shovel for mining.
1972	WABCO 3200 off-highway truck of more than two hundred tons.
1975	Deere JD-750 and 755 hydrostatic bulldozer and track loader.
1978	Caterpillar D10 track-type tractor with elevated-sprocket, flexible undercarriage.
1986	Demag H485 hydraulic front shovel of more than five hundred tons.
1995	Komatsu 930E off-highway truck of more than three hundred tons.

Of the principal earthmoving equipment companies that existed at the end of World War II, only Caterpillar remains as an independent company. The others have dwindled, lost their identity through mergers and acquisitions, or disappeared, yet the opportunity created by enormous economic growth has attracted numerous dynamic new entrants into the industry. In the mid-1990s the number of participants in the earthmoving equipment business was at an all-time high, and vigorous competitors were based in North America, Europe, and Japan. Dominated in 1946 by a few American companies, the industry has become worldwide.

Will the industry and its participants continue to grow in the years ahead or will there be a diminishing need for earthmoving equipment? United Nations mid-point projections show world population reaching about 8.5 billion by 2025, a nearly 50 percent increase from 1995. Meeting the needs of this increased population for food, water, housing, raw materials of all kinds, transportation, and communications would seem to assure the future of the industry. Most population growth, however, will occur in the newly emerging and less developed countries that surely will want their own national sources for earthmoving equipment. Western and Japanese manufacturers who fail to respond will do so at their peril. Meanwhile, in the industrialized world, with mature infrastructures and slow-growing populations, demand for the heavier types of construction equipment will continue its downward trend. Offsetting that will be the needs of the worldwide mining industry for ever-larger machines. Opportunities will continue to exist for earthmoving equipment companies that are responsive to such needs.

The Industry and Organized Labor

During the nineteenth-century beginnings of the agricultural implement industry, each implement was virtually handmade using hand-forged metal parts and fitting them with wooden pieces crafted by a skilled carpenter. As implements grew in complexity, castings were required, drawing in foundrymen (molders) and patternmakers, and machinists were needed to shape and drill the castings. Into the late 1800s little effort was expended to achieve close tolerances or interchangeable parts, so even assembly was a skilled job of filing and fitting pieces. But manufacturers throughout the latter half of the nineteenth century were striving to design implements and organize factories in ways that would minimize the need for scarce skilled labor. As machine tools improved and more special-purpose tools, jigs, and fixtures came into use, manufacturers were able to substitute semiskilled and unskilled workers for skilled labor. They were also able to lower costs without sacrificing and usually improving quality. Thus, the American farm implement industry was transformed in the late 1800s from one employing primarily skilled craftsmen to one employing largely unskilled or semiskilled workers with a small, elite minority of craftsmen.[1]

It was these craftsmen—the molders, patternmakers, machinists, carpenters, and other trades—that formed "locals" to represent collectively their respective craftsman members in bargaining with the owners. Owners quickly learned that a strike by a handful of well-organized and unified key skilled workers could shut down the work of many times their number of unskilled and semiskilled workers. And so, however reluctantly, companies were forced to begin bargaining with the locals, usually affiliated with the American Federation of Labor that had been organized in 1886. But the unions were rarely able to extract formal recognition from owners, nearly all of whom maintained strong anti-union stances.[2]

After the formation of International Harvester in 1902, the company experienced serious labor disruptions in 1903, 1916, and 1919 and each time was able to defeat the unions. Most skilled tradesmen at Harvester either belonged to or sympathized with unions, but no industrial union representing all workers came close to gaining a foothold. Strikes were almost always over wages and hours and attempts to gain union shops. Benefits had not yet entered the bargaining arena, but ironically companies used what are now recognized as fringe benefits to fight unionism. Over the years, Harvester and other companies in the industry provided profit-sharing, stock, sickness and accident plans, pensions, and various employee welfare programs in the vain hope that such things would keep unions out, but they were not successful.[3] Paternalism was the order of the day, especially at companies like Deere, Case, and Holt that were located in smaller communities. Deere and Case placed great importance on the principle of dealing with workers as individuals and went to the extent of having each sign a printed contract.[4]

Economic gains produced by strike-induced bargaining attracted new members to the AFL unions, so that by 1914 membership had reached two million. During World War I, pressure for increased production and avoidance of work stoppages gave unions good organizing opportunities, and AFL membership by 1920 had doubled to more than four million. In that year, union membership embraced 18.9 percent of nonagricultural employment, but, significantly, 78 percent of all union membership was in craft organizations. The mass of unskilled and semiskilled workers in the rapidly developing steel, automotive, chemical, electrical, agricultural, and heavy machinery industries remained unorganized. Only a few industrial unions such as the United Mine Workers, the Western Federation of Miners, and the Brewery Workers existed in which membership was not based on a particular skill but was open to all workers within the industry, regardless of skill.[5]

Sensing that its anti-union tactics were futile, in 1918 Harvester co-opted the concept of the industrial union by establishing "works councils" that gave the appearance of worker representation but for all practical purposes were controlled by management. These were strongly opposed by the AFL in the strike of 1919, but nevertheless remained when the strike was over. Despite union opposition, the works councils at Harvester were effective in averting labor problems until the NLRB ruled that they were company-dominated, forcing Harvester to disband them in 1937. They were then replaced by independent unions that lasted four more years until another NLRB ruling forced representational elections in 1941.[6]

Although unions lost some membership during the 1920s, the situation at the beginning of the depression was essentially unchanged: Skilled craft unions making up the AFL continued to dominate the American labor movement and the machinery industry remained unorganized.

The Rise of Industrial Unionism, 1934–41

One of the first acts of the New Deal was the passage of the National Industrial Recovery Act of 1933, which, among other things, strongly encouraged collective bargaining by unions. That put great pressure on the AFL to begin chartering industrial unions, but the structure of the AFL, with its near-exclusive emphasis on craft unions, did not lend itself to industrial unionism. For two years little was done. Then, in 1935 an industrial unionist faction could be restrained no longer, and the breakaway Committee for Industrial Organization (CIO) was formed under the leadership of John L. Lewis, president of the United Mine Workers. The CIO immediately began issuing charters for the formation of new industrial unions in the automotive, steel, chemical, electrical, machinery, and other industries, arousing deep hostility among the AFL unions. After several unsuccessful attempts at reconciliation, in 1937 the CIO unions, most of them recently formed, were expelled from the AFL. In 1938 the CIO converted itself to a federation as the Congress of Industrial Organizations, and the nation had two rival labor federations, one craft, one industrial.

It was against this background that an AFL charter was issued to William Collins in 1934 to organize a General Motors local. The year 1935 saw the birth of the United Auto Workers–CIO when Collins switched allegiance to the CIO. The young union won a major victory in 1937, when, after using a new sit-down strike tactic at GM's Flint, Michigan, plant, it gained recognition as bargaining agent for union workers at General Motors. Chrysler soon followed, and although Ford held out for four years by 1941 the UAW-CIO was almost unchallenged in the automotive industry. With a leadership liberally sprinkled with socialists and communists, the UAW under R. J. Thomas was noted for its militancy and strong left-wing political agenda in the early 1940s.[7]

Also in 1937, the Steel Workers Organizing Committee succeeded in organizing U.S. Steel, and industrial unionism became firmly implanted on the American labor scene. By the end of 1937 the CIO claimed almost two million members.[8]

Organizing efforts began in the farm equipment industry in 1934 at J. I. Case in Racine, and by 1935 campaigns were underway at all major manufacturers. Leon Clausen, president of Case, was rabidly opposed to unions and fought bitterly to keep them out, taking strikes in 1934 and 1935 and a six-month strike in 1936–37, but in 1937 the UAW-CIO won recognition at Racine and Rockford. Ultimately, the UAW swept up all the Case plants, organizing Rock Island in 1941 and Burlington in 1942. But although the UAW won recognition as the bargaining agent for its members it did not win a union shop; thus the company remained free to deal individually with workers who did not choose to join.[9]

Allis-Chalmers, although not strictly a farm and earthmoving equipment manufacturer, was also an early target. In 1935 Harold Christoffel obtained an AFL charter to organize all Milwaukee A-C employees not eligible for a craft union, but the AFL proved ineffectual in organizing unskilled workers and no progress was made. Attracted by the success of the industrial unions, Christoffel pushed a change of affiliation to the UAW-CIO, and that union quickly won recognition. Milwaukee Local 248, UAW-CIO was certified in 1938, beginning a decade of turbulent labor relations for A-C as the communist-dominated local carried out its political agenda. Allis-Chalmers's three electrical plants were organized by the United Electrical Workers–CIO, another union that would later prove to be communist-dominated, and its farm and earthmoving equipment plants at LaPorte, Indiana, and Springfield, Illinois, were organized by the leftist Farm Equipment Workers–CIO. That gave Allis-Chalmers a full line-up of left-leaning or communist-dominated unions to deal with. It would pay a heavy price before it was free of the burden.[10]

Trouble began quickly when in 1939 Local 248 struck for thirty days over the issue of a union shop. That strike failed but was followed in 1941 by a seventy-six-day strike in which it was subsequently established that leadership of the local had conducted a fraudulent strike vote. Because A-C had important defense contracts, the federal government stepped in to settle the strike.[11]

This was but one example of the numerous strikes and obstructionist tactics conducted by communist-dominated and left-leaning unions against defense contractors during the period of World War II—before the German attack on the Soviet Union in June 1941. Such tactics ceased immediately after the Soviet Union entered the war, these same union locals becoming model citizens and strong critics of any activity that might hamper war production.

The UAW registered another success when it won a representational election at International Harvester's Ft. Wayne, Indiana, truck plant in 1940, the first major penetration by the UAW at IH, but the UAW made almost no headway in organizing Harvester's implement plants.[12]

Forming the Farm Equipment Workers Union

While the UAW was preoccupied in the mid-1930s with organizing the automotive industry, a rival union was forming to challenge it in the agricultural and earthmoving equipment industries. A spin-off of the Steel Workers Organizing Committee (CIO), this group, calling itself the Farm Equipment Workers Organizing Committee, would later evolve into the United Farm Equipment and Machine Workers of America (CIO), another radical leftist union that would be a powerful force in the farm and heavy equipment industries for a decade and a half.[13]

International Harvester's Tractor Works in Chicago, one of the largest plants in the farm equipment industry, was the first target of the Farm Equipment Workers (UFE), and after a year of effort and over the strenuous resistance of management the UFE succeeded in winning an election there in 1938. But progress was slow at the other six IH farm equipment plants until early 1941, when the NLRB ruled that Harvester's independent unions, which had replaced the works councils in 1937, were company-dominated and constituted an unfair labor practice. The six plants were now wide open to UFE organizing efforts, but the CIO-affiliated UFE had to contend with the AFL, which already represented the skilled trades and planned to organize all the workers.

Management, knowing it was going to lose to one or the other of the unions, favored the less militant AFL over the radical UFE. Perhaps that was why the UFE won subsequent representational elections in four of the six plants: McCormick Works and West Pullman in the Chicago area and East Moline and Rock Falls, Illinois. That left only Milwaukee and the Moline Farmall plant to the AFL. The events of 1941 made the UFE the dominant union at IH, and by the end of the war it represented almost thirty thousand of the sixty-nine thousand total work force.[14]

The War Years

By the end of 1941 unions had enjoyed mixed success in organizing the farm equipment industry, but the country's entry into the war quickly changed all that. To assure labor peace in the war industries, in early 1942 the federal government extracted an agreement from management and labor under which strikes and lockouts would be prohibited and wages would be controlled within a narrow band. To administer wartime industrial labor relations, the War Labor Board (WLB) was set up and given sweeping powers. To compensate unions for forgoing use of their principal weapon, the strike, the WLB established a climate that strongly discouraged companies from resisting union organizing efforts. Once organized, the unions, with the tacit or sometimes overt support of the WLB, were able to wrest contracts from management that included concessions on such issues as maintenance of membership, dues checkoff, and union shops that would have otherwise been gained only through long and arduous bargaining. Conflicts over wages were settled by WLB edict. By the end of 1943 the farm and earthmoving equipment industries were, for all practical purposes, fully organized.

Conflict in the Quad Cities

It was in the Quad Cities (Moline, Rock Island, Davenport, and Bettendorf) that the UFE and the UAW acted out their bitter rivalry in the 1940s in the farm equipment industry. Moline was the headquarters and center of Deere manufacturing operations, with five plants and a sales branch located there. IH had two plants, and Case and Minneapolis-Moline one each.

Deere's labor relations had been relatively peaceful during the 1930s despite unsuccessful union organizing efforts. The company continued its practice of individual contracts with each worker until 1939, when the NLRB ruled that a contract clause effectively barring union membership was illegal. Still, unions did not penetrate a major Deere plant until 1942, when the UAW won a certification election over the UFE at Ottumwa, Iowa. Under the favorable organizing climate established by the WLB the remaining Deere plants were unionized in quick succession. The Moline-area Harvester

Works, Spreader Works, and foundry went UAW, and the Planter Works went UFE. In 1943 the UAW won at the Waterloo tractor plant, but the UFE took the Moline Plow Works and the Deere's Branch Office.[15] And so the stage was set for the bitter postwar struggle between the UFE and the UAW in the Quad Cities.

The UFE and Caterpillar

Caterpillar, with one large plant in East Peoria and a small one in San Leandro, California, had successfully resisted unions until it, like Deere, was caught up in wartime labor conditions, and East Peoria was organized by the UFE in 1942.[16] The AFL Machinists (IAM) took San Leandro.

Postwar, 1945–55

During the war the influence of the War Labor Board had kept industry work stoppages to a minimum, but unions, chafing under the wartime restrictions on wage increases, believed they had fallen behind the cost of living and were determined to catch up as soon as the war ended. For example, Grant Oakes, president of the UFE, announced in September 1945 that the union would demand a 30 percent increase everywhere it had bargaining rights, which took in IH, Deere, A-C, Oliver, and Caterpillar.[17] Other labor leaders had similar goals, and beginning in the fourth quarter of 1945 the nation began to experience an unprecedented wave of strikes.

Reuther and the UAW

General Motors was the UAW's first postwar automotive target, but when a 113-day strike was settled in early 1946 the union obtained only an 18.5 cent per hour increase and the dues checkoff, items other unions had gotten without long strikes. Rank-and-file discontent with the settlement, among other things, resulted in the ouster of R. J. Thomas and the election of Walter Reuther as president at the union's 1946 convention. But Reuther was forced to work with a hostile executive board controlled by a leftist Thomas faction. In a ploy to regain control, in early 1947 that faction proposed a merger with the smaller UFE in the belief that doing so would provide the necessary votes to take over at the next convention. The UAW's membership voted down the merger in a referendum, however. These maneuvers culminated in 1947 in the landslide reelection of Reuther and gave him unchallenged control of the union. He was to become the dominant figure in industrial unionism in the United States until his tragic death in an airplane crash in 1970.[18]

Postwar Strife in the Equipment Industry

In December 1945 the UAW walked out at Case's four major plants in a strike that lasted 440 days at Racine, the longest in the company's history. Although the other plants settled in the fall, a bitter strike continued at Racine, marked by considerable picket line violence. After missing a full selling season of the strongest demand for farm equipment ever experienced in the United States, Case president Leon Clausen finally agreed to bargain, and with the aid of a federal mediator the strike ended in March 1947. Although receiving some concessions from Case, the union gave up its key demands for a union shop and dues checkoff. Overall, it was a defeat for the UAW, which was unable to obtain another strike vote at Case until 1960. That year the union found itself still negotiating with Case for a union shop, dues checkoff, a cost of living adjustment (COLA), an annual improvement factor, and other items that the UAW had won as long as ten years earlier from other companies.[19]

In the spring of 1946 Allis-Chalmers was hit by strikes at all plants simultaneously by the UAW, UFE, and United Electrical Workers (UEW). All but West Allis, controlled by the radical Local 248-UAW led by Harold Christoffel, were settled by fall. The West Allis strike continued for eleven months and had even more picket line violence than Racine. With every major farm equipment manufacturer either slowed or completely shut down by walkouts in the spring of 1946, farmers, expecting a free supply situation with the war's end, began clamoring for an end to the strikes. Harry S. Truman announced plans in June for the federal seizure of Case and A-C. Congress was unreceptive, however, and the idea was dropped.[20] During congressional hearings that year, revelations of the communist affiliations of Local 248 leadership triggered a back-to-work movement by the majority of workers. Sensing defeat, Christoffel called off the strike, but in the meantime the local had been decertified by the NLRB.[21]

In June 1947 the Taft-Hartley Act became law and provided for, among other things, the filing of non-communist affidavits by union leaders, subject to perjury charges. That action forced the resignation of the leadership of Local 248, and the local was placed under the administration of the UAW

International, which quickly won recertification from the NLRB. Thus ended a period of labor turbulence for Allis-Chalmers unmatched in any of its competitors, but at a heavy price for the company. Its 1946 sales were only one-third of 1945's at a time when its competitors' sales were booming.[22]

Harvester and a Militant Local

A part of International Harvester's postwar expansion plans was the decision to be aggressive in entering the construction equipment business, but it needed additional manufacturing space to accomplish that. A suitable government surplus plant became available in late 1945 in Melrose Park, a Chicago suburb. The plant, built in 1941, had been operated by Buick to produce aircraft engines. What Harvester could not foresee in purchasing the plant was that it was also "buying" a union local that would bedevil the company for the next thirty-five years. Local 6, UAW-CIO, had established itself in the plant early in the war in a climate of mistrust and hostility stemming from the GM-UAW battles of the late 1930s. Within wartime WLB restrictions the local was one of the most militant in the UAW. Unable to use the strike against Buick, it resorted to flooding the grievance system as a means of demonstrating its militancy. It would use the same tactics against Harvester, and the UFE Harvester locals, not to be outdone, adopted similar tactics.

After a short break when the Buick operation was wound down, Local 6 quickly regained recognition in 1946 after the Harvester takeover. With the exception of 1949, every contract negotiation through 1958 was accompanied by strikes—in 1946, 1947, 1948, 1950, 1955, and 1958. In addition, a seventy-seven-day strike occurred in 1952, a non-contract year, over job classifications and piece rates.[23]

The UFE took thirty thousand Harvester workers out on strike in mid-January 1946 while UAW-led strikes were going on simultaneously at Case and A-C. The Harvester strike was settled April 18 without government intervention, but the UFE failed to win its key demand for continuation of the wartime WLB-imposed maintenance of membership clause.[24]

UAW-UFE Rivalry at Deere

No sooner had the war ended in the Quad Cities than strikes began at Deere. Initially, walkouts began in August at the UAW-controlled Harvester

Works and Spreader Works but soon spread to the UFE-controlled Plow Works. Then Union Malleable (the Deere foundry) and the Ottumwa plant were taken out by the UAW. The issues were primarily economic, but the UAW also wanted companywide bargaining. Deere, following its tradition of decentralization, insisted on separate talks for each plant. The UAW locals signed two-year contracts in early November for a 10 percent wage increase, essentially what the company originally offered, but the UFE stayed out another month before taking roughly the same package. It was not the only occasion in the Quad Cities when one union tried to outdo the other in demonstrating militancy. Deere was no sooner back to work than the UAW took out Case's Rock Island plant in a three-month strike, and in January 1946 the FE struck International Harvester's East Moline plant.

In 1947 Deere avoided a strike by accepting an agreement similar to the one previously negotiated by the UAW with the automotive industry (the "pattern agreement"), and the UFE followed suit. But the UAW-UFE rivalry was heating up. In a successful raid at the Dubuque plant, the UAW won out over the UFE in a 1947 representational vote. That intensified the UFE's drive to outperform the UAW in obtaining concessions from management. But in late 1948 the UAW beat out the UFE again when the UAW won the election at J. I. Case's new Bettendorf plant, which had almost two thousand workers.

The year 1949 was a pivotal one for the UFE. The UAW aggressively attempted to raid its locals, and the UFE battled back. Meanwhile, the companies were in the middle, trying to negotiate new contracts. The UAW seemed to be making headway against the UFE at Deere's Plow Works and succeeded in getting an NLRB representational election, but to the intense chagrin of the UAW the UFE overwhelmingly retained bargaining rights. It was to be the only good news for the UFE that year. At the CIO convention in 1949 ten unions charged with being communist-dominated were expelled, including the UFE and the large UEW. The UFE, a small splinter union compared to the UAW, recognized its isolation and voted to merge with the UEW, which shared its political orientation.

Deere was the UAW's target company in the 1949 negotiations as the unions attempted to establish a pattern agreement for bargaining with other equipment manufacturers. A contract covering seven plants was signed without a strike and contained no major concessions to the union, although it did have a clause permitting the reopening of negotiations after a year. The UFE signed a similar agreement at the Plow Works.[25]

Pattern Agreements at Harvester and Deere

The 1950 Harvester-UAW contract was the first to be negotiated centrally, and the union, without a strike, won a pension plan. Later that year, however, after the watershed agreement with GM, the UAW immediately reopened negotiations with Harvester, and a seventy-seven-day strike ensued. The union wanted and received a pattern agreement modeled on the GM contract, which included a modified union shop, company-paid pensions, an annual improvement factor, and the cost of living adjustment. Harvester, like GM, won a five-year agreement.[26] The two key concessions GM granted in 1950 were company-paid pensions and a modified union shop. The annual improvement factor, intended to recognize putative increases in productivity, and a COLA had been conceded by GM in 1948, but after 1950 they were to become embedded in almost all UAW contracts. The UAW's determination in 1950 to obtain a contract at Harvester patterned after the GM agreement indicated the fundamental strategy the union would follow: to draw the automotive and machinery industries into pattern agreements and, once that was accomplished, never to allow them to escape.

After the GM agreement of 1950 the UAW also reopened the Deere contract. In addition to the annual improvement factor, a COLA, and joint control of the pension plan, it wanted companywide bargaining and a master contract. Deere wanted a five-year contract with a no-strike pledge. A strike at all UAW locations began on September 1 and lasted 110 days. The union obtained a GM pattern contract but not joint control of pensions and gave a limited no-strike pledge. Deere won a five-year agreement.[27] By 1955, when the contract was due for renegotiation, the UFE was no longer a factor at Deere, which removed the competitive element that had complicated earlier negotiations.

Yet after months of negotiations a four-and-a-half-month strike occurred in 1956, with Deere resisting but finally accepting the 1955 industry pattern agreement.[28] It would be the last major work stoppage at Deere until strikes of nearly six weeks in both 1967 and 1976. After the 1956 strike Deere was generally the most conciliatory and accommodating company in the industry for the next thirty years. For that reason it was frequently the UAW's target company in the farm and construction equipment industries.

The UAW Takeover at Caterpillar

Caterpillar's postwar labor relations were both simplified and complicated by its position as essentially a one-plant manufacturer. That resulted in one large bargaining unit: Peoria Local 105 of the UFE. After a twenty-eight-day strike in 1946, a two-year contract was signed, the major provision of which was reduction in the work week from forty-eight to forty hours.[29] But the passage of the Taft-Hartley Act in 1947 complicated the UFE's position in 1948 because of local leadership's refusal to sign non-communist affidavits. That brought about an NLRB election and the end of the UFE at Caterpillar. In a hotly contested election, the UAW-CIO defeated the UAW-AFL; what resulted was the certification of the UAW-CIO as bargaining agent at Caterpillar's East Peoria plant in June 1948.[30] The certification marked the beginning of the most adversarial long-term relationship between the UAW and any of the major corporations with which it bargained.

After an initial two-year contract was signed in 1949, in 1951 the UAW attempted but failed to bring Caterpillar in line with the contracts it had gotten with the car makers, Deere, and International in 1950. Initially, the union demanded a 28 cent general increase; the company offered 8 cents. After a two-month strike of twenty-two thousand workers, the union settled for 13.5 cents and a cost of living adjustment in 1952.[31] A two-year agreement was signed in 1952 and extended to correspond to the end of five-year UAW agreements with the Big Three, Deere, and IH. With the 1955 contract Caterpillar for the first time fell in line with the pattern agreement on wages and benefits established in Detroit.[32] With the 1955 agreement the UAW and the automotive and equipment industries began a tradition of three-year contracts that would last into the 1980s.

But all was not rosy for the UAW at Caterpillar. During the company's postwar expansion program the first major plant outside the Peoria area, in Joliet, Illinois, was opened in 1951, and the UAW lost the representational election to the Machinists Union, IAM-AFL, which also had bargaining rights at the smaller San Leandro, California, plant as well as the Trackson Company in Milwaukee, which Caterpillar acquired the same year. With few exceptions, over the years Caterpillar IAM locals would be content to follow the lead of the UAW and ride on whatever agreement it struck.

The UAW had better luck at Caterpillar's Decatur, Illinois, plant, which opened in 1954. Although the rival UAW-AFL was strong in the Decatur area, the UAW-CIO was able to win bargaining rights, as it did at other major new Caterpillar plants opened in the late 1950s at York, Pennsylvania, and Aurora, Illinois.[33] When the AFL and CIO merged in 1955, the UAW-AFL became a part of the Allied Industrial Workers of America.[34]

The Demise of the UFE

Although the UAW dominated the UFE at Deere, the opposite was true at International Harvester. The UAW controlled Melrose Park and the truck plants, but the UFE was dominant almost everywhere else. As late as 1952 the UFE claimed twenty-eight thousand members at Harvester compared to twenty-four thousand for the UAW. The intense rivalry between the unions severely complicated bargaining at IH but also had advantages. When one union struck the other kept working, and Harvester was seldom completely shut down. On balance, however, management regarded the radical-leftist UFE as the greater evil and looked for an opportunity to break the union at IH.[35]

In 1950, after the UFE had already signed a two-year agreement with Harvester, the UAW won a groundbreaking pattern contract at IH. The UFE had been upstaged and was determined to outdo the UAW in 1952. After negotiations broke down, the UFE went out on August 22 but could not have picked a worse time to strike. The country was in the throes of anti-communist hysteria, and the evasive performance of the leadership of the UFE and its UEW parent before congressional committees that year had raised doubts among rank-and-file members. Sensing the union's weakness, Harvester management took a tough position at the bargaining table. After an eighty-seven-day strike, the UFE, realizing it would not win in a show-down representational election against the UAW at IH, accepted defeat and signed a less favorable contract than the one IH had with the UAW. Effectively, that broke the UFE as a national union.[36]

Pat Greathouse, director of the UAW's midwestern Region 4, had led the union's battle with the UFE in the farm and construction equipment industries during the late 1940s and early 1950s. After the UFE was broken by its 1952 defeat at Harvester, Greathouse, who had become head of the UAW's "ag-imp" department, began a campaign to persuade UFE leaders at the local level to bring their locals into the UAW. By the time the UAW's contracts were due for renegotiation in 1955 he had succeeded in inducing many to affiliate with the UAW; the UFE disappeared from the American labor scene.[37]

Supplemental Unemployment Benefits

The UAW achieved another revolutionary breakthrough in the 1955 negotiations with the automotive and machinery industries when Ford, the automotive target company, granted supplemental unemployment benefits (SUB). It was the opening wedge leading to Reuther's goal of the guaranteed annual wage. SUB were originally conceived to supplement state unemployment compensation when car makers shut down for their annual model change. When first negotiated, SUB provided that companies, for each hour worked under the contract, would contribute 5 cents to a fund that would pay workers 65 percent of their normal pay for the first four weeks and 60 percent for the succeeding twenty-two weeks. (By 1967 that had been negotiated upward to 95 percent and fifty-two weeks.) Although the other manufacturers professed to be shocked by Ford's concession, the benefits were nevertheless incorporated into the pattern agreement that the automotive and machinery industries accepted in 1955.[38]

In 1954, with the encouragement of Harvester management, the UAW established the Harvester Department, chaired by Leonard Woodcock, UAW vice president. Henceforth, negotiations between the company and the union would be centralized on major policy issues. The change facilitated negotiations in 1955. After a short strike, the company acquiesced to the Detroit pattern and signed a three-year master contract that granted, among other things, the union shop and SUB.[39]

Summary, 1945–55

The postwar period to 1955 saw the UAW-CIO gradually overpower and absorb the UFE, its only serious rival in the farm and construction equipment industries. By the mid-1950s Caterpillar, Deere, Case, Massey-Ferguson, Oliver, International Harvester, and Euclid were, with few exceptions, bargaining exclusively with the UAW, as were Allis-Chalmers's farm and construction equipment divisions. The AFL Boilermakers represented workers at LeTourneau-Westinghouse in Peoria.

The ten-year period was bisected by the watershed 1950 GM agreement. The first five postwar years were marked by internecine struggles within the UAW, the battle between the UAW and UFE, bitter opposition from management, and the UAW's gropings for a strategy. The 1950 negotiations with the automotive and equipment industries made the strategy crystal clear: industrywide pattern bargaining. Thus, in industries that had few sellers, all doing business in the same marketplace, labor costs would move in lock step, and no company would be permitted to gain competitive advantage at the bargaining table.

Worldwide economic conditions in 1950, with Europe and Japan still prostrate, lent a superficial logic to the concept but only so long as U.S. producers were relatively free from competition not subject to the same pattern agreements. By 1955 the rapidly recovering foreign auto producers were preparing to challenge Detroit in the U.S. market. European and Japanese machinery manufacturers—although not yet capable of challenging the likes of Caterpillar, International Harvester, and Deere in North America—were growing ever more competitive in their home markets and those of developing countries. Unable to escape the grip of the UAW pattern agreements, the U.S. machinery industry began to sense a decline in competitiveness in export markets.

By the end of 1955 the UAW pattern agreement generally prevailing in the machinery industry included a union shop, dues checkoff, an annual improvement factor, a COLA, five or six paid holidays, supplemental unemployment benefits, improved non-contributory pensions, and substantial movement toward eventual comprehensive medical benefits. During the next twenty-five years the UAW, in the words of Samuel Gompers, would want "more and then still more."[40]

The Comfortable Years, 1956–79

By the mid-1950s management of machinery companies had grudgingly conceded the unions' right to exist in plants and bargain collectively for wages and benefits but was still outraged at union economic demands that, according to the companies, outstripped increases in productivity. That attitude was reflected in Caterpillar's annual reports of the period, which almost always included a polemic on union demands and used phrases such as "unrestrained monopoly power" and "extortionate demands" (of unions) and expressed alarm at the resulting escalation in prices and the "dangerous inflationary effects."[41] But it was ingenuous to think the UAW would be deterred in its economic demands by such considerations. It was intent on making its blue-collar workers full-fledged members of the middle class, and in that goal it succeeded remarkably well. Throughout these years the economy did support the steadily increasing wages and benefits extracted by the UAW without runaway inflation. Yet a price would have to be paid in the future for the growing rigidities in work rules, the featherbedding limits on productivity, the proliferating job classifications, and the adversarial climate fostered by union militants and usually reciprocated by shop management.

A Shifting UAW Emphasis

Having established a pattern of negotiating generous wage and benefit increases at contract time as well as regular cost-of-living increases, the UAW in the late 1950s began to place greater emphasis on gaining increased paid time off and on noneconomic issues: overtime scheduling, subcontracting, grievance procedures, job classifications, seniority rights, layoff, downgrade and bumping procedures, transfer rights, and increases in company-paid union representatives. Management felt that such issues went to the heart of its right to manage and met union efforts to put them on the bargaining table with strong resistance. But the UAW persisted, and little by little the issues became the subjects of negotiations and the union gained concessions. Between 1955 and 1980, the sticking point in negotiations more often than not could be traced to noneconomic demands.

Twenty Years of Pattern

After thirteen years of frustration, in 1960 the UAW finally was able to win a strike vote at Case and a strike ensued. But Case, under pressure from its bankers, was cleaning up its balance sheet and thus happy for an opportunity to reduce inventories. After six months both sides agreed to mediation, but the final agreement still did not include the union shop and dues checkoff. It was not until 1962, after the retirement of Case's old guard top management, that the union obtained dues checkoff and two years later a union shop. By the end of 1966, working with more flexible management, the UAW was finally able to win an agreement approximating what it had obtained as much as sixteen years earlier with GM and others, including a COLA and a master contract that covered all seven of Case's facilities. But it was not until 1974 that the union succeeded in getting a true pattern agreement at Case.[42]

Meanwhile, Caterpillar and the union continued their troubled relationship. In 1958, after strikes of seven, eight, and nine weeks at Peoria, York, and Decatur, Caterpillar and the UAW settled for the pattern economic package established by the union with the Big Three but refused to yield a key union demand for a master contract. Caterpillar had been the target of the UAW ag-imp department, and the company charged the UAW International with attempting to obtain more from Caterpillar than it had won in Detroit to establish a more advantageous pattern for bargaining with Harvester, Deere, and Allis-Chalmers, which were not on strike. These companies subsequently settled for the Caterpillar package without serious labor stoppages. In 1961 strikes of six to twenty-four working days at various locations resulted in the signing of another pattern agreement. The next contract year, 1964, saw a three-week strike in February over production standards, but the new agreement, for the first time negotiated centrally, was signed in the fall, with negligible work stoppages. But in late 1965 Decatur went out for two months over work standards and job classification disputes. The company also experienced a seventeen-day strike at all UAW facilities in 1967 before a contract was signed.[43]

After twelve years of trying, the UAW obtained a master contract at Caterpillar in 1970 without a strike. The company studiously refrained from calling it a master contract, referring to it as a "central agreement," but it covered 30,500 workers. Likewise, contracts were signed in 1973 and 1976 without major strikes, the latter year covering thirty-four thousand workers. The 1973 contract included a "thirty-and-out" retirement provision, dental care, and some limitations on compulsory overtime.[44]

In keeping with tradition, in 1958 Harvester was unable to obtain an agreement without a strike, this one of two months beginning on November 13. With the demise of the UFE, many rank-and-file former UFE members at Harvester remained bitter. Grievances continued to be the sticking point, but this time top bargainers from Harvester and the UAW resolved to cooperate in putting an end to the long grievance war. The plan was to settle grievances quickly on the spot before they entered the system. The plan worked and ended fifteen years of guerrilla warfare in Harvester plants. Thus began a period of conciliation and accommodation in Harvester-UAW relations. Termed the "New Look," it was to last until 1979.[45] While Harvester enjoyed twenty years of relative labor peace compared to its history of confrontation with its unions, it did so at the price of concessions in the area of work rules that would prove extremely costly in the long run.

After the long strike of 1955, Deere's labor relations had been relatively peaceful until 1967 contract negotiations resulted in a six-week strike in the fall at all UAW locations. Although Deere was able to obtain agreements without strikes in 1971 (for the 1970 contract year) and 1973, in 1976 it was selected as the UAW's target for the machinery industry and a thirty-nine-day strike resulted. The outcome, an agreement the UAW said was the best ever in the industry, served as a pattern that other companies subsequently accepted.[46]

The Chrysler Bailout

The year 1976 was to be the last year of relatively easy gains by the UAW. The first signs of trouble were at Chrysler, which, as the weakest of the Big Three, was the first to be seriously affected financially by the inroads of Japanese imports. By 1979 Chrysler was calling on all constituents—bankers, suppliers, dealers, management, and union employees—to contribute to keeping the company going. Only by negotiating an unprecedented $1.5 billion loan guarantee by the federal government did the company stave off bankruptcy. The UAW stripped out nearly $1 billion from its recently negotiated three-year contract as a contribution to the bailout plan. After forty years of taking, it was the UAW's first experience with give-backs involving what had been considered sacrosanct gains. In an ironic reversal of pattern bargaining, concessions made to Chrysler were soon demanded by GM and Ford. The demand for "equality of sacrifice," heard from union leadership for the first time, was to be repeated with increasing frequency during the 1980s.[47]

In the machinery industry, 1979 was to be the last year in which contract negotiations followed the historic pattern. A recession beginning in late 1980 and the onslaught of Japanese competition aided by a grossly undervalued yen meant that things would never be the same again in the U.S. earthmoving equipment industry.

In Peoria, UAW Local 974 struck on October 1, 1979, the day of contract expiration, and stayed out until December 19, the longest strike to date at Caterpillar. Much of the background leading to the strike had to do with an internal struggle within the local between militant and moderate factions. Although the strike was not sanctioned by the International and no strike benefits were paid, all seven other Caterpillar UAW locals joined it some three weeks later. Issues involved the number of company-paid, full-time union representatives; control of overtime; subcontracting; and work assignments. But the company claimed to have given away nothing of importance. The economic side followed pattern, and the final three-year agreement covered forty thousand workers.[48] Simultaneously, Deere in the Quad Cities was hit by a strike, but a pattern settlement was reached in three weeks.[49]

The Final Harvester Strike

The 1979 labor event of the greatest importance, however, was at Harvester, where the UAW was on strike from November 1, 1979, to April 20, 1980—172 days. A new CEO, Archie McCardell, was determined to lower Harvester's labor costs, which management believed to be out of line with those of competitors, a self-inflicted problem due to Harvester's past concessions to the union. The overriding issue was compulsory overtime, which the company had previously bargained away. The union bitterly resisted what it regarded as takeaways, and in the end Harvester got back very little.[50] It took serious losses in the fourth quarter of 1979 and the first quarter of 1980.

The company was hardly back to work when the recession struck with devastating suddenness, triggering more losses and culminating in the sale of its construction equipment business to Dresser in 1982. Although Harvester had serious management and financial problems of long-standing that in all likelihood would have resulted in the eventual breakup of the company, there is no doubt that the long strike of 1979–80 accelerated the process.

Summary, 1956–79

Compared to the postwar decade, the years between 1956 and 1979 were ones of relative tranquility in labor relations. The unions were firmly in place and had achieved a high degree of security through the union shop. The merger of the AFL and CIO in 1955 had largely put an end to interunion raiding as well as the ability of management to play off one union against another. The UAW was paramount in the automotive, farm, and construction equipment industries. In the few places where the UAW writ did not run, other unions were content to follow its lead. In addition to spectacular gains in wages and benefits during the period, the UAW began placing more emphasis on gaining additional paid time off and on noneconomic issues such as work rules, layoff procedures, company-paid union representation, and other similar matters. Despite stubborn resistance from management, concessions were gained. The companies appeared to have no alternative but the strategy of a fighting retreat before the aggressive thrusts of the UAW until Chrysler's near-bankruptcy in the late 1970s brought the first give-backs in the union's history to save jobs. Chrysler's problems were but a portent of things to come during the 1980s, however.

The Decline of Union Power, 1980–95

Union strategies to save jobs had come too late. High wages and benefits, inflexible work rules, and confrontational tactics had taken their toll over twenty years. Inept corporate management had also made a major contribution to union job losses throughout American industry in the 1970s. Myopia, complacency, and incompetence are only a few of the adjectives appropriate to describe much of the management of American industry during the period. Beginning in the early 1970s, significant job losses to imports began to occur in the heavily unionized automotive, steel, metal working, garment, and electronic industries, but management's response, with a few exceptions, was to ask the government for protection in the form of quotas, "voluntary" agreements, or higher tariffs. Between 1970 and 1979 membership in unions affiliated with the AFL-CIO fell from 15,978,000 to 13,621,000, with industrial unions taking a disproportionate share of the reduction. Membership leveled off during the 1980s in the thirteen to fourteen million range, but strong increases in government employee and teachers unions masked a continuing drop in industrial unions.[51] The UAW went from about 1.5 million members in 1978 to 840,000 in 1991.[52]

Not only did unions lose in absolute numbers but the union share of nonagricultural employment dropped steadily from a high of 35.8 percent in 1945 to only 16.1 percent in 1991.[53] Yet despite the loss nationally, industrial unions' bargaining strength remained unimpaired in the traditional strongholds of steel, rubber, electrical, automotive, and farm and construction equipment.

By 1980 construction equipment manufacturing in the United States was down to three major players: Caterpillar, Case, and Deere. International Harvester, a weak fourth, had been looking for a way out of the business but not yet found a buyer. Allis-Chalmers and Fiat S.p.A. had pooled construction equipment businesses in 1974 in a joint venture, Fiat-Allis, and by 1982 most F-A manufacturing was centered in Italy and Brazil. WABCO, Clark, Terex, and Euclid continued as short-line manufacturers.

Collapse of the Equipment Industry

Demand for construction equipment had been excellent throughout the 1970s, with most companies experiencing an almost unbroken succession of year-upon-year stair-step increases in sales and profits. According to annual corporate reports, U.S. employment levels peaked in the farm and construction equipment industries between 1979 and 1980, reaching almost seventy thousand at Caterpillar, more than fifty thousand at Deere, and seventeen thousand at Case. Union membership, running counter to the national trend, paralleled employment increases. The bubble was about to burst, however. By mid-1980 all indications were that the U.S. economy was headed into a recession, but no one in management or labor had an inkling of how profoundly the next five years would change the nation's construction equipment industry.

To adjust production schedules in the face of adverse economic signs, layoffs began in the industry in the first half of 1980. Caterpillar laid off 5,600, but as a result of layoff and downgrading provisions in the union contract some twenty thousand employees were moved to different jobs.[54] Year-end 1980 employment at Deere was reduced by more than four thousand from 1979.[55] Yet it appeared that the recession would be shallow and short for 1981 sales; profits remained strong, and some recalls occurred. But it was not to be. Instead of a predicted upturn in the latter half of 1982, industry sales fell disastrously during the year and precipitated massive layoffs. Deere's year-end employment fell by 12,500, and Caterpillar's dropped 23,500—all in the United States.[56]

Also in 1982, a contract year, the UAW targeted Caterpillar. After weeks of fruitless negotiations, a strike began at all UAW locations on October 1 and involved 20,400 active UAW members compared to the forty thousand three years earlier. Increasingly, the company had been feeling the bite of competition from Komatsu and had identified Komatsu's substantially lower labor costs as a principal cause. Caterpillar framed the issue as one of cost containment and claimed that its labor costs, including fringe benefits, were about double those in Japan. The company also believed that the UAW had negotiated more favorable agreements to the automotive industry and some competitors in the earthmoving equipment industry (Euclid, Terex and Dresser) than it demanded from Caterpillar.

At this point, unfavorable economic conditions prevailed worldwide, and demand for earthmoving equipment was at the lowest level in recent memory. Under such conditions a strike would apply little or no short-term economic leverage on Caterpillar, which had overseas plants and dealers with adequate inventories to meet what little demand existed. Thus, conditions were ripe for a long and bitter strike.

After a 205-day strike set a new record for Caterpillar, the UAW Bargaining Committee reluctantly allowed the membership to vote on the last company offer. Despite the committee's recommendation against approval, a contract ratified in late April eliminated the annual improvement factor, something that had been embedded in UAW contracts since the early 1950s. In its stead the union agreed to a profit-sharing plan, but with a guaranteed amount for 1984, the first year. The company also won a reduction in paid personal time off. A cost of living adjustment was continued as before, and the agreement was to run for thirty-seven months.[57]

Deere and others, working under contract extensions, quickly signed pattern contracts with the UAW, and the non-UAW plants followed suit.

Job Losses at Harvester

Throughout the early 1980s, International Harvester had been drastically downsizing in a desperate effort to survive. The 1979 agreement with the UAW was reopened in 1981, and Harvester demanded concessions to save jobs. Negotiations dragged, however, when the company failed to meet union demands for "equality of sacrifice" from management. In May 1982 a new 2½ year agreement was reached that included some concessions by the UAW that the company said would be worth $200 million over the life of the contract. At this point, ten thousand of the twenty-eight thousand Harvester UAW workers had been laid off.[58] By late 1984, when an agreement was reached to sell its farm equipment business to Case, only one major Harvester farm plant in the United States, that in East Moline, remained to be included in the package. From a total worldwide employment of almost ninety-eight thousand on October 31, 1979, only fifteen thousand remained on the payroll of Navistar, the surviving corporation, on October 31, 1986.[59]

Soon after the purchase and in a move to rationalize operations, Case closed its Terre Haute, Rock Island, and Bettendorf plants, entailing a further work force reduction of 4,900. In bargaining over the closings with the UAW, Case obtained a wage freeze and reduction in job classifications in return for full employment security for hourly workers.[60]

Caterpillar and the UAW

After the financial battering workers had taken in strikes of eighty days in 1979 and 205 days in 1982–83, Caterpillar UAW members chose more moderate leadership before the next contract negotiations. The company also appeared to soften its position so that a contract was signed in July 1986 without a strike. The new contract, to run twenty-seven months through September 30, 1988, covered 16,200 employees, a drop of 4,200 (about 20 percent) from the 1983 agreement. UAW jobs at Caterpillar were now only 40 percent of what they had been at the 1979 high. Job security was uppermost in the minds of UAW negotiators. In return for a reduction in job classifications, the union won a degree of layoff protection through some limitations on the company's rights to reduce employment. Uncharacteristically, the usually docile IAM at Caterpillar's Joliet plant chose to demonstrate independence and struck for four weeks. Eventually it accepted a contract that it had previously rejected.[61]

Deere and Pattern Bargaining

Meanwhile, the U.S. farm equipment industry was experiencing an even more drastic downturn than the construction equipment industry. Beginning in 1980, retail demand declined for six consecutive years. Deere saw sales slide from a peak of $5.5 billion in 1980 to $3.5 billion in 1986; employment dropped from more than sixty-five thousand in 1979 to 37,900 in 1986. The company was in no mood to sign a new labor agreement, which it felt would increase costs. In a reversal of roles it stated that it would not sign a "pattern settlement based on the contract negotiated with Caterpillar this past summer." The UAW struck four key Deere plants on August 23, and Deere responded by closing its remaining UAW plants. Although the farm economy continued weak, Deere attributed the loss of $333 million in the 1986 fourth quarter and 1987 first quarter to the strike. Thus, Deere began 1987, its sesquicentennial year, in the midst of the longest strike in its history. After a shutdown of 162 days, a settlement was reached February 1, 1987, although neither side claimed victory and Deere suffered construction equipment market share losses.[62]

A Quiet Period

The industries with which it bargained were experiencing tough times, and the UAW found itself under continuing pressure for give-backs. Wanting to minimize the time it was locked into concessions, the International opted for two-year agreements in 1986 and hoped for better times in 1988.

A five-year period of relative labor peace in the UAW's industries began in 1986. The union bywords became "job security," and the union endorsed new cooperative programs with management in an effort to preserve jobs. Quality circles were in and strikes were out. Corporate annual reports waxed ecstatic about new employee satisfaction programs; face-to-face meetings between workers and factory management were to improve operations and employee morale. But many of the hard core among both labor and management harbored reservations about the traditional adversarial relationship ever changing. In this environment, new three-year contracts were signed in 1988 throughout the UAW industries without major disruptions. The union's overriding concern, job security, was reflected in negotiating efforts to lock in existing jobs under all circumstances.

The Storm at Caterpillar

When negotiations opened in 1991 between the UAW and the Big Three, the U.S. economy was again in the midst of another recession, but despite that it appeared that the car makers had successfully weathered the 1980s. The union approached these negotiations with something like its old confidence, and agreements were reached in Detroit without significant disruptions. It then turned to Deere, the target company of the UAW ag-imp department, and an agreement was reached, following the Detroit pattern, without a strike.[63]

It was now Caterpillar's turn. But after two contracts without strikes and five years of labor peace, the militants were back in control of Local 974, the UAW's flagship Caterpillar local. Bill Casstevens, secretary-treasurer of the UAW International, said that Caterpillar needed an "attitude adjustment," and it was clear the UAW was spoiling for a fight with its old adversary. But it was not the same Caterpillar that for more than forty years had strenuously resisted the UAW strategy of pattern bargaining but nonetheless had signed a long series of just such agreements. With new, more aggressive top management and modernized manufacturing operations, there were signs that this time things were going to be different.

With the expiration of the contract on September 30, 1991, the union agreed to a week-to-week extension until the Deere negotiations were concluded and Casstevens, the chief negotiator, would be free to turn his attentions to Caterpillar. When that occurred, union demands were presented in the form of the freshly signed pattern agreement with Deere and were quickly rejected by Caterpillar. Caterpillar then modified its original offer, but the union rejected it. A strike began on November 3 at selected critical locations. The company responded by announcing a lockout at most locations not on strike but continued to build and ship products using salaried personnel and retirees. On February 16, 1992, Caterpillar lifted the lockout and invited striking workers to return but had few takers. Three days later the company tabled what it called its final offer, which the union rejected.

At this point Caterpillar had experienced the rejection of three offers and in addition had rejected the union's sole offer of the Deere pattern agreement.[64] On March 5 the company officially declared negotiations at an impasse. If a dispute is an economic strike, then under federal labor law declaring an impasse clears the way for the hiring of replacement workers. If, however, a strike concerns unfair labor practices, permanent replacement workers cannot legally be employed.[65] The UAW's response was to deny that negotiations were at an impasse. But when that failed to shake the company's resolve, the union shifted to the rather dubious claim that the dispute had all along been an unfair labor practices strike.

The company, now taking a very tough line, on April 1 announced that it was sending letters to all UAW employees, inviting striking workers to return to work the following Monday, April 6, under the terms of the company's final offer. It also announced that it would begin advertising for replacement workers to fill the jobs of striking workers who failed to return.[66]

Caterpillar had thrown down the gauntlet to the UAW, and the unprecedented challenge to a powerful union attracted the attention of the national media and Washington politicians. Liberal Democrats, in an uproar, renewed their promise of legislation to prohibit the hiring of replacement workers but could do nothing to forestall the impending collision. As the fateful day approached, interest groups around the nation were watching intently, while tensions had never been so high in the Peoria area.

Caterpillar was clearly disappointed when only four hundred crossed the picket line that Monday. The strikers, eyeing each other warily, were awaiting developments, but gradually the number trickling in to work rose. A week later the company reported that a thousand were back to work. In the meantime, the company was swamped by thousands of responses to its job advertisements. In light of these disquieting developments, the union decided to accept an earlier company proposal to bring in the Federal Mediation and Conciliation Service. Negotiations, with the involvement of FMCS, were set to begin April 13 in Hinsdale, a Chicago suburb.[67]

Back to Work

After two days of talks in which neither party tabled a new offer, Bill Casstevens faced up to harsh reality and ordered the strikers back to work. It was billed by the FMCS as a compromise: The union would return to work in return for the company dropping plans to hire replacement workers.[68] But the union had blinked first, and the strikers knew it.

By the end of May, all the strikers were back, working without a contract under provisions of the company's final offer. Negotiations were re-opened April 30 but went nowhere. At this point, the union announced its new "in-plant" strategy in which members would "work to rule" and pursue slow-down and obstructionist tactics to reduce production and bring the company to its knees. Only the militant minority engaged in these tactics and production was not seriously impeded, but unrest in the shop resulted in the filing of more than a hundred unfair labor practice grievances with the NLRB over a two-year period.[69]

The Second Caterpillar Strike

Having now laid the necessary basis, on June 21, 1994, the UAW International took its members out in what it declared was an unfair labor practices strike, secure in the belief that under these conditions the company could not legally hire replacement workers.[70] The company responded by again mobilizing salaried employees and retirees and this time adding temporary replacement workers. Market demand was strong, with most popular products on allocation, but soon the makeshift work force had the plants running at capacity despite union claims to the contrary.[71]

As it gradually filtered through to a demoralized union membership that the strike was having little effect on the company, line-crossers began trickling back to work. Sensing the mood, the International raised weekly strike pay from $100 to $300.[72] In July 1995, a few days after the first anniversary of the strike, the company announced its sixth consecutive quarter of record profits.[73] Clearly, the strike was not applying the intended economic leverage on Caterpillar.

In the meantime, with the passage of three years, the Deere contract was up for renegotiation in the fall of 1994. Recognizing that it was vulnerable because of the unresolved Caterpillar strike, the UAW moved cautiously. Although 90 percent of the 10,500 union workers rejected Deere's first offer, the UAW International refrained from calling a strike.[74] Sensing their advantage, the Deere negotiators took a tough line and refused to move from their original offer. Talks were broken off. Faced with the possibility of another Caterpillar-like impasse, after four months a more conciliatory UAW came back to the bargaining table, and a new three-year contract was ratified on March 5, 1995. The union accepted a two-tier wage system in which new hires would come in at 70 percent of the current starting level. There would be no wage increases over the life of the contract, but three annual lump sum payments, totaling 10 percent, were provided. A COLA would continue as before. Despite the UAW's long history of resisting incentive pay plans, Deere gained agreement to an incentive plan called the "Continuous Improvement Pay Plan" (CIPP), which rewarded increased productivity. Although the UAW called it a good contract, the Deere agreement included some things the union had rejected out of hand in the Caterpillar negotiations. Still, the union claimed it had reached another pattern agreement with Deere.[75]

The summer of 1995 saw the passing of the UAW's old guard. At its annual convention, Owen Bieber, president, and Bill Casstevens, secretary-treasurer, stepped down. Stephen Yokich, UAW vice president in charge of the key General Motors department, was elected to succeed Bieber. Yokich, no stranger to the ag-imp department, had led negotiations for the union in the long strike at Caterpillar in 1982–83 and the renegotiation of Harvester's contract in 1982. He quickly made it clear that reaching a settlement with Caterpillar would be one of his top priorities.[76]

The End of the Strike

Talks were soon reopened, with negotiations being conducted quietly at secret locations around the Midwest. Both sides refrained from news releases, but rumors flew. In late November, 1995 it was reported that Caterpillar was about to present the union with another proposal, its sixth, and the membership would be permitted to vote on it. That did happen on the weekend of December 2–3, but before the vote the UAW International headquarters informed its membership that the strike was being called off—regardless of the outcome. The 8,700 strikers (4,100 had returned to work) overwhelmingly rejected the offer and faced the prospect of returning to work without a contract. After four years of bitter strife, union workers were getting no more and perhaps less than they could have gotten at the outset before Caterpillar proved it could successfully operate without them. Major provisions of the Caterpillar offer included a six-year contract, no wage increases for the life of the contract except for a COLA, two-tier wages for new hires, flexible work schedules, and the company's right to use part time and temporary employees in the shop. Workers would have job security for the life of the contract, and pension benefits were improved. The company's preferred-provider medical plan was retained.[77]

It was a major setback for the UAW when for the first time in nearly fifty years a manufacturer had successfully resisted accepting a pattern agreement. The outcome was certain to fuel speculation about the future of pattern bargaining in the automotive industry and elsewhere.

Conclusion

After forty-five years of almost uninterrupted successes, organized labor in the farm and earthmoving equipment industries began to see its power erode during the early 1980s as the flood of imports, business consolidations, financial failures, downsizing, and changing corporate strategies drastically reduced membership. These conditions forced the UAW to shift from its traditionally aggressive stance to a more defensive posture in which job security became paramount. But the UAW held tenaciously to the basic strategy it had adopted right after World War II—pattern bargaining.

Through fifteen to twenty years of downsizing and the workings of the seniority system, U.S. companies in the steel, electrical, rubber, automotive, and equipment industries found themselves in the 1990s with aging work forces. Recognizing this, the companies believed it was important that they obtain concessions from the unions before a new generation of workers took over. Thus pressure on the unions increased steadily.

The first major challenge to pattern bargaining came in 1991 with the opening of contract negotiations at Caterpillar, a company which, unlike the automotive and farm equipment industries, relied on exports from the United States for a major part of its business. As the earthmoving equipment industry's only worldwide competitor from a U.S. base, Caterpillar believed that it was vital to rein in its pattern labor costs to remain competitive with overseas rivals. The four-year test of wills between Caterpillar and the UAW was watched intently by both business and labor, and the outcome sent ominous signals to Big Labor. Only time will reveal the full significance of these events.

NOTES

ONE   Creating the Need

1. Hadfield, *World Canals*, 39–43.

2. For early American canals, see Bourne, *Floating West*, and Shaw, *Canals for a Nation*.

3. Shaw, *Canals for a Nation*, 235.

4. Ibid., 230.

5. Wixom, *American Roadbuilders Association* [hereafter *ARBA*] *Pictorial History of Roadbuilding*, 36, 43.

6. Shaw, *Canals for a Nation*, 228.

7. Frey, ed., *Railroads in the Nineteenth Century*, xxxii.

8. For the Suez Canal, see Burchell, *Building the Suez Canal*, and Kinross, *Between Two Seas*.

9. Thompson, "American Contributions to the French Panama Canal Venture."

10. For the Panama Canal, see Lee, *Panama Canal*, and McCullough, *Path between the Seas*.

11. Wixom, *ARBA Pictorial History of Roadbuilding*, 47, 64.

12. "List of Exhibitors, First Road Show, November 1909," July 23, 1959, Construction Industry Manufacturers Association (CIMA), Milwaukee.

13. Wixom, *ARBA Pictorial History of Roadbuilding*, 50–51.

14. Ibid., 86.

15. For early congressional action on roads, see Wixom, *ARBA Pictorial History of Roadbuilding*, 86, and U.S. Department of Transportation, *America's Highways*.

16. Wixom, *ARBA Pictorial History of Roadbuilding*, 124–31.

17. "Retrospectives," *Engineering News-Record*, Jan. 4, 1993, 30.

18. "Retrospectives," *Engineering News-Record*, Jan. 5, 1989, 33.

19. Ibid., 36.

20. U.S. Department of Interior, Water and Power Resources, *Project Data*, 45, 79–84, 1049.

21. Wolf, *Big Dams and Other Dreams*, 3–59.

22. Cullen, *Rivers in Harness*, 134, 135; U.S. Department of the Interior, Water and Power Resources, *Project Data*, 209.

23. U.S. Department of the Interior, Water and Power Resources, "Preface" and "Statistical Summary," in *Project Data*, v, 1369–437.

24. "Retrospectives," *Engineering News-Record*, Jan. 5, 1989, 45.

25. Cullen, *Rivers in Harness*, 135.

26. Warne, *The Bureau of Reclamation*, 162–73.

27. "Retrospectives," *Engineering News-Record*, Jan. 5, 1989, 48.

28. Wixom, *ARBA Pictorial History of Roadbuilding*, 96.

29. Ibid., 44–54.

30. Ibid., 31–33.

31. Ibid., 41.

32. Ibid., 41, 43.

33. Ibid., 41.

34. Ibid., 136.

35. For the interstate highway program, see Wixom, *ARBA Pictorial History of Roadbuilding*, ch. 10, and U.S. Department of Transportation, *America's Highways*.

36. Cullen, *Rivers in Harness*, 92–114.

37. U.S. Department of Commerce, Bureau of the Census, *Historical Statistics of the United States, Colonial Times to 1970*, series M, 205–20, 600; Reynolds, "Iron Ore Ranges," 195.

38. For the story of the discovery of the Mesabi Range, see DeKruif, *Seven Iron Men*.

39. Reynolds, "Iron Mining Machines and Techniques," 189–94; Reynolds, "Iron Ore Ranges," 194–98.

40. Reynolds, "Iron Ore Supplies," 231–33.

41. Flawn, *Mineral Resources*, 76, 77.

42. For the Guggenheim family's involvement in copper mining and Bingham Canyon, see Hoyt, *The Guggenheims and the American Dream*; see also the *Wall Street Journal*, July 13, 1971.

43. Annual report, 1993, Phelps Dodge Corporation.

44. U.S. Department of Commerce, Bureau of the Census, *Historical Statistics of the United States, Colonial Times to 1970*, series M, 93–106, 589, series M, 123–37, 592; U.S. Department of Commerce, Bureau of the Census, *Statistical Abstract*, 1991, 709.

45. U.S. Department of Commerce, Bureau of the Census, *Statistical Abstract*, 1994, 721.

46. Orlemann, *Giant Earth-Moving Equipment*, 69.

47. U.S. Department of Commerce, Bureau of the Census, *Statistical Abstract*, 1996, 695.

TWO   The Beginnings, 1831–1945

1. Marsh, *A Corporate Tragedy*, 15–29.

2. Ibid., 30.

3. Ibid., 38–42.

4. Ibid., 45.

5. Williams, *Fordson, Farmall, and Poppin' Johnny,* 7–11.

6. Wendel, *150 Years of International Harvester,* 258, 259.

7. Gray, *The Agricultural Tractor,* 2:21.

8. Broehl, *John Deere's Company,* 479.

9. Gray, *The Agricultural Tractor,* 2:21; Williams, *Fordson, Farmall, and Poppin' Johnny,* 68.

10. Broehl, *John Deere's Company,* 479; Williams, *Fordson, Farmall, and Poppin' Johnny,* 85–89.

11. Wendel, *150 Years of International Harvester,* 329–42.

12. Ibid., 413.

13. Ibid., 342–44.

14. Marsh, *A Corporate Tragedy,* 57.

15. Peterson, *An Industrial Heritage,* 1–16.

16. Ibid., 41–63.

17. Ibid., 90–95.

18. Ibid., 104.

19. Ibid., 107.

20. Ibid., 108.

21. Ibid., 131.

22. Ibid., 112.

23. Ibid., 149–52.

24. Ibid., 245, 252.

25. Annual reports, 1925–30, Caterpillar Tractor Co.

26. Peterson, *An Industrial Heritage,* 253.

27. Wendel, *The Allis-Chalmers Story,* 347.

28. Ibid., 199, 200.

29. Ibid., 347, 348.

30. Ibid., 348.

31. Caterpillar named the product the Lifetime-Lubricated track roller.

32. Gray, *The Agricultural Tractor,* 2:17.

33. Peterson, *An Industrial Heritage,* 254.

34. Ibid., 252.

35. Ibid., 257.

36. Ibid., 273.

37. Broehl, *John Deere's Company,* 528.

38. Peterson, *An Industrial Heritage,* 313.

39. Wik, *Benjamin Holt and Caterpillar,* 48.

40. Leffingwell, *Caterpillar,* 30, 31.

41. Wik, *Benjamin Holt and Caterpillar,* 111.

42. Ibid., 21.

43. Leffingwell, *Caterpillar*, 38.

44. Ibid., 38, 41; Wik, *Benjamin Holt and Caterpillar*, 60–64.

45. Wik, *Benjamin Holt and Caterpillar*, 69–72.

46. Leffingwell, *Caterpillar*, 12–25.

47. Ibid., 41–44.

48. Leffingwell and Wik differ on the price Holt paid. In his discussion of the transaction, Leffingwell, *Caterpillar*, 42–44, gives the price as $750,000. Wik, however, states it as being "approximately $1 million." *Benjamin Holt and Caterpillar*, 58. He also states (108) that "the Best Manufacturing Company was sold to the Holts for $325,000." No authority is cited for the two higher figures, but Wik cites primary sources for the $325,000 figure. Caterpillar publications are silent on this point. Possibly the transaction involved assumption of debt by Holt.

49. Caterpillar Inc., *The Caterpillar Story*, 18.

50. Ibid., 17.

51. Leffingwell, *Caterpillar*, 54.

52. Ibid., 62.

53. Wik, *Benjamin Holt and Caterpillar*, 63.

54. Caterpillar Inc., *The Caterpillar Story*, 26.

55. Payne, ed., *Benjamin Holt*, 66.

56. Wik, *Benjamin Holt and Caterpillar*, 98.

57. Leffingwell, *Caterpillar*, 83.

58. Ibid., 94.

59. Wik, *Benjamin Holt and Caterpillar*, 102; Leffingwell, *Caterpillar*, 88.

60. Wik, *Benjamin Holt and Caterpillar*, 105, 106; annual report, 1925, Caterpillar Tractor Co.; *Peoria Star*, May 4, 1925.

61. Annual report, 1925, Caterpillar Tractor Co.

62. Caterpillar Inc., *The Caterpillar Story*, 29.

63. Annual report, 1929, Caterpillar Tractor Co.

64. Wendell, *Encyclopedia of American Farm Tractors*, 29, 39–41, 54, 176, 204, 205, 285, 286; Gray, *The American Farm Tractor*, 1:40–46.

65. Gray, *The American Farm Tractor*, 2:53.

66. Annual report, 1928, Caterpillar Tractor Co.

67. Caterpillar, *The Caterpillar Story*, 40, 41; Caterpillar Inc., *Caterpillar Model Identification Guide*, 1991.

68. For the story of the development of the diesel engine, see Grosser, *Diesel*.

69. Leffingwell, *Caterpillar*, 97–105; Caterpillar Inc., *The Caterpillar Story*, 36–39.

70. Leffingwell, *Caterpillar*, 107.

71. In 1936 the prices for FOB Peoria were $2,450 for the RD4, $3,375 for the RD6, $4,600 for the RD7, and $6,650 for the RD8. See Stephens, ed., *Farm Tractors, 1926–1956*, 152, 153.

72. Ibid., 183–88.

73. Annual report, 1935, Caterpillar Tractor Co.

74. Annual report, 1936, Caterpillar Tractor Co.

75. Annual report, 1956, Caterpillar Tractor Co.

76. Caterpillar Inc., *The Caterpillar Story,* 35.

77. Annual report, 1941, Caterpillar Tractor Co.

78. Ibid.

79. Ibid.

80. See LeTourneau, *Mover of Men and Mountains,* chs. 1–9 for LeTourneau's early life.

81. Ibid., chs. 9–10.

82. Gowenlock, *The LeTourneau Legend,* 15.

83. Annual report, 1943, R. G. LeTourneau Inc.

84. LeTourneau, *Mover of Men and Mountains,* 169–73.

85. Gowenlock, *The LeTourneau Legend,* 30–34. LeTourneau's first use of the apron was in his 1932 Model A Carryall scraper, but in this design the apron was also used as the ejector, pushing the material out the rear of the scraper. In the Model B Carryall (also 1932), the apron was hinged so it could be raised and lowered to the cutting edge. The rear wall of the scraper formed the ejector, which moved forward to push out the material. This was the configuration subsequently adopted by almost all manufacturers of cable-operated scrapers.

86. Ibid., 193, 195, 198.

87. Ibid., 199.

88. Ibid., 200; annual report, 1943, R.G. LeTourneau Inc.

89. LeTourneau, *Mover of Men and Mountains,* 204, 205; annual report, 1943, R. G. LeTourneau Inc.

90. LeTourneau, *Mover of Men and Mountains,* 215, 216.

91. Ibid., 216–19.

92. Ibid., 232; "Retrospectives," *Engineering News-Record,* Jan. 4, 1990, 59.

93. LeTourneau, *Mover of Men and Mountains,* 220–22.

94. Ibid., 230.

95. Annual report, 1943, R. G. LeTourneau Inc.

96. Van Tassel and Grabowski, eds., *The Encyclopedia of Cleveland History,* 104.

97. Ibid., 195.

98. According to Leffingwell, *Caterpillar,* 85, Rollin White's first successful tractor, the Model H, was modeled closely on a small Best tractor, the Model 8-16, which, like other early Best crawlers, incorporated a differential.

99. To protect farmers from exaggerated claims by some manufacturers, the University of Nebraska initiated an annual performance testing program in 1920. Results were made public, and although participation was voluntary, tractors that had not undergone the test became suspect in farmers' eyes.

100. Stephens, ed., *Farm Tractors, 1926–1956,* 24, 25, 38, 39, 74, 127.

101. Ibid., 153–56.

102. Van Tassel and Grabowski, eds., *The Encyclopedia of Cleveland History*, 196.

103. Ibid., 382; Frantz, "Forty Years of Euclid Scraper Development."

104. Anderson, *One Hundred Booming Years*, 11–47.

105. Payne, *Initiative in Energy*, 29–31.

106. "The Story behind Our Trademark," Harnischfeger Industries brochure, n.p., author's possession.

107. Anderson, *One Hundred Booming Years*, 48.

108. Orlemann, *Giant Earth-Moving Equipment*, 16–18.

109. Ibid., 18.

110. Broehl, *John Deere's Company*, 27–29, 44, 65–70, 75.

111. Ibid., 125, 126.

112. Ibid., 161, 162.

113. Ibid., 200, 201.

114. Ibid., 230–35.

115. Ibid., 313, 362.

116. Ibid., 797.

117. Ibid., 328–32.

118. Ibid., 343.

119. McMillan and Jones, *John Deere Tractors and Equipment, 1837–1959*, 24–28; Broehl, *John Deere's Company*, 403–7.

120. Deere & Company, *How Johnny Popper Replaced the Horse*, 7.

121. Broehl, *John Deere's Company*, 804.

122. Wendel, *Encyclopedia of American Farm Tractors*, 83–85, 86; McMillan and Jones, *John Deere Tractors and Equipment, 1837–1959*, 19–21, 30–32; Broehl, *John Deere's Company*, 520.

123. Broehl, *John Deere's Company*, 496.

124. Ibid., 534, 535.

125. Ibid., 537.

126. Ibid., 570; McMillan and Jones, *John Deere Tractors and Equipment, 1837–1959*, 38.

127. Holbrook, *Machines of Plenty*, 22.

128. Ibid., 23–27.

129. Ibid., 29.

130. Ibid., 33.

131. Holmes, *J. I. Case*, 6.

132. Holbrook, *Machines of Plenty*, 46.

133. Ibid., 52.

134. Holmes, *J. I. Case*, 18.

135. Holbrook, *Machines of Plenty*, 59, 60; McKinley, *Wheels of Farm Progress*, 30.

136. McKinley, *Wheels of Farm Progress*, 29.

137. Holmes, *J. I. Case*, 17.

138. Ibid., 32, 33.

139. Ibid., 20.

140. Ibid., 21.

141. Ibid., 24.

142. Ibid., 182.

143. Neufield, *A Global Corporation*, 23, 24.

144. Holmes, *J. I. Case*, 44, 45.

145. Ibid., 45.

146. Broehl, *John Deere's Company*, 451.

147. Holmes, *J. I. Case*, 48.

148. Ibid., 56.

149. Ibid., 57.

150. Broehl, *John Deere's Company*, 528.

151. Neufield, *A Global Corporation*, 15, 16, 17.

152. Ibid., 4.

153. Ibid., 21, 22.

154. Ibid., 24.

155. Ibid., 23, 24.

156. Ibid., 25.

157. Ibid., 30.

158. Ibid., 30–32.

159. Ibid., 51.

160. Ibid., 37.

161. Ibid., 51.

162. Ibid., 37.

163. Broehl, *John Deere's Company*, 546, 547.

164. Van Tassel and Grabowski, eds., *The Encyclopedia of Cleveland History*, 195, 196.

165. Caterpillar Inc., *The Caterpillar Story*, 46–50.

166. Gowenlock, *The LeTourneau Legend*, 108, 109.

167. LeTourneau, *Mover of Men and Mountains*, 3.

168. Wendel, *150 Years of International Harvester*, 407–9.

169. Marsh, *A Corporate Tragedy*, 72–74.

170. Broehl, *John Deere's Company*, 548–54.

171. Holmes, *J. I. Case*, 64.

172. Peterson, *An Industrial Heritage*, 330–41.

173. Ibid., 330.

174. Annual report, 1956, Caterpillar Tractor Co.; annual report, 1944, R. G. LeTourneau Inc.

175. Marsh, *A Corporate Tragedy*, 71.

176. Annual report, 1956, Caterpillar Tractor Co.

177. Annual report, 1944, Caterpillar Tractor Co.
178. Annual report, 1944, R. G. LeTourneau Inc.

THREE   The Postwar Decade, 1946–55

1. U.S. Department of Commerce, Bureau of the Census, *Historical Statistics of the United States, Colonial Times to 1970,* table F31, 226, 227.
2. U.S. Department of Commerce, Bureau of the Census, *Historical Statistics of the United States, Colonial Times to 1970,* series F, 130–43, 233.
3. *New York Times,* July 3, 1945.
4. *New York Times,* Sept. 7, 1945.
5. *New York Times,* June 4, 1952.
6. *New York Times,* Sept. 13, 1951.
7. *New York Times,* Sept. 9, 1945.
8. *New York Times,* Oct. 2, 1952.
9. Neufield, *A Global Corporation,* 108–10, 118, 122–25.
10. Broehl, *John Deere's Company,* 581–588.
11. Lapica, ed., *Facts-on-File Yearbook, 1950,* 292.
12. Lapica, ed., *Facts-on-File Yearbook, 1951,* 6.
13. *New York Times,* March 7, 1946.
14. Marsh, *A Corporate Tragedy,* 74.
15. *New York Times,* Sept. 28, 1955.
16. *New York Times,* March 1, 1947.
17. Marsh, *A Corporate Tragedy,* 114–17.
18. *New York Times,* March 3, 1949.
19. Marsh, *A Corporate Tragedy,* 78.
20. Ibid., 77–79.
21. Ibid., 118.
22. Ibid., 119.
23. Ibid., 120, 121.
24. *Wall Street Journal,* Sept. 12, 1974.
25. Annual report, 1946, Caterpillar Tractor Co.
26. Annual report, 1947, Caterpillar Tractor Co.
27. Annual report, 1949, Caterpillar Tractor Co.
28. Annual reports, 1950, 1951, Caterpillar Tractor Co.
29. Annual report, 1955, Caterpillar Tractor Co.
30. Annual report, 1950, Caterpillar Tractor Co.
31. Annual report, 1954, Caterpillar Tractor Co.
32. Annual report, 1955, Caterpillar Tractor Co.
33. Ibid.
34. Caterpillar Inc., *Caterpillar Model Identification Guide, 1991.*
35. Ibid.

36. Ibid.

37. Annual report, 1951, Caterpillar Tractor Co.

38. Caterpillar Inc., *Caterpillar Model Identification Guide, 1991.*

39. Ibid.

40. Ibid.

41. Ibid.

42. Peterson, *An Industrial Heritage,* 296, 330, 346, 347.

43. Ibid., 347, 351.

44. *New York Times,* Nov. 2, 1953.

45. *New York Times,* March 7, 1952.

46. Peterson, *An Industrial Heritage,* 346.

47. Wendel, *The Allis-Chalmers Story,* 201.

48. Ibid., 348.

49. "Together . . . to Serve You Better," Fiat-Allis ConExpo '75 advertising brochure.

50. Wendel, *The Allis-Chalmer Story,* 178, 179.

51. Ibid., 205, 206; *New York Times,* Aug. 12, 1952.

52. Peterson, *An Industrial Heritage,* 349.

53. *New York Times,* Sept. 11, Nov. 2, 1953.

54. Annual report, 1944, R. G. LeTourneau Inc.

55. Ibid.

56. Annual report, 1947, R. G. LeTourneau Inc.

57. Annual report, 1948, R. G. LeTourneau Inc.

58. Gowenlock, *The LeTourneau Legend,* 110, 111.

59. Annual report, 1947, R. G. LeTourneau Inc. and interim report through Aug. 31, 1948.

60. Annual report, 1950, R. G. LeTourneau Inc.

61. *New York Times,* May 10, 1953.

62. "George Westinghouse," in *Railroads in the Nineteenth Century,* ed. Frey, 430–36.

63. Annual report, 1953, LeTourneau-Westinghouse.

64. Annual report, 1954, LeTourneau-Westinghouse.

65. Annual report, 1955, LeTourneau-Westinghouse.

66. Frantz, "Forty Years of Euclid Scraper Development."

67. Orlemann, *Euclid and Terex Earthmoving Machines,* 21.

68. Van Tassel and Grabowski, eds., *The Encyclopedia of Cleveland History,* 382.

69. *New York Times,* Aug. 8, 1953.

70. *New York Times,* Nov. 18, 1955.

71. Wendel, *Encyclopedia of American Farm Tractors,* 124.

72. As diesel engine technology has since evolved, the four-cycle design has proven capable of matching the two-cycle in weight-to-horsepower and is generally accepted as superior in other desirable characteristics.

73. Sloan, *My Years with General Motors,* 365–77.

74. Ibid.

75. Frantz, "Forty Years of Euclid Scraper Development."

76. Wendel, *Oliver Hart-Parr,* 15, 16, 107, 123.

77. Stephens, ed., *Farm Tractors, 1926–1956,* 153; Wendel, *Oliver Hart-Parr,* 24–29.

78. Van Tassel and Grabowski, eds., *The Encyclopedia of Cleveland History,* 196.

79. Wendel, *Oliver Hart-Parr,* 265–75.

80. Ibid., 123.

81. "Clark Equipment Company," in *International Directory of Company Histories,* ed. Kepos, 8:114–16.

82. *New York Times,* Feb. 24, 1953.

83. *New York Times,* Feb. 14, 1954.

84. *New York Times,* Feb. 16, 1955.

85. Orlemann, *Giant Earth-Moving Equipment,* 97.

86. U.S. Department of Commerce, Bureau of the Census, *Historical Statistics of the United States, Colonial Times to 1970,* series P, 231–300, 695.

87. Broehl, *John Deere's Company,* 604, 670.

88. Holmes, *J. I. Case,* 90, 91.

89. *New York Times,* Feb. 16, 1946.

90. Broehl, *John Deere's Company,* 570, 571.

91. Ibid., 572.

92. Ibid., 596–600, 603.

93. Ibid., 600–602.

94. Ibid., 603–8.

95. Neufield, *A Global Corporation,* 64, 65.

96. Ibid., chs. 7, 8.

97. Holmes, *J. I. Case,* 74.

98. Ibid., 86.

99. "From Road Show to ConExpo: A Brief History," news release, March 1993, Construction Industry Manufacturers Association (CIMA), Milwaukee.

100. *New York Times,* July 17, 1948.

101. *Engineering News-Record,* July 29, 1948.

FOUR   The Interstate Decade, 1956–65

1. *New York Times,* June 21, 22, 27, 30, 1956.

2. *New York Times,* Aug. 19, 1957.

3. *New York Times,* Jan. 9, 1958.

4. *New York Times,* Sept. 22, 1959.

5. *New York Times,* Aug. 4, 1958.

6. *New York Times,* Oct. 13, 1961.

7. *New York Times*, Jan. 7, 1962.

8. *New York Times*, Jan. 23, 1964.

9. "Retrospectives," *Engineering News-Record*, Jan. 4, 1990, 62; "Retrospectives," *Engineering News-Record*, Jan. 25, 1962, 46. According to a Euclid advertisement (*Engineering News-Record*, May 24, 1962, 4–5), the joint venture purchased 142 Euclid hauling units for this project.

10. *New York Times*, Jan. 19, 1959.

11. U.S. Department of Commerce, Bureau of the Census, *Historical Statistics of the United States, Colonial Times to 1970*, series F, 130–43.

12. Holmes, *J. I. Case*, 90; Holbrook, *Machines of Plenty*, 243.

13. Holmes, *J. I. Case*, 85, 86.

14. *New York Times*, Feb. 22, 1956.

15. Holmes, *J. I. Case*, 91.

16. *New York Times*, Sept. 7, Oct. 28, Nov. 16, 1956; Holmes, *J. I. Case*, 96–98.

17. Holmes, *J. I. Case*, 99, 102–3.

18. Ibid., 99–101.

19. Ibid., 119, 122.

20. Ibid., 119.

21. Ibid., 129, 131.

22. Ibid.

23. Ibid., 104–6.

24. Ibid., 106.

25. Ibid., 108.

26. *New York Times*, Feb. 2, 1960.

27. Holmes, *J. I. Case*, 108.

28. *New York Times*, April 3, 1964.

29. Holmes, *J. I. Case*, 125, 126.

30. *New York Times*, April 3, 1964.

31. Trade advertising, *Engineering and Mining Journal*, May 1965.

32. Holmes, *J. I. Case*, 131.

33. Broehl, *John Deere's Company*, 635–41.

34. Ibid., 620–23.

35. Ibid., 626–35, 806.

36. Ibid., 594.

37. McMillan and Jones, *John Deere Tractors and Equipment, 1837–1959*, 174–87.

38. McMillan and Harrington, *John Deere Tractors and Equipment, 1960–1990*, 97.

39. "Exhibitors 1957 Road Show," news release, Jan. 16, 1957, Construction Industry Manufacturers Association (CIMA), Milwaukee.

40. McMillan and Harrington, *John Deere Tractors and Equipment, 1960–1990*, 101, 102.

41. Broehl, *John Deere's Company*, 765.

42. McMillan and Harrington, *John Deere Tractors and Equipment, 1960–1990*, 98.

43. Ibid., 99–101.

44. Ibid., 101.

45. Broehl, *John Deere's Company*, 647.

46. *New York Times*, Nov. 16, 1957.

47. Neufield, *A Global Corporation*, 266, 267.

48. *New York Times*, Nov. 16, 1957.

49. *New York Times*, Feb. 14, 1959; Neufield, *A Global Corporation*, 327–29.

50. Neufield, *A Global Corporation*, 318.

51. Ibid., 353–55.

52. Ibid., 268.

53. Annual report, 1965, Caterpillar Tractor Co.

54. Annual report, 1956, Caterpillar Tractor Co.

55. Annual report, 1958, Caterpillar Tractor Co.

56. Annual report, 1960, Caterpillar Tractor Co.

57. *New York Times*, Sept. 2, 1965.

58. Annual reports, 1956–65, Caterpillar Tractor Co.

59. Caterpillar Inc., *Caterpillar Model Identification Guide, 1991*.

60. Annual report, 1957, Caterpillar Tractor Co.

61. Annual reports, 1956, 1965, Caterpillar Tractor Co.

62. Caterpillar Inc., *Caterpillar Model Identification Guide, 1991*; annual reports, 1958, 1962, 1974, Caterpillar Tractor Co..

63. *New York Times*, July 24, 1965; annual report, 1965, Caterpillar Tractor Co.

64. Annual report, 1963, Caterpillar Tractor Co.

65. Annual report, 1962, Caterpillar Tractor Co.

66. Annual report, 1965, Caterpillar Tractor Co.

67. *New York Times*, Jan. 28, 1952.

68. *New York Times*, Jan. 8, 1960.

69. Marsh, *A Corporate Tragedy*, 81.

70. *New York Times*, Jan. 8, 1960.

71. Marsh, *A Corporate Tragedy*, 115, 116.

72. Ibid., 108–11.

73. *New York Times*, March 8, 1960.

74. Marsh, *A Corporate Tragedy*, 119.

75. Trade advertising, *Engineering and Mining Journal*, March 1957.

76. Trade advertising, *Engineering and Mining Journal*, August 1965.

77. Marsh, *A Corporate Tragedy*, 119.

78. Ibid., 121.

79. Trade advertising, *Engineering and Mining Journal*, July 1965.

80. Trade advertising, *Engineering and Mining Journal*, Dec. 1961.

81. Marsh, *A Corporate Tragedy*, 112, 113, 123.

82. Peterson, *An Industrial Heritage*, 353–55.

83. Ibid., 361.

84. Ibid., 355.

85. *New York Times*, Oct. 6, 1959; Peterson, *An Industrial Heritage*, 361.

86. Peterson, *An Industrial Heritage*, 81.

87. Wendel, *The Allis-Chalmers Story*, 179.

88. Peterson, *An Industrial Heritage*, 367.

89. *New York Times*, Sept. 29, 1956, Sept. 5, 1959.

90. Orlemann, *Euclid and Terex Earth-Moving Machines*, 67.

91. *New York Times*, Oct. 17, 1959.

92. Trade advertising, *Engineering and Mining Journal*, June 1965.

93. Trade advertising, *Engineering and Mining Journal*, October 1962.

94. Annual reports, 1956–65, LeTourneau-Westinghouse.

95. Annual reports, 1957, 1958, LeTourneau-Westinghouse.

96. *Engineering and Mining Journal*, Oct. 1965.

97. *New York Times*, May 9, 1961.

98. Gowenlock, *The LeTourneau Legend*, 258.

99. Ibid., 262–70.

100. Ibid., 274.

101. Ibid., 280–85.

102. *New York Times*, March 19, 1960.

103. *New York Times*, Nov. 1, 1960.

104. *New York Times*, Nov. 2, 1961.

105. Wendel, *Oliver Hart-Parr*, 54–61.

106. Ibid., 275.

107. *New York Times*, March 19, 1960.

108. Trade advertising, *Engineering News-Record*, Feb. 7, 1957.

109. Trade advertising, *Engineering News-Record*, July 5, 1962, 31.

110. *New York Times*, March 11, 1965.

111. "Komatsu," in *International Directory of Company Histories*, ed. Hast, 3:545–46, also in *International Directory of Company Histories*, ed. Grant, 16:309–11 (an update); *Komatsu Corporate Fact Book*, 1992.

112. *Komatsu Corporate Fact Book*, 1992.

113. Ibid.

114. *Wall Street Journal*, Feb. 24, 1982.

115. *Komatsu Corporate Fact Book*, 1992.

116. *Engineering News-Record*, Feb. 7, 1957; *Engineering and Mining Journal*, March 1957; "Exhibitors 1957 Road Show," news release, Jan. 16, 1957, Construction Industry Manufacturers Association (CIMA), Milwaukee.

117. *Engineering News-Record*, Feb. 14, 21, 1963; *Engineering and Mining Journal*, March, 1963; "List of Exhibitors," news release, Feb. 1, 1963, Construction Industry Manufacturers Association (CIMA), Milwaukee.

118. *New York Times*, Jan. 21, 1966.

FIVE   The Industry Matures, 1966–75

1. U.S. Department of Commerce, Bureau of the Census, *Statistical Abstract, 1988*, 450.

2. Ibid., 449.

3. Ibid., 407.

4. *New York Times*, Nov. 24, 1966.

5. *New York Times*, Feb. 2, 1975.

6. *New York Times*, Aug. 14, 1973.

7. *New York Times*, Dec. 14, 1968.

8. *New York Times*, Feb. 2, 1975.

9. *Engineering News-Record*, Jan. 2, 1975.

10. *Wall Street Journal*, Jan. 26. 1970.

11. *Wall Street Journal*, June 13, 14, 1974, Feb. 26, 1975, July 1, 1976; *Engineering News-Records*, Jan. 2, 1975.

12. *Engineering and Mining Journal*, April, 1967.

13. *Wall Street Journal*, July 13, 1971.

14. *Engineering and Mining Journal*, March, 1973.

15. *Wall Street Journal*, March 24, 1972.

16. *Engineering and Mining Journal*, March, 1965.

17. Annual reports, 1966, 1972, 1975, Caterpillar Tractor Co.

18. Ibid.

19. Annual reports, 1965, 1975, Caterpillar Tractor Co.

20. Annual reports, 1969, 1973, 1974, 1975, Caterpillar Tractor Co.

21. *Wall Street Journal*, June 13, 1974.

22. *Wall Street Journal*, Dec. 10, 1971.

23. "This Is Caterpillar," corporate brochure, 1977.

24. Annual reports, 1965, 1975, Caterpillar Tractor Co.

25. *Wall Street Journal*, July 12, 1967, Jan. 24, Feb. 28, March 27, 30, 1968.

26. *Wall Street Journal*, June 8, 1970.

27. *Wall Street Journal*, Aug. 17, 1972.

28. *Wall Street Journal*, Oct. 4, 1972.

29. Caterpillar Inc., *Caterpillar Model Identification Guide, 1991*.

30. *Engineering and Mining Journal*, Oct. 1965.

31. Caterpillar Inc., *Caterpillar Model Identification Guide, 1991*.

32. Ibid.

33. Ibid.

34. Ibid.; annual report, 1972, Caterpillar Tractor Co.

35. Annual report, 1960, Caterpillar Tractor Co.

36. Annual report, 1968, Caterpillar Tractor Co.

37. Annual report, 1975, Caterpillar Tractor Co.

38. Annual report, 1965, 1975, Caterpillar Tractor Co.

39. Annual report, 1974, Caterpillar Tractor Co.

40. Holmes, *J. I. Case*, 136.

41. Ibid., 137.

42. Ibid.

43. Ibid., 143.

44. Ibid., 139.

45. Broehl, *John Deere's Company*, 808.

46. Holmes, *J. I. Case*, 139, 140.

47. Ibid., 137, 138.

48. *Wall Street Journal*, Sept. 16, 1969.

49. Holmes, *J. I. Case*, 146, 147.

50. Ibid., 143.

51. Ibid., 143–46.

52. Ibid., 159.

53. *Wall Street Journal*, July 10, 1972; Holmes, *J. I. Case*, 145.

54. Holmes, *J. I. Case*, 145.

55. Ibid., 142.

56. Trade advertising, *Engineering News-Record*, Jan. 16, 1975.

57. Holmes, *J. I. Case*, 151, 152.

58. Ibid., 152.

59. Ibid., 142.

60. Ibid., 160.

61. Holbrook, *Machines of Plenty*, 267.

62. *Wall Street Journal*, March 5, 1967, Dec. 16, 1970.

63. Broehl, *John Deere's Company*, 806.

64. Ibid., 682.

65. Ibid., 683–89.

66. McMillan and Harrington, *John Deere Tractors and Equipment*, 1960–1990, 102.

67. Ibid., 102, 103.

68. Ibid., 103.

69. *New York Times*, March 5, 1967; McMillan and Harrington, *John Deere Tractors and Equipment*, 1960–1990, 99.

70. *Wall Street Journal*, May 14, 1973.

71. *Wall Street Journal*, Sept. 9, 1974.

72. McMillan and Harrington, *John Deere Tractors and Equipment*, 1960–1990, 104.

73. Annual report, 1984, Deere & Company.

74. Ibid.

75. Broehl, *John Deere's Company*, 692.

76. *Wall Street Journal*, Aug. 20, 1967.

77. *Wall Street Journal*, Aug. 11, 1967.

78. *Wall Street Journal*, Aug. 20, 1967; Peterson, *An Industrial Heritage*, 379.

79. Peterson, *An Industrial Heritage*, 379–96; *Wall Street Journal*, March 1, Dec. 31, 1968, March 4, 1969.

80. Peterson, *An Industrial Heritage*, 410; *Wall Street Journal*, March 4, 1969, Feb. 25, 1970, Feb. 2, 1971.

81. *Wall Street Journal*, July 13, 1973.

82. Ibid.

83. Annual reports, 1966, 1971, 1975, International Harvester Company, Deere & Company, and Caterpillar Tractor Co.

84. Marsh, *A Corporate Tragedy*, 141–43.

85. Ibid., 167, 191.

86. *Wall Street Journal*, Oct. 19, 1973; Derber, *Labor in Illinois*, 123.

87. Trade advertising, *Engineering News-Record*, May 13, 1976, 34, 35.

88. *Wall Street Journal*, June 22, 1970.

89. *Wall Street Journal*, Sept. 12, 1974.

90. Annual reports, 1971, 1974, 1975, International Harvester Company.

91. *Wall Street Journal*, Feb. 6, 1975.

92. *Wall Street Journal*, May 17, June 1, 1968, Dec. 11, 1969.

93. Annual report, 1967, WABCO.

94. Ibid.

95. Trade advertising, *Engineering and Mining Journal*, Feb. 1973, 28–29.

96. Trade advertising, *Engineering News-Record*, April 26, 1962, 124; ConExpo '69 reports, *Engineering News-Record*, Feb. 6, 1969, 98–113, Feb. 20, 1969, 27.

97. ConExpo '69 report, *Engineering News-Record*, Feb. 6, 1969, 98–113.

98. Annual reports, 1966, 1971, 1972, 1974, 1975, American Standard Inc.

99. "Clark Equipment Company," in *International Directory of Company Histories*, ed. Kepos, 8:114–16; *Wall Street Journal*, July 1, 1969.

100. *Wall Street Journal*, April 2, 1971.

101. ConExpo '75 report, *Engineering News-Record*, Feb. 20, 1975, 32–38.

102. *Wall Street Journal*, Jan. 16, 1975.

103. *Wall Street Journal*, Jan. 12, 1972, Jan. 30, 1974, Feb. 4, 1976.

104. *Wall Street Journal*, May 14, 1967.

105. Neufield, *A Global Corporation*, 168.

106. Ibid., 356.

107. ConExpo '69 report, *Engineering News-Record*, Feb. 6, 1969, 98–113.

108. "Varity Corporation," in *International Directory of Company Histories,* ed. Hast, 3:650.

109. *Wall Street Journal,* March 2, 1970.

110. *Wall Street Journal,* July 15, 1974.

111. Kudrle, *Agricultural Tractors,* 129.

112. *Wall Street Journal,* July 15, 1974.

113. ConExpo '75 report, *Engineering News-Record,* Feb. 20, 1975, 32–38.

114. Report of June 1981, Corporate Intelligence Group.

115. *Wall Street Journal,* Dec. 16, 1976.

116. *Wall Street Journal,* Aug. 3, 4, 1967, Feb. 6, June 23, 1968.

117. Orlemann, *Euclid and Terex Earth-Moving Machine,* 71–74, 75, 79.

118. ConExpo '75 report, *Engineering News-Record,* Feb. 20, 1975, 32–38.

119. *New York Times,* June 23, 1968.

120. Ibid.

121. *Wall Street Journal,* Jan. 28, 1971.

122. Ibid.; *Wall Street Journal,* March 18, 1971.

123. *Wall Street Journal,* April 28, Oct. 29, 1971.

124. *Wall Street Journal,* March 8, Nov. 14, 1975.

125. *Wall Street Journal,* Sept. 1, 1971.

126. ConExpo '75 report, *Engineering News-Record,* Feb. 20, 1975, 32–38.

127. Payne, *Initiative in Energy,* ch. 2 and 110–14, 178, 232.

128. Ibid., ch. 4.

129. *Wall Street Journal,* March 1, 1972; Payne, *Initiative in Energy,* 331; annual report, 1972, American Standard Inc.

130. Payne, *Initiative in Energy,* 339–44.

131. Ibid., 342.

132. Ibid., 345.

133. Ibid., 356.

134. *Wall Street Journal,* April 29, May 6, 1981.

135. *Wall Street Journal,* Feb. 24, 1982.

136. *Komatsu Corporate Fact Book, 1992.*

137. Ibid.

138. Annual report, 1975, Komatsu Ltd.

139. ConExpo reports, *Engineering News-Record,* Feb. 21, 1963, Feb. 6, 1969; L-W advertisement, *Engineering and Mining Journal,* March 1965.

140. Gowenlock, *The LeTourneau Legend,* 110.

141. Ibid., 77, 112.

142. Ibid., 190.

143. For the story of the development of pneumatic tires, see O'Reilly, *The Goodyear Story.*

144. Caterpillar Inc., *Caterpillar Model Identification Guide, 1991.*

145. ConExpo '69 report, *Engineering News-Record*, Feb. 6, 1969, 98–113, Feb. 20, 1969, 27.

146. ConExpo '75 report, *Engineering News-Record*, Feb. 20, 1975, 32–38.

SIX   The Pinnacle and the Fall, 1976–85

1. U.S. Department of Commerce, Bureau of the Census, *Statistical Abstract, 1986,* 445.

2. Ibid., 449, 450.

3. "Credit (General)," *New York Times Index, 1980,* 321.

4. U.S. Department of Commerce, Bureau of the Census, *Statistical Abstract, 1986,* 407.

5. U.S. Department of Commerce, Bureau of the Census, *Statistical Abstract, 1994,* 728.

6. *New York Times*, Nov. 14, 1976, July 19, 1981.

7. *New York Times,* April 13, 1980.

8. *New York Times,* Dec. 7, Dec. 24, 1982, Jan 7, 1983.

9. *New York Times,* April 9, 1984. Also see "Water," *New York Times Index, 1977,* 1464–66, for numerous articles on the Carter administration's efforts to cancel CAP.

10. *Wall Street Journal,* July 1, Dec. 9, 1976; *Engineering News-Record*, Jan. 27, 1977.

11. *Wall Street Journal* exchange rate tables, Aug. 16, 1971, Jan. 2, 1975, Jan. 2, 1979, Jan. 2, 1981.

12. *Wall Street Journal,* Feb. 19, 1980.

13. Embankment volumes, generating capacity, and other specifics are from the *International Water Power and Dam Construction Handbook* (1990).

14. Annual report, 1985, Caterpillar Tractor Co.

15. *Engineering News-Record*, Jan. 15, 1981, 51.

16. *Engineering News-Record*, Jan. 8, 1981, 19.

17. *Engineering News-Record*, Nov. 13, 1980, 25.

18. *New York Times,* June 2, 1983.

19. *Wall Street Journal* exchange rate tables, Aug. 16, 1971, Jan. 2, 1985, March 1, 1985.

20. *Wall Street Journal,* April 19, 1976.

21. Annual report, 1981, Caterpillar Tractor Co.

22. Ibid.

23. Annual report, 1978, Caterpillar Tractor Co.

24. Annual reports, 1976, 1981, Caterpillar Tractor Co.

25. Ibid.

26. Annual reports, 1973–81, Caterpillar Tractor Co.

27. *Wall Street Journal,* Feb. 20, May 15, May 18, 1981.

28. *Wall Street Journal,* Aug. 3, 1981.

29. Annual report, 1982, Caterpillar Tractor Co.

30. Annual report, 1983, Caterpillar Tractor Co.

31. *Wall Street Journal,* Aug. 12, 1983.

32. Annual report, 1983, Caterpillar Tractor Co.

33. Annual report, 1985, Caterpillar Tractor Co.

34. *Wall Street Journal,* July 3, 1979.

35. Annual report, 1983, Caterpillar Tractor Co.

36. *Wall Street Journal,* Feb. 12, June 4, July 30, Dec. 11, 1981; annual report, 1981, Caterpillar Tractor Co.

37. *Wall Street Journal,* Feb. 12, 1981, Feb. 3, 1982.

38. Caterpillar Inc., *Caterpillar Model Identification Guide, 1991;* annual report, 1985, Caterpillar Tractor Co.

39. Caterpillar Inc., *Caterpillar Model Identification Guide, 1991;* annual report, 1977, Caterpillar Tractor Co.

40. Caterpillar Inc., *Caterpillar Model Identification Guide, 1991.*

41. Ibid.

42. Annual reports, 1984, 1985, Caterpillar Tractor Co.

43. Annual report, 1985, Caterpillar Tractor Co.

44. *Wall Street Journal,* Nov. 30, 1984.

45. *Wall Street Journal,* Feb. 24, 1982.

46. Trade advertising, *Engineering News-Record,* June 19, 1986, 70–71, Nov. 6, 1986, 76–77.

47. Ibid.; ConExpo '81 report, *Engineering News-Record,* Feb. 5, 1981, 15–16.

48. *Wall Street Journal,* Jan. 10, 1979.

49. *Komatsu Corporate Fact Book, 1993; Wall Street Journal,* Feb. 13, 1985.

50. *Wall Street Journal,* Dec. 18, 1985.

51. Annual report, 1983, Komatsu Ltd.

52. *Komatsu Corporate Fact Book, 1993;* annual report, 1985, Caterpillar Tractor Co.

53. Holbrook, *Machines of Plenty,* 263; Holmes, *J. I. Case,* 149.

54. Holmes, *J. I. Case,* 150.

55. Case company history, at [http://www.casecorp/corporate/history/].

56. *Wall Street Journal,* May 20, 1977; Holmes, *J. I. Case,* 160–62.

57. *Wall Street Journal,* March 19, 1984.

58. Holmes, *J. I. Case,* 156, 157.

59. Ibid., 169.

60. *Wall Street Journal,* Oct. 15, 1979; Holmes, *J. I. Case,* 165.

61. Annual report, 1984, Tenneco Inc.

62. Holmes, *J. I. Case*, 170.

63. *Wall Street Journal*, Nov. 23, 1984.

64. *Wall Street Journal*, Nov. 27, 1984.

65. Ibid.; Holmes, *J. I. Case*, 172–76.

66. Annual report, 1985, Tenneco Inc.

67. Annual reports, 1976–85, J. I. Case.

68. Annual reports, 1976–81, Deere & Company.

69. *Wall Street Journal*, Nov. 3, 1978.

70. *Wall Street Journal*, May 24, 1979.

71. Broehl, *John Deere's Company*, 731.

72. The ranking of the top companies by worldwide earthmoving equipment sales in 1978 was Caterpillar, Komatsu, Case, Deere, International Harvester, Fiat-Allis, Terex (est.), Massey-Ferguson, and IBH. IH slightly surpassed Deere in 1979. The ranking in 1981 was Caterpillar, Komatsu, Case, IBH, Fiat-Allis, Deere, and IH, with Massey-Ferguson competing only in the loader-backhoe business.

73. Annual reports, 1979–85, Deere & Company.

74. McMillan and Harrington, *John Deere Tractors and Equipment, 1960–1990*, 104–7; *Engineering News-Record*, March 25, 1976, 26, July 2, 1981, back cover.

75. Ibid., 108; annual report, 1983, Deere & Company.

76. McMillan and Harrington, *John Deere Tractors and Equipment, 1960–1990*, 106.

77. Annual report, 1984, Deere & Company.

78. *Wall Street Journal*, June 25, 1982.

79. *Wall Street Journal*, Aug. 20, 1982.

80. Annual report, 1985, Deere & Company.

81. *Wall Street Journal*, June 29, 1977; Payne, *Initiative in Energy*, 361–63.

82. Annual reports, 1975–82, Dresser Industries, Inc.

83. *Wall Street Journal*, Nov. 2, 1982; annual report, 1983, International Harvester Company.

84. Annual report, 1986, Dresser Industries, Inc.

85. Annual reports, 1984, 1985, Dresser Industries, Inc.

86. *Wall Street Journal*, Feb. 4, 1977, Jan. 24, 1978, June 12, 1980.

87. *Wall Street Journal*, Aug. 22, 1978.

88. *Wall Street Journal*, March 6, 1981.

89. *Wall Street Journal*, June 29, 1981.

90. *Wall Street Journal*, Oct. 7, 1982.

91. Trade advertising, *Highway and Heavy Construction*, Feb. 1982, 32.

92. *Wall Street Journal*, Jan. 6, 1984.

93. *Wall Street Journal*, April 3, 1984.

94. Trade advertising, *Engineering News-Record*, Feb. 12, 1987, 50–67.

95. Annual report, 1981, Fiat-Allis.

96. *Wall Street Journal*, June 17, Dec. 5, 1980.

97. *Wall Street Journal,* June 11, 1980, Jan. 15, Dec. 23, 1981, Feb. 23, April 22, May 4, 1982.

98. *Wall Street Journal,* Sept. 28, 1982.

99. *Wall Street Journal,* Sept. 17, 28, 1982.

100. *Wall Street Journal,* Nov. 11, 1985.

101. Annual reports, 1983, 1984, Fiat-Allis.

102. Annual report, 1985, Fiat-Allis.

103. Marsh, *A Corporate Tragedy,* 163–65, 168–73, 258.

104. Ibid., 13, 173–75; *Wall Street Journal,* Aug. 4, Dec. 21, 1977.

105. *Wall Street Journal,* July 24, Dec. 7, 8, 1978.

106. *Wall Street Journal,* Dec. 21, 1979.

107. Marsh, *A Corporate Tragedy,* 208, 210–23; *Wall Street Journal,* Nov. 2, 1979.

108. *Wall Street Journal,* March 12, April 23, May 16, 1979; Marsh, *A Corporate Tragedy,* 210–23.

109. *Wall Street Journal,* Dec. 2, 15, 19, 1980.

110. Marsh, *A Corporate Tragedy,* 235; *Wall Street Journal,* Nov. 3, 1980, Jan. 26, 1981.

111. *Wall Street Journal,* Feb. 20, March 16, Sept. 21, 28, Dec. 11, 23, 1981; Marsh, *A Corporate Tragedy,* 244–57.

112. *Wall Street Journal,* May 15, 18, Oct. 6, 1981.

113. Annual report, 1981, International Harvester Company.

114. Annual reports, 1979, 1980, International Harvester Company.

115. *Wall Street Journal,* May 15, 1981.

116. *Wall Street Journal,* March 16, 1981.

117. Annual report, 1981, International Harvester Company.

118. *Wall Street Journal,* Feb. 24, 1982.

119. *Wall Street Journal,* Feb. 25, 1982.

120. *Wall Street Journal,* Aug. 25, 1982.

121. Annual report, 1983, International Harvester Company.

122. *Wall Street Journal,* Oct. 10, 13, 1982.

123. *Wall Street Journal,* Feb. 25, May 4, Oct. 14, 1983.

124. Annual report, 1984, International Harvester Company; *Wall Street Journal,* Dec. 16, 1983.

125. Annual report, 1984, International Harvester Company; Marsh, *A Corporate Tragedy,* 296–98; *Wall Street Journal,* Nov. 27, 1984.

126. Annual report, 1979, International Harvester Company; annual report, 1985, Navistar International Corp.

127. *Wall Street Journal,* March 19, May 5, 1976.

128. *Wall Street Journal,* July 19, Sept. 7, 16, 30, 1976.

129. *Wall Street Journal,* Oct. 21, 1976.

130. *Wall Street Journal,* March 19, 1980.

131. *Wall Street Journal,* Sept. 5, Nov. 20, Dec. 10, 1980, Sept. 1, 1981.

132. *Wall Street Journal,* Dec. 16, 1976, Dec. 19, 1977, Feb. 16, 1978.

133. *Wall Street Journal,* Dec. 16, 1976.

134. *Wall Street Journal,* Feb. 16, 1978.

135. *Wall Street Journal,* Dec. 20, 1978.

136. *Wall Street Journal,* Jan. 25, 1979.

137. *Wall Street Journal,* May 14, Oct. 3, 1980.

138. *Wall Street Journal,* Dec. 11, 1978.

139. *Wall Street Journal,* Jan. 25, 1979.

140. "Varity Corporation," in *International Directory of Company Histories,* ed. Hast, 3:650.

141. *Wall Street Journal,* Nov. 28, 1979.

142. Annual reports, 1980, 1985, Massey-Ferguson Ltd., and 1991, Varity Corp.

143. *Financial Times,* July 2, Sept. 9, 1992; report of Sept. 30, 1992, Corporate Intelligence Group.

144. Annual report, 1994, Varity Corporation.

145. *Wall Street Journal,* Oct. 2, 1980.

146. *Wall Street Journal,* July 17, 1980.

147. Ibid.

148. *Wall Street Journal,* Sept. 25, Sept. 30, 1980.

149. *Wall Street Journal,* Jan. 31, 1982.

150. *Wall Street Journal,* May 1, 1981.

151. *Wall Street Journal,* Aug. 9, 25, 1982.

152. *Wall Street Journal,* Nov. 7, 1983.

153. *Wall Street Journal,* Nov. 25, 1983.

154. *Wall Street Journal,* Nov. 25, 1983, Feb. 2, 1984.

155. *Wall Street Journal,* Sept. 7, 1984.

156. *Wall Street Journal,* Feb. 2, 1984.

157. *Wall Street Journal,* Nov. 30, 1984.

158. Annual reports, 1976–80, American Standard Inc.

159. Annual reports, 1981–83, American Standard Inc..

160. Annual report, 1984, American Standard Inc.; annual report, 1986, Dresser Industries, Inc.

161. "Off-Road Trucks in Construction," and "Small Jobs Create New Market for Articulated Dump Trucks," *Highway and Heavy Construction,* Nov. 1985, 42–43.

162. *Komatsu Corporate Fact Book, 1994.*

163. Orlemann, *Giant Earth-Moving Equipment,* 97–102.

164. "ConExpo '81—Building through the Twentieth Century," news release PR 78–211, n.d., Construction Industry Manufacturers Association (CIMA), Milwaukee; ConExpo '81 report, *Highway and Heavy Construction,* Feb. 1981.

SEVEN   Recovery and Renewal, 1986–95

1. U.S. Department of Commerce, Bureau of the Census, *Statistical Abstract, 1986*, 445.

2. U.S. Department of Commerce, Bureau of the Census, *Statistical Abstract, 1994*, 501.

3. *Wall Street Journal* exchange rate tables, Feb. 13, 1985–April 18, 1995.

4. U.S. Department of Commerce, Bureau of the Census, *Statistical Abstract, 1994*, 728.

5. Annual reports, Caterpillar Inc., 1981–88, and Deere & Company, 1970–85.

6. *New York Times*, March 21, 1987.

7. *New York Times*, Nov. 26, 28, 1991.

8. *Engineering News-Record*, May 10, 1990, Oct. 7, 1991, Sept. 7, 1992.

9. *Wall Street Journal*, Dec. 13, 1995.

10. *Engineering News-Record*, Jan. 7, 1990.

11. *Engineering News-Record*, March 17, 1988.

12. *Engineering News-Record*, Nov. 23, 1992.

13. *Wall Street Journal,* May 31, 1996.

14. Annual reports, 1982–86, Caterpillar Tractor Co. and Caterpillar Inc.

15. For the story of the closure of the Glasgow plant, see Woolfson and Foster, *Track Record.*

16. Notice and proxy statement, Feb. 12, 1986, Caterpillar Inc.

17. Annual report, 1986, Caterpillar Inc.

18. Annual reports, 1984–90, Caterpillar Tractor Co. and Caterpillar Inc.

19. Second-quarter report to stockholders, 1990, Caterpillar Inc.

20. Annual reports, 1989, 1990, Caterpillar Inc.

21. Notice and proxy statement, Feb. 20, 1991, Caterpillar Inc., segment information.

22. Notice and proxy statement, Feb. 14, 1992, Caterpillar Inc., A-22.

23. Ibid., A-12.

24. Notice and proxy statement, Feb. 19, 1993, Caterpillar Inc., A-22, A-13. The Statement of Financial Accounting Standards (SFAS) was established by the Financial Accounting Standards Board, which required all corporations to adopt the new, more conservative method of establishing reserves for postretirement benefits other than pensions.

25. Annual report, 1993, Caterpillar Inc.

26. Notice and proxy statement, Feb. 25, 1994, Caterpillar Inc., A-14.

27. Annual reports, 1994 and 1995, Caterpillar Inc.

28. Notice and proxy statement, March 1, 1996, Caterpillar Inc., A-30.

29. Notice and proxy statement, Feb. 25, 1994, Caterpillar Inc., A-15; notice and proxy statement, March 1, 1996, Caterpillar Inc., A-30.

30. Caterpillar Inc., *The Caterpillar Story,* 71.

31. Annual reports, 1991, 1992, 1993, Caterpillar Inc.

32. Notice and proxy statements, 1987, 1991, Caterpillar Inc. CM yen sales are converted from U.S. dollars using average exchange rates for 1987 and 1991.

33. Caterpillar Inc., *Caterpillar Model Identification Guide, 1991.*

34. Annual report, 1987, Caterpillar Inc.; Caterpillar Inc., *The Caterpillar Story,* 71; Caterpillar Inc., *Caterpillar Performance Handbook,* 22d ed., 2–6.

35. Caterpillar Inc., *Caterpillar Model Identification Guide, 1991.*

36. *Peoria Journal Star,* July 2, 1996.

37. Caterpillar Inc., *The Caterpillar Story,* 71.

38. Caterpillar Inc., *Caterpillar Model Identification Guide, 1991.*

39. Ibid.

40. Trade advertising, *Engineering and Mining Journal,* May 1994, 26–27, and June 1995, 39.

41. *Wall Street Journal,* April 16, 18, 1991.

42. Caterpillar Inc., *Caterpillar Model Identification Guide, 1991.*

43. Notice and proxy statement, Feb. 14, 1992, Caterpillar Inc., A-12.

44. Annual report, 1993, Caterpillar Inc.

45. "Market Shares," Wood-Manfredi report, March 1997.

46. *Komatsu Corporate Fact Book, 1993.*

47. *Wall Street Journal,* Aug. 17, 18, 1988.

48. Komatsu Dresser consolidated statement of operations, 1991; annual report, 1991, Dresser Industries, Inc.

49. Prospectus, 1992, Indresco; annual report, 1992, Dresser Industries, Inc.

50. *Moody's Industrial Manual, 1996.*

51. *Peoria Journal Star,* Aug. 31, 1994.

52. *Komatsu Corporate Fact Book, 1993.*

53. *Peoria Journal Star,* Jan. 9, 1996.

54. *Komatsu Corporate Fact Book, 1993.*

55. *Peoria Journal Star,* Nov. 9, 1995.

56. Annual report, 1995, Komatsu Ltd.

57. *Komatsu Corporate Fact Book, 1993.*

58. *Wall Street Journal,* Aug. 28, 1989.

59. *Komatsu Corporate Fact Book, 1993.*

60. *Wall Street Journal,* Aug. 2, 1989.

61. *Komatsu Corporate Fact Book, 1993.*

62. Ibid.

63. Ibid.

64. Ibid.

65. *Wall Street Journal,* Oct. 27, 1993.

66. *Komatsu Corporate Fact Book, 1993.*

67. Ibid.

68. Ibid.

69. Trade advertising, *Highway and Heavy Construction,* Aug. 1985, 60–61, Oct. 1985, 22–23, March 1989, 38–39, and April 1989, 76, and *Engineering News-Record,* Feb. 28, 1994, 20–21, and March 21, 1994, A-13.

70. Trade advertising, *Engineering and Mining Journal,* June 1991, 68.

71. "News and Trends," *Caterpillar World,* Dec. 1994, 18.

72. "Buyer's Guide," *Construction Equipment,* March 1996.

73. Annual report, 1989, Komatsu Ltd.

74. Annual report, 1995, Komatsu Ltd.

75. Ibid.

76. *Komatsu Corporate Fact Book, 1993.*

77. Annual report, 1995, Komatsu Ltd.

78. *Caterpillar Folks,* July 6, 1995.

79. Annual reports, 1981, International Harvester Company and American Standard Inc.

80. Annual reports, 1983–87, Dresser Industries, Inc.

81. Prospectus, 1992, Indresco.

82. Annual report, 1990, Dresser Industries, Inc.

83. Annual report, 1992, Dresser Industries, Inc.

84. *Moody's Industrial Manual, 1996.*

85. Annual reports, 1982–87, Deere & Company.

86. Annual report, 1986, Deere & Company.

87. Annual report, 1987, Deere & Company.

88. Annual reports, 1981–90, Deere & Company.

89. Annual reports, 1987, 1988, Deere & Company.

90. Annual reports, 1985, 1995, Deere & Company.

91. *Wall Street Journal,* March 30, 1987.

92. *Wall Street Journal,* June 19, 1989.

93. Annual report, 1989, Deere & Company.

94. Annual report, 1993, Deere & Company.

95. "Deere & Company," in *International Directory of Company Histories,* ed. Hast, 3:462–64.

96. *Wall Street Journal,* July 2, 1986.

97. Annual reports, 1989–93, Deere & Company.

98. Annual reports, 1979, 1994, 1995, Deere & Company.

99. *Wall Street Journal,* Dec. 10, 1987; McMillan and Harrington, *John Deere Tractors and Equipment, 1960–1990,* 108.

100. Annual report, 1995, Deere & Company.

101. *Wall Street Journal,* Nov. 7, 1991.

102. Annual report, Wood-Manfredi, April 1992.

103. McMillan and Harrington, *John Deere Tractors and Equipment, 1960–1990,* 107, 108; annual report, 1995, Deere & Company.

104. "Buyer's Guide," *Construction Equipment,* March 1996.

105. Annual report, 1995, Deere & Company.

106. *Wall Street Journal,* Aug. 31, 1989, May 31, 1990.

107. Holmes, *J. I. Case,* 183.

108. Annual report, 1985, Tenneco Inc.

109. Annual reports, 1982, 1988, Tenneco Inc.

110. *Wall Street Journal,* Dec. 12, 1988.

111. Holmes, *J. I. Case,* 176–78.

112. Ibid., 187, 188; annual reports, 1988–90, Tenneco Inc.

113. Holmes, *J. I. Case,* 188–90; *Wall Street Journal,* July 23, 1992.

114. Annual report, 1991, Tenneco Inc.

115. Holmes, *J. I. Case,* 190; *Wall Street Journal,* July 23, 1992.

116. Holmes, *J. I. Case,* 191, 192.

117. Holmes, *J. I. Case,* 192; Prospectus, June 24, 1994, Case Equipment Corporation, 67.

118. *Wall Street Journal,* March 23, May 6, 1993; annual report, 1992, Tenneco Inc.

119. Prospectus, June 24, 1994, Case Equipment Corporation, 18.

120. "Case Digs Out from Way Under," *Newsweek,* Aug. 14, 1995.

121. Annual report, 1993, Tenneco Inc.

122. Prospectus, June 24, 1994, Case Equipment Corporation; *Wall Street Journal,* June 27, Oct. 31, 1994.

123. *Wall Street Journal,* Oct. 31, 1994, July 26, 1995, Feb. 23, 1996.

124. *Wall Street Journal,* Nov. 21, 1995.

125. Prospectus, June 24, 1994, Case Equipment Corporation, 67.

126. Annual reports, 1994, 1995, Case Equipment Corporation.

127. Annual reports, 1986, 1990, 1992–95, Tenneco Inc.; Prospectus, June 24, 1994, Case Equipment Corporation.

128. *Wall Street Journal,* Dec. 15, 1986.

129. Annual reports, 1986, 1987, Tenneco Inc.

130. Holmes, *J. I. Case,* 191; *Construction Equipment,* Case advertising brochure CE051113, 1993.

131. Annual report, 1995, Case Equipment Corporation.

132. *Construction Equipment,* Case advertising brochure CE051113, 1993.

133. "Market Shares," Wood-Manfredi report, March 1997.

134. Ibid.

135. *Construction Equipment,* Case advertising brochure CE051113, 1993; annual report, 1995, Case Equipment Corporation.

136. Annual report, 1995, Case Equipment Corporation.

137. *Wall Street Journal,* Jan. 24, 1985.

138. Trade advertising, *Highway and Heavy Construction,* July 1986, 30, 31, and Oct. 1986, 36, 37.

139. Annual report, 1992, Clark Equipment Company.

140. "Spotlight—Hydraulic Excavators," *Highway and Heavy Construction,* July 1986, 30–31, Oct. 1986, 36–37.

141. Annual report, 1989, Akermans-Verkstad AB.

142. 10-K report, 1990, Clark Equipment Company.

143. 10-K report, 1992, Clark Equipment Company.

144. 10-K report, 1994, Clark Equipment Company.

145. Annual reports, 1993, 1994, Clark Equipment Company; corporate review, 1994, Volvo Construction Equipment Group.

146. 10-K report, 1992, Clark Equipment Company.

147. Corporate review, 1994, Volvo Construction Equipment Group.

148. Annual report, 1990, Clark Equipment Company.

149. Ibid.

150. Annual report, 1992, Clark Equipment Company.

151. Ibid.

152. 10-K and annual reports, 1994, Clark Equipment Company.

153. *Wall Street Journal,* Jan. 27, March 7, 1995.

154. *Wall Street Journal,* March 29, May 30, 1995.

155. Corporate review, 1995, Volvo Construction Equipment Group.

156. "Market Shares," Wood-Manfredi report, March 1997.

157. The material on Terex acquisitions is from "Terex Corporation," in *International Directory of Company Histories,* ed. Kepos, 7:513–15; "The Accounting Questions at Terex," 148; 10-K report, 1989, Terex Corporation; and *Moody's Industrial Manual, 1996.*

158. Milwaukee County Historical Society database.

159. *Wall Street Journal,* Feb. 4, 1986.

160. Annual reports, 1988, 1989, 1991, Terex Corporation.

161. Annual report, 1993, Terex Corporation.

162. Annual report, 1994, Terex Corporation.

163. Prospectus, 1990, Terex Corporation.

164. Trade advertising, *Engineering News-Record,* Jan. 25, 1962, and *Engineering and Mining Journal,* Jan. 1961, 88, Feb. 1961, 43, March 1967, 76–77, April 1967, 27, and June 1967, 94–95.

165. Business Wire Service report, March 11, 1996.

166. *Wall Street Journal,* May 2, 1986.

167. Annual report, 1986, Fiat-Allis.

168. Off-Highway Research Report, Corporate Intelligence Group, Jan. 31, 1994.

169. "Fiat-Geotech," in Off-Highway Research Report, Corporate Intelligence Group, Construction, Mining and Industrial Equipment in Europe, Sept. 1989.

170. *Wall Street Journal,* May 8, 1991.

171. *Wall Street Journal,* Sept. 22, 1993.

172. *Financial Times,* Feb. 12, 1990.

173. "Machinery Outlook," Wood-Manfredi report, Dec. 1994.

174. Off-Highway Research Report, Corporate Intelligence Group, Jan. 31, 1994.

175. *Standard and Poor Corporation Records-1996.*

176. Material on Liebherr from: "Liebherr," Off-Highway Research Report, Corporate Intelligence Group, Construction, Mining and Industrial Equipment in Europe, Feb. 1991; "Machinery Outlook—Europe," Wood-Manfredi report, April 1995; and *Contract Journal,* June 1, 1995, 33.

177. Material on JCB from "JCB Inc.," Off-Highway Research Report, Corporate Intelligence Group, Construction Equipment Industry in North America, July 1995; *Financial Times,* April 4, 7, Oct. 23, 1995; and Yengst, "Trendlines," *Diesel Progress,* Sept. 1995, 4.

178. Orlemann, *Giant Earth-Moving Equipment,* 18.

179. Milwaukee County Historical Society database.

180. *New York Times,* May 26, 1953.

181. *Wall Street Journal,* July 19, 1971.

182. *New York Times,* March 12, 1946.

183. Orlemann, *Giant Earth-Moving Equipment,* 18.

184. Ibid., 15; trade advertising, *Engineering and Mining Journal,* March 1961, 1; Anderson, *One Hundred Booming Years,* 75, 86.

185. Orlemann, *Giant Earth-Moving Equipment,* 15, 20, 27.

186. Ibid., 16, 23, 24, 29; "Shovels and Excavators," *Engineering and Mining Journal,* Oct. 1990, 30–31.

187. Orlemann, *Giant Earth-Moving Equipment,* 33, 63.

188. "Harnischfeger Industries, Inc.," *Moody's Industrial Manual,* 1996.

189. Anderson, *One Hundred Booming Years,* 167–82; Orlemann, *Giant Earth-Moving Equipment,* 80–81.

190. Annual report, 1993, Harnischfeger Industries, Inc.

191. White, "New Trends in Surface Mining Equipment," *Engineering and Mining Journal,* Jan. 1987, 27–29; Anderson, *One Hundred Booming Years,* 74.

192. *Wall Street Journal,* Dec. 8, 1983.

193. *Wall Street Journal,* Feb. 1, 1984.

194. Milwaukee County Historical Society database.

195. Annual report, 1985, Dresser Industries.

196. "Bucyrus International, Inc.," *Moody's Industrial Manual,* 1996.

197. Milwaukee County Historical Society database; "Harnischfeger Industries, Inc.," *Moody's Industrial Manual,* 1996.

198. Of the major hydraulic excavator manufacturers, only Poclain, Liebherr, and O&K do not fall within these categories.

199. ConExpo '87 reports, *Engineering News-Record,* Dec. 11, 1986, 22–25, Feb. 12, 1987, 36–37, 40–41, March 5, 1987, 10–11.

200. "93 Exposition Directory and Reference," ConExpo brochure, n.d., Construction Industry Manufacturers Association (CIMA), Milwaukee.

201. *Caterpillar Folks,* April 14, 1995.

202. *Financial Times,* April 7, 1995.

EIGHT   Perspectives

1. Kudrle, *Agricultural Tractors,* ch. 7.

2. Ibid., 127.

3. Annual report, 1995, Caterpillar Inc.

4. U.S. Department of Commerce, Bureau of the Census, *Statistical Abstract, 1996,* table 752, 494; *Historical Statistics of the United States, Colonial Times to 1970,* series E, 23–39.

5. Federal Highway Administration, *Price Trends for Federal-Aid Highway Construction,* table PT-201, April 1997 [a quarterly publication prepared by the Federal-Aid and Design Division, Office of Engineering].

APPENDIX   The Industry and Organized Labor

1. Hounsell, *From the American System to Mass Production, 1800–1932,* ch. 4.

2. Hildebrand, *American Unionism.*

3. Ozanne, *A Century of Labor-Management Relations at McCormick and International Harvester.*

4. Broehl, *John Deere's Company,* 529; Holmes, *J. I. Case,* 73.

5. Hildebrand, *American Unionism.*

6. Marsh, *A Corporate Tragedy,* 62–64, 67.

7. Cormier and Eaton, *Reuther,* chs. 7, 8, 9.

8. Hildebrand, *American Unionism.*

9. Holmes, *J. I. Case,* 73, 74.

10. Peterson, *An Industrial Heritage,* 321, 322, 343.

11. Ibid., 323, 341, 342.

12. Marsh, *A Corporate Tragedy,* 66.

13. Ibid., 67.

14. Ibid., 67–70.

15. Broehl, *John Deere's Company,* 555, 556.

16. Derber, *Labor in Illinois,* 295.

17. *New York Times,* Sept. 17, 1945.

18. Cormier and Eaton, *Reuther,* 246–48 and chs. 16, 17.

19. Holmes, *J. I. Case,* 74–77.

20. *New York Times,* June 7, Aug. 13, 1946.

21. Peterson, *An Industrial Heritage,* 343–45.

22. Ibid., 346.

23. Derber, *Labor in Illinois,* ch. 4D.

24. *New York Times,* Jan. 22, 1946; Marsh, *A Corporate Tragedy,* 83.

25. Broehl, *John Deere's Company,* 573–581; Derber, *Labor in Illinois,* 275–78.

26. Derber, *Labor in Illinois,* 114. Despite the firm five-year agreement, in 1952, Reuther forced a reopening of negotiations in the automotive industry, claiming that the Korean War had introduced new conditions.

27. Broehl, *John Deere's Company,* 581.

28. Derber, *Labor in Illinois,* 279.

29. Annual report, 1946, Caterpillar Tractor Co.

30. Annual report, 1949, Caterpillar Tractor Co.; Derber, *Labor in Illinois,* 296.

31. *Peoria Journal Star,* Sept. 28, 1951.

32. Annual reports, 1952, 1955, Caterpillar Tractor Co.

33. Annual report, 1958, Caterpillar Tractor Co.

34. Derber, *Labor in Illinois,* 309.

35. Marsh, *A Corporate Tragedy,* 84.

36. Ibid., 85–87.

37. Ibid., 89, 90.

38. Cormier and Eaton, *Reuther,* 331–35.

39. Derber, *Labor in Illinois,* 116, 117.

40. Hildebrand, *American Unionism.*

41. Annual reports, 1957–61, Caterpillar Tractor Co.

42. Holmes, *J. I. Case,* 108, 117, 141.

43. Annual reports, 1958, 1961, 1964, 1965, 1967, Caterpillar Tractor Co.

44. Annual reports, 1970, 1973, 1976, Caterpillar Tractor Co.

45. Marsh, *A Corporate Tragedy,* 90–92; Derber, *Labor in Illinois,* 118, 119.

46. Derber, *Labor in Illinois,* 281, 282.

47. Moritz and Seaman, *Going for Broke,* 314, 333–35.

48. Annual report, 1979, Caterpillar Tractor Co.; Derber, *Labor in Illinois,* 306.

49. Derber, *Labor in Illinois,* 282, 283.

50. Ibid., 123–26; Marsh, *A Corporate Tragedy,* 210–23.

51. U.S. Department of Commerce, Bureau of the Census, *Statistical Abstract,* 1990, table 687, 418, 1992, table 670, 421; U.S. Department of Labor, Bureau of Labor Statistics, *Handbook of Labor Statistics—1978,* table 150, 507.

52. U.S. Department of Commerce, Bureau of the Census, *Statistical Abstract,* 1992, table 670, 421.

53. U.S. Department of Commerce, Bureau of the Census, *Historical Statistics of the United States, Colonial Times to 1970,* series D, 741–45; Jacobs, ed., *Handbook of Labor Statistics—Second Edition,* 321.

54. Annual report, 1989, Caterpillar Inc.

55. Annual report, 1984, Deere & Company.

56. Annual reports, 1982, Caterpillar Tractor Co. and Deere & Company.

57. Annual report, 1983, Caterpillar Tractor Co.

58. *Wall Street Journal,* Nov. 27, 1981, April 30, 1982.

59. Annual report, 1979, International Harvester Company; annual report, 1986, Navistar.

60. Holmes, *J. I. Case,* 175–77.

61. Annual report, 1986, Caterpillar Inc.; "Caterpillar," in *International Directory of Company Histories,* ed. Hast, 3:450.

62. Annual reports, 1986, 1987, Deere & Company.

63. Annual report, 1991, Deere & Company.

64. Annual reports, 1991, 1992, Caterpillar Inc.; *Peoria Journal Star,* Feb. 17, 20, 1992.

65. *Peoria Journal Star,* March 6, 1992.

66. *Peoria Journal Star,* April 2, 1992.

67. *Peoria Journal Star,* April 7, 9, 14, 1992

68. *Peoria Journal Star,* April 15, 1992.

69. *Peoria Journal Star,* June 22, 1994.

70. Ibid.; *Wall Street Journal,* June 22, 1994.

71. Annual report, 1994, Caterpillar Inc.

72. *Wall Street Journal,* Aug. 1, 1994.

73. Second-quarter report to stockholders, 1995, Caterpillar Inc.

74. *Business Week,* Oct. 31, 1994.

75. Off-Highway Research Report, Corporate Intelligence Group, Feb. 28, 1995.

76. *Wall Street Journal,* June 15, 27, 1995.

77. *Wall Street Journal,* Nov. 20, 21, 28, 30, Dec. 4, 7, 12, 1995.

BIBLIOGRAPHY

Books and Articles

"The Accounting Question at Terex." *Business Week*, Oct. 12, 1992, 148.

Anderson, George B. *One Hundred Booming Years: A History of Bucyrus-Erie Company, 1880–1980*. Milwaukee: Bucyrus-Erie Company, 1980.

Bourne, Russell. *Floating West: The Erie and Other American Canals*. New York: W. W. Norton, 1992.

Broehl, Wayne G. *John Deere's Company*. Garden City: Doubleday, 1984.

Burchell, S. C. *Building the Suez Canal*. New York: Harper and Row, 1966.

Caterpillar Inc. *Caterpillar Model Identification Guide, 1991*. Peoria: Caterpillar, 1991.

———. *Caterpillar Performance Handbook*. 22d ed. Peoria: Caterpillar, 1991.

———. *The Caterpillar Story*. Peoria: Caterpillar, 1990.

———. *Century of Change*. Peoria: Caterpillar, 1984.

Cormier, Frank, and William J. Eaton. *Reuther*. Englewood Cliffs: Prentice-Hall, 1970.

Cullen, Allan H. *Rivers in Harness: The Story of Dams*. Philadelphia: Chilton Books, 1962.

Deere and Company. *How Johnny Popper Replaced the Horse*. Moline: Deere and Company, 1988.

DeKruif, Paul. *Seven Iron Men*. New York: Harcourt, Brace, 1929.

Derber, Milton. *Labor in Illinois: The Affluent Years, 1945–80*. Urbana: University of Illinois Press, 1989.

Flawn, Peter T. *Mineral Resources*. New York: Rand McNally, 1966.

Frantz, Don. "Forty Years of Euclid Scraper Development: A Photo Essay, 1924–1964." *Equipment Echoes*, no. 31 (Dec. 1993): 8–13.

Frey, Robert L., ed. *Railroads in the Nineteenth Century*. Encyclopedia of American Business History and Biography Series. New York: Facts On File, 1988.

Gowenlock, Philip G. *The LeTourneau Legend*. Brisbane: Paddington Publications, 1996.

Grant, Tina, ed. *International Directory of Company Histories*. Vol. 16. Chicago: St. James Press, 19

Gray, Roy B. *The Agricultural Tractor.* Vols. 1 and 2. St. Joseph, Mich.: American Society of Agricultural Engineers, 1975.

Grosser, Morton. *Diesel: The Man and the Engine.* New York: Atheneum, 1978.

Hadfield, Charles. *World Canals: Inland Navigation Past and Present.* New York: Facts On File, 1986.

Hast, Adele, ed. *International Directory of Company Histories.* Vol. 3. Chicago: St. James Press, 1988.

Hildebrand, George H. *American Unionism: An Historical and Analytical Survey.* Reading, Mass.: Addison-Wesley, 1979.

Holbrook, Stewart H. *Machines of Plenty.* Updated by Richard G. Charlton. Racine: J. I. Case, 1977.

Holmes, Michael S. *J. I. Case: The First 150 Years.* Racine: J. I. Case, 1992.

Hounsell, David A. *From the American System to Mass Production, 1800–1932.* Baltimore: Johns Hopkins University Press, 1984.

Hoyt, Edwin P. *The Guggenheims and the American Dream.* New York: Funk and Wagnalls, 1967.

International Water Power and Dam Construction Handbook. Sutton, Surrey: Reed Business Publications, 1990.

Kepos, Paula, ed. *International Directory of Company Histories.* Vol. 8. Detroit: St. James Press, 1994.

Kinross, Lord. *Between Two Seas: The Creation of the Suez Canal.* New York: William Morrow, 1969.

Komatsu Corporate Fact Book, 1992, 1993. Komatsu Corporate Publication.

Kudrle, Bobert T. *Agricultural Tractors: A World Industry Study.* Cambridge: Ballinger Publishing, 1975.

Jacobs, Eva E., ed. *Handbook of Labor Statistics—Second Edition.* Lanham: Bernan Press, 1998.

Lapica, R. E., ed. *Facts On File Yearbook—1950* and *1951.* Vols. 10 and 11. New York: Facts on File, 1951, 1952.

Lee, W. Storrs. *Panama Canal: The Strength to Move a Mountain.* New York: C. P. Putnam's Sons, 1958.

Leffingwell, R. *Caterpillar.* Osceola, Wis.: Motorbooks International, 1994.

LeTourneau, Robert G. *Mover of Men and Mountains: Autobiography of R. G. LeTourneau.* Englewood Cliffs: Prentice-Hall, 1960.

Marsh, Barbara. *A Corporate Tragedy.* Garden City: Doubleday, 1985.

Martin, Albro. *Railroads Triumphant: The Growth, Rejection, and Rebirth of a Vital American Force.* New York: Oxford University Press, 1992.

McCullough, David. *The Path between the Seas: The Creation of the Panama Canal, 1870–1914.* New York: Simon and Schuster, 1977.

McKinley, Marvin. *Wheels of Farm Progress.* St. Joseph, Mich.: American Society of Agricultural Engineers, 1980.

McMillan, Don, and Russell Jones. *John Deere Tractors and Equipment, 1837–1959.* St. Joseph, Mich.: American Society of Agricultural Engineers, 1988.

McMillan, Don, and Roy Harrington. *John Deere Tractors and Equipment, 1960–1990.* St. Joseph, Mich.: American Society of Agricultural Engineers, 1991.

Moritz, Michael, and Barrett Seaman. *Going for Broke: The Chrysler Story.* Garden City: Doubleday, 1981.

Neufeld, E. P. *A Global Corporation: A History of the International Development of Massey-Ferguson Limited.* Toronto: University of Toronto Press, 1969.

O'Reilly, Maurice. *The Goodyear Story.* Elmsford, N.Y.: Benjamin, 1984.

Orlemann, Eric C. *Euclid and Terex Earth-Moving Machines.* Osceola, Wis.: Motorbooks International, 1997

———. *Giant Earth-Moving Equipment.* Osceola, Wis.: Motorbooks International, 1995.

Owens, Marguerite. *The Tennessee Vallley Authority.* Westport: Praeger Publishers, 1973.

Ozanne, Robert. *A Century of Labor-Management Relations at McCormick and International Harvester.* Madison: University of Wisconsin Press, 1967.

Paskoff, Paul F., ed. *Iron and Steel Industry in the Nineteenth Century.* Encyclopedia of American Business History and Biography Series. New York: Facts On File, 1989.

Payne, Darwin. *Initiative in Energy: Dresser Industries, Inc., 1880–1978.* New York: Simon and Schuster, 1979.

Payne, Walter A., ed. *Benjamin Holt: The Story of the Caterpillar Tractor.* Stockton: University of the Pacific, 1982.

Peterson, Walter F. *An Industrial Heritage: Allis-Chalmers Corporation.* Milwaukee: Milwaukee County Historical Society, 1978.

Quick, Graeme, and Wesley Buchele. *The Grain Harvesters.* St. Joseph, Mich.: American Society of Agricultural Engineers, 1978.

Reynolds, Terry S. "Iron Mining Machines and Techniques." In *Iron Industry in the Nineteenth Century,* ed. Paul F. Paskoff, 189–94. Encyplopedia of American Business History and Biography Series. New York: Facts On File, 1989.

———. "Iron Ore Ranges." In *Iron and Steel Industry in the Nineteenth Century,* ed. Paul F. Paskoff, 194–98. Encyclopedia of American Business History and Biography Series. New York: Facts On File, 1989.

———. "Iron Ore Supplies." In *Iron and Steel Industry in the Twentieth Century,* ed. Paul F. Paskoff, 231–33. Encyplopedia of American Business History and Biography Series. New York: Facts On File, 1994.

Seely, Bruce E., ed. *Iron and Steel in the Twentieth Century.* Encyclopedia of American Business History and Biography Series. New York: Facts On File, 1994.

Shaw, Ronald E. *Canals for a Nation: The Canal Era in the United States, 1790–1860.* Lexington: University Press of Kentucky, 1990.

Sloan, Alfred P. *My Years with General Motors*. London: Pan Books, 1963.

"Spotlight—Hydraulic Excavators." *Highway and Heavy Construction*, Beg. 1986, 54–60.

Stephens, Randy, ed. *Farm Tractors, 1916–1925*. Implement and Tractor Collector's Series. Overland Park: Intertec, 1991.

———. *Farm Tractors, 1926–1956*. Implement and Tractor Collector's Series. Overland Park: Intertec, 1990.

Thompson, John. "American Contributions to the French Panama Canal Venture." *Equipment Echoes*, no. 51 (Spring 1998): 19–24.

U.S. Department of Commerce, Bureau of the Census. *Historical Statistics of the United States, Colonial Times to 1970*. Washington, D.C.: Government Printing Office, 1975.

———. *Statistical Abstract of the United States of America*. Washington, D.C.: Government Printing Office, 1970–79, 1986, 1988, 1991, 1992, 1994, 1996.

U.S. Department of the Interior, Water and Power Resources Service. *Project Data*. Denver: Government Printing Office, 1981.

U.S. Department of Labor, Bureau of Labor Statistics. *Handbook of Labor Statistics, 1978*. Washington: Government Printing Office, 1978.

U.S. Department of Transportation. *America's Highways, 1776–1976: A History of the Federal-Aid Program*. Washington, D.C.: Government Printing Office, 1976.

Van Tassel, David D., and John J. Grabowski, eds. *The Encyclopedia of Cleveland History*. Bloomington: Indiana University Press, 1987.

Warne, William E. *The Bureau of Reclamation*. Westport: Praeger Publishers, 1973.

Wendel, C. H. *The Allis-Chalmers Story*. Osceola, Wis.: Motorbooks International, 1993.

———. *The Encyclopedia of American Farm Tractors*. Osceola, Wis.: Motorbooks International, 1992.

———. *Oliver Hart-Parr*. Osceola, Wis.: Motorbooks International, 1993.

———. *150 Years of International Harvester*. Osceola, Wis.: Motorbooks International, 1993.

White, Lane. "New Trends in Surface Mining Equipment." *Engineering and Mining Journal*, Jan. 1987.

Wik, Reynold M. *Benjamin Holt and Caterpillar: Tracks and Combines*. St. Joseph, Mich.: American Society of Agricultural Engineers, 1984.

Williams, Robert C. *Fordson, Farmall, and Poppin' Johnny: A History of the Farm Tractor and Its Impact on America*. Urbana: University of Illinois Press, 1987.

Wixom, Charles W. *American Roadbuilders Association Pictorial History of Roadbuilding*. Washington, D.C.: American Roadbuilders Association, 1975.

Wolf, Donald E. *Big Dams and Other Dreams: The Six Companies Story*. Norman: University of Oklahoma Press, 1996.

Woolfson, Charles, and John Foster. *Track Record: The Story of the Caterpillar Occupation*. London: Verso Press, 1989.

Worster, Donald. *Rivers of Empire: Water, Aridity and the Growth of the American West*. New York: Pantheon Books, 1985.

Yengst, Charles R. "Trendlines. JCB: How a Household Name in England Has Become a Global Player." *Diesel Progress*, Sept. 1995.

Newspapers and Other Periodicals

Business Week, Caterpillar Folks, Caterpillar World [a corporate quarterly publication], *Construction Equipment, Contract Journal, Engineering and Mining Journal, Engineering News-Record, Financial Times, Highway and Heavy Construction, Equipment Echoes* [Historical Construction Equipment Association quarterly publication], *Moody's Industrial Manual, 1996, Newsweek, New York Times*, Peoria *Journal Star*, Peoria *Star, Standard & Poor Corporate Records, Wall Street Journal, World Mining Equipment*.

Corporate Annual Reports and 10-K Reports

Akermans Verkstad AB, Allis-Chalmers, American Standard Inc., Case Corporation, Caterpillar Tractor Co., Caterpillar Inc., Clark Equipment Co., Deere & Company, Dresser Industries, Inc., Fiat-Allis, Harnischfeger Industries, Inc., Indresco Inc., International Harvester Co., J. I. Case Inc., Komatsu Ltd., Massey-Ferguson Ltd., Navistar International Corp., Orenstein & Koppel AG, Phelps Dodge Corporation, R. G. LeTourneau, Inc., Tenneco Inc., Terex Corporation, Volvo Construction Equipment, WABCO.

INDEX

Armington, George, 81
Armington, Raymond Q.: as general manager of Euclid Division, 130
articulated dumpers. *See* dumpers
Atkinson, Guy F., 145
Aurora Engine Co., 50
Austin-Western motor graders: acquisition by Clark Equipment Co., 220; discontinuance, 273
auxiliary equipment manufacturers: of Caterpillar, 67; of IH, 84; of A-C, 124

backhoe-loader. *See* loader-backhoe
Baker, Murray M., 52; role in Holt-Best merger, 59
Baldwin-Lima-Hamilton Co.: acquisition by Clark Equipment Co., 220
Bamford, Joseph C., 357
Bamford, Sir Anthony, 357, 359
Barber-Greene Co.: acquisition by Caterpillar, 316
Bates Tractor Co.: as early crawler competitor, 60
Becherer, Hans: as Deere CEO, 332
Bechtel, W. A., 13
Bessemer Process: 25, and direct-shipping ore, 26
Best, Clarence Leo: and formation of C. L. Best Gas Traction Co., 53; as first Caterpillar chairman, 59
Best [C. L.] Gas Tractor Co. (C. L. Best Gas Traction Co.): formation, 53; rivalry with Holt, 53, 57; introduction of first crawler, 57; introduction of Models 60 and 30, 57; merger with Holt, 59
Best, Daniel: and Holt Manufacturing Co., 53
Bingham Canyon Mine: and Kennecott Copper Co., 28; 29
Blackie, William, 164, 166; as Caterpillar CEO, 196
Blake, Eli Whitney: and invention of jaw-crusher, 17
bottom-dump wagon: introduction by Euclid, 19, 81, 384
Bucyrus-Erie Co. (Bucyrus Steam Shovel and Dredge Co., Bucyrus International): formation, 83; merger with Vulcan Steam Shovel Co., 83; merger with Erie Steam Shovel Co., 83; acquisition of Armstrong Drill Co., 83: as auxiliary

equipment manufacturer to IH, 84, 360; joint venture with Komatsu, 183, 231; loss of construction market, 359; mining opportunities, 360; and growth in shovel sizes, 360–61; financial reverses, 363; restructuring, 363; formation of Bucyrus International, Inc., 364
Buda Co.: acquisition by Allis-Chalmers, 124
bulldozer: and R. G. LeTourneau, 70, 384
Bureau of Reclamation: establishment, 28; involvement in Central Valley Project, 29; accomplishments, 29; and Pick-Sloan Plan, 31
Butterworth, William: as Deere CEO, 87, 88, 89

canals: Midi, 3; Erie, 3–4; Potomac, 3; Chesapeake and Ohio, 3; Pennsylvania Mainline, 4; Suez, 17; Panama, 19; Wiley-Dondero, 22; Soo, 33
Case Corp. (J. I. Case, Case Equipment Corp., J. I. Case Threshing Machine Co.): as exhibitor at first Road Show, 10; incorporation, 93; entry into farm tractor business, 93; recapitalization, 94; Leon Clausen as president, 94, 148; acquisition of Emerson-Brantingham Corp., 95; acquisition of Rock Island Plow, 95; impact of combine harvester on, 95; and World War II, 104; and federal restraint of trade lawsuit, 111; and postwar strike, 139; merger with American Tractor Co., 148; introduction of loader-backhoe, 149; role of Rojtman in, 148, 150; and company stores, 152, 336; acquisition by Kern County Land Co., 153; growth of product line, 153, 204, 205; acquisition by Tenneco, 203; acquisition of Drott, 203; Ketelson as CEO, 204; overseas expansion, 205; acquisition of Poclain, 264, 338; formation of Consolidated Diesel Corp., 265; financial reverses of, 266; acquisition of IH farm equipment, 266; operating losses, 334; Tenneco investments in, 334; first restructuring, 335; Mead as CEO, 335; second restructuring, 335; spin-off by Tenneco, 336; Rosso as CEO, 336; return to profitability, 336; restructuring of product line, 337; and Sumitomo ex-

auxiliary equipment manufacturer to Caterpillar, 67; acquisition by Allis-Chalmers, 124

Lenz, Randolph W.: acquisitions, 346–48; formation of Terex Corp., 347

LeTourneau, Robert G.: early life, 68; development of cable-controlled bulldozer, 70; development of scraper, 72; introduction of Tournapull, 39, 74; death, 180; role in off-highway tire development, 235. *See also* R. G. LeTourneau, Inc.

LeTourneau-Westinghouse (Division of Westinghouse Airbrake): formation, 127; entry into elevating scrapers, 219, 235; acquisition of Adams Motor Grader, 127; introduction of Haulpak truck, 177; acquisition by American Standard, 217. *See also* WABCO

Liebherr: and hydrostatic products, 295, 355; large hydraulic front shovels, 297, 354; origins, 354; product line, 354; North American operations, 356; acquisition of Wiseda Co., 355, 356, competitive position, 356

loader-backhoes: and Case, 149, 386; Caterpillar introduction, 256; JCB as pioneer, 357, 386

———, models: *Case:* Model 320, 149; Models 430, 530, and 80-Series Construction Kings, 150; L-Series, 338; *Deere:* Models JD300, JD400, and JD700A, 157

Lombard, Alvin O., 49, 384

machine allocation: postwar, 110; and Caterpillar, 159, 197

Marathon Manufacturing Co.: acquisition of R. G. LeTourneau, Inc., 180

Marion Power Shovel Co. (Marion Steam Shovel Co.): formation, 83; acquisition by Dresser, 271, 363; loss of construction market, 359; mining opportunities, 360; growth in shovel size, 360–61

Martinson, Oscar J.: and walking mechanism for draglines, 84

Massey-Ferguson (Massey-Harris): formation, 96; acquisition of Case Plow Works, 94, 97; and overseas manufacturing, 98; and depression years, 98; and self-propelled combine, 99; and Massey-Harris Harvest Brigade, 99; merger with

Ferguson, 139; entry into earthmoving equipment business, 158; acquisition of Perkins, Landini, 158; introduction of mid-range equipment, 223; acquisition of Hanomag, 223; and dealers, 224; financial reverses, 286, 288; sale of Hanomag, 287; and formation of Varity, 288. *See also* Varity Corp.

McAdam, John L.: and development of macadam roads, 16

McCaffrey, John: as IH CEO, 114, 168; retirement, 169

McCardell, Archie R.: as IH CEO, 279, 281; and UAW, 280, 407; ouster, 283

McCormick, Brooks: as IH CEO, 214, 217, 279

McCormick, Cyrus Hall: introduction of first reaper, 37; dealer franchise system, 37, 372; death, 38

McCormick, Cyrus Hall, Jr.: entry into business, 37; resignation as IH CEO, 64

McCormick, Fowler: as IH CEO, 42; resignation, 114

McCormick Harvesting Machine Co., 60

Mead, Dana G.: as Case CEO, 335; as Tenneco CEO, 336

Melrose Co.: acquisition by Clark Equipment Co., 220, 343, 344

Mesabi Range: discovery, 25, 26; production from, 27

mini excavators, 297

Monarch Tractor Co.: acquisition by Allis-Chalmers, 46; as early crawler tractor competitor, 61

Morenci Mine: daily production, 29

Morgan, Lee L., 196; as Caterpillar CEO, 251; as gas turbine advocate and acquisition of Solar Turbine, 251; retirement, 254

Morrison-Knudsen Co. (M-K), 13

motor graders: and introduction of leaning wheel by Adams, 35; introduction of Auto Patrol by Caterpillar, 62, 384; introduction by Deere of JD570, 208, 386; introduction by Caterpillar of Series G, 201; and Austin-Western, 220, 273

Moxy dumper: and Komatsu, 322

National Labor Relations Board, 391
National League for Good Roads: establishment, 10

William R. Haycraft is a retired marketing executive of Caterpillar Inc. He holds a degree in civil engineering from Auburn University. *Yellow Steel* is his first book. He lives with his wife, Carol, in Peoria, Illinois.

Typeset in 10/13 Sabon
with Univers display
Designed by Kathleen Szawiola
Composed by Jim Proefrock
at the University of Illinois Press
Manufactured by Cushing-Malloy, Inc.

University of Illinois Press
1325 South Oak Street
Champaign, IL 61820-6903
www.press.uillinois.edu